The Incarnate Imagination

The Incarnate Imagination:

Essays in Theology, The Arts and Social Sciences

In Honor of Andrew Greeley A Festschrift

Edited by Ingrid H. Shafer

Bowling Green State University Popular Press
Bowling Green, Ohio 43403

Copyright © 1988 by Bowling Green State University Popular Press

Library of Congress Catalogue Card No.: 87-73481

ISBN: 0-87972-418-8 Clothbound
      0-87972-419-6 Paperback

Cover design by Gary Dumm

Contents

Preface

Ray B. Browne

Every so often—though far too infrequently—there comes along a person who speaks to—and through several of the media—many, perhaps most, of the positive aspects of the good in people. That individual becomes, in the most affirmative senses of the word, a *modern* person, aware of the complexities of present-day life, of the dynamics of present-day cultures, and determined to respond to them in every way he/she is capable of responding. That individual becomes a cultured individual, in the sense that he/she responds to the cultures around him/her.

Such an individual is Andrew M. Greeley. He has responded to the challenges and opportunities of the world—both present-day and eternal, as he sees it—as both an academic and as a creative artist. He has succeeded in both areas because he has not been restricted or hidebound by either. Instead of seeing these media as ends in themselves, Greeley has used them as means to greater ends.

That he has succeeded in his endeavors is vouched for by the breadth of the contributors to this *festschrift*. These are the academics who vouch for Fr. Greeley's effect on them and the parts of culture that they observe. A far greater voucher comes from the millions of readers of Greeley's creative works who attest through their purchases that Greeley's words are reaching them and touching them and moving them. With their purchases and reading habits they attest to the degree to which Greeley speaks to their needs as they slog through life and the manner in which he helps transform the sad song of disappointed mankind into a hymn of morning and hope.

A single life could hardly be expected to do more.

Introduction

Ingrid H. Shafer

Even under the "best" of circumstances—an honoree known solely among "fellow-disciplinarians"—the editor of a *Festschrift* confronts a very special problem: how to avoid the danger of presiding over the gestation of a collection of essays linked by little more than their authors' respect for the honoree. This volume, on the other hand, is a tribute to one who, in the (only slightly hyperbolic) words of his friend John Shea, "has infiltrated every section of the Dewey Decimal System." Thus it is hardly surprising that the twenty-five contributors represent ten major disciplines, from A (Art) to—well, not Z (alas, no zoologist volunteered)— but T (Theology). In order to minimize potential fragmentation, contributors were asked to address, at least tangentially, some dimension of the creative imagination as it pertained to their specialty.

The creative imagination seemed an appropriate focus, since much of Andrew Greeley's work involved not only empirical research and theoretical reflection on the imaginative realm, but, in his stories and poems, proceeds directly from his own inner landscape. He is one, to cite David Tracy, who "has not only named but produced crocuses." This emphasis on the imagination is in turn consistent with Greeley's identity as priest, his Catholic Incarnationalism which insists on literally *seeing* the Divine and the human *together (analogia entis)*, and is closely related to the Romantic vision of Spirit and Nature joined in and through the imagination.

In addition, the creative imagination cuts across disciplinary boundaries, or, more appropriately, lurks in the very matrix of every individual's psyche and every culture, affecting all aspects of human endeavor, at once discovering and generating connections, patterns, transformations, images. Jean-Paul Sartre describes in his autobiography how as a young boy he was drawn to writing by the compulsion to "pluck the pictures" from within his head and give them reality outside of himself. It is ultimately this same sort of primal drive which engenders everything from a flint scraper or limerick or wedding gown to the *Summa Contra Gentiles*, *Romeo and Juliet*, Rubens' *The Garden of Love*, and the DNA Double Helix. We create our individual lives and our social worlds by turning pictures into stories and stories into theories and theories back into stories and images.

1

2 The Incarnate Imagination

The essays and images in this volume were not selected: they happened. Since they were primarily meant as tributes, all would be included; given time constraints, none could be revised. As they arrived, one by one, original art works and stories, sociological studies, literary criticism and theological reflection, the editor worried and wondered: would this outpouring of scholarly respect for Andrew Greeley, this spontaneous collection, however excellent each of the individual pieces, merge into an organic whole, or would it end up like the words and syllables plucked randomly from telephone books by the Dadaists? She "listened" to the texts and herself. The very limitations of operating within the boundaries of the given became a challenge and horizon. She arranged and re-arranged the pieces, playfully working a jigsaw puzzle whose continually changing form she dimly intuited with no assurance that the pieces would fit. Finally, a configuration emerged which seemed both her doing and demanded by the submissions themselves: a "story" with a beginning, middle, and end. An end which, like one of her favorite symbols, the uroboros, returned to the beginning.

In the first essay of Part One (Creative Imagination and the Individual), Erika Fromm speculates that an androgynous personality with the ability to "let go" may be the key to creative imagination, and discusses original research based on the analysis of journal narratives showing that self-hypnosis enhances creative imagery considerably for those individuals capable of a fantasy life. Next, Martin Marty lists several ways historians use imagination, comparing them to poets who are inwardly driven and engaged in "creative irrelevance" as they tell stories which are at once frivolous and meaningful. Through creative imagination they find a specialty, a method, a language; through imagination they leap from "trace to event," artifact to story. He urges historians to "leave the [index] cards in another room...write the story one feels impelled to tell." Both Fromm and Marty touch on a theme which will appear, in numerous variations, throughout this volume: the essential association of the creative imagination to the process of opening up, making connections, joining, merging, linking. Both also introduce the major co-theme, inextricably united to the former: the importance of story telling.

Part Two (Creative Imagination and Society) also consists of two essays. In the spirit of Clifford Geertz, Harrison White argues that in order to map the patterns of social interaction and deal with the subtly complex metaphors of social configurations, social scientists need to develop an appropriate algebraic rather than the traditional metric analytic framework. Teresa Sullivan presents research showing that as expected, given the religious emphasis on the bureaucratic virtues of obedience, reliability, and conformity, contemporary Catholic immigrants are less likely than non-Catholic immigrants to display the "economic creativity" associated with self-employment. Surprisingly, however, the few who are self-employed are more successful than all other groups except for Islamic males.

Fran Gillespie, S.J., expands and embroiders upon Peter-Hans Kolvenbach's *Go Forth and Teach: The Characteristics of American Catholic Education* in the first essay of Part Three (Creative Imagination and Higher Education). Gillespie develops a contemporary yet Ignatian vision of the Catholic university as hybrid child of mixed parentage—the teaching Church *and* the secular state. In his contribution, David Riesman suggests that effective academic leaders should possess intellectual breadth, moral courage, and such qualities as determination, resourcefulness, patience, the capacity to balance administrative responsibilities with direct involvement in academic affairs, and the willingness to tackle the "two culture" divide.

Part Four (Creative Imagination and the Institutional Church) presents two related papers demonstrating serious discrepancies between the positions of American bishops and the Catholic laity. Henry Kenski and William Lockwood report their findings of weak support of the Catholic laity for the official "seamless garment" (sanctity of life) positions in the areas of social, economic, and foreign policy. Like Margaret Kenski, they see an urgent need for re-imagining American Catholicism. Margaret Kenski considers the reluctance of the American hierarchy to oppose Vatican policies and support equality for women within the Church a serious and politically imprudent failure of imagination, since on social, economic and political issues except for abortion, women are more likely than men to agree with the bishops' position.

In the first essay of Part Five (Creative Imagination and Art) Albert Bergesen reminds linguistic cultural analysts of the fundamental interdependence of the multiple worlds we inhabit and chides them for working within self contained systems of signs isolated from the real world, thus divorcing the cultural from the economic. He then looks at the impact of economic factors on art. He argues that as art succeeds in the market, the artistic community grows close knit and self conscious, causing it to develop "ingroup codes of discourse" which engender more and more formally abstract works of "art for art's sake," unintelligible to outsiders. This precipitates a decrease in economic return which in turn leads to a gradual shift once again toward a greater emphasis on content over form, increased popularity, and the beginning of yet another such cycle.

Charles Scribner III is the first contributor to address the "linking" motif in its most powerful manifestation in human life: sexual love. He takes us on a guided tour through metaphorical landscapes from Rubens' exuberant Baroque celebration of married passion, the *Garden of Love*, through Watteau's a evanescent *Pilgrimage to Cythera* (Venus's sacred island), to Fragonard's Rococo four-part series, *The Progress of Love*, and the final act of Mozart's *The Marriage of Figaro*. All of those artistic renderings, Scribner suggests, evoke heaven-on-earth, the reconciliation of the divine and the human, *agape* and *eros*.

Part Six (Creative Imagination and Literature) consists of essays by Michael Marsden, Joseph Feeney, S.J., Charles Fanning, and Joseph Blotner. Like Bergesen, Marsden focuses on an aspect of the "high" culture/"low" culture dichotomy. He argues that successful popular writers function in contemporary literate society the way folk story *tellers* function in pre-literate societies, and are precisely for that reason generally misunderstood by print-obsessed literary critics. Possessed by their stories, these latter day bards dialogue with their audience, weave their magic spells, and structure new-old tales to the patterns of their culture, bringing people into the warm circle of the communal hearth, the story's "fire" sparked as private imagination twirls within and against the pre-established form of genre tradition.

"The relationship between the writer and the reader is a sacred one" as he "moves people from a relative state of isolation into the larger community of human concern."

Feeney develops a model of the Catholic imagination in contemporary America which consists of four varieties: the esthetic (Bach preludes: brocaded vestiments; candles and incense), the financial (*quid-pro-quo* mentality; God as vending machine), the ritual (holy water and novenas; communal ritual), and the athletic (God as the Great Coach) mode. He then applies his model to the fiction of Mary Gordon, Tom McHale and Andre Dubus.

Fanning discusses James T. Farrell's 2500 page O'Neill—O'Flaherty pentalogy as the "most thoroughly realized embodiment in American literature of three generations of Irish American life," rendered a single, coherent work of art by Farrell's skillful interweaving of the "outer stream of social life" (deaths in the family) and the "inner stream of consciousness" (solitary reveries).

Blotner takes us into William Faulkner's religious sensibility which included the melding of such seeming contradictions as speaking of Christianity as a "fairy tale" and saying a conventional prayer before dinner; considering "art...the salvation of mankind" and purchasing a twelve-volume Cambridge edition of the Bible he could not afford. While Faulkner rejected a personal God, atheism, divine grace, and life after death, he affirmed "a God who is the most complete expression of mankind, a God who rests in both the eternity and the now," and wrote (at least in part) in order to leave a scratch on the "wall of oblivion" for someone to read a thousand years hence.

In Part Seven (Creative Imagination and Scripture), Scripture is explored from a Jewish and a Catholic perspective. It seems both ironic and momentous that it is Jacob Neusner who alone of all the contributors directly confronts the ultimate level of fusion, that between human beings and God. He demonstrates that unlike the mere "you" of prayer found in the initial writings of the Judaism of the dual Torah, God appears in the Babylonian Talmud (ca. 600 C.E.) as a fully formed personality, an *incarnate* God, consubstantial with humanity not only in physical, mental and emotional traits (albeit on a cosmic scale), but also (and especially) in being bound to the standards of human society; God who celebrates Israel as Israel celebrates God; "God unique in heaven, Israel unique on earth, the one like the other and matched only by the other—and both finding ultimate embodiment in the sage."

Roland E. Murphy, O. Carm. adds a highly significant dimension to the marriage metaphor by arguing that the literal historical meaning of the Song of Songs as human love poem and the traditional meaning of this love poem as symbol of the love between God and God's people need not be viewed as mutually exclusive. Murphy suggests that the traditional meaning is valid precisely on the basis of the symbolism of human sexual love. He finds evidence in the Hebrew text (8:6) that sexual love as described in the Song is somehow associated with the Lord as Lover, and considers it unfortunate that the traditional meaning was allowed to eclipse the literal meaning, leading to an impoverished Christian attitude toward sex.

Essays by David Tracy, Lawrence Cunningham, Hans Küng, Mary G. Durkin, and John Shea make up Part Eight (Creative Imagination and Theology). In his paper, Tracy lays the foundation for a post-modern marriage of art to theology, of adding aesthetic criteria as a major component in the determination of theological criteria through the uncovery/retrieval of embedded imaginative possibilities present in the analogical (albeit second-order reflective) language of Thomas Aquinas by paralleling it to metaphoric first-order symbolic language (as understood by Paul Ricoeur).

Vatican II, according to Cunningham, precipitated a major shift in emphasis from a strongly iconic to a more verbal matrix for the Catholic imagination; from sacred space to sacred time; from church as a place for the Sacramental Christ (and "Prisoner of the Tabernacle") toward Christ evoked in and through liturgy as performed with the active participation of the congregation; from the priest as custodian of the sacred mysteries facing the High One to the priest facing the world, expected to reach out and communicate those mysteries to the people. Like the Kenskis, he argues that the institutional church has thus far failed to grasp the opportunity afforded by this shift with its profound implications for pastoral theology and the education of future clergy who will be called upon to be at once priests and poets, capable of calling up the *Urworte* (primordial words) of transcendental mystery and ultimate purpose.

After noting that for many contemporary people the traditional rituals of the church have become walls between God and themselves, Hans Küng adds an ecumenical perspective to the linking motif by suggesting that for us, as children of the Semitic prophetic tradition, discovering God anew might mean learning from the Indian mystic tradition. Opening ourselves to God as the wholly immanent transcendence allows us to recover him as a God of love, a "God with a human face" precisely in this secularized, rational, pluralistic world by seeing more in the everyday than the everyday itself through such experiences as "being stopped," "being held," or not "feeling completely at home" on earth. Experiencing God anew in an attitude of reasoning trust as the mid-point of our lives opens up our eyes to our own reality in new ways of seeing and permits us to honor and praise God in a new way: "in responsible service to the world and in a true service of worship."

Around the description of an Irish wedding, and in a manner complementary to that of Roland Murphy, Mary G. Durkin weaves theological reflections on the Catholic understanding of human sexuality as based on the *Genesis* account of creation and *The Song of Songs*. Pastoral theologians need to appeal to the creative imagination of their people and remind them of this very special source of grace which is always available to married lovers and can become a constant source of intimacy renewal.

Instead of reflecting on narrative theology. Shea *is* himself the Priest/Poet-Poet/Priest as he speaks in the voices of the two brothers and the father of the Prodigal Son parable, and tells three contemporary stories of the love of God, stories from and to the heart, about everyday people doing everyday things: a cheerfully patient father whose "children needed him;" a little girl determined to make passing strangers happy, and "get them" no matter how hard they might resist; a good woman who can't forgive herself for being human and finds Nazareth and self-acceptance in a soup kitchen among street people.

In part Nine (Creative Imagination at Play) Alice Rossi captures the inner worlds of women, not from without, through statistical tables and multiple regression analysis, but by telling her personal story of the universal experience of preparing for a daughter's wedding; of grandmother, mother, and daughter "under a tree on a sunny Sunday afternoon, silk threaded needles in hand, stitching their memories, hopes, and dreams into the happiest, most beautiful gown the family has yet produced;" of the gown which "had worked its charm in merging past and present" and "worked yet another one, for it spoke to the future and its fruit in a fourth generation to come."

With her delightfully irreverent "Limericks on the Study of Religion," Wendy O'Flaherty adds a vital dimension, often forgotten in "serious" discussions of creativity (albeit noted by fellow historian of religion, Marty as "creative irrelevance"): its *essential* child-like playfulness, its rootedness in liberating laughter, poking fun, *having* fun. O'Flaherty reminds us of the power of non-malicious humor to dissolve tension, join opposites, and show us that none of our constructs (however lofty) are immune to being toppled.

Finally, interweaving the various methods and themes of contributors, Ingrid Shafer turns full circle to the beginning of the volume and imaginatively enters the world of one of Professor Fromm's journal narrators by shifting out of highly abstract third level discourse into recording her feelings and impressions during a trance-like state in which present merges with the past and her personal mythology is imaginatively linked to cosmic archetypes and the Christian story.

John David Mooney's artistic vision of Andrew Greeley represents a perfect coalescence of both foci of this volume. It flows out of his creative imagination— the painter's eye capturing his subject's eye, and mouth and edge of jaw, going beneath the surface, plumbing the depths of the other, and somehow, magically— using every resource from technical command of his medium to personal knowledge of the man round whom his imagination swirls—dissolving, diffusing, dissipating, as Coleridge put it, in order to re-create, no, *create* a new Andrew Greeley, one like none who ever existed, and yet one who, an illusion on paper, is—truth. Let us now turn to the man whom this volume honors.

This *Festschrift* celebrates the life and work of a man whom the future may well count among the Fathers (and, hopefully, Mothers) of the new-old Postmodern Church, along with such as Karl Rahner, Theilhard de Chardin, John Courtney Murray, Henri de Lubac, Hans Küng, David Tracy, G. K. Chesterton, and others yet unrecognized or even unborn. The names of contributors to this volume speak for themselves. Among them are some of the most renowned scholars in numerous disciplines, men and women who respect Andrew Greeley, the priest/bard/scholar; Jews, Protestants, Agnostics, and Catholics who are proud to call the man their friend. The very diversity of those who have made this tribute possible is symbolic of both Greeley's truly "catholic" vision and the trajectory the Church will have to travel if the post-Vatican Two reactionary fortress builders are to be thwarted from obstinately continuing to preach, as David Tracy wrote in *The Analogical Imagination*, "a truth that can ignore all the truths disclosed in the classics of other religions and secular cultures, save the one truth the despised 'world' has taught them all two well—the truth of power in its myriad forms, from the sword of religious wars to the bureaucratization of the spirit in contemporary fundamentalist and dogmatic empires."

Poring over Greeley's hundred odd books plus countless articles and columns (all probably on laser disk or its descendant), those who ponder the forces which shaped the crucial twentieth century transitions of the Church can be imagined to trace this brilliant Celt's pilgrimage through the dark corridors of the authoritarian Church, the humid jungles of academe, and the labyrinth of his own preconscious. They will encounter a man of many facets and faces, a follower of Christ and Socratic gadfly, a Don Quixote battling wind mills, a leprechaun Grail quester in pursuit of the Magic Cup, a troubadour romancing his Lady, a Peter Pan poking fun, a pugnacious male at once resisting and yielding to the gentle, feminine aspects of his psyche, a Renaissance man in the fullest sense of the term. Finally, the jigsaw puzzle pieces will fall into a coherent pattern, the complex modes and moods of Andrew Greeley will coalesce into a single master narrative—that of a quintessential (very human though hardly "average") *priest*, a priest, passionately in love with God, people and the Catholic Church, and like all passionate lovers only too eager to do battle for the cause.

Astride his word processor, armed with the sharp lance of Irish wit, trained in the arenas of academia and Church, a veteran of countless intellectual tournaments, skirmishes, and wars, this crusader for humanely loving rationality will be noted to have used literally *any* expression or image—from calling Thomas a'Kempis a "mean spirited, passive aggressive little anti-intellectual" to referring to love-making as *menage a trois* with God the Divine Voyeur, in order to rescue Christianity from two thousand years of dualism and shatter the complacent shell of conventionally dead piety.

As that of the pilgrim, his story will emerge as the common human journey from unity through fragmentation, alienation, and bitterness toward uncertain but possible reintegration and homecoming. As that of a man, his story will be read as capturing the passage of the maturing male psyche from challenging aggressiveness toward tenderness and sensitivity. As that of the priest, his story will be a chronicle of the turbulent decades of the American Church within the context of global Catholicism during the second half of the twentieth century. As that of the social scientist, his story will evoke that of a photographer, unwilling to retouch his subject's realistic and occasionally unflattering likeness. Finally, as that of the bard, his story will be seen as having turned full circle: the priest without a parish who transformed sociological insights into tales about Karl Rahner's kind of incarnate God-in-all-things will be remembered as minister to an otherwise largely un-churched reader congregation of millions. As Archbishop Jean Jadot (Apostolic Delegate to the U.S. 1972-1980 who was prevented by ill health to contribute to this volume) wrote in a recent letter to the editor of his volume: "God's ways are mysterious. And everybody receives his/her charisms. Andrew has really an extraordinary one."

Paradoxically (or maybe predictably), that very same man will be reported to have been reviled as psychopathic money grubbing peddler of pop porn and romantic trash by a strange alliance of right and left wing clerical, literary, and feminist dogmatists who automatically dismissed writings of popular appeal, particularly if they also reflected a (Catholic) vision of a meaningful and gracious cosmos.

The future may well consider Greeley's autobiography, *Confessions of a Parish Priest*, a Catholic classic in the tradition of St. Augustine and Cardinal Newman (whose personal motto, *cor ad cor loquitur*, might be Greeley's as well). Much will probably be made of the Augustinian association. After all, it is with Augustine, Ambrose and Jerome (another pugnacious scholar) that Hellenic dualism and despair mingled with the essentially world affirming, joyous "good news" of the Gospels, an unholy marriage which precipitated centuries of emphasis on the corruption of the flesh, the evils of passion, the sanctity of virginity, the inferiority of women. Augustine responded to the pluralism of his age by severing the realms of spirit and flesh in the name of what he considered a "pure" love devoid of concupiscence. Greeley will be counted among those who responded to the pluralism of the twentieth century by recovering, out of the stories and symbols of the Catholic tradition, an alternate vision, one which reconciles (as the Incarnation was meant to reconcile) flesh and spirit, *agape* and *eros*. Both Augustine and Greeley focus on the power of grace. In stark contrast to his not quite ex-Manichean predecessor, however, Greeley sees grace operating in and through the physical and most specifically the sexually loving and archetypally feminine dimensions of life.

During and since the Renaissance, the Catholic God image shifted from emphasis on the Transcendent God of the ancient and medieval traditions toward emphasis on the "enfleshment" of God, divine "humanation" (*Menschwerdung*), the Christ envisioned as "Son of Man." With Rubens (as Charles Scribner III reminds us in his paper) this intuitive incarnationalism would explode in a riot of color and light, angel-winged cupids and pagan deities gathered together to celebrate fruitful nuptial passion, allowing nature and all of history to serve as the "bread and wine" in a cosmic eucharistic consecration which even the fortress mentality of the Counter Reformation could not stifle. To apply Rudolf Otto's categories, the Holy has come to be experienced less in terms of *tremendum* than *fascinans* as we begin to see in the human face the *imago Dei*. As Hans Küng notes in his article, God can neither be empirically perceived nor logically deduced. Nevertheless, God is somehow embedded in our everyday experience, "verified," like love, within the experiential horizons of our lives—where S/HE can be recovered for the postmodern world in Ricoeur's second naiveté through what Greeley has called the religious imagination which is closely related to David Tracy's analogical imagination.

"My suggestion is," writes Father John Shea in his contribution to this volume, "the love of God is the hidden unity of Andy's prodigious writings," which is after all, as Shea reminds us "the central conviction of Christian faith—God is love." Again and again, in sociological analyses, theological reflections, and stories Andrew Greeley insists and imaginatively demonstrates that divine love is most directly experienced in our human relationships, particularly through the passionate love which binds men and women to one another and frees them to become fully themselves. Thus the two thematic strands of this volume, the creative imagination and Andrew Greeley, coalesce into the double helix of passionate, life engendering love, incarnate reflection of that *hesed* (love) which according to the *midrashim* created the universe and continues to govern it in association with *zedek* (righteousness).

The current "diaspora" of the Church offers promise of her eventual metamorphosis from a hardened chrysalis stage into a living leaven of love intimately involved in and drawing sustenance from the workings of the world which she seeks to comprehend and transform from within. No matter how desperately dogmatists are laboring to shore up their crumbling fortress, the Incarnation will no longer be denied, and one of the ways in which this "experimental moment," this "crisis of representation" can be harnessed constructively, consists in taking every possible opportunity to translate abstract theological insights for the public at large, to carry the dialogue into the world outside the disintegrating citadel walls. This is the task Andrew Greeley set for himself as early as 1961, in his second published book, *Strangers in the House: Catholic Youth in America*. After insisting that city and nature, the technical and the numinous, the profane and religious must be harmonized, he wrote: "A new cosmos must be built, a cosmos in which nature and technology are seen as restored in Christ. Technology will not be abandoned, the big city will not be deserted, but *both must be sanctified*. How this is to be done, where we must begin, I do not know. To suggest answers to these problems is the work of the poet, the metaphysician, and the theologian" (64).

Seen in this perspective, the modern period can be interpreted not as one of creeping secularization but as one of the progressive and universal appropriation of the Incarnation. Our age allows us to discover God in and through nature, science, technology, scholarship, the arts, literature and human relationships—*if* post-Cartesian anthropocentrism is linked with Incarnational theology. The time has come, Greeley realizes, for humanity to recover beyond the paternal God of moral proscriptions the maternal God of unconditional acceptance and the androgynous God of fiercely tender passion.

"So Greels, Quixots, have you found the Grail and the princess?" the narrator asks himself in the final chapter of volume one of Greeley's memoir. "Not yet," the author quips, "but now I think I know where they are." We can only hope that the Church as a whole will indeed imaginatively come to share Father Greeley's vision of the graciousness of the Really Real and evolve into a community which supports rather than controls, which resists envy, and puts power in the service of love. Not in our life-time. Or in that of our children. But maybe...just maybe...God (Herself) willing, by the year 2088. Too late for Andrew Greeley himself, and all the martyrs of the post-Vatican Two reaction, but possibly in time to allow the Church finally to become, at the dawn of her third millennium, what she has been meant to be from the beginning: a living world-transforming presence, a sacrament of God's abiding love.

Andrew Greeley:
A Pictorial Tribute

John David Mooney

PART ONE

Self-Hypnosis and the Creative Imagination[1]

Erika Fromm

Some years ago, Andrew Greeley, who was then a sociologist colleague of mine at the University of Chicago and a great expert on questionnaires, helped me design a questionnaire for a study of self-hypnosis. In turn, I offered to let him experience what it feels like to be hypnotized and to teach him the art of self-hypnosis.

Hypnosis is an altered state of consciousness in which imagery and creativity are heightened. Andy was a marvelous hypnotic subject. He rose to the occasion like brilliant, multicolored fireworks. Hypnosis released in him the ability to make creative use of his vivid fantasy and imagery, and to write highly successful novels (Greeley, 14).

Because Andy was a consultant in the earliest phase of my planning the research studies on self-hypnosis, and because self-hypnosis enhanced Andy's own use of creative imagination, it seems appropriate to me to report in this Festschrift on some of the research done on this topic in my laboratory during the last fifteen years.

In a longitudinal study of self-hypnosis, thirty-three subjects practiced self-hypnosis one hour per day for four weeks. The subjects recorded daily in a journal three aspects of the self-hypnosis experiences following each self-hypnosis session: 1) the subjective impression of their self-hypnotic experiences for each particular day; 2) the self-suggestions attempted; and 3) a report on the depth of their trance as measured by the Extended North Carolina Scale (Tart, 1970) near the beginning, approximately in the middle, and towards the end of the hour.

The present study is based on the analysis of the journal narratives. It is an extension of our research on the phenomena and characteristics of self-hypnosis published earlier (Fromm, et al., 1981), which dealt *mainly* with the results of the self-hypnosis questionnaires Andrew Greeley had helped us to construct.

The journals were divided into three groups based on the subjects' overall success in self-hypnosis, as perceived by the subjects themselves: Group A consisted of three subjects who had highly successful self-hypnosis session; Group B encompassed twenty-seven subjects who felt their sessions were successful; and Group C contained three subjects who defined their self-hypnosis experiences as unsuccessful. The most noteworthy parts of three journals, one from each group, will be presented and discussed here.

The diaries of the three highly successful subjects are extremely interesting, imaginative and colorful. Those of the three unsuccessful subjects are boring because they are totally without fantasy.

Scoring categories had been developed from the quantitative results of the self-hypnosis questionnaires (Fromm et al., 1981). Many of these were also used in the analyses of the diaries. But in analyzing the diaries we were also open to the possibility of finding new categories. Indeed, several new categories emerged: Insight, Strong Affect, Dissociation, Amnesia, and Ego Inactivity. This last category was scored whenever a subject would note that he was just relaxing, having no thoughts or memories or imagery; doing nothing; experiencing nothing else but relaxation.

As we had done before, we established two categories: Structure and Content.

The Structural Category embraces the following areas:

Concentrative Attention
Expansive Attention
Ego Activity
Ego Receptivity
Absorption
Fading of the General Reality Orientation
Trance Depth
Vacillation of Trance Depth

Concentrative Attention was scored when the subject focussed attention on one particular thought, image, or memory during the session and sustained this concentration for some length of time. Expansive Attention was scored when the subject freely allowed many different thoughts, memories or objects spontaneously to enter his attentional field, either simultaneously or in rapid succession. Rich and varied imagery always was found in states of Expansive Attention.

Ego Activity in our self-hypnosis research was defined as a voluntary mental activity occurring during trance, such as the subject's making a decision or giving himself suggestions. Both concentrated attention and specific suggestions indicate the presence of Ego Activity. Ego Activity is an ego syntonic state. In Ego Receptivity, on the other hand, a person allows thoughts or feelings to come into awareness which otherwise are below the threshold of consciousness. Expansive Attention and Absorption often accompany the presence of Ego Receptivity. Ego Receptivity implies that the "gate" to the primary process thoughts and images, i.e. fantastic, irreal imagery, has been opened. Ego Receptivity in general is also an ego syntonic state, that is, a state in which the person feels comfortable, in contrast to Ego Passivity, a state in which a person feels helplessly overwhelmed, either by his own drives, by reality, or by his guilty conscience.

We scored "Absorption" whenever the hypnotic subjects indicated in their diaries that in the trance they had been totally fascinated or engrossed by the experience. Frequently this went hand in hand with a childlike wonder or amazement, or an esthetic experience.

Another structural characteristic of hypnosis and of self-hypnosis is what in the hypnosis literature has been called (Shor, 1959) the Fading of the General Reality Orientation (GRO). In medium-deep or deep trance, people often more or less lose awareness of their actual surroundings. Inner reality or fantasy becomes so real that outer reality fades. The fading of the General Reality Orientation is related to the concentrated quality of attention, to absorption, and to the depth of trance. The depth of trance can be measured quite precisely by means of various tests; it also can vacillate within the same session.

To our surprise, diary entries which could be scored as GRO or Absorption were very rare. In the questionnaires which had been given at the end of four weeks of self-hypnosis, we had asked our subjects specific questions about these areas. Their answers showed that the GRO and Absorption were very important structural factors. But only a few subjects spontaneously mentioned in their diaries that they were so absorbed in the experiment that the General Reality Orientation seemed to fade into the background. We felt that to become spontaneously aware of Absorption and the GRO requires a good deal of psychological sophistication, more sophistication than our naive subjects had. In their diaries they tended to report what they had *done* each day (giving themselves suggestions, working on their own problems, etc.) or the content of what they had experienced such as vivid imagery, strong affect, or an age regression. They reported Absorption and the GRO, but only when specifically asked about them after the month-long experiment was over.

The Content Categories we established on the basis of the analyses of the diaries were as follows:

Imagery
Age Regression
Personal Memories
Dreams (usually induced by self-suggestion0
Strong Affect
Working on Problems
Suggestion of Motor Phenomena
Suggestion of Sensory Phenomena

Most of the Content Categories are self-explanatory. The only one that may need explanation is Age Regression. In Age Regression a person *re-experiences* or *relives*—as opposed to remembering—an event from his/her own past. The person actually reports *being* in a past situation at a younger age and re-experiencing the affect and other phenomena of that time, for instance, sensory and motor phenomena. The "adult part" or "observing ego" may remain in the present situation while the "child part" regresses to an earlier time. For instance, the subject may say, "I *am* 3 years old and *am* playing in the sandbox with my friend Billy, throwing sand at him. I have fun. But I, the adult, am also in your office, sitting in that deep, comfortable chair, and watching the little boy, me, playing in the sandbox."

Having presented a short overview of our method and findings, let us now sample three diaries, and note the differences we have observed between our *very* successful, our successful, and lastly our unsuccessful subjects. We shall start with a subject from our largest group, Group B (twenty-eight out of a total of thirty-three subjects), the successful subjects; then proceed to the very successful, and last to the unsuccessful group.

Subject 108, a Successful subject, developed a great deal of imagery, particularly between the seventh and the twenty-third day. He also made a task for himself to dream a dream every day, that is, to *suggest* to himself that he dream a dream.

Already on the second day subject 108 experienced vacillations between Ego Activity and Ego Receptivity, as well as between Attention Concentration and Expansive Attention:

I closed my eyes and continued to observe the colors and patterns on my eyelids. I was able to suggest seeing various colors, especially blue and magenta. I also observed several patterns and shapes moving and changing against the color background. Oddly, the more I tried to focus my attention on these patterns, the fewer and less interesting the patterns became. I continued to watch the patterns but without paying strict attention to them. In general, most of the shapes were abstract or geometric, but occasionally I would recognize a person's face or body or some other object. These images continued to appear, as if they were being generated effortlessly by my mind. I found this stream of images and patterns intriguing and satisfying.

On day 4, subject 108 became frustrated because the harder he tried to concentrate on the suggestions that he gave to himself, the less he succeeded in deepening the trance. He still wanted to control the experience.

On Day 7, he finally added Imagery to Ego Activity to deepen the trance, quickly followed by Ego Inactivity, and Ego Receptivity. He let it happen rather than trying to force it, and thus became much more successful in his endeavor to deepen the trance.

On Day 8 he allowed even more Ego Receptivity, which led to Imagery; and he used less Ego Activity and control.

In this session I decided to take a less structured approach to any deepening suggestions. After induction (of trance) I concentrated solely on my breathing—I tried to see it as an involuntary and effortless process, and I tried to concentrate on the movement of air through the nose and lungs. This was very relaxing, and before long my concentration was diverted by many types of spontaneous images.

On Day 9 he again allowed more Ego Receptivity and Expansion of Attention. This led to a wealth of imagery, a beautiful dream, the latent content of which exemplifies Self-Hypnosis as a Regression in the Service of the Ego

I spent rather longer than usual in trying to go deeper, but it seemed that trying even in this abstract way was not very effective for producing a deep trance. As soon as I stopped concentrating on my breathing, imagery began to occur spontaneously. There was such a quantity of imagery that I felt I didn't have time to evaluate or explore it—I could relax and observe. It was if my imagination was overflowing with miscellaneous ideas.

My dream for this period was somewhat disjointed and discontinuous. First I am with a group of people—they seem to be my friends, although I don't recognize any of them. We are on our way to a sports arena to watch some kind of professional game. We arrive and buy our tickets and walk into the arena through a long series of dingy corridors. When we get inside there are only a few people present, although the arena is huge. While I am talking to my friends, I suddenly notice the playing field has changed to grass and the "inside" of the arena is actually "outside." Further, everyone is now dancing on the grass—I think this is very puzzling. But I don't mention it to anyone. My next image is that I am dancing myself—swinging a girl around very fast like I used to do playing as a child.

But he continued to struggle between the tendency to want to control all of his experiences and the rising knowledge that he should let go. Because he could not really relinquish control, he was unable to learn that letting go, i.e., Ego Receptivity and Expansive Attention, would lead deeper and faster into the profound stages of trance he wanted to achieve, than would Ego Activity and Attention Concentration.

Subject 108 was a talented subject. But unlike subject 081, the *highly* successful subject we shall discuss next, he also was a person to whom control meant a great deal. This prevented him from being *very* successful in self-hypnosis.

Contrast subject 108's report with the narrative of subject 081, one of our excellent (High) subjects who was not a bit concerned about "letting go." This subject, in reality, was an eighteen-year-old girl, but her imagination encompassed a wide range of ages. Here is an excerpt from Day 3:

Again I spent more time in a quiet trance with occasional thoughts running through. I regressed to a baby, first newborn, then 8 months, and then two years old, and then 9, and back to 18. As newborn I hardly moved. I just lay there and looked around the room. Everything looked new and big. At 8 months I moved more and sucked my hand and made sounds. At 2 I rocked and repeated "Mommy" and "Daddy" and made odd sounds. By the time I was nine I was bargaining with the popsicle man to give me a popsicle and some dry ice. I then went back up to 18. I was a cat for a few minutes and did a lot of purring. The most interesting part tonight was being a baby. Not being able to talk or sit up, just gurgle.

Effortlessly, this subject went into all kinds of interesting experiences and imagery, but kept enough control (again effortlessly) to get herself out of uncomfortable hypnotic situations and into more enjoyable ones as in the following example, Day 6:

First of all today I suggested I was a prisoner in my room. I was going to be in it alone for a year. I went around, pacing, touching the walls and doors nervously.

I became quite upset. I sat down and dreamed I was in a dungeon with bread and water being thrown in to me.

Then I was no longer a prisoner in my room or in a dungeon, I was in a harem. Just lying around lazily doing nothing except draw, bathe, munch, talk, and was sitting in total luxury. Then it appeared that some of my friends were in it. Then I was in a tent in the desert by myself. The dry cool wind was blowing over my body. I was a dancer; I was tired but cool after a hot day. Then I became wounded, a dying person on a battlefield with dead bodies around me. It was so very awful and hideous that I quickly changed before I fully took on the suggestion. At this point a deck of cards was shuffled right before me. An old woman was telling my fortune. I didn't want to hear it, however, so I picked up the cards. Also, today my back hurt; so I suggested this pain wasn't there, and it felt better.

The highlights today were being in a harem and lying in the tent just because I found it pleasurable. However, being in prison made me very upset and I almost cried. It was terrible to think of being completely alone in the room for a year. I also disliked being a dying person today on a battlefield and I'm glad I didn't get into it (although I think I should have).

Most of the experiences of subject 081 were delightful and interesting to her. They also give the reader the strong impression that the subject always experienced Deep Absorption and the GRO. But she rarely mentioned Absorption and the GRO in her diary.

This eighteen-year-old girl, in her typical adolescent identity struggle (Erikson, 1980), used the self-hypnosis experience to put herself into many niches and life roles in order to find one that would fit her.

Here are some more examples showing subject 081's rich imagery. On Day 16 she reflected:

Today I went into trance for 10 minutes and decided to become an old woman. I had some crocheting next to me that I was doing, and so I started it. I was talking to a grandchild—telling a story. I was very old. I moved creakily and slowly. Every chain I made crocheting was an effort. I was telling a story about my brother and a woman. I told it carefully, and each word was said so slowly that I'd forget what the entire sentence was. I got tired telling the story and crocheting, so I told my grandchild to let me rest. I went back into a restful trance. I really like becoming different characters. I go into a trance and either decide what character I want to be ahead of time, or just let whatever happens happen. I count to 5 or so, and then suddenly I'm that person. I get more and more into the role as time goes on. When I have no character in mind I count and then just start talking. Soon I realize what person I am, and it seems natural. I can then just slide into new roles each as real as the last. My feelings become those of the new person. I laugh, think, cry, gossip over my new character's concerns. I suddenly know all sorts of different people involved in her life. It's really interesting, and I enjoy doing it.

Of our two Low self-hypnosis subjects, one (subject 091) was too cerebral. He constantly observed himself, analyzing what he was doing or not able to do, and tried to find a computer-like system that would enable him to be both ego active (giving himself instructions) and able to let go and be ego receptive. The other, subject 045, did nothing else but give himself suggestions, most of them the same that he had received in hetero-hypnosis and often noting for each one in his diary whether it was successful or unsuccessful. By a "plus" he indicated that he was successful; by a "minus" he indicated that with this particular task he had been unsuccessful. Here are some typical excerpts from subject 045s diary.

Day 4:

+ left hand light...floating
- whole body floating
- dream
+ memory of kindergarten shopping trip
+ mental chess game
+ taste of corned beef sandwich

Ability to concentrate definitely heightened. Chess game sufficient although not astounding. Still unable to experience dream. Felt distracted by minor noises in room (some noisy plumbing, mostly).

Day 14:

At the end of the 2nd week, these sessions seem to be getting less, rather than more interesting; and I am having more and more trouble using up an hour.

Day 23:

I fell asleep after about 30 minutes of trance during which I gave myself no specific suggestions. I still can't quite tell the difference between trance and this light, normal sleep.

Poor self-hypnotic subjects like subject 045 lack the ability for Imagery, Ego Receptivity, Expansive Attention, and creative experiences in self-hypnosis. It may be possible to teach them self-hypnosis for the control of pain by teaching them to divert their Concentrative Attention to pleasant thoughts or memories. But I doubt that they can use self-hypnosis creatively for producing art, for working on emotional problems, even for diminishing anxiety. I believe that the successful and very successful self-hypnosis subjects can work on their problems by means of their ability to listen and look at that which comes up from within (Ego Receptivity), by their being capable of Expansive Attention, and above all by their having facile imaginations and little need to defend against Strong Affect.

Results

Results of our studies indicated that imagery is the most important aspect of self-hypnosis. The presence of imagery was a dramatic common denominator among all but three of our subjects' self-hypnosis experiences. It may be considered to be a marker of the self-hypnotic state itself: the more imagery, particularly the more primary process imagery, the deeper is the trance. Indeed, one of the studies done by our research group has shown that imagery in self-hypnosis positively correlates with the depth of trance (Kahn, Fromm, Lombard & Sossi).

Another of our studies, (Lombard, Kahn & Fromm) showed that imagery in self-hypnosis is a multidimensional phenomenon. Vivid realism of the image on the one hand, and the fantastic quality of imagery on the other, emerged as key features. A significant correlation was found between vivid-realistic imagery and primary process (i.e., fantastic) imagery, suggesting that these two are intertwined in self-hypnosis, yet qualitatively distinct constructs.

There were some very clear gender differences in imagery produced during self-hypnosis. Although our female as well as our male subjects were highly hypnotizable and manifested many similar personality characteristics—they all were sensitive people, intellectually curious, and esthetically oriented—the production of self-hypnotic imagery differed significantly between females and males. Male subjects produced significantly less vivid-realistic and primary process imagery than the female subjects did.

Results from other studies have also shown sex differences in the amount of non-hypnotic and of hetero-hypnotic imagery produced by males and females. Van Dyne and Stava (1981) found that female subjects experienced more vivid hypnotic imagery than male subjects did. Crawford (1982), found that women have more vivid waking-state imagery than males do. Pine and Holt (1960), Fromm *et al* (1981), Bowers (1971), and Coe, St. Jean & Burger (1980) also found that the vividness or the amount of imagery produced by women is greater than that produced by male subjects. In our present study we came to a similar conclusion. Despite the fact that according to personality tests we had given to our subjects there were great similarities between our male and our female groups, women produced more vivid and fantastic self-hypnosis imagery than did the men.

For the female subjects in our research project "impulse Expression and Control" and "Outgoingness" were positively correlated with primary process imagery. Our results suggest that the ability to express impulses rather than to rigidly control them, and a dramatic, forceful, risk-taking stance were positively associated with primary process imagery. The self-hypnotic imagery experienced by our female subjects appears to have been related to their impulse life. This finding contrasts with Bowers' (1971) hypothesis that female fantasy is oriented around environmental factors, while male fantasy is impulse-oriented.

The integration of masculine and feminine personality characteristics is perhaps the key to creative imagination. Males who have integrated both their imaginal (or "feminine") characteristics with their analytical, "masculine" attributes may be more likely to be highly aware of their imagery than those who have not. That is, the subjects' gender and the presence of personality characteristics associated with some measure of opposite sexual identifications may have contributed to the production of vivid-realistic and primary process imagery in our subjects. Among the female subjects, those who were able to express their impulses, and were outgoing, forthright, and adventurous, produced more primary process imagery than other female subjects. So did the highly sensitive, artistic males. These patterns reflect an integration of masculine and feminine personality characteristics and may be attributed to unconscious opposite sexual identifications. The presence of such strong trends in a relatively small sample indicates the findings are meaningful and worthy of further investigation.

Our results show that a strong enhancement of creative imagery is the most important aspect of self-hypnosis. The increase in imagery and the much greater variety of structural and content categories used in the self-hypnotic experience differentiate the diaries of the Successful and Highly Successful subjects from those of the poorer ones.

Note

[1]Certain parts of this paper were presented at the 9th International Congress of Hypnosis and Psychosomatic Medicine in Glasgow, Scotland, in August, 1982, and published under the title "Representations of Self-Hypnosis in Personal Narratives" in Waxman, D., Misra, P.C., Gibson, M., and Basker, M.A., *Modern Trends in Hypnosis.* New York: Plenum Press, 1985.

References

Bowers, K.S. "Sex and Susceptibility as Moderator Variables in the Relationship of Creativity and Hypnotic Susceptibility." *Journal of Abnormal Psychology*, 78 (1971): 93-100.

Coe, W.C., St. Jean, A.L., and Burger, J.M. "Hypnosis and the Enhancement of Visual Imagery. *International Journal of Clinical and Experimental Hypnosis*, 28 (1980): 225-243.

Crawford, H. J. Hypnotizability, Daydreaming Styles, Imagery Vividness, and Absorption: A Multidimensional Study. *Journal of Personality and Social Psychology*, 42 (1982): 915-926.

Erikson, E. *Identity and the Life Cycle.* New York: W. W. Norton & Company, 1980. (A reissue; originally published in *Psychological Issues*, 1, 1959).

Fromm, E., Brown, D. P., Hurt, S. W., Oberlander, J. Z., Boxer, A. M., & Pfeifer, G. The Phenomena and Characteristics of Self-hypnosis. *International Journal of Clinical and Experimental Hypnosis*, 29 (1981): 189-254.

Fromm, E., Oberlander, M. I., and Gruenewald, D. Perceptual and Cognitive Processes in Different States of Consciousness: The Waking State and Hypnosis. *Journal of Projective Techniques and Personality Assessment*, 34 (1970): 375-387.

Greeley, A. *Confessions of a Parish Priest.* New York: Simon and Schuster, 1986.

Kahn, S., Fromm, E., Lombard L. & Sossi, M. (in press). The relation of self-reports of hypnotic depth in self-hypnosis to hypnotic susceptibility and imagery production. *International Journal of Clinical and Experimental Hypnosis.*

Lombard, L., Kahn, S., & Fromm, E. (in press). The Role of Imagery in Self-hypnosis: Its Relationship to Personality Characteristics and Gender. *International Journal of Clinical and Experimental Hypnosis.*

Pine, F. and Holt, R. R. Creativity and Primary Process: A Study of Adaptive Regression. *Journal of Abnormal and Social Psychology*, 61 (1960): 370-379.

Shor, R. E. Hypnosis and the Concept of the Generalized Reality Orientation. *American Journal of Psychotherapy*, 13 (1959): 582-602.

Tart, C. C. Self-report Scales of Hypnotic Depth. *International Journal of Clinical and Experimental Hypnosis*, 18, (1970): 105-125.

Van Dyne, W. T. and Stava, L. J. (1981). Analysis of relationships among hypnotic susceptibility, personality type, and vividness of mental imagery. *Psychological Reports, 48*, (1981): 23-26.

Creative Imagination in Writing Religious History

Martin E. Marty

Since only .0013 percent of the American people make a living writing religious history (of the Judaeo-and Christian brands), there is little point in turning this chapter into a "how to write" exercise. Assuming that each author has ten readers, which means .013 percent of the population, there is not much more point in using it as a "how to read" program, if we have only one genre of formal literature in mind. Yet for all the people who are believers within the Western religious tradition, or who are affected by the tradition—which means 100% of the people— it is valid to reflect on what it means to retrieve stories from the past and tell them afresh.

The Crucial Contribution of History

Judaism and Christianity, it is often noted, are faiths that are through and through historical. This means that the drama of such faiths does not occur in the realm of Platonic ideas, Gnostic emanations, or realms above. The hidden Yahweh lays bear a holy arm, and the wielding of that arm is felt in battles in Canaan, wanderings of Israel, or the dance of the whirlwind. The letter to the Hebrews reminds Christians that "it was not to angels that God subjected the world to come," but to someone who "partook of the same nature" as children of flesh and blood. The Christian story deals with one who "had to be made like his brethren in every respect," including having armpits and tears, digestive processes and the joy of human company.

Believers may do what they wish with the Christian story, including systematize conclusions drawn from it or turn it into dogma and laws. Think of the imaginative leaps it takes to do just that! You'd never believe it! Yet a billion people do. It is not likely however, that they believe the dogmas or follow the laws because these converted or held the loyalties of that billion. The story grasped them.

The Place of Story in Human Life

The story. When a couple of people fall in love with each other, we expect soon to see them talking over candlelight at a restaurant, or locked in conversation as well as embrace in an automobile or on a sofa or at the beach. If they are using

25

the hours to grow in love and understanding, it is not likely that one is asking the other, "Please tell me the ten principles by which you live!" or "Give me your philosophy of life!" More likely they are saying something like, "Tell me your story!" Or, "I think you ought to know that I was abused as a child, and it will take some time to tell that." Or "You must know that I was happy in love before, but my fiance died, and I've never felt quite secure since then again." They grow together to build a two-person community by telling stories.

So do believing communities. A congregation is a place where people hear stories about Joshua and David, John the Baptist and Jesus. While memory fades when there are few readers or hearers or tellers of the story, it is still possible to presume that "the Good Samaritan" or "the Good Shepherd" or "the Psalmist" or "the Suffering Servant" means something to people whose faith in God is born of stories told in the Bible. It is possible to presume that to hear of "the Crusades" or "the Inquisition," of "Saint Francis" or "Martin Luther," events or people who belong to the tradition in post-biblical times, also connotes something based on stories in the minds of believers. The transaction goes less, "Tell me the ten principles by which Saint Francis lived!" and more, "Tell me the story of Saint Francis."

Particulars and the Christian Story

To deal with a story means to deal with particulars. G. K. Chesterton once said, or it was probably he who said, or he might have been the one who said something like, "If you want to draw a long-legged, long-necked, spotted animal and write "alligator" under the picture, that is your freedom." But it won't designate anything recognizable to readers who have familiarity with the animal kingdom. If you want to communicate, you have to write "giraffe" under such a picture, and "alligator" under appropriate other pictures.

Similarly, you have a right to say that the moon is made of Gruyere cheese— a mark of imagination, since in such illustrations it usually gets written off as green cheese—and that all who are Christians believe that gremlins dance on pinheads and pinpoints. But the choice to do that will not communicate much of anything except that you have freedom. If you want to talk to the Christian community about its origins, you have to base your stories on the stories that gave birth to such community, stories like those in the Bible or that derive from the biblical experience and community.

Such stories are not random. Once they occurred or were believed to have occurred, they get bonded to the experience of the believing community. They may be forgotten by many, but they are always potentially retrievable. They can be embellished, beautified, elaborated, uglified, just as the giraffe can be appliqued on black fabric, spraypainted with Day-Glo, or engraved with a steelpoint in surrealistic distortions. Yet they still have to designate or connote something that connects with specific acts.

These acts, the believing communities say, deal with the ways an eternal and invisible God creates and falls in love with the workings of time. These acts become the story of the creation and shaping, the nurture and chastening, the saving and mission of Israel. They focus, for Christians, in not only the oddly-by-Godly chosen

Jews, but in a particular Jew, a rabbi of Nazareth. You cannot stumble on the details of such a story by accident and imagination.

With the Aid of Monkeys and Chessboards

Bring on the monkeys. I invite them in whenever particularity, odds, and chance come into play. We used to be told that if you gave a monkey a typewriter and an infinite amount of time, sooner or later he would type the works of Shakespeare, or at least *Hamlet*, or a scene from that play. (A comedy troupe urged instant solution: get an infinite number of monkeys and typewriters and they would produce such a work at once.) Mathematicians, however, have pointed out that on such a random basis, it would take a monkey with a word-processor trillions of years to hit, by chance, only the words on the spine of the book itself, *The Works of William Shakespeare* or the line, "To be or not to be, that is the question." The monkeys remind us that the complex story behind the believing community is inherited, derived, locked into history, in need of telling and hearing.

The mere presence of the story, however, does not exhaust the need for imagination. Here comes variety in the telling. Clear off the monkeys and bring on the chessboard, my other favored device for illustrating choice and option. We are told that if we wanted to play all the varieties of the first eleven moves of chess on each side, we would have to call in all the people now alive and have had them begin a game every few minutes since the time of Christ in order to exhaust the opportunities. (For such an exercise we would have to think with the Stephen Hawking of several years ago that time moves in both directions, that we can "remember the future" and project events backward, but that is not the part of the exercise that is the present point). More recently I have read that to exhaust all the moves on the whole chessboard one would have to entertain as many options as there neutrons in our universe. Infinite!

The Locations of Readers and Hearers

So with the telling of the story that historians draw upon. It is one thing to hear it told by a homilist in a suburban mass and another to have it rendered by an angry feminist. It is one thing to hear it on a bed in a cancer ward and another to hear it after the birth of a first child. It is one thing to have it reworked in a folk song and another in a baroque mass. It is all kinds of things in the hands of theologians, philosophers, God-killers, poets, parents. Or professional historians.

Think of the creative imagination it takes to decide to make a living as such an historian. Picture the tombstone of such as me. It could read: "Here Lies Martin E. Marty. Born February 5, 1928. Died February 5, 2018. He told stories for a living." [Note, in passing, that the birth date is the same as that of one Father Andrew Greeley, who is two hours younger and should outlive me by two hours, after which we join the company of Aquarians in their corner of the mansions above. But that is another story.] "He told stories." He was an historian. It could have shown other kinds of imagination. "He had an M.B.A." or "He played Glockenspiel." Or "He sent men into battle to get killed." How frivolous it seems to make one's living telling elements of the Christian story. If frivolous, then, to someone who has a desperate interest in finding meaning in life and would like to think it worthwhile, how imaginative.

Imagination in Specialty-Choosing

After one has chosen to respond to the vocation of being an historian of the Christian story, the imaginative work really begins. Take the issue of specialty. The homilist or Confraternity of Christian Doctrine instructor may generalize with the biblical story, to have some awareness of all its parts, especially when they come around in weekly Lectionary texts or as background to some lesson for high schoolers. (I think it takes more imagination to pull off a good homily or hold the attention of teenagers for an hour than to write a critically well-reviewed monograph on Christian history but that, once again, is another story.) The professional historian uses imagination to find a period, a zone of interest, a topic, a specialty.

Jacob Burckhardt once wrote that history is an account of what one age finds worthy of notice in another. Our generation may be interested in aspects of "the Servant Church" or "the People of God on pilgrimage" just as another generation may have turned to stories of "the triumph of leaders within the tall towers of total Christendom." But within a generation there is also choice. One specializes in the life of Empress Theodora and another in her relation to the Monophysite Controversy and still another in the history of St. Agnes' Parish. It takes creative imagination to stick with the story, since most people will not turn to it. Here the religious historian has to be inwardly driven, as must the poet in Dylan Thomas's understanding. His or her "craft and sullen art" is about lovers who lie abed oblivious to and uninterested in the poems about lovers who lie abed. Most Christians may not feel the need and probably do not need all the stories of all the historians. One may not get the notice of a colleague in the next office. Why expect a Uruguayan peasant to care?

On Relevance and "Stopping to Think"

While pursuing historical writing, or any of the humanities, one is engaged in acts of what John Henry Newman called "creative irrelevance." Yet there is also some sustenance in the record itself: one knows that now and again the apparently irrelevant suddenly turns relevant. Alfred Schutz has spoken of intrinsic and imposed relevances. Intrinsic relevance has to do with what is contrived to meet a situation. It would be intrinsically relevant for me to help achieve a means of successfully ending the AIDS plague. But there can also be imposed relevance. I may go about my work in a laboratory almost as if pursuing science for science's sake—and then find that someone uses one of my discoveries to help address the AIDS treatment or cure.

So with Christian stories. They may begin in almost studied irrelevance and suddenly be of use to the community. For an example: at mid-century a number of us seminarians celebrated an invented theologian, Franz Bibfeldt. We took him seriously. In 1951 one of us noticed that it was the 1500th anniversary of the Council of Chalcedon. No one seemed to care. We Bibfeldtians did. With the delight insiders in on a hoax share, we announced that the Bibfeldt Circle would read papers on that Council. My topic, for instance, was "The Concept of Substance at the Council of Chalcedon." We took the assignments seriously, learned something that gave us pleasure and taught us something, and then closed the books. A year later the Faith and Order Commission people of the new World Council of Churches announced that Christians could not move forward in making statements about the divinity and humanity of Christ without first revisiting the intentions of the theologians back at the Council of Chalcedon. We were ready to go, far ahead of the story and the pack that would tell it.

When does the product of the crafty and sullenly artful but creatively irrelevant historian-story teller become potentially relevant? G. J. Renier, a great historian and thinker about history, suggested when: when society "stops to think." History is a story and nothing but a story. It is the story of the human in society past. One can go about business on a routine basis. When a crisis or an opportunity comes, then one consults what historians have been keeping alive through their preservation of archives, their research and organization of stories, their writing and publishing. The Second Vatican Council found a Catholic church in crisis and facing opportunity. Its scholars drew on neglected elements of biblical and later Christian story in order to gain precedent and courage for acting in the future. They would have nothing on which to draw had the scholars chosen to burn the records, spread the contagion of ecclesiastical amnesia, or been neglectful. They had used their imagination and therefore Pope John XXIII and Pope Paul VI and bishops and a half million faithful had resources to do things that meant the writing of a new chapter and more in the Christian history.

The Choice of Genre and Method

The choice of genre in historical writing is also a part of creative imagination within this vocation. One concentrates, by instinct and training and practice, on, say, intellectual or social or cultural history, and in a lifetime begins to get good at some part of it. An historian will draw on the modes of others and, please God, will not be 'pure' since historical work is never pure; she will have elements of several genres in her story. Yet there is usually a prime accent. An illustration will help clarify this point. (Note here as several times already in this essay: when an historian wants to make a point, he tells another story).

Several years ago thirteen members of our faculty were airlifted to storied Tuebingen, the German university town, ("now, Hans Kueng's") for a conference. I had heard that one year philosophers George Wilhelm Friedrich Hegel and Friedrich Wilhelm Joseph von Schelling and poet Johann Christian Friedrich Hoelderlein had roomed together in the dormitory of the Evangelical Seminary there. I also had heard that Ferdinand Christian Baur, the founder of modern Christian "history of theology" who taught there had to read, not write, early on winter mornings. He was too kind to wake the servants to light the fire and too professorial to do so himself, so he could not dip his pen into the ink; it was frozen. I located what I think was the dormitory room (though its present denizens were oblivious to the fact and uninterested in hearing about it) and the Baurian home study. Come see them, I urged my colleague, a peerless historian of Christian thought in the Hegel-Schelling-Hoelderlein-Baur era. To my astonishment I had to hear that he had no interest in giants' dormitory rooms and inkwells; he taught their ideas, not their biographies and social history.

Our historical imaginations had difficulty touching at the moment. I granted that overall it is far more important to know the intellectual history of Hegel and Baur than to find their dormitories and inkstands. Yet to a social or cultural historian, the past retrieved by such sites also tells important things. It helps draw attention to the concentration of brain power in an era and in a place and evokes questions as to why we are so dumb and dull today. It helps tell what was the status of a professor then, compared to that of professors now who can write in the morning even if they do not wait for the servants to turn up the thermostat and to turn on the word-processor.

On Being an Historical Historian

Tuebingen, by the way, by and large, made its choice, and honors theology, intellectual historians, historical theologians, and historians of theology. When conference time came, I found that the writers of the program had a hard time defining my kind of historian. They learned that I teach the same kind of history as one teaches in history departments. In some puzzlement, evidently, someone on the committee invented the designation: "Martin E. Marty, Professor of Historical History." Or, as the great pioneer of historical history in 19th century Germany, Leopold von Ranke would have it, I was "nur ein gewoehnlicher Historiker," just a conventional historian—and not a philosopher of history.

Yet conventional historians have to use their imaginations. Andrew Greeley can tell you that it sometimes takes more intellectual energy for him to tell a story than it does to take a sociological survey. It is work as well as play to stick to narrative, to have a taste for people and places that are inaccessible to us except in imagination that seeks to recreate their made-up or "actual" past. Mention of that brings us to the most risky, frightening, and, if one thinks about it, almost defeating aspect of historical work—and one that grows in risk and urgency when the historian deals with desperately urgent matters like the stories behind peoples' faith—the leap from present to past and from trace to event.

Is There a Past? There Are Only Traces

Here creative imagination most comes into play. The non-historian may not often think of this, and the historian would go mad if she thought too often about it but the entire venture is based on a leap from trace to event. Let the madness spread: Arthur Danto has suggested that it would be philosophically difficult if not impossible to prove that the world was not created by an instantaneous act five seconds ago. The best clues we have that it did not are our own remembered existences through longer time and the existence of the past tense. Why need it if it did not designate such passage through time? But, I have to say still another time, that is another story for another day. We have a sufficiently difficult jump ahead of us.

Here, to the point, it is: past events are, in themselves, simply and irretrievably lost. They do not, by themselves, exist. We are wholly dependent on the traces they leave, traces associated with them, for any stories we would tell. Here is a monument, there a bill of sale, here a pyramid, there a tomb, and still there, a library of documents. We are dependent upon artifacts or witnesses. We cannot know with complete assurance that the traces were not left to mislead, to beguile, to seduce, to distract us. Whoever has followed congressional heroes during times of Constitutional arguments and governmental scandal, knows how legitimate documents get shredded, how manufactured events get invented through contrived documents, how random traces—audio tapes of conversations, for instance—give us upsetting "truths." Do we know that what was shredded would have given us a different story than the one the shredders invent would tell us? Almost certainly so. Do we know that voices on tapes were not fabricated, faked by actors? Certainly not, but there are good reasons to have some sense of reliance on them. Yet just as they are subject to varied interpretations, by Republicans and Democrats, for instance, so one loses a sense of stability and certainly of "objectivity" in the traces or sources and in the interpretive community.

The Issue of Assumptions and Preconceptions

Suppose one can get over the hang-ups that can come when one stops worrying about whether the past actually existed and, secondly, about how we are dependent upon traces and cannot get at past events. There are still creatively imaginative leaps ahead. For instance, there is the matter of a priori, presuppositions and assumptions. These always color the account of the first witnesses who leave us the traces to events as well as to the later company of historians who revisit the traces and leave their interpretations. The phenomenologist asks us to "bracket" such presuppositions. He does not say we can do away with them, but only that we can somehow become aware of some aspect of them. Yet go away they will not. R. G. Collingwood once said that the kind of history we write tells us much about the kind of persons we are. One might also say that the kind of history we write tells something of what we believe.

This does not mean that all Christian history is written by Christian dogmatic ideologues. Much good Christian history, be it remembered, is written by people who may not be Christian, may not be convinced by the Christian story, at all. And one soon catches in the act the one who does not "bracket" faith commitments and who imposes them on a story. Thus I could say to my history department colleagues: "Here is the true story. I know I don't have documents to back it up at crucial moments, but I am 'born again,' so I have a good feel for the story. I have a commitment to a doctrine of Providence, and can say that a provident God gives me facts about the past that are inaccessible to you. Because this God is provident, I who have faith in him can tell about outcomes that are lost to you." Those colleagues would say, "That's all very interesting, Marty. But either you are living in the centuries you write about—we moderns don't think that way—

or we should get you an appointment in the psychiatric clinic, because you have a dangerous set of delusions, or you ought to transfer departments, because whatever else you are doing it is not research and writing history. You are not, as they say at Tuebingen, an historical historian."

Historical historians, more than some of them know, do import interpretations or philosophies of history, however pure they would be. Thus the positivist believed— and believes, for dinosaurs do exist in our profession, and fossils survive, and in some departments outnumber living types—that they can be utterly objective, neutral, devoted to ordering facts, and presenting the past as it was. Yet the choice of being a positivist is a commitment; it relies on ambitious architectures of the imagination, deft mental sleight-of-hand acts, and not a little chutzpah or ignorance of metaphysics. Most other historians recognize that somehow who they are and what they believe colors their work. If what they believe is not conscious, it still belongs to them. The model of this is Jose Ortega y Gasset's concept of *creencias*, which are ideas so deep we do not know we have them; they are not the beliefs that we hold but the beliefs that we are.

Often beliefs connecting one with Jewish and Christian stories are seen as the only obscuring, blighting, and prejudicing ones. In 1978 at Ball State University there was held a conference on "interpretations of history." These included "behavioralism," "feminism," "black," and "Marxist" interpretations alongside Jewish and Christian perspectives. I enjoyed reminding the audience that the modern university is nervous about none of the above except the Jewish and Christian. Why do these make people nervous? Because they connect with philosophies of history in the sense that one's expectation of the future (Messiah? Eschaton?) color one's understanding of the present. The Christian drama is based in notions that the human drama accessible to historians connects also with an unseen, eternal Actor who imparts meaning or makes possible some finding of meaning in the otherwise random, temporal flux.

Shocking. But are not the other philosophies of history also based upon some such concepts of the whole of history? The Marxist messianic moment has not arrived; it belongs to the future, but assurance that it is coming colors one's interpretation of the present. The black and feminist understandings are based on the concept that past suppression and enslavement endow a story with distinctively if not even uniquely valid meaning, accessible only or chiefly to those who have endured oppression or who are heirs of those who did. Indeed, we might all, or almost all, come to an understanding of the value of such story, but, says the heir of Holocaust victim or suburban male alienation or immigrant snubbings, there are also other stories. Christianity itself is about suffering, even when told by middle class males with academic tenure, who may bring their own individual and collective memories of suffering to their writing of the plot.

Honoring the Sufferers

Christianity is about suffering. So is Judaism. So is the human story at large. The creative imagination of the historian comes into play in endeavors to recreate or represent some account of that story. Theodor Adorno has said that since human history is the story of suffering, and suffering acquires some of its dignity by being remembered, to choose to forget, to repudiate history and tradition, is a dehumanizing act. So the historian in the Jewish and Christian traditions somehow comes to terms not only with a distinctive set of philosophies of history, but with the need to do justice to the dimensions of human experience in which not everything turns out well. All the people of more than a century ago died. Most of them did not want to die. They did not get what they wanted. Most of them presumably died in pain. The fact that the pain occurred long ago did not lessen it; indeed, pre-anesthesia it may have been greater than is pain today. Yet those believers "died in faith," in a faith expressed in the Hebrew Scriptures with cries such as "Though he slay me, yet will I trust him!" To make such cries and faith and pain intelligible in another kind of time and place demands creative imagination on the part of those who would tell their stories, would be historians.

Theories of Behavior in Christian History

Creative imagination also comes into play in that the traces that are left do not and cannot tell us all that we would like to know about a past event. They cannot reproduce or keep alive for us all aspects of the mindsets of the past. Take the most crucial event or test for the Christian historian, the determinative act that the faithful call "the Resurrection of Christ." There are some notable theologians, as notable as Germany's Wolfhart Pannenberg, who suggest that this resurrection is as assured and accessible an event of the past as are many other ancient events. There is witness to an empty tomb. There is the existence of a believing community of transformed disciples. His arguments about how faith connects with historical proof here, however, are so intricate that theologian Daniel Fuller speculates: one must have a Ph.D. in philosophy of history and historical method in order thus to be a believer.

No, people believed, said Fuller, for other reasons. Some contemporaries suggest that if the Shroud of Turin is proven to be authentic, faith will spread. I wonder. Suppose it had attached to it a trademark or bill that it came from Sam's Linen Shop in Jerusalem, purchased in the Passover Season around 29 A.D., and that it bore all the authentic marks of dried blood etc., would faith be born? If faith were thus born, would not the disciples, who could easily have preserved it and would have to have, if the cloth would be authentic, have run all over Asia Minor waving it and saying, "He is risen?" No, all we have to go on are witnesses. Fuller reminds us that at Antioch people believed because they found apostle Barnabas plausible as a good man, full of the Holy Spirit. His character and credibility, the quality of his life and risky testimony—all these led "many" to believe.

The historian, in this case the author of Luke-Acts and thus the pioneer in the Christian historical profession, tells that story. Yet the imagination that tells subsequent stories based on such traces and accounts has only begun to be brought into play thereafter. In order to make sense of it, the historian brings some understanding of human behavior into play. Robert Berkhofer has argued that one cannot "do" history without having some explicit or implicit, informed or misformed, concept of why humans act as they do. Yet past actors, in this case

Barnabas and the hearers at Antioch, are not available for extensive psychological examination. The historian does not have the psychoanalyst's advantage of having the client or subject on the couch, available for endless hours of intimate questioning. We have only a few lines about Barnabas and a few chapters about the spread of early Christianity.

Instead, to make sense of such a story, we stand at the side of Wilhelm Dilthey and R. G. Collingwood and other great hermeneuticians of historical writing, and say that we must somehow use imagination to create analogues for past events and interpretations. To do so does not prove the existence of God or the truth of the Christian story. (Whoever thinks such proofs are the goal of the Christian historian had better seek other media, and probably has already done so.) To do so may make intelligible past actions. We know how faith comes in the present world: chiefly when credible people testify who are already plausible to us, perhaps because their testimony is given at risk (as in the case of the persecuted, those imprisoned for their faith, those who risk status in specific intellectual communities). From such knowledge we can "back up" to make sense of earlier experiences. Thus Dilthey says that the "modern" cannot have Luther's kind of religious experience. (Some moderns can and do!) That is, they will not writhe before God in guilt and make a river of tears their nightly pillow-soaker. They will not feel threatened by a God who is too near. But by analogy, they can come into the zone where Luther's experience makes sense. Paul Tillich would say that today one does this by describing the terror of numbness created by a sense not of the too-nearness but of the absence of God. When one is thus rendered alert, it is possible to find Luther's story intelligible. What is important to note here is that the story is told and heard against the background of experience we bring about what people do find believable and when they believe.

The Creative Researcher

I have restricted my comments about creative imagination in the writing of history to what might be called the archaeology of the subject. We have set out to disinter the understandings that stand well behind the ordinary act of writing. It would be possible to go on from there to describe many kinds of taken-for-granted creative activity that we find in the better historians. They may have to be creative about grantspersonship, a barbarism for the act of writing successful grant applications to get funds for research in far off deserts and monasteries. Whoever has read many of these as member of juries in granting agencies knows that here as seldom the historian, the "conventional historian," the "historical historian," most likely shows the novelist's art of fiction-writing.

So she gets to go to where the traces and documents are. Finding one's way through archives, doing research, compiling notes—all these call for certain kinds of creativity, though often no more is evoked than were the subject locusts or marigolds or anything else that can be found, studied, and classified. The creative moment returns, I argue and try to teach my students and follow myself, when one "takes command" of the research. Those dominated by superabundance of notes on 3 x 5 inch cards may never find a story. They may only feel a responsibility to classify what they have laboriously copied, without ever having taken time to tell their story based upon such research. Leave the cards in another room, I urge; write the story one feels impelled to tell, for entertainment or edification or intrinsically, having it all grow out of the research and one's own lived experience. Then return to the cards to see what was missed, distorted, overlooked, or wrong. There the exact quotations and the footnoted substantiating materials come into play. To each her own method: there is no one correct way. Yet to do justice to the tears and laughter, the commitments and paradoxes of Jewish and Christian believers and members in faith communities, acts of imagination come into play.

The Rhetoric of Christian History

Finally, one comes to the threshold of another topic involving creative imagination: the rhetoric of history, whether spoken or written. Christian historians often do not get to be effective because they lack rhetorical power. Often the professionals have to stand aside, however much they know, because the amateurs tell the story better. I do not know how to impart creative abilities to people who do good research, argue well, explain sufficiently, and fail to hold interest. I do know that some barriers to being interesting can be minimized.

One of these is the conventions of the trade. In many graduate schools and journals young historians are encouraged to be as uninteresting as possible. They must impress by choosing incredibly arcane and specialized topics, master them, and write unintelligibly intellectual-looking articles on them for publication in lugubrious and unread journals. Only thus can they pass from assistant to associate to full professor. Some day some of them become presidents of historical organizations and are expected in their presidential addresses to reflect on their craft. To the surprise of many, they often turn out also to have been interesting people who bring strange, provocative, even outlandish perspectives to their work. It is probably good that they do not get to show this much interestingness until they have paid the dues of the craft—accuracy, steadfastness, industry, attention to detail.

The pathos lies, however, in the fact that while historians write about people, and people are intrinsically interesting, they sometimes do this writing in such ways that people and their past become boring. In the coming generation if the historical historians are to achieve what they might, they will—alongside deliverers of homilies, teachers of children, builders of community, and leaders of movements—reexplore the arts of rhetoric, or persuasive speech and writing. It is likely that to do so they will have to explore the power and character of myth and symbol, rite and ceremony, dream and vision, in the lives of the ordinary people who were members of the believing community. Or who read about them now. Some of such writers will find it profitable to have hung out with mythosymbolic enactors of rite and ceremony. For instance, among them, with Andrew Greeley, who has for some decades been standing for such enactments and achievements among us.

PART TWO

Modelling Ideology as Configurations for Action[1]

Harrison C. White

I wish to suggest a way in which mathematical formulation can capture aspects of the subtle interplay of culture with social process. Many have expressed dissatisfaction with current approaches to this interplay. In the words of Clifford Geertz "...the absence of any analytic framework with which to deal with figurative language...(has) reduced sociologists to viewing ideologies as elaborate cries of pain...." (207).

My basic claim is that a person when urgently concerned with his social locale conceives it as a configuration of specific actors joined one to another by basic sorts of ties. A child, upon the birth of a sibling, does this early. Adults take, as guides to construing a configuration, not only earlier experiences but also images of social configurations in their cultures—whether formal, as from a drama, or newspaper story, or from everyday language and shared experience. Such guides are metaphors—mappings between own social locale and cultural image.

Before developing my point—which can be seen as building tangible plumbing for the poetic flows of culture analysts—let us see how even the basic claim has surprising sharpness. it may be neglected just because the tangible mathematical plumbing required to make it good is not familiar.

Robert Axelrod recently coded the Hitler-Chamberlain argumentation of 1938 into 653 "assertions" concerning 174 "concept variables." Each assertion consists of a cause, a connector, and an effect. In his words: "Since the effect variable of one assertion can be the cause variable of another assertion, arguments can be represented as chains of assertions. The easiest way to visualize the complex structure that can result is to represent the concept variables as points, and represent the connections between them as arrows...." These chains were terminated by the one-third of the assertions, called value assertions, which led to German or British national utility.

I argue that Axelrod's vision of this ideological confrontation *is* shaped by a mathematical technique, path analysis but is inappropriately shaped. His "concept variables" are in fact such as "oppression of Sudeten Germans," "fulfillment by Hitler of promises to Germans," "Czechoslovakia as a spearhead in the side of Germany," "Czechoslovakian alliances with other countries," "French and British readiness to go to war over the Sudetenland," "worldwide support of German." "His "connectors" are positive, negative, or no effect. The shaping by path analysis seems arbitrary, and Axelrod indeed does report in some puzzlement finding very little of that interweaving of chains which is at the heart of path models—and of course there are no actual numeric coefficients for paths.

Euclidean graphs reminiscent of economics or metallurgical phase diagrams are Charles Tilly's choice for analyzing collective actions, *From Mobilization to Revolution*. To him, too, some mathematical conception seems essential to capture the complexities of social interaction mediated by ideology. Again the use of variables appears awkward, and no actual calculations seem feasible. To me, a sure sign of inappropriate mathematical formulation is the absence of urges to specific computations.

Instead of metric variables, I advocate trying algebraic representation of ties among actors as our mathematical framework, leading to new sorts of predictions and calculations—mappings, homomorphisms, congruences. Configurations of a few basic relations among a set of actors are the heart of Tilly's mobilization-repression dynamics, and these configurations are ill-summarized by "heights" of variables.

An observer's view of an urgent social configuration is inadequate for repressing and predicting the social process underway. Actors will be bringing to bear their own views of the configuration. Individuals, in shaping their views, seek and choose guidance in metaphors, from configurations portrayed in their culture. Control of the menu of metaphors available, as ideologies, gives great though indirect power to the class able to effect it. At the same time a metaphor guides a person to other persons perceived as in the same position: they may together shape their own particular view of the configuration around them and in so doing combine and alter metaphors with some small impact on the existing menu. An observer *can* summarize the concrete pattern of relations which emerges, reflecting a least common denominator of various metaphors as applied by individuals in the concrete population.

Before sketching the particular operationalization which colleagues and I have developed, available for calculations on specific data, I ask you to judge whether the scheme above is not consistent with that of Geertz, who calls for "thick description" in disdain of overly sociologized and mechanical approaches to interplay between culture and social process. The very subtleties and complexities he emphasizes cry out to my mind for explicit and thus mathematical formulation. In his words ". . . we are reduced to insinuating theories because we lack the power to state them" (24).

My text for this purpose pieces together other quotes from Geertz's 1973 selection of essays:

Culture patterns have an intrinsic double aspect: they give meaning, that is objective conceptual form, to social and psychological reality both by shaping themselves to it and by shaping it to themselves (93).

Cultural acts, the construction, apprehension, and utilization of symbolic forms, are social events like any other; they are as public as marriage and as observable as agriculture (91).

...our mental task shifts from a gathering of information about the pattern of events in the external world per se toward a determining of the affective significance, the emotional impact of that pattern of events.... The reading of Kafka's novels enables us to form a distinct and well-defined attitude toward modern bureaucracy....Not only ideas, but emotions, too, are cultural artifacts in man (81).

The perceptions of the structural congruence between one set of processes, activities, relations, entities, and so on, and another set for which it acts as a program...—symbol— of the programmed, is the essence of human thought (94).

The climax, for my purposes, are these words:

...(consider) ideologies as systems of interacting symbols, as patterns of interworking meanings.... Not only is the semantic structure of the (ideological) figure a good deal more complex than it appears on the surface, but an analysis of that structure forces one into tracing a multiplicity of referential connections between it and social reality, so that the final picture is one of a configuration of dissimilar meanings out of whose interworking both the expressive power and the rhetorical force of the final symbol derive. This interworking is itself a social process.... (206-213)

First, I lay out the elements of the mathematical representation developed by the research group with which I was associated.

The actors a given person sees implicated with him in an urgent situation need not be the same as, though they will overlap with, those seen by another person. They may not all be particular individuals. Siegwart Lindenberg recently found that newspaper reporters in major stories perceived over a third of the major actors as various kinds of abstract, situational or anonymous entities; also organizations and positions in them were more numerous than individuals as such.

In sizing up his social configuration an actor will discriminate only a few types of ties from himself to, and among, other actors. We may assume like Axelrod just ties which help and hinder, or those plus neutral familiarity; the individual will not make such analytic distinctions as between affective and cognitive. The major assumption in our present models is that all actors discriminate the *same* few types of ties.

On the other side of the metaphor, in an icon, persons can see a dramatic configuration portrayed in analogous terms. Icon, of course, means symbol, which also has a concrete meaning. By the nature of an icon there will be fewer actors involved and general agreement on which pairs each type of tie obtains between. A person comes to identify himself with some actor in the icon through seeking guidance from it.

Now to a brief sketch of the calculations. There is one on each side of the metaphor, and a correspondence is induced between them. The basic step is computing the incidence between pairs of actors of each possible kind of compound of the types of ties. This is a Boolean calculation, which does not discriminate numbers or strengths of paths of the given kind of compound tie between a given pair. It yields a description of how the configuration interlocks, a description not requiring numerical discriminations beyond the intuitive scope of the person being considered.

The key idea, in completing calculation for the person's own view of the configuration, is due to Christopher Winship, who also emphasized the descriptive array just defined, which I call a Winship box. This idea is to search for persons who are automorphically equivalent, that is with the same abstract structuring of compound ties, whether or not the actual persons so reached are the same. Automorphic equivalence is *not* decided directly by perfect match, but by comparative discrimination of a sort that may simulate intuitive processes. Cluster algorithms are used which work from numerical distances defined upon the results of searches in the Winship box. Philippa Pattison collaborated in this development.

The results can be stated. A set of equations, from a given person's point of view, which state approximate equivalences among types of compound tie. These equivalences also hold from the point of view of other persons found automorphically equivalent to the first—whether or not one knows, or is tied, to another. Thus we argue they have objective standing: they state an abstract position—held in a field of standard types of ties, even though the computation builds from a subjective point of view. Social class in the Marxist sense is such an abstract position. An analogous algebra can be computed for each actor in the icon more easily and perhaps with no approximations necessary.

Now to the main point. The guidance a person can obtain from an icon is by a correspondence between his class position and one he finds in the icon. (The correspondence may be a negative one, in which case it is better called irony.) In our mathematical parse of this intuitive search for correspondence, a person's algebra is mapped from that of an actor in the icon. The person may have but a vague apprehension of his class position. If our mathematical simulation has truth, his class position, though in some sense qualitative, is not easy to discern from his concrete configuration, especially not unless his perceptions of ties among others are sharp, and not then unless and as he identifies and compares notes with equivalent persons. A correspondence, a mapping from a class position in the icon, can yield and influence his search. More, it can shift his identification, in our terms his algebra equations, or reach in still further and coax changes in his perception of ties themselves. Over time, the reverse can occur, and persons beginning to be conscious of a distinctive new class position may produce or induce changes in the menu of icons. There is no implification that all persons find a class position or that the icons are adequate.

Class position once identified will tend to persist until urgent pressure or disorienting change in context fuels renewed search. In a *particular* population bound in tangible interaction, persisting class positions of various persons must come to terms. Earlier work of our research group, on block-models and their algebra, dealt with this situation, where not just role equivalence but concrete positional equivalence is at issue (White, Boorman and Breiger; Boorman and White).

I can but mention two of the substantial empirical difficulties implicit in this sketch. Sociometric field techniques have not proved effective in getting at a person's perceptions of others' ties. Such ties between others are crucial to the given person's I-algebra which we construct analytically through tracing compound ties of given types through other persons. At least to start, we will assume that the ties persons perceive are those reported by the other persons involved.

Many of the actors perceived in a social configuration will not be individuals, and content analysis techniques must be relied on for those direct ties. Here Lindenberg's results, cited earlier, raise a second difficulty, again about construction of compound ties: he finds that abstract actors are twice as common as targets of action than as initiators.

One way to summarize our aim is as a reinterpretation of the ambitious early work of Sutton et al.[2], which they summarize well in a sentence Geertz also notes: "Ideology is a patterned reaction to the patterned strains of a social role" (307).

*   *   *

Even this bare sketch is cumbersome. My earlier extensive quotes from Geertz and remarks on other formal analyses of ideology were designed to convince you that effective modelling in this area requires a heavy framework. Now before ending, I should persuade you that the term, metaphor, is borrowed honestly.

Max Black gives this classic example of a metaphor: "The poor are the Negroes of Europe" (26). Insertion of "like me" after poor turns it into a shorthand form of metaphor in my usage. In Black's words: "The metaphor selects, emphasizes, suppresses, and organizes features of the principal subject by applying a system of 'commonplaces' about the subsidiary subject" (44-5). This is close to the view of Paul Henle:

In the metaphor it is not merely that there are parallel situations—the same elements in the same arrangement, but also that there is a felt similarity between the corresponding components.... Thus the aptness of metaphor depends on the capability of elaborating it—of extending the parallel structure....[it] can be spun out, following a line of analogy, or even several lines at once. (180)

I move one side of metaphor down from a literary to a real life situation, and I emphasize relational, network aspects, rather than categorical attributes for each of the two subjects. Having done so, I can assimilate other, linguistic insights from Henle. My metaphors, like his word inflections, cause a kind of forced observation by the user—to use the verb he must note time order or the noun, sex; to use the metaphor he must note relations among others in his ken. Yet still available are the insights of literary critics. That my usage is not foreign to their approach is suggested by this remark of Ian Watt "...that typical device of comedy, total ignorance by one character of the intentions of the other as a result of a misunderstanding between third parties..." (263). Or by the successful play of the 1960s, MacBird. Or by Lukacs' contrast of drama to the historical novel, or Auerbach's views on figural as contrasted with rhetorical literature.

Still more important, I wish to persuade you, in ending, that estimation through metaphor captures much of what people actually do, and need to do. Metaphor is not a made-up concept, it was derived by observing how speakers moved men in Greek assemblies considering urgent public matters touching all. V. I. Lenin laid down that workers can acquire political class consciousness only outside the sphere of relations between workers and employers: icons are needed. Masterson asserts that Black's metaphors capture what scientists do to find a new way of seeing. (80) Finally, consider this patronizing tale by Herbert Simon:

...I have heard the chairman of the board of a very large and successful American corporation discuss the procedures his company used for reaching decisions on questions of highest importance—questions that reach the level of the board of directors. At a loss for words or a scheme of analysis, he had to resort to a homely and inadequate parable about the decision processes he had observed in a shopping expedition with is wife. And so it goes. We talk about organization in terms not unlike those used by a Ubangi medicine man to discuss disease...." (xiv)

And so indeed it goes, I argue—the chairman was at no loss for a scheme, he used a metaphorical scheme sufficiently subtle, and powerful, that we social scientists are as yet unable to pin down.

Notes

[1]Financial support under NSF grant SOG 76 24394 is gratefully acknowledged, as is crucial help from Professor Ronald L. Breiger and from Cynthia A. White.
[2]*The American Business Creed.*

References

Auerbach, Erich. *Mimesis.* Princeton: University Press, 1953.

Axelrod, Robert. "Argumentation in Foreign Policy Decision Making." Institute of Public Policy, University of Michigan, Discussion Paper No. 90, 1976.

Black, Max. *Models and Metaphors.* Ithaca: Cornell University Press, 1962.

Boorman, Scott and Harrison. C. White. "Social Structure from Multiple Networks, II. Role Structures." *American Journal of Sociology,* 81 (1976): 1385-1446.

Geertz, Clifford. *The Interpretation of Cultures.* New York: Basic Books, Inc., 1973.

Henle, Paul (ed.). *Language, Thought and Culture.* Ann Arbor: University of Michigan Press, 1958.

Lindenberg, Seegwart. "Actor Analysis and Depersonalization." *Mens En Maatschappij,* 51, 2(1976): 152-178.

Lukacs, Georg. *The Historical Novel.* New York: Penguin Books, 1962 (1939).

Masterman, Margaret. "The Nature of a Paradigm." In I. Lakatos and A. Musgrave (eds.) *Criticism and the Growth of Knowledge. Cambridge: Cambridge University Press, 1979.*

Simon, Herbert A. *Administrative Behavior. Boston: The Free Press, 1957.*

Sutton, Francis X., Seymour E. Harris, Carl Kaysen, and James Tobin. *The American Business Creed.* Boston: Harvard University Press, 1956.

Tilly, Charles. *From Mobilization to Revolution,* Working Paper 156, Center for Research on Social Organization, University of Michigan, 1977.

Watt, Ian. *The Rise of the Novel.* Berkeley: University of California Press, 1957.

White, Harrison C., Scott A. Boorman, and Ronald L. Breiger. "Social Structure from Multiple Networks, I. Blockmodels of Roles and Positions." *American Journal of Sociology,* 81 (1976): 730-780.

Religion, Immigrants, and Entrepreneurship: Economic Creativity and Cultural Background

Teresa A. Sullivan

When summer temperatures rise, parked cars all over the country now sport bright, corrugated cardboard folders that shield the dashboard from the sun. The cardboard folders have made multimillionaires of the two young Israeli immigrants who developed and marketed them. Many would see this as one fulfillment of the American dream, but relatively few would classify the incident as *economic creativity*—this despite efforts to identify creativity in all its musical, artistic, verbal, spatial and other aspects. Yet the creative imagination is surely no less imaginative nor creative for being turned to practical ends. This short essay addresses economic creativity in the form of entrepreneurship among immigrants. Although few immigrants will be as successful as the two Israelis, their risk-taking and initiative are economically creative and their economic consequences little understood.

Why immigrants? Immigrants are "not like us" (Greeley, 1971) in many ways, but one of the most interesting ways is their propensity for self-employment. In an economy in which small businesses are thought to be withering, the resurgence of immigrant enterprise is a notable countertrend. In 1980, while only 7.0% of U.S. workers were self-employed, 16.8% of the immigrant workers were self-employed. Entrepreneurship is an economic resource that immigrants can bring to the U.S. economy even if their skin color, education, or linguistic ability eliminate other jobs for them. Recognizing the economic potential of such immigrants, U.S. immigration policy once provided for admission of some immigrants who were willing to invest in a U.S. business (Cafferty, Chiswick, Greeley, and Sullivan 146), and Canadian policy still provides for entrepreneur visas. Today, although other priorities now determine admission to the U.S., disproportionate numbers of immigrants are self-employed. Far from taking jobs from the native-born, these immigrants create new jobs for themselves and their employees.

Economic creativity is linked to nationality and ethnicity. There are "commercial cultures" that encourage new economic ventures, and there are ethnic strategies for generating income (Sullivan, 1986, Light). In addition, a "cultural division of labor" may relegate some lines of work to some ethnic groups. Examples include Jewish moneylenders in the Middle Ages and Chinese grocers in the Mississippi Delta (Loewen). Not surprisingly, then, there are variations in the degree of economic success experienced among immigrant groups (Greeley, 1974).

Religion and Immigrant Entrepreneurship

Within the classical sociological tradition it was the relationship of religion, not ethnicity, to economic success that generated the most interest. The classic work in this tradition was Max Weber's *Protestant Ethic and the Spirit of Capitalism.* Weber's thesis, much simplified, is that Puritan theology generated in believers an anxiety about salvation. Behavior that tended to make one successful in business, such as working long hours and frugally reinvesting the profits, was also seen as virtuous and relieved the anxiety. Thus, success in business was also seen as mark of divine election. Most of these early businessmen were merchants, factors, and other members of the petite bourgeousie, for whom economic creativity could also be classified as a charism.

Although later critics disputed the point, Catholicism could be seen as far less conducive to successful business. In large part, this was attributed to the communal orientation of Catholicism that emphasizes, for example, priestly intercession and communal celebrations (which wasted profits!). In addition, the centralized, bureaucratic Roman Church rewarded good corporate bureaucrats among its priests (for concrete examples, see Greeley, 1986). It may also have encouraged corporate bureaucratic virtues among its laity. Obedience, reliability, and conformity are desirable attributes for both employees and for Catholic laypersons. Innovativeness and risk-taking are not. Thus, one might expect that Catholic immigrants would be less likely than either Protestants and Jews to be self-employed.

This does not imply that Catholics in the United States would be unsuccessful. Indeed, they would be likely to excel as employees, and they arrived just as good employees were most needed. The peak periods of European Catholic immigration coincided with the emergence of large corporations and the gradual decline of smaller, less efficient firms. The Catholic immigrants settled in large cities, and their eventual acquisition of skills in accounting, public administration, and law made them key personnel for many companies. And as Greeley has demonstrated, they and their children and grandchildren have been very successful by any financial standard.

The pattern characteristic of today's Catholic immigrants is still unknown. No longer principally European in origin, today's Catholic immigrants are more likely to come from Latin America, the Caribbean, and the Philippines. At the same time, the religious diversity of the immigrant pool has also increased. One result of the 1965 amendments to the Immigration and Nationality Act was to reopen immigration to Asia and to the Islamic countries of the Middle East and Africa. In most cases, the numbers of immigrants from any one nationality or ethnic group are too small to permit detailed analysis (Sullivan, 1987). But religion is a master cultural force that affects multiple nationalities, and almost no attention has been paid to the differences among religious groups in immigrant success. This insight has motivated the current study.

Data and Methods

The decennial United States census provides the largest sample of immigrants available for study. Because immigrants are a relatively small proportion of the United States population, most sample surveys will contain far too few immigrants for analysis, and this is especially true if a minority group among the immigrants is the focus (e.g., the self-employed or a specific nationality). It is necessary, therefore, to turn to the United States census for this study. The data used here consists of a five percent sample of the immigrants who completed the "long form" in the 1980 enumeration. The Public Use Microdata Samples (or PUMS) contain the actual responses for each person, so that the characteristics of different immigrants may be studied in relationship to one another.

Religion, however, is one item that is not contained in the United States census, and so the identification of religion with specific immigrants must be based on their country of birth and a strong assumption that the immigrants were influenced by the dominant religion of their home country. Thus, Latin Americans are generally considered Catholic and Saudi Arabians are generally considered Islamic. The third group separately identified is Eastern Asia, the area generally influenced by Confucianism and Buddhism. The "other" category includes the mostly Protestant countries of Europe, which together provide relatively few immigrants, and also countries with religious diversity, such as India, Lebanon, Vietnam, or Canada. There were also a few countries with a majority religion but whose immigrants to the U.S. are likely to be from a minority religion. Malaysia is an example; some preliminary analysis showed that a high percentage of Malaysian immigrants to the United States were ethnically Chinese and thus unlikely to subscribe to the Islam which is the majority religion in Malaysia. Table 1 shows, with greater detail, the categorization of place of birth that was used.

Multiple regression analysis was used to predict the annual earnings of the immigrants in 1979 using a number of variables that have previously proven to be indicators of financial success. Among the most important is education, scored in years of completed schooling, which ranges from an average 10.4 years for Catholic males to 15.2 years for Islamic males. Labor market experience, which is approximated by age less total years of school less five, ranges from a high of 25.6 for Catholic males to a low of 18.7 for Islamic males. The square of experience is also used as a predictor variable because the effect of experience is often best modeled quadratically; its effect is expected to be negative. Additional variables expected to positively affect earnings are weeks worked in 1979, ability to speak the English language well, being married, and estimated number of years since migration. The census indicates a range of years during which the person immigrated (e.g., 1965 to 1970). The "years since migration" variable is estimated by subtracting the median of that range from 1980. Thus, the immigrant who entered the country between 1965 and 1970 would receive a score of 12.5 for years since migration.

Table 1
Classification of Place of Birth by Majority Religion

Catholic	Islamic	Oriental
Azores	Afghanistan	China
Belgium	Algeria	Hong Kong
Cuba	Bahrain	Japan
Dominican Republic	Egypt	Kampuchea
France	Iraq	Korea, N. and S.
French Carribbean	Iran	Laos
Ireland	Indonesia	Macau
Italy	Jordan	Mongolia
Lithuania	Kuwait	Taiwan
Madeira	Libya	Thailand
Mexico	Morocco	Singapore
Poland	Qatar	
Portugal	Oman	
San Marino	Pakistan	
Spain	Saudi Arabia	
Vatican City	Sudan	
Yugoslavia	Syria	
South America	Tunisia	
except Fr. Guiana,	Turkey	
Guyana, Surinam	United Arab Emirates	
Central America	W. Sahara	
except Belize	Yemen	
	Yemen, Democratic	

Other refers to all other countries

The "other" category of immigrants have the longest residence in the U.S., a mean of 17 years for men and 18 years for women.

Longer U.S. labor market experience is expected to be positively associated with higher earnings. The square of years since migration is used for the same reason as the square of years of experience, and also expected to be negative. Variables are also included for rural residence and Southern residence, usually associated with lower earnings. The Catholic immigrants are most likely to live in the South, presumably because so many of the recent Latin American immigrants are located in states such as Florida and Texas.

The final predictor variable is self-employment and refers to persons who reported themselves self-employed in either an incorporated or an unincorporated business. About 18% of the Catholic males were self-employed, versus 25% of the "others," 28% of the Oriental males, and 31% of the Islamic males. Females were much less likely to be self-employed: 7% of Catholics, 11% of "other" and Islamic females, and 15% of Orientals. The means and standard deviations for these variables are listed for each religion group, by sex, in the appendix table.

The dependent variable in this analysis is annual earnings in 1979, which is one measure of economic success. Annual earnings beyond the "open-ended interval" used by the Census Bureau—that is, any earnings so high that the Census Bureau refused to report them for privacy reasons—were coded as 1.5 times the highest reported level. Before controlling for any of the other variables, it is apparent that the earnings for the Catholic immigrants, both male and female, are the lowest: $15,200 for males and $7,900 for females. Islamic males earn the highest for males, $21,300, and "other" females have the highest earnings among the women: $9008.

The purpose of the multiple regression analysis is to examine the contribution of each of the predictor variables to the earnings of the immigrants. The numbers in Table 2 are unstandardized regression coefficients, and each one may be interpreted as the contribution to earnings, controlling for the other variables. Thus, to take one example, each week worked in 1979 meant an additional $275 for a Catholic male and an additional $409 for an Islamic male. Speaking English well added $1281 for a Catholic male, other things constant. The statistic labeled R2 indicates how much of the variance in earnings can be explained by the predictor variables. In six of the equations, between one-fifth and one-fourth of the variance is explained; among Islamics, we explain 27% of the variance for males and 33% of the variance for females.

Given our interest in economic creativity and the potential "pay-off" to self-employment, the most interesting datum in Table 2 is the coefficient associated with self-employment. In every case, the coefficient is large, positive, and significant. It is largest for Islamic males: they earn, on average, over $11,200 more if they are self-employed. Catholic and "other" males are similar in earning about $6600 more if they are self-employed. Surprisingly perhaps, given their image as entrepreneurs, Oriental males realized only $4400 as their return to self-employment. Catholic women were the least likely to be self-employed, but it paid off more for them than for the others: a self-employed Catholic immigrant woman realized $1700 from her self-employment, even after all the other variables are controlled.

Table 2
Regression of Income on Predictor Variables, by Predominant Religion of
Country of Origin, Immigrant in the United States, 1980.

Predictor Variables	Other	Catholic	Oriental	Islamic
(Males)				
Self-Employment	6,555.1**	6,629.6**	4,406.0**	11,255.2**
Weeks Worked 79	405.7**	274.8**	317.7**	409.2**
Education (yrs.)	1,560.6**	922.5**	1,061.0**	1,943.1**
Married	3,257.4**	2,740.4**	2,640.2**	1,421.2
Rural	713.8	1,327.2**	11,807.1**	1,276.8
Experience	952.3**	467.2**	736.8**	928.9**
Experience-Sq.	-14.5**	-6.8**	-11.7**	-11.4**
Langwell	482.4	1,280.9**	3,965.6**	-2,208.9
YSM	252.4**	211.5**	502.1**	573.3**
YSM-sq	-4.5**	-2.4**	-11.5**	-12.8*
South	-657.2*	-739.3**	-775.7	79.8
constant	-38,196.1**	-19,756.4**	-29,202.7**	-44,453.3**
F-Sig.	.0000	.0000	.0000	.0000
R-sq	.21	.24	.23	.27
Mean Earnings	21,481	15,243	18,385	21,327
n =	33,047	44,400	7,259	3,405
(Females)				
Self-Employment	972.0**	1,676.6**	1,267.0**	1,143.3
Weeks Worked 79	221.4**	179.8**	195.4**	226.3**
Education (yrs.)	580.5**	399.2**	385.9**	559.9**
Married	-1,123.3**	-24.9	-206.1	-416.3
Rural	-1,499.4**	-232.9	-2,185.1**	1,511.4
Experience	79.6**	8.1	-14.2	61.3
Experience-Sq.	-1.1**	0.1	0.4	0.2
Langwell	-241.5	676.0**	862.7**	525.0
YSM	56.6**	189.7**	217.7**	129.9
YSM-sq	-1.8**	-5.6**	-5.2**	-5.2
South	-643.3**	-763.8**	-924.5**	-217.3
constant	-7,954.5**	-5,456.1**	-29,202.7**	-9,490.6**
F-Sig.	.0000	.0000	.0000	.0000
R-sq	.22	.25	.22	.33
Mean Earnings	9,008	7,879	8,547	8,913
n =	25,912	29,727	6,457	1,188

Source: PUMS - A 5% Sample, 1980
* - sig at .05
** - sig at .01
Note: Universe consist of civilian labor force members ages 25 to 64, excluding unpaid family workers

Table 3
Decomposition of Differences in Earnings among Immigrants by Predominant
Religion of Country of Origin, by Sex, United States, 1980

Groups (Income Diff.)	Difference intercept	Rate of Return	Char.s	Interact	Error
Males					
Other vs. Catholic (6,237.31)	-18,440	18,534	4,375	1,765	3.43
Other vs. Oriental (3,095.57)	-8,993	11,051	2,469	-1,430	-1.66
Other vs. Islamic (153.32)	6,257	-6,702	583	12	3.07
Catholic vs. Oriental (-3,141.74)	9,446	-9,437	-3,066	-80	-5.09
Catholic vs Islamic (-6,084.00)	24,697	-27,179	-6,264	2,662	-0.37
Oriental vs. Islamic (-2,942.25)	15,251	-17,058	-392	-747	4.73
Female					
Other vs. Catholic (1,128.98)	-2,498	2,196	1,282	149	-0.01
Other vs. Oriental (461.61)	-1,994	1,959	747	-249	-2.13
Other vs. Islamic (95.07)	1,536	-1,701	371	-111	-0.28
Catholic vs. Oriental (-667.37)	505	-390	-653	-127	-2.12
Catholic vs Islamic (-1,033.91)	4,034	-4,103	-1,137	172	-0.27
Oriental vs. Islamic (-366.54)	3,530	-3,651	-210	-37	1.85

Source: Table 2 and Appendix Table
Note: Universe consist of civilian labor force members ages 25 to 64, excluding unpaid family workers

This is $400 more than Oriental women, $500 more than Islamic women, and $700 more than "other" women. From this analysis, it appears that although Catholics are less likely to be self-employed, when they are self-employed they are successful at it. Only Islamic males are more successful. And the Orientals, long touted as the "golden minority" for their industrious small enterprises, realize lower returns from them than do the Catholics.

Although the Catholic self-employed received a higher rate of return to self-employment, there are relatively fewer of them, and they also do not receive equivalent rates of return on many other variables, including number of weeks worked, education, experience, and experience in the United States labor market. Moreover, they tend to have lower human capital "endowments" in terms of education and English language use. Thus, Catholics still earn substantially less than other immigrants. But what is the reason? Is it the lower level of education and other resources that they bring with them, or is it their rate of return to these resources? (The former are indicated by the values in the appendix table and the latter by the values of the coefficients in Table 2).

One way that we can analyze the reasons for the differences is to decompose the differences among the regression equations in Table 2. This is done in Table 3. The largest difference, between "other males" and Catholic males, is $6200, and this difference is due principally to the difference in rate of return and only secondarily to the characteristics of the Catholics. Catholic males earn less than Oriental and Islamic males both because of their lower rates of return and because their human capital characteristics are less conducive to high earnings. But in every case, it is the conversion of the resources into earnings in which the Catholics are at the greatest disadvantage. Self-employment is an exception: it is a characteristic that Catholic immigrants are more able than others to turn to their advantage. But the "routine" human capital variables of education, experience, language, and so on are less successfully converted by Catholics into earnings.

Discussion

To what extent does this analysis really say anything about religion, and to what extent is it "merely" an indication of the relative lack of success among Mexicans, the largest single Catholic immigrant group? It is not merely a "Mexican" effect, because in other analyses, not shown here, the rate of return to self-employment for Mexican immigrants is always substantially *lower* than that for Asian immigrants, exactly the opposite of the result shown here. It is true, however, that the Mexican immigrants here in the United States in 1980 are likely to have lower education and other skill levels than the immigrants from other countries. One reason for this may be the relative "openness" of the U.S. border to Mexicans, regardless of skill, and the emphasis (after 1965) on skill levels for the admission of Asians and Africans. These differences may begin to diminish, however, as recent legal changes and changes in the composition of African and Asian immigrants make family reunification the primary basis for admission to the United States. This will tend to reduce the higher skill levels of many of immigrants classified here as "other," "Oriental," and "Islamic."

Appendix Table
Mean Values and Standard Deviation of Variables Used in Income Regression
for Each Immigrant Group Classified by Predominant Religion of Origin Country

Variables	Other	Catholic	Oriental	Islamic
(Males)				
Income	21480.59	15243.27	18385.01	21327.27
	(20649.98)	(15952.12)	(19545.65)	(24734.53)
Education	13.72	10.40	14.40	15.18
	(4.04)	(5.08)	(4.72)	(4.15)
Experience	23.89	25.55	20.41	18.68
	(12.36)	(12.19)	(11.86)	(11.27)
Exp - Sq.	723.41	801.44	557.44	475.72
	(644.22)	(687.53)	(610.89)	(538.49)
Weeks 79	46.48	44.83	44.76	43.84
	(12.20)	(13.58)	(13.90)	(14.89)
Langwell	.95	.68	.74	.94
	(.23)	(.47)	(.44)	(.24)
Married	.80	.83	.83	.75
	(.40)	(.37)	(.38)	(.43)
YSM	17.24	14.71	10.81	10.86
	(10.25)	(9.11)	(8.89)	(8.15)
YSM-Sq	402.18	299.33	194.44	184.38
	(349.41)	(305.67)	(276.53)	(240.95)
Self-Employed	.25	.18	.28	.31
	(.43)	(.38)	(.45)	(.46)
Rural	.06	.03	.01	.02
	(.24)	(.17)	(.11)	(.14)
South	.17	.21	.13	.19
	(.37)	(.41)	(.34)	(.39)
N of Cases	33047	44400	7259	3405
(Female)				
Income	9008.13	7879.15	8546.52	8913.06
	(8912.05)	(7945.05)	(8828.86)	(8511.92)
Education	12.79	10.74	12.30	13.67
	(3.39)	(4.77)	(4.70)	(4.03)
Experience	24.90	24.90	21.97	20.86
	(11.95)	(12.07)	(12.02)	(11.65)
Exp-Sq.	762.75	765.72	627.25	570.82
	(630.56)	(662.86)	(629.30)	(561.46)
Weeks 79	41.65	40.13	40.70	38.36
	(16.14)	(17.00)	(16.36)	(18.21)
Langwell	.95	.68	.70	.90
	(.22)	(.47)	(.46)	(.30)
Married	.70	.70	.79	.72
	(.46)	(.46)	(.41)	(.45)
YSM	18.05	14.47	11.63	12.52
	(9.79)	(8.82)	(8.40)	(8.79)
YSM-Sq	421.46	287.13	205.87	233.87
	(341.59)	(296.06)	(256.20)	(271.47)
Self-Employed	.11	.07	.15	.11
	(.31)	(.26)	(.35)	(.31)
Rural	.06	.02	.02	.02
	(.23)	(.14)	(.15)	(.13)
South	.18	.22	.16	.17
	(.38)	(.41)	(.37)	(.38)
N of Cases	25912	29727	6457	1188

Source: PUMS - A 5% Sample, 1980
Note: Universe consist of civilian labor force members ages 25 to 64, excluding unpaid family workers

It is more problematic to discern the relative role of a religious tradition in these findings, but religious diversity is a topic that is never far from discussions of immigration. United States' immigration policy has been closely tied to issues of culture, religion, and economics. Most restrictionist policies have been based on fear of economic competition and justified by concerns about religious, linguistic, or ethnic diversity. Without recourse to Weber, much of the opposition to continued Catholic immigration at the turn of the century was based on fear that Catholics were "cheap labor" who would take jobs away from the native-born. This theme comes up again and again in the context of contemporary Latin American immigration. Self-employment offers the immigrant a way to short-circuit this fear among the native-born.

By contrast, Asians have graduated from "Yellow Peril" to "golden minority." Some of the changed perception of Asians may be linked to admiration for their entrepreneurship. In an employee society, entrepreneurship sharply segments the scope of competition and the possibility of mobilization along ethnic or religious lines. In a few exceptional cases, such as the violence among native-born and Vietnamese shrimp fishers along the Texas coast, direct competition has emerged in an economic segment that has historically been dominated by native-born small business owners. Such segments, however, appear to be relatively small and perhaps shrinking.

Conclusion

As expected, Catholic immigrants are less likely than other immigrant groups to display the "economic creativity" associated with self-employment. Contrary to expectations, however, both Catholic immigrant males and females have higher rates of return to self-employment; that is, for the few who are self-employed, the self-employment pays off at a higher rate than it does for those from other religious groups. Catholic immigrants tend to have lower earnings than immigrants from other religious backgrounds because they bring to the labor market less favorable characteristics and, more importantly, because they are less successful in converting these characteristics into earnings. If more of them were self-employed, it appears that their earnings profiles would improve.

Acknowledgements

This research was supported by a grant from the Rockefeller Foundation. I am deeply indebted to Stephen D. McCracken, my research assistant, whose own formidable knowledge of Brazil helped me in thinking through these ideas, and whose computer assistance was invaluable. My work on this essay was greatly facilitated by a summer Research Fellowship at the East-West Population Institute, East-West Center, Honalulu, Hawaii.

References

Cafferty, Pastora S. J., Barry R. Chiswick, Andrew M. Greeley, and Teresa A. Sullivan, *The Dilemma of American Immigration*. New Brunswick, NJ: Transaction, 1983.

Greeley, Andrew M. *Confessions of a Parish Priest*. New York: Simon and Schuster, 1986.

_____ *Ethnicity in the United States: A Preliminary Reconnaissance*. New York: Wiley, 1974.

_____ *Why Can't They Be Like Us?* New York: E. P. Dutton, 1971.

Light, Ivan H. *Ethnic Enterprise in America*. Berkeley: University of California Press, 1972.

Loewen, James W. *The Mississippi Chinese: Between Black and White*. Cambridge: Harvard University Press, 1971.

Sullivan, Teresa A. "Documenting Immigration: A Comparison of Research on Asian and Hispanic Immigrants." J. T. Fawcett and B. V. Carino, eds. *Pacific Bridges: The New Immigration from Asia and the Pacific Islands*: New York Center for Migration Studies, 1987. 427-451.

_____ "Stratification of the Labor Market under Conditions of Continuing Immigration." in R. de la Garza and H. L. Browning, eds. *Mexican Immigrants and Mexican Americans*. Austin: University of Texas Press, 1986. 56-63.

Weber, Max. *The Protestant Ethic and the Spirit of Capitalism*. Talcott Parsons, trans. New York: Scribner's, 1958 (1905).

PART THREE

Towards a Vision for a Catholic and Ignatian University in America

Fran Gillespie, S.J.

Introduction

The imagination of Fr. Greeley has soared far, wide and high over the landscapes of sociology, theology, education, literature—including poetry, political science—including ecclesial politics, psychology—including his autobiography, and economics—including a recent study of shortfalls in Catholic tithing. His perspicacious gaze has not been unselective in that it forever homes in on his Catholic Church—the parish, the laity, the priesthood, the episcopacy, the papacy, Mary, and my area of interest which I shall take up below, the Catholic school. As if anyone needed reminding, Fr. Greeley's focus betrays his inveterate sacerdotal stripe just as his tone of voice often betrays more the outspoken prophet of a God on high than the complacent, dulcimer tones of a church bureaucrat royal. Such is my image of him anyway, and I share it fraternally as one who is also a Catholic priest sociologist whose parental lineage also hails from Ireland's west coast.

The Imagination: A Few Of Its Modalities

One can refer to the imagination under modalities such as sociological, artistic, philosophical, theological, mystical, religious, "episcopal" and so forth. For instance, one can refer to C. Wright Mill's imaginative linking of one's biography with one's historical situation; to Van Gogh's impressionism; to Plato's image of himself as the obstetrician of his interlocutor's ideas; to David Tracy's use of the "analogical" imagination; to Julian of Norwich's image of God Our Mother; to Joseph Feeney's four modes of adult Catholic imagination (see his essay elsewhere in this *Festschrift*), or to Eugene Kennedy's treatment of the "episcopal" imagination among the American hierarchy. All of these have their place, but it is the modality that deals with "the mind's eye" or "vision" that I shall take up here.

Fr. Greeley sketched a vision for Catholic education in an essay he wrote two decades ago, and in the process revealed what I call his selective gaze and prophetic tone (1970:27):

the principal problem of Catholic education is a collapse of morale, a loss of nerve based on the absence of a theoretical perspective which would give direction and purpose to the Catholic educational system. Catholic educators themselves have lost confidence in what they are doing because they are not able to fit their efforts into some larger system of values.

The theoretical vision that Fr. Greeley proceeded to sketch for Catholic education in that essay imaginatively mixed three themes: innovation, comedy and love. I shall briefly illustrate his use of the latter. Fr. Greeley begins this part of his essay by citing Christ's mandate to love one another (John 13:35), and next emphasizes that all church members, especially Bishops, are called to be Christlike lovers, and then, sounding like the prophet Micah, writes about love and education this way (1970:41).:

"because of the Church's commitment to love, the teachers in Catholic schools ought to be better lovers than teachers at other schools... One would also assume the Catholic commitment to love would make it necessary for the Catholic schools, faculty, administrators and students alike, to be deeply involved in serving Christ where he is to be found among the poor."

The Problem

But times and schools and Catholics and maybe even love have changed over the two decades since Fr. Greeley adumbrated that vision. There is, therefore, a need to elaborate anew a vision for Catholic schools—from the grammar schools up through the universities. There is an ongoing need, in fact, to rework our visions and dreams—as Father Hesburgh once put it:

"All too soon the present day with its dreams and plans becomes part of the past. Not always are the dreams fulfilled and the plans realized. This does not mean that we cease to dream and refuse to plan. [We] built on a dream which had its roots in Faith. When dreams fail because of rushing time, we renew our Faith and point to things Eternal. A greater future will come from the same Faith that built the past."

The area of Catholic schooling that I shall focus on is neither the grammar school nor the high school—though I have taught grade school for two years and I know what it is to stand in front of high school students with nothing more than my lecture and a piece of chalk and an eraser to defend myself! The area that I shall focus on is Catholic higher education where I taught for ten years before renouncing tenure and leaving in large part for want of a vision of the sort that Fr. Greeley long ago prophesied was lacking. I believe with him that Catholic higher education is still in desperate need of a vision, one that will enable all those who work in it, Catholic and non-Catholic alike, who esteem it as ministry or in Weberian terms view it as a "beruf," to subsume what they are doing under an overarching system of values. At the very least the vision needs an updating and a clearer elaboration of its Christocentric and Catholic character.

To be more precise, the problem is not with the lack of a vision for the Catholic university *per se*. If that was all that was lacking then one could benefit from reacquainting oneself with Cardinal Newman's timeless vision of a university, or grapple with applying David Hassel's challenging vision, or "baptize" (an old Catholic trick) the new and thought-provoking opus from Ernest Boyer and the Carnegie Commission, or simply to reawaken oneself with insights from the many partial visions that are around (Lucey; Healy; Ellis; Watkins; Hesburgh; Gannon; Byron; Buckley; O'Hare; O'Meara; Riesman; Schroth; Pope John Paul II; USCC. No, the problem more precisely is to elaborate a vision for a *Catholic university in America* in a way that respects the independence of these two nouns and one adjective while shaping them into meaningful language for discourse (Appleyard). Or to use another image, the task is to devise a vision that can keep these three spheres of influence orbiting in a dynamic equilibrium.

Finding an imagination that can unify this trinity of sovereign institutions is no easy task. How to accomplish such a feat given such factors as: the academic institution's unbounded freedom to search for truth and explore knowledge endlessly; the organic bond between the *magisterium* of the Catholic Church and a Catholic university; the State which has the power to bestow a university's charter, grant it funds and ultimately through the offices of its Secretary of Education authorize its accreditation? The problem is seemingly intractable for the solution implies a feat of *e tribus, unum*.

Pressures From The Church And From The State

Catholic universities in America, for the want of a clear and shared vision of their identity and mission, are often placed in a vulnerable position. They seem at times to be squeezed by pressures on both sides from Church and State. For instance, witness the negative reactions of the 100 Catholic university presidents to the recent draft of a Schema for a pontifical document on Catholic universities worldwide. It was issued from the Vatican Congregation for Catholic Education headed by Cardinal Baum. Witness also the uncharacteristically bold statement from a subset of these, viz., the presidents of Jesuit colleges and universities who asked that the Schema, as it stood, simply not be published because it neither encouraged nor promoted the Catholic university, but if it had to be published, then it should be substantially modified because it was flawed in its content and would be disastrous in its consequences. Better no vision at all than a myopic one was the refrain heard from this presidential chorus.

On the other hand, Catholic universities feel they have to withstand pressures from the State. Such is the case when government funds come with strings that would seem to tie knots around an institution's adherence to some Catholic teachings. For instance, when universities such as Georgetown choose to deny gays on campus official status, or when universities choose to prevent abortions at university health centers. It is not hard to see, given such pressures, how easy it becomes for some Catholic universities to capitulate to one lobby or the other.

The University's Temptation to Capitulate on its Unique Identity

In urging the elaboration of a vision I am ever mindful of the history of some universities in America that were formerly sectarian. When one looks at what may be the master trend for sectarian higher education in America, it seems clear that the pressure to capitulate to the State is significantly greater than the pressure to remain Church affiliated. Just observe the current non-sectarian status of Harvard founded by the Puritans, of Yale founded by the Congregationalists, of Brown founded by the Baptists, of King's College (Colombia) founded by the Episcopalians, not to mention Princeton, Queen's College (Rutgers), and several others. Can the larger, more prestigious Catholic universities escape such an outcome? Can even the smaller ones—witness the present status of formerly Catholic Webster University? Indeed, do they even want to escape it?

To be sure, some sectarian universities still stand firm in their church affiliated relationship. Some Catholic colleges are trying to reaffirm their Catholic characters, such as St. Benedict's (O'Connell,) St. Michael's (Reiss,), Creighton University (Hauser,) and Assumption (Tessitore), though this is not to say that they have solved the problem of keeping the three entities of "university," "Catholic," and "America" functioning in dynamic equilibrium. On the other hand, universities such as Villanova, Marquette, St. Louis, Duquesne, and Fordham, to name a few, seem to speak of their Catholic identity in increasingly muted terms. They feel they have good reasons for doing so. Fordham, for example, along with several other Catholic universities in the State of New York, behaves as if were constrained to place the candle of its Catholic identity under a secular bushel basket in order to accommodate the Bundy funds. Even Notre Dame university has not escaped criticism of weakening its Catholic identity (Jones), though Fr. Hesburgh declares rather enigmatically that Notre Dame is more "professedly" Catholic than ever.

All Catholic Universities in America are of a Mixed Marriage

But capitulation to either pressure group should not be the answer for a university that is to be Catholic in America. I think a necessary first step in preparing a vision for a Catholic university is to acknowledge and to accept resolutely the tensions emanating from church and state and prepare itself to live with them. In the Catholic church's centuries old association with Catholic universities, tensions are as common as spring and summer thunderstorms. Universities must face the fact that historically the Church's intermittent quarrels with its Catholic universities have even entailed "prolonged and impassioned controversies between faculties and the local bishop, as well as occasioning disputes that involved the pope" (Ellis). Whatsmore, church historian Msgr. John Tracy Ellis, familiar as anyone with the history of this relationship plays the role of a Dutch uncle cautioning Catholic universities that "for the foreseeable future the task of the Catholic universities of the United States...will be an exacting and trying experience."

And it goes without saying that the same sort of historical tensions obtaining between Catholic universities and American society can also be documented e.g., the anti-Catholicism in America in the 1890s, 1920s, and 1950s. And while, to be sure, some claim that "no First Amendment problem seems ever to have arisen with regard to higher education." (Whitehead), others disagree, citing the American Court's jaundiced view of a campus that becomes "pervasively sectarian" (e.g., see the cases of Tilton vs. Richardson, 1971 or Roemer v. Board of Public Works, 1976). Consequently, no matter from which side these tensions and pressures come, and they will be coming for the duration, acknowledging them as a persistent fact of Catholic university life in America is the first step for elaborating any vision.

To put the matter more positively, another fact of the matter is that part of the identity of Catholic universities in America is their relationship to the teaching Church, and part of their identity in democratic America is as a secular identity under civil authority—like a city (Healy). Thus a Catholic university in America must take a second step of affirming both its Catholic and non-catholic parentage. But before it really can come of age and move forward in wisdom and grace honoring as it does both its separated parents (to indulge an image) it must be furnished a theoretical perspective which would give it direction, purpose and inspiration.

Towards A Vision for a Subset of Catholic Universities in America

What I propose can be regarded as one vision among many possible visions. The scope of my vision is modest in that it is not primarily focused on the universe of all Catholic colleges and universities in the United States.[1] Rather it primarily focuses on the constellation of 28 colleges and universities that are putatively Catholic and Jesuit. As a Jesuit priest and alumnus of two Jesuit colleges as well as a former faculty member and chairperson at a Jesuit university, I prefer to confine my focus to that area about which I feel less ignorant.

The point of departure for my vision is the recently published document on Jesuit education entitled *Go Forth and Teach: The Characteristics of Jesuit Education* (Kolvenbach). This document, published under the auspices of the General of the Society of Jesus, identifies 28 characteristics flowing from nine principles that comprise St. Ignatius of Loyola's vision of the world. It was seven years in the making and was produced by an international commission on the apostolate of Jesuit Education. This group of Jesuits and laity first met in Rome in 1980 to discuss the topic of Jesuit "secondary" education. The document has gone through numerous drafts and has benefited from consultation from the worldwide network of Jesuit schools in India, Japan, Australia, South America, North America, Europe and Africa. It is not meant to be a new *Ratio Studiorum*—the 16th century document which furnished the vision for the successful running of Jesuit schools throughout Christendom and beyond. It is offered to earnest seekers of educational visions, and this is important to note, "not as definitive or final, for that would be very difficult or even impossible"). Rather the document is offered to extend "a common vision and a common sense of purpose" to all who collaborate in educational institutions of the Society of Jesus".

I do not say that the Kolvenbach document is a *sine qua non* for all visions of Catholic and Jesuit colleges and universities in America, but I believe it is paradigmatic for elaborating any such vision. It contains most of the essential elements that would comprise such visions, though, to be sure, they can be arranged and emphasized in other ways. I believe that the Ignatian imagination underlying the vision in this document is one successful vision for keeping the trinity of sovereign institutions of "university," "Church," and "State" orbiting in a dynamic equilibrium.

Mutatis Mutandis

Given its genesis, there is the risk, on one hand, that some will be tempted to summarily dismiss the document as sophomorish and jejune, arguing that at best it is applicable only to some parts of Jesuit secondary education in the United States. Some Jesuit presidents of the so-called 28 Catholic and Jesuit universities might even be included among these. Jesuit presidents, like other Catholic university presidents, perceive themselves directly answerable only to their Boards but evidently not to their Provincials or their local Bishops. Hence, they can become unduly selective in their perceptions. At times, they can be inordinately attached to the views of the "university" and to the "State" while correspondingly detached from the viewpoints of the Catholic Church and the Society of Jesus[2] to which they are in some sense organically linked. Ons the other hand, it is of paramount importance that all observe the flashing *caveat: mutatis mutandis* before picking up the Kolvenbach document to read. In other words, the format, style and content of the document is reasonably malleable and adaptable (though not to say Procrustean). The letter from the General of the Jesuits introducing the document explicitly says as much: "Those working in other Jesuit educational institutions, especially in *universities*...should make the adaptations that are needed, or develop from this present document *a new one* that will fit their situation more appropriately". There is ample room, therefore, for all higher education personnel to approach the vision in this document critically, skeptically, openly and imaginatively.

I myself have observed the caveat of "making the necessary changes" to the document in elaborating my version of a vision. For instance, I choose to refer to it not as Jesuit but as an Ignatian[3] vision for Catholic and Jesuit universities. Also, as those who have already read the document in its entirety will soon detect, I use my own heremeneutics and exegesis of the document. For instance, I have rearranged the format dividing it into nine parts and have used categories which should be familiar to all those in Catholic higher education who have ever framed a school's mission statement, or prepared its catalogue, or dealt with handbooks for the faculty and students. Categories such as Christo-centric, in service to the Catholic Church, the role of the faculty, the formation of students, collaboration, governance, campus environment, and so forth are used. On the other hand, I omitted mention of the main Ignatian principles underlying the document, paraphrased some statements, took exegetical liberties by rearranging the format of the document, and deleted some statements I deemed not really unique to Ignatian colleges and universities. For instance, deleted from my version of the vision are such statements as the following (the numbers at the end refer to passages in the Kolvenbach document):

Students should develop effective communication skills (29);

Ignatian education takes into account the developmental stages of growth (73);

That it seeks to motivate students to become lifelong learners and to teach them "to learn how to learn" (45);

That students are to grow in their ability to reason reflectively, logically and critically (26);

The curriculum is centered on the person rather than on the material to be taught (42);

Students are enabled to evaluate the pervasive influence of the mass media (30);

All of the above, of course, are constitutive of a university worth its name. But rather than include them and similar common denominator statements from the Kolvenbach document, I omit them because they can be found in any number of non-Catholic liberal arts colleges and universities in America (no matter what the admission offices at Jesuit universities claim to the contrary).

On the other hand, I observe the Kolvenbach's document's use of a certain helpful syntax: "...to avoid a constant repetition of the idealistic 'wishes to be,' or the judgmental 'should be,' the characteristics are written in the categorical indicative: Jesuit education is" (16).

The characteristics I have selected for inclusion in my vision are selected ever mindful of the dynamic tensions emanating from the "university," "Church," "State" trinity mentioned earlier. At the same time, I have concentrated on the "Catholic" element more than the "university" or the "State" element for three reasons: (1) limitations of space, (2) because these other two elements are more readily found elsewhere, and (3) because agreement is less difficult to reach on secular topics than religious topics. Naturally, I expect some elements pertaining to the "Catholic" orbit of influence to cause friction and sparks. In fact, the very ordering of the statements below is, in general, done in a way that goes from the most to the least provocative. That they will occasion discussions, some more spirited than others, is to be expected. However, the statements, or "perspectives" as I prefer to call them, do provide a necessary faith vocabulary for use in the limbo situation that now exists in Catholic and Jesuit higher education. For Americans with the habit of heart of paraphrasing even explicitly religious phenomena in secular and purely professional terms (Bellah, et al.), I hope such faith language is a helpful start on the way to elaborating the vision needed for Catholic higher education. The perspectives I present are designed to be applicable (and arguably so) to Catholic Jesuit universities. It goes without saying that readers are free to regard each and every excerpt as a sort of null hypothesis which they can, as it were, uphold or reject on the basis of some body of evidence they care to adduce.

Elements in a Vision for a Catholic and Ignatian University in America

Part 1.0 Explicitly Christ-Centered

    1.1 Christ is proposed as the model of human life. Everyone can draw inspiration and learn about commitment from the life and teaching of Jesus (61).

1.2 Ignatian education promotes a faith that is centered on the historical person of Christ, which therefore leads to a commitment to imitate him as the "Man for others" (70).

1.3 Out of a desire to follow Christ's way of proceeding, students in Ignatian universities are expected to undergo personal preparation, dedicating themselves to study, to personal formation, and ultimately to action (111).

1.4 The aim of Ignatian education is the formation of principled, value oriented persons for others after the example of Jesus Christ (93).

1.5 Christian members of the educational community strive for personal friendship with Jesus (62).

1.6 Pastoral care for Christians in the university community centers on Christ present among them. Students encounter the person of Christ as friend and guide; they come to know him through Scripture, sacraments, personal and communal prayer, in play and work, in other persons. They are led to the service of others in imitation of Christ the Man for others (63, 64).

1.7 Making the Spiritual Exercises is encouraged as a way of knowing Christ better, loving him, and following him (65).

1.8 Worship and reverence are part of the life of the university community; they are expressed in personal prayer and in appropriate community forms of worship (36).

1.9 For those students and adults who want to know Christ more completely and model their lives on him more closely, opportunities such as the Christian Life Communities are available (104).

1.10 The concern for total human development which is the "Christian humanism" of Ignatian education includes the recognition of sin and its effects in the life of each person (54).

Part 2.0 For Service to the Roman Catholic Church

2.1 Loyalty to and service of the Church, the people of God, will be communicated to the entire educational community in an Ignatian university (94).

2.2 Ignatian education—while respecting the conscience and the convictions of each student—is faithful to the teachings of the Church, especially in moral and religious formation (95).

2.3 The Ignatian university is an apostolic instrument of the Church (128).

2.4 As part of the mission given by the Church to the Jesuits, an Ignatian university does everything it can to resist atheism vigorously with united forces (35).

2.5 As part of its service of the church an Ignatian university will...cooperate with the local Bishop. For example, important decisions about university policy take into account the pastoral orientation of the local church...and consider their possible effect on the local church... (97).

2.6 An Ignatian university works in cooperation with local parishes (98).

2.7 For Catholic students Ignatian education offers a knowledge and love for the Church (102).

2.8 In ways proper to a university, concrete experiences of church life are available to all students through participation in church projects and activities (103).

2.9 In an Ignatian university there is a willingness on the part of both lay people and Jesuits...to work together as a single *apostolic* body in the formation of students. Thus, there is a sharing of vision, purpose and *apostolic* effort (119).

2.10 Ignatian education still remains an instrument to help students know and respond to God better (93).

2.11 In Ignatian universities, the integrating factor in the process of discovering God and understanding the true meaning of human life is theology as presented through religious and spiritual education. Religious and spiritual formation is integral to Jesuit education; it is not added to, or separate from, the educational process (34).

2.12 The curriculum includes a critical analysis of society in a way that Christian principles are a part of the analysis. Reference points for this analysis are the Hebrew and Christian Bibles, Church teachings, and human science (78).

Part 3.0 Characteristics of its Faculty

3.1 As far as possible, the university chooses as qualified leaders of the educational community persons who can teach and give witness to the teachings of Christ presented by the Catholic Church (95).

3.2 As far as possible, persons chosen to join the educational community of an Ignatian university will be men and women capable of understanding its distinctive nature and of contributing to the implementation of characteristics that result from the Ignatian vision (122).

3.3 Teaching in an Ignatian university is a ministry in the Church (93).

3.4 Teachers assist students in their growth by helping them to reflect on personal experiences so that they can understand their own experience of God (56).

3.5 Since every program in the university can be a means to discover God, all teachers share a responsibility for the religious dimension of the university (34).

3.6 Lay teachers, especially those active in parish activities can help students participate in Church projects and activities, and can communicate to students the current emphasis on the apostolate of lay people (103).

3.7 The teacher is to help each student become an independent learner, to assume the responsibility for his or her own education (45).

3.8 Teachers are more than academic guides. They are involved in the lives of the students, taking a personal interest in the intellectual, affective, moral and spiritual development of every student. "Cura personalis" (concern for the individual person) remains a basic characteristic of Ignatian education (43).

3.9 Teachers try to become more aware of justice issues so that they can provide students with the intellectual, moral and spiritual formation that will make students agents of social change (78).

3.10 The intellectual formation students receive is based on competent and well motivated teaching (26).

Part 4.0 Characteristics of its Students

4.1 The goal of Ignatian education today is not to prepare a socio-economic elite, but rather to educate leaders in service. The Ignatian university, therefore, will help students develop the qualities of mind and heart that will enable them—in whatever station they assume in life—to work with others for the good of all in the service of the Kingdom of God (110).

4.2 The pursuit of academic excellence is necessary but not sufficient in an Ignatian university. The aim is on the fullest possible development of every dimension of the person, linked to the development of a sense of values and commitment to the service of others (107).

4.3 The success of Ignatian education is measured not in terms of academic performance of students or professional competence of teachers, but rather in terms of the ways in which students will make use of their formation in the service of others *ad maiorem Dei gloriam* (37).

4.4 An objective of Ignatian education is to assist in the fullest possible development of all the God given talents of each individual person as a member of the human community (25).

4.5 Ignatian education helps students realize that talents are gifts to be developed, not for self-satisfaction or self-gain, but rather, with the help of God, for the good of the human community (82).

4.6 Ignatian education promotes an attitude of mind that sees service of others as more self-fulfilling than success or prosperity (83).

4.7 Ignatian education includes formation in values...it includes the training of character and the formation of the will (51).

4.8 It involves a process of education that takes place in a moral context whereby knowledge is joined to virtue (52).

4.9 In an Ignatian university a framework of inquiry in which a value system is acquired through a process of wrestling with competing points of view is legitimate (53).

4.10 In Ignatian education particular care is given to the development of the imaginative, the affective and the creative dimensions of each student so as to enrich learning and prevent it from being merely intellectual. These dimensions are also a way to discover God and God's self-revelation through beauty (28).

4.11 The intellectual, imaginative, affective, creative, and physical development of each student...all can help students to discover God active in history and in creation (36).

4.12 Ignatian education encourages and assists each student to respond to her or his own personal call from God, a vocation of service in personal and professional life—whether in marriage, religious, priestly or single life (66).

4.13 Ignatian education challenges students to try to put into practice—in concrete activity—the values they have received in their formation (73).

Part 5.0 Pluralism: An Important Asset to the Campus Community

5.1 Members of various faiths and cultures are viewed as a welcome part of the Ignatian educational community (61).

5.2 Ignatian education promotes dialogue between faith and culture and between faith and science. It encourages contact with and genuine appreciation of other cultures while being creatively critical of the contributions and deficiencies of each (38).

5.3 The purposes and ideals of members of other faiths can be in harmony with the goals of the Ignatian university and they can commit themselves to these goals for the development of the students and for the betterment of society (94).

5.4 The endeavor in Ignatian education is to build a solidarity with others that transcends race, culture and even religion (33).

5.5 Pastoral care is made available to all members of the educational community in order to awaken and strengthen their personal faith commitment (63).

5.6 The Ignatian university community encourages collaboration in ecumenical activities (100).

Part 6.0 Social Justice: Ignatian Formation in its Theory and Praxis

6.1 Ignatian education asks its students and graduates alike for a commitment to the struggle for a more human world, to the goal of a new type of person in a new kind of society in which each individual has the opportunity to be fully human (76).

6.2 In an Ignatian university the focus is on a process of education for justice that will make the commitment to work for justice in adult life more effective (77).

6.3 There are opportunities in Ignatian education for actual contact with the world of injustice (80).

6.4 Ignatian education tries to have students realize that persons and structures can change together with a commitment to work for those changes in a way that will help to build more just human structures (58).

6.5 Ignatian education makes a preferential option for the economic poor, the handicapped, the marginalized and all others unable to live a life of full human dignity (85).

6.6 The poor form the context of Ignatian education...its educational planning is from the perspective of the poor (88).

6.7 Students in Ignatian universities are provided opportunities for contact (conjoined with reflection) with their poor sisters and brothers (89).

6.8 The aim of Ignatian education is the fullest possible development of every dimension of the person, linked to the development of a sense of values and a commitment to the service of others which gives priority to the needs of the poor and is willing to sacrifice self-interest for the promotion of justice (107).

6.9 The decisive action called for today is the faith that does justice, including action for peace (74, 75).

Part 7.0 A Festive Campus Ambience

7.1 The ambience of the Ignatian university offers the opportunity for a faith response to God, and presents such a response as something truly human and not opposed to reason. Most of all it recognizes faith is never imposed (38).

7.2 Enmeshed in a world of excessive competitiveness, evidenced by individualism, consumerism, and success at all costs, the Ignatian university urges its students to distinguish themselves by their ability to work together, to be sensitive to the feelings of one another, to be committed to the service of others shown in the way they help one another—all of which cannot thrive in an atmosphere of academic competition where one's personal qualities are judged only by comparison to those of others (112).

7.3 Students' personal development through the training of character and will, overcoming selfishness and lack of concern for others, are aided by the necessary regulations of an Ignatian university, including a fair system of discipline (52).

7.4 Ignatian education encourages a healthy patriotism but never an unquestioning acceptance of national values (39).

7.5 The university structure reflects the new society that the Ignatian vision, through its education, is trying to construct (142).

7.6 Sports programs in the final analysis promote cooperation with others, and allow students in Ignatian universities to accept both success and failure graciously (31).

7.7 Good manners are expected in an Ignatian university (33).

Part 8.0 Collaboration and Consultation Integral to Governance

8.1 All those sharing responsibility for the governance of the Ignatian university, in application of the principle of subsidiarity, form a directive team (140).

8.2 All members of the board are familiar with the aims of the Ignatian university and with the vision of Ignatius on which these aims are based (130).

8.3 Teacher, staff, and administrators collaborate with other universities and educational agencies to discover more effective institutional policies, educational processes and pedagogical methods (115).

8.4 Collaboration with the laity in a common mission is a goal of an Ignatian university (118).

8.5 In order to promote a common sense of purpose applied to the concrete circumstances of school life, faculty, staff, and administrators communicate with one another regularly on personal, professional and religious levels (123).

8.6 Parents are a constituency within the educational community of Ignatian universities, and they are offered opportunities to participate in advisory councils (131).

8.7 Parents are informed about the commitment of Ignatian education to a faith that does justice (133).

8.8 The alumni/ae are members of the "community working in service of the kingdom" and an Ignatian university has a special responsibility to guide their ongoing formation (135).

Part 9.0 The Society of Jesus: The Jesuit Influence

9.1 If the university is authorized to use the name "Jesuit," then sufficient authority and control remains in the hands of the Society of Jesus to enable it to respond to a call of the Church through its institutions and to ensure that the university continues to be faithful to its traditions (141).

9.2 Neither individual Jesuits nor the Society of Jesus has any power of decision making not defined in the statutes of the Ignatian university (129).

9.3 Whether the president of a "Jesuit" university be a layperson or a Jesuit, the responsibility entrusted to him or her always includes a mission that comes ultimately from the Society of Jesus. This mission, as it relates to the Ignatian character of the school, is subject to periodic evaluation by the Society of Jesus. (138).

9.4 The role of the president of the university includes that of an apostolic leader. He or she is to aid the development of a common Ignatian vision, and is responsible for the distinctively Ignatian character of the education (139).

9.5 Effective authority can be exercised by anyone, Jesuit or lay, who has a knowledge of, sympathy for, identification with and commitment to the Ignatian character of education (141).

9.6 Jesuits are active in promoting lay-Jesuit collaboration in the school such that they are willing to play a subordinate, supporting, anonymous role, and willing to learn how to serve from those they seek to serve (121).

Conclusion

The vision proposed above is presented without further commentary, though each and every "perspective" within it invites extended annotations, comments, and qualifications. Here is where all parties interested in elaborating a vision for working in an American university which identifies itself as Catholic and Jesuit, must do their part. Specifically, they must participate in some such process as that described by Appleyard and which he says has enjoyed some success at Boston College. An Ignatian vision for any given university can not be effectively elaborated without such a process of lay and Jesuit collaboration—where "lay" is not confined to the customary Vatican usage but includes non-Catholics as well as Catholics. With such a collaborative process in place, an Ignatian vision will hopefully follow, and once the vision, then soon after the release of the energies of the God graced love for truth, learning, and teaching envisioned long ago in Fr. Greeley's imagination.

Notes

[1]By way of defining my terms, I am referring to the 235 Catholic colleges and universities in America but not to institutions established by the Holy See which bestow degrees that only the Holy See can give (such as seminaries or the *sui generis* Catholic University of America in Washington, DC.)

[2]It should not be forgotten that the Society of Jesus permits the use of its copyrighted name to any university that would call itself "Jesuit." All 28 of the schools seem eager to appropriate the copyrighted name when it comes to attracting students from cohorts of traditional college age (which are now declining). Witness the recent change of name of Wheeling College to Wheeling Jesuit College. Independent marketing for some of the schools has found that the name "Jesuit" sells because it is readily perceived as part of a tradition of quality education. That "Jesuit" also involves inseparable linkage to the Society of Jesus (not to mention to the Catholic Church) is a fact that tends to be often downplayed by those 28.

[3]Ignatian is a term that can be predicated of any Christian who shares the world view of Ignatius (especially as it is experienced in his Spiritual Exercises). Jesuit is a narrower canonical term and refers to the approximately 26,000 members of the Society of Jesus.

References

Appleyard, J.A. "The Language We Use: Talking About Religious Experience." *Studies in the Spirituality of Jesuits*, 19.2 (1987).

Bellah, Robert N., Richard Madsen, William M. Sullivan, Ann Swidler, et. al. *Habits of the Heart: Individualism and Commitment in American Life*. Berkeley: University of California Press, 1985.

Boyer, Ernest L. *College: The Undergraduate Experience in America*. New York: Harper & Row, 1987.

Brown, William and Andrew Greeley. *Can Catholic Schools Survive?* New York: Sheed and Ward, 1970.

Buckley, Michael. "Jesuit, Catholic Higher Education: Some Tentative Theses." *Review for Religious*, May/June (1983): 339-349.

Byron, William. "Our Goals Statement: Occasional Papers on Catholic Higher Education." D.C.: Association of Catholic Colleges and Universities, 1976.

_____ "Liberal Learning and the Future of Families." *America*, June, 142. 23 (1980): 499-502.

Ellis, John Tracey. "The Catholic Church and Her Universities: A View from History." *Current Issues in Catholic Higher Education*, 8 (1987): 3-9.

_____ "The Catholic Liberal Arts College: Has It A Future?" *Current Issues in a Catholic Higher Education* 3 (1982): 3-9.

Gannon, Thomas. "A Catholic University." *Commonweal* 104, No. 2 (1977): 41.

Hassel, David J. *City of Wisdom*. Chicago: Loyola University Press, 1983.

Hauser, Richard. "Creighton University: Still Catholic and Jesuit." *Lumen Vitae*, XL, No. 3, (1985).

Healy, Timothy. "The Usages of Freedom." *Current Issues in Catholic Higher Education.* 8 (1987): 35-38.

Healy, Timothy. "God's Better Beauty." *Georgetown University Annual Report*, pp. 1-8, Office of University Relations, December 1984. D.C.: Georgetown University.

_____ "The Ignatian Heritage and Today's College." *America*, 25 Jan. 1977.

Hesburgh, Theodore. *The Catholic University: A Modern Appraisal.* South Bend: Notre Dame Press, 1970.

_____ "Catholic Education in America," *America*, Oct. 1986:

Jones, E. Michael. "Is Notre Dame Still Catholic?" *Fidelity*, 1984: 19-24.

Kennedy, Eugene. *Re-imagining American Catholicism.* New York: Vantage Books, 1986.

Kolvenbach, Peter-Hans. *Go Forth and Teach: The Characteristics of Jesuit Education.* D. C.: Jesuit Secondary Education Association, 1987.

Lucey, Gregory. *The Meaning and Maintenance of Catholicity as a Distinctive Characteristic of American Catholic Education: A Case Study.* (Unpublished Ph.D. Dissertation, University of Wisconsin), 1978.

Mills, C. Wright. *The Power Elite.* New York: Oxford University Press, 1956.

Newman, John. *The Idea of A University.* New York: Longmans, Green and Company, 1923.

O'Brien, David. "Effect of Religiosity on Sex Attitudes, Experience and Contraception among University Students." *Journal of Sex and Mental Therapy*, 10.1 (1981): 57-62.

O'Connell, Colman. "The Mission of the College of St. Benedict: Its Catholic Character." *Current Issues in Catholic Higher Education*, Vol. 8.1 (1986).

O'Hare, Joseph. "A Conversation with Fordham's New President." *Fordham Magazine*, 17.7 (1984): 10-14.

O'Meara, Timothy. "The Notre Dame Long-Range Plan." *Leadership Roles of Chief Academic Officers*, David Brown, editor. San Francisco. Jossey-Bass, 1984. 85-90.

Pope, John Paul II. "Excellence, Truth, and Freedom in Catholic Universities." *Origins*, 9. 19 (1979).

Reiss, Paul J. "Saint Michael's College: Its Catholic Character and Academic Freedom." *Current Issues in Catholic Higher Education*, 8.1 (1986).

Schroth, Raymond. "Tough Choices on Campus." *Commonweal*, March 22, 1986: 170-175.

Tessitore, Aristide. "Catholic Higher Education as an Assumptionist Apostolate." *CMSM Documentation*, No. 46 (1986).

Tetlow, Joseph A. "The Jesuit Vision in Higher Education: Perspectives and Contexts." *Studies*, Vol. XV. No. 5 Nov. and Vol. XVI. No. 1 Jan. (1983).

United States Catholic Conference. *Catholic Higher Education and the Pastoral Mission of the Church.* D.C.: United States Catholic Conference, 1980.

Whitehead, Kenneth. "Religiously Affiliated Colleges and American Freedom." *America*, Feb. 7, 1987: 96ff.

Some Observations on Leadership in the Liberal Arts College

David Riesman

As a non-hierarchical society, America has always had to depend on leadership arising out of the democratic and egalitarian plain. At the same time, as Tocqueville observed and as indeed much of American history from the colonists' rebellion onward testifies, Americans fear and resist authority. Boys learn very young one of the slogans of American individualism: "You're not the boss of me!" The self-selection of academics, as distinct from those attracted to work in business or in the civil service, heightens these all-American tendencies so that some faculty members even in small liberal arts colleges are not loyal to their departments or their subspecialties, but are solipsistic small businessmen. In an essay-review of Michael Maccoby's *The Gamesman* in *Change* a few years ago, I commented that I had met more jungle fighters (one of his leadership types) in academic than corporate life, where there are team-oriented gamesmen and a few institutional loyalists (Maccoby refers to the latter with inappropriate derogatory connotation as "company men"). Concern for the quality of leadership is at once endemic and cyclical in American life.

Today there is a particular preoccupation with leadership and followership. I believe this reflects the odd combination of extravagantly sanguine boosterism in the general economy and among some academic entrepreneurs and the recognition that large deficits, provocative and divisive foreign policies, and awareness of inability to solve or even to understand how one might solve many major domestic problems create an anxious mood among the reflective, and a subcurrent of anxiety even among the outwardly buoyant. Moreover, the delegitimation of leadership and trust in established institutions and established leaders that began with the civil rights movements as these moved North, the anti-Vietnam war movements, the women's movements, and the reaction against all these on the part of cultural and religious conservatives, has heightened the distrust of experts and of established hierarchies in the society at large, and particularly in the more selective liberal arts colleges and universities, where the acids of modernity have added their corrosive power to the extant individualism. There is thus both a call for leadership and a fear of it.

The call for leadership has commonly a nostalgic aura about it. Some of our most influential social critics, liberals or Left-leaning in their general outlook on society, such as Robert Bellah and his colleagues (in the book *Habits of the Heart*) and Christopher Lasch and those who might call themselves communitarian liberals, sometimes look back in their writings to Abraham Lincoln as an undoubted leader who called on the nation to remain a nation and, as his presidency proceeded, to live up to its highest ideals of liberty, equality, and justice.

The widespread expectation that college presidents should be leaders in exhibiting by their actions and by what they say about them, the qualities of moral vision and leadership within and beyond their institutions, is partly an inheritance from the days of the president as clergyman or priest; there are still such clerics who are presidents, but they are rare. In fact, the most eminent among them, Father Theodore Hesburgh, C.S.C., of Notre Dame, or the younger and less world-renowned Father Timothy Healy, S.J., of Georgetown University, are cited by many observers to illustrate the kind of leadership we have lost. The intensity of the quest for such leadership ranges far beyond the academy, in part because of the judgment that such leaders are absent from the larger political arena or are merely media creations composed of speech writers' addresses combined with photo opportunities. In fact, there is a considerable number of very able and courageous and even inventive governors in the various states; however, the "nationalization" of American society through mobility, the media, and the jet plane tends to focus questions of leadership on the national scene and hence often on senators and congressmen trained in the law or in other isolating settings who have shown capacity to run a staff of ten and win interest beyond their home base without having had experiences that would prepare them to be team builders, let alone institutional loyalists at the national level.

Some time ago I had a letter from the chairman of the presidential search committee of a liberal arts college, one of the small independent colleges which are in peril. With 1500 students and long affiliated with one of the smaller denominations, it has a non-metropolitan locale in a Rust Belt state. It belongs to the cohort of "colleges in peril" described in general terms in Gilbert T. Sewall's "Small Independent Colleges in America."[1] When asked to nominate someone who might be a president of the college, I had recommended a man who combines cultivation with forcefulness, a person of integrity though not quixotic. The chairman wrote me that the college was too precariously situated to take a chance on someone with such high expectations, especially in his dedication to the liberal arts and sciences as against what has been termed the shopping-mall or cafeteria college. The chairman wondered if the college could survive the person I had recommended, even while recognizing that this person would help bring the college national visibility. I suspect there was something else that the chairman, a board member, did not report: namely, that faculty members may claim that they want a president who is a leader and a person of moral sensibility, but they may well feel intimidated by just such a person who, if energetic and alert, would not put up with instances of slovenly behavior—for instance, grade inflation to woo students into one's own bailiwick.

Actually, the search procedures we use to pick college and university presidents sometimes seem almost designed to weed out potential leaders, however one may define leadership. This is especially so if candidates are brought to the campus, where different constituencies, to put it in vulgar terms, can "feel the merchandise," putting candidates who should be treated as prospects in the position of being supplicants, tempted to make political pitches they believe will appeal to faculty without turning off trustees, and to students without turning off faculty. The study of search procedures on which Judith Block McLaughlin and I have been engaged for half a dozen years makes clear that leadership is essential in chairing the search committee, if one is to avoid lowest-common-denominator choices and to conduct a process which will court desirable individuals; otherwise the process is one of screening ambitious applicants for whom a presidency is either a step up or a step out of a currently impossible situation.

If one examines simultaneously, as I have been doing, both the leadership of some liberal arts colleges, and searches for all sorts of colleges, there are certain identifiable categories one can distinguish, and assess in terms of larger questions of what would be optimal in a specific setting. There are the "turnaround" presidents who do not need to be magnanimous or visionary, but energetic, entrepreneurial, and prepared to be disliked, even hated, by faculty. Such presidents depend absolutely on the full support of their boards.[2] In the terms Michael Maccoby uses in his forthcoming book, *Why Work: Motivating the New Generation*, these individuals could be described as Defenders, rescuing an institution at whatever cost in personal equanimity, but without being necessarily wedded to the institution in any transcendent way; commonly, they are also experts, who know finance and fund-raising, understand the all-important role of admissions and the visibility that may enhance admissions, and who leave diurnal academic work mainly to their deans while reviewing such indices as tenure ratios, teaching loads, and salaries. Some have been extremely inventive as entrepreneurs outside the institution. Dan West, who is much more than a Defender, though he is also that, is President of Arkansas College in Batesville, Arkansas; he has been effective in using venture capital in real estate development to advance a precariously funded college. Grinnell College has done fabulously in this respect.

There is another type or group of presidents, also experts and entrepreneurs, who come into institutions that are doing reasonably well but which have been somewhat stagnant and are perhaps in the long run likely to suffer in competition with more rambunctiously managed competitors. These presidents are ambitious for themselves and their colleges; they want to move them into another level of distinction. George Harmon at Millsaps College in Jackson, Mississippi; Neal Berte at Birmingham-Southern College; Ronald Calgaard at Trinity University in San Antonio, all belong to a group of presidents who have pushed their colleges, using the leverage of grants from foundations and corporations and private donors vastly to upgrade facilities, including dormitories; to move recruiting of students and their financing to another level of price-war competition; to recruit professors of more energy as well as greater academic reputation. In general, these men accept the going definitions of what is a superior liberal arts college, and seek to meet those definitions by careful appreciation of faculty sensibilities without being too inhibited by these. In their pronouncements, perhaps notably so in the Southern settings mentioned by way of illustration, they will speak of values and of building character. They often have inspirational gifts, and their vision is so far beyond where the college is now and yet still within reasonable reach, that they are not seen as quixotic. They combine managerial with inspirational talents.

Absent from discussions of presidential leadership are the qualities of self-development and the wish to remain alert to incipient ethical and cultural issues which are not part of the daily grist of academic life. I have been struck in looking at presidential searches to see that it has hardly ever been mentioned as a criterion in the list of virtues and skills sought for in a new president that the new incumbent should be a mentor to his or her subordinates and should in turn seek mentoring— by reading and reflection, through brief sabbaticals, through meeting with peers— to improve his or her intellectual and moral capacities. We can talk all we like about justice and honor and concern for others, but life presents us with unanticipated settings to respond to which we must be morally and intellectually alert as few of us are in any society.

Several examples may suggest what I have in mind. Notre Dame is one of the few institutions which maintains an honor code, requiring fellow students to turn in a violator; without such a provision, maintained to this day at the University of Virginia despite a continuing drumbeat of opposition, an honor code cannot be truly effective, but, as often happens, will become another cause for cynicism as violators go unreported. A few years ago, a prominent black athlete, the mainstay of his team, was in the women's dormitories after the hour when men are supposed to be out of them. The student resident assistant saw him; so did several other students. These latter were all white. The resident assistant feared to turn the student in, and so did those who had observed him. In such settings, the fear to be thought racist is an inhibition—a kind of perverse Affirmative Action. But several students came to Father Hesburgh, reported what had occurred, and declared their inability to take the case through the proper procedural steps.[3] Hesburgh immediately told the students that he believed the honor code had put too great a burden on them; he would handle the situation himself. He called in the athlete, explained that he was dismissing him immediately, and that if the athlete spent a year in useful work and brought back a report on such work, he could be re-admitted, but without scholarship. (There is a happy outcome to the story, for the student was grateful to Father Hesburgh for not condescending to him, spent a fruitful year, and returned to complete his baccalaureate degree.) I think of another instance where a suicide occurred on the campus of a small liberal arts college in New England. The President was in Florida making a round of visits to alumni groups and soliciting contributions. Rather than return immediately to campus, he allowed his Dean of Students to handle the matter. The shock of the occasion led to the plummeting of morale on campus. A more morally and intellectually alert president might have realized the importance of his returning at once, whatever the immediate costs.

One situation which has caught many college and university presidents unprepared (as well as many other leaders of public and private affairs) is where in a fitfully and unevenly reviving burst of faculty-student activism, protests arise over something that the college is or is not engaged in doing. Examples come from instances of efforts to prevent a CIA recruiter from coming to the campus of a liberal arts college, where neither students nor faculty differentiate the "dirty tricks" branches of the CIA from its analytical sides. The coercion that has often occurred where a CIA recruiter has been blocked from meeting with students is not only a disruption of the work of the career office, but an effort to put the university on record on one side of a political and moral line, and the "bad guys" on the other side, including of course students who might be interested in a career with the CIA and faculty members who no more want the CIA interfered with than they would like CIA interference with their own research.

The occasional efforts to block CIA recruiters from campus are a pale refraction of the much more fervent and more violence-prone battles over what was alleged to be college and university complicity in the Vietnam war in the years after the first teach-in was held at the University of Michigan in 1965—regrettably not an educational effort intended to illuminate all the complexities of Southeast Asia and of American internal debates over the Cold War and the "loss of China," but rather mass meetings to mobilize sentiment leading to action. To a person like myself, who has since 1945 devoted his civic energies primarily to the problems and possibilities of controlling the race for nuclear arsenals, it is at once puzzling and saddening that presidents are not presented with issues arising out of that threat to human existence itself, but have, vis-a-vis the policies of the United States government, been able to deal only with peripheral issues such as CIA recruiting, or the effort on some campuses to restore ROTC; however, in a very few major research universities presidents have been presented with the question as to whether scientists should be prohibited from research and development of the so-called Strategic Defense Initiative. Many scientists at Cornell, MIT, and elsewhere have as individuals signed self-denying ordinances vis-a-vis such research, which they believe to be in fact provocative and extravagantly improbable as an actual shield. Even so, holding such views myself, I would be opposed to a college or university's taking a stand on this issue as an institution, for I hold to the view that the task of academic institutions is to preserve a free forum for ideas and for research (which would permit ruling out classified research as inappropriate, although I do not regard that issue as a simple one),[4] with presidents seeing themselves, along with the board of trustees, as custodians of resources for future generations of faculty and students—maintaining this position even on issues involving the question of nuclear winter and the end of the human adventure.

A few college and university presidents have entered this arena of war and peace, in order to encourage teaching and research in some aspects of its formidable intricacies. Adele Simmons, President of Hampshire College, herself a knowledgeable student of non-American societies, has sought to organize teaching in war and peace studies in the Five College Consortium (Amherst College, Hampshire College, Mount Holyoke College, Smith College, and the University of Massachusetts-

Amherst), as well as contributing to public discussion of the issue. James Gardner, President of Lewis & Clark College, has appreciated the importance of Soviet-American exchanges. Against cautionary advice both from the State Department and some Trustees, he went to Moscow immediately after the downing of the Korean airliner in order to facilitate a program of exchanges which then brought Georgy Arbatov and other Soviet students of American society to the Portland area. Such efforts run the risk of arousing local anti-Soviet reactions, whether from Jewish groups or from other subgroups vigilantly on the lookout for opportunities to attack Communism and the well-known evils of Soviet society. President Gardner had the advantage of coming to this arena after long experience in international affairs at the Ford Foundation, including having a chance as the Foundation's Latin American representative to spend years in the major South American countries seeing how the United States looks from outside its borders. Thus he had some basis in intellectual preparation for seeking moral clarity in the opportunities and the risks his program of exchange was potentially creating for Lewis & Clark College.[5]

As I write these lines, the overwhelming issue on many campuses is one for which most college presidents were unprepared intellectually and, in many cases, morally as well, even though it is hardly novel, and that is the issue of ethical investment (and hence the call for ethical divestment) vis-a-vis securities of companies doing business in South Africa.[6] The issue of ethical behavior of a college as employer, investor, landlord, and neighbor has been around and agitated here and there for a very long time. But so far as I can see, especially in the South African divestiture issue, presidents and boards of trustees have not adequately prepared themselves to confront such issues as they arise. In many cases they have sacrificed their responsibilities as stewards for the future for the sake of making moral statements in the present, which appeal to vocal and increasingly volatile students, faculty members, a minority of alumni, and liberal and radical preachers and politicians. I leave aside in this discussion all the many complexities of the issue as an intrinsic one of political pragmatism and public morality. On the campuses, however, the issue quickly becomes one of whether divestment will help or hurt South African blacks, help or hurt apartheid or the divergences from it practiced by many American corporations, and all the problems of a multi-tribal society that is in some respects an advanced industrial and in spots liberal democracy, and in other respects a less developed African country which includes two dominant white tribes. What is troubling to me is the way in which presidents, along with other administrators and to a lesser degree boards of trustees have been drawn into the nearly infinite intricacies of the issue (as it might be judged by well-informed observers from countries without a history of slavery) as an opportunity to show that the college's leaders are not insensible to dramaturgically inflamed choices between the righteous and the damned. Building shanties on a campus has some of the same graphic symbolism as that practiced in the anti-Vietnam war movement—symbolism which turned to an anti-American ugliness and violence whose provocative nature may have strengthened the war party at the time.[7]

Robert Edwards, when President of Carleton College (1977-86), exhibited a rare clarity concerning the problems confronted by an academic institution which seeks to use its role as an investor to make a statement of its values and, in the minds of some, to influence corporate and national policies. He has asked, for example, whether a college wants to say to its graduating seniors that they would be evil persons, did they go to work for companies judged by a majority of the campus to be complicitous and unethical. Should the college itself receive grants or scholarship assistance from such companies? Should, as some Right Wing students and a tiny number of faculty members have now begun to claim, investments be abandoned in companies doing business in Soviet Bloc countries? And what about companies selling to South Africa, or selling products to the Soviet Union or Poland—already the Right Wing is seeking to boycott Pepsi-Cola for doing business with Communists?

It is obvious that I cannot explore the complexities of the issues themselves here; my effort is to illustrate particular qualities of presidential alertness, at once practical and moral (and ethics to be meaningful must always bear on practical life), prepared by previous thought for issues which then suddenly arise when the rolling wave of activism, often nationally manipulated to catch the media, hits the particular campus.

When shanties were erected on the Dartmouth College campus, the argument made for them was that they were educational, awakening individuals to what the protestors regarded as the pre-eminent moral issue of the epoch. I am suggesting that the presidents can use the same issue, at the hazard of being abused as racists, non-consultative, non-majoritarian, and undemocratic—of all these, the greatest sting is "racist"—to educate faculty (commonly leaders on campus political issues, though not always in the limelight) and students about the long-run purposes of higher education and the significance of reluctance to turn political issues into moral ones and thus issues on which there are only good guys, bad guys, and neuters. (In a putsch the "neuters" are usually inactive, fearing intimidation by the "good guys.")

The politicization of the campus, whether by the Right Wing or today more commonly by the liberal-Left, has for many presidents whose principal concern is with the prospects of their institutions become an immense distraction.

I want to turn now to what presidents in the relatively small number of independent colleges primarily devoted to the liberal arts and sciences can do to improve the academic and intellectual vibrancy of their institutions, and what sorts of leadership they need to pursue that goal. Presidents must concern themselves with fund-raising and, even in the most favored institutions, with admissions policy, while in many less favored ones they make a mistake not to put enrollment and retention of students as their first priority, seeing to it that the dean of admissions reports directly to them rather than through a vice president or provost. They must themselves help recruit top admissions and financial aid people, consider what can be done through institutional research to learn about the college's potential attractions for students and what can legitimately be done to make it more attractive without succumbing completely to consumerism.[8]

Some brave presidents have recognized that, to maintain the quality of their student body in a period of demographic decline in their area, when they are not heading colleges as abundantly overapplied as Williams or Amherst, it would be wise to plan on a somewhat smaller student body with commensurate faculty and staff, thus retaining and even improving selectivity. James Powell, the President of Franklin & Marshall College, has proposed just such considerations, even though at present the College has 3600 applicants, of whom it accepts 55 per cent for a yield of 500 acceptances. Jill Conway, before her retirement as President of Smith College, made a similar proposal. The initial reaction to such a notion is commonly outrage: how could so marvelous an institution as ours, still eagerly sought after, possibly decline unless through fault of presidential leadership! It is more comfortable for sitting presidents to leave such issues to their successors, just as it is more comfortable for them to undermaintain their institutions while pleasing the faculty through raises and students and their parents through generous financial aid. Indeed, there are many presidents who act the way corporate managers do when the latter are judged not on the long-run health of the corporation but on its "bottom line" showing on a quarterly or even monthly basis, and on the price of its stock kept high enough to minimize the risk of takeovers.

Such considerations can only allude to the reasons why I believe that presidents' capacities for leadership can best be assessed by their peers, that is, other presidents or former presidents. A still unpublished study of presidential assessment based on a single detailed case study and on interviews with presidents and trustees illustrates how unlikely it is to find disinterested assessment of presidents among trustees, faculty members, students, and staff.[9] To be sure, the judgments of people with partial or what Veblen would have called one-eyed views of the president, though sometimes frivolous and not uncommonly vindictive, are not irrelevant. But they must be weighed from the perspective of the sociology of knowledge and understanding of the limitations of the observer. I can speak for myself here. Without the slightest wish ever to become a president, I have had an interest in the college presidency from my undergraduate days onward; and having become a sociologist as a second career without passing through the socialization processes of a Ph.D. program, I know that I sometimes find it hard to sympathize with the antagonism of faculty (especially in the more selective and high-prestige institutions) toward their presidents, a number of whom I have known as friends as well as through my research. I know that I must discount my own perspective if I am not to be unfair to faculty reactions.

The effort of college and university presidents to occupy the "bully pulpit," to speak out on national issues, represents continuity from earlier traditions of such leadership. In addition to Father Hesburgh, William Friday at Chapel Hill, Clark Kerr at Berkeley, Robert M. Hutchins at Chicago have been examples of this mode. When a few years ago A. Bartlett Giamatti attacked the Moral Majority for claiming that it was a majority or that it had a monopoly of morality, he won only tepid applause from many academic and intellectual people, who were grateful that he had said this but who did not believe it would cause the President of Yale any grief. It appeared to be almost as innocuous, coming from an Eastern

76   The Incarnate Imagination

Seaboard university, as would be an attack on racism. Such a judgment was mistaken: Giamatti received a deluge of irate letters from alumni, including influential ones, who criticized him for speaking out on an issue more controversial than he had perhaps imagined, and who accused him of taking toward evangelical religion the supercilious view of Eastern intellectual elites. The episode illustrates the degree to which what *The Lonely Crowd* referred to in 1950 as veto groups are ceaselessly vigilant and potentially influential. Room for maneuver in the national forum is not easily won or sustained.

John Silber, the philosopher and polemicist, former Dean of the University of Texas-Austin, now since 1971 President of Boston University, has been prepared to endure and it would seem at times almost happy to invite the antagonism of many members of his own faculty of arts and sciences. By serving the University magnificently in terms of its financial underpinning, the distinction of its faculties, and the increase in numbers and quality of its applicants, and over time by building support on his own Board of Trustees, Silber has consolidated his position; indeed in a sense he is locked into it, because the faculty antagonism is so strong that other university presidential search committees would be most unlikely to propose him, despite his evident gifts, and try to lure him from his present battlement. On Central America, on American foreign policy generally, on the kinds of academic conduct and civility which should be cultivated—on these and other issues Silber has spoken with force, intelligence, and candor. In 1985, he offered to manage the Boston public schools—an interesting proposal worth serious consideration, but quickly dismissed as condescending and hostile because of the widespread suspicion of its source. Silber has concerned himself not only with national issues of foreign policy, but also with educational policy; thus, he revived the idea of a national student loan bank which would be amortized through repayment and which would free students (far more than do the present limited subsidies and loans) to go where they wish, free of state boundaries and family finances.

Clark Kerr and others have criticized college presidents for being too exclusively oriented extramurally, and too little concerned with specifically academic issues, with the climate of research, of learning and of teaching on the campus.[10] He and others refer to the implicit verdict to the same effect rendered by those academic deans and academic vice presidents who decline to become candidates for the presidency, believing it would take them almost entirely into the arenas of fundraising, public relations, and in effect peripatetic talk show host.[11] I am confining my discussion here to liberal arts colleges which are residential, with 3,000 students or fewer, where it is possible for a president directly to influence the academic tone rather than having to work primarily, as in a complex university or a comprehensive college, through his or her influence on the choice of deputy administrators or middle management. I want to illustrate the kinds of things presidents can do and occasionally manage to do in cooperation with the dean or academic vice president/provost.

During his time as President of the two St. John's Colleges at Annapolis and Santa Fe, Edwin Delattre did not seek to undermine the strongly entrenched program of Great Books. However, he noted that students in the course of their seminars learned to talk well but wrote almost nothing. He was not unaware that writing by American students in college is often confined to courses in English or to remedial courses, except for those who write theses or essays in particular programs. Delattre challenged the Tutors to create more opportunities for student writing. They resisted, basing their case on the oral traditions of Plato's Academy and on some observations attributed to Socrates in one of the Platonic dialogues. Delattre kept pressing, insisting that American students in general, and shockingly St. John's College students, were handicapped in their inability to compose a cogent written argument. The point here is not the degree of his success, which was rather modest, but the determined effort, which suffered from a lack of decanal support at either campus. In this as in other instances, the successor presidents now being chosen for Annapolis and for Santa Fe may perhaps reap the benefits of Delattre's pressures. Indeed, his judgment that there should be a president for each campus, a topic on which he had to persuade many Trustees and many unwilling Tutors, was based on his recognition that a commuting president who was also raising money and doing all the other needful things extramurally was handicapped in the perseverence necessary to overcome a resistance that is particularly strong at a college that was once and still remains innovative in its uncompromising purity, and as a result runs the danger of becoming something of a frozen experiment.

Robert Edwards, already referred to in another context, faced almost the opposite situation at Carleton College. There students do a great deal of writing as a regular part of their course work, and the quality of that writing is judged by many faculty members in the different fields of scholarship and not only in courses in literature or composition. However, Edwards recognized that in Carleton's small classes with almost too accessible professors, often on a first-name basis with their students, the latter were not always well prepared for presentations of self in less nurturant and friendly forums. Correspondingly, it was possible that even outstanding Carleton students were handicapped in competing for Rhodes Scholarships and similar national fellowship competitions, and might suffer also from diminution of regard in interviews for jobs or places in graduate and professional programs. I am speaking here of something concededly marginal, which a number of the faculty members at Carleton were inclined to dismiss, sometimes viewing Carleton students as the more admirable if they were less polished than some of Edwards's fellow Princeton or Harvard Law alumni. Still, when by patient persuasion Edwards was able to institute a voluntary forensic program, some faculty critics were surprised to see how many students wanted to take advantage of it.

Patience is especially requisite in colleges in rural or small-town locales, where every move the president makes has reverberation throughout the locale. When she was President of Mary Baldwin College in Staunton, Virginia, Virginia Lester discovered—and she is not the only president to have made such a discovery— that her food service manager had strong connections in Staunton, as well as ties to older faculty, and of course faculty members have ties to one another which would be strained not only by efforts at retrenchment, but also by anything interpreted as a "Great Leap Forward."

In some of the liberal arts colleges I have studied, the president has not been permitted to bring in from outside an academic dean granted tenure in an appropriate department. In part this has been because the faculty believe they will have more control over a dean who cannot count on a permanent place among them. But in part it reflects the resistance of these colleges to bringing in anyone with tenure, even to a department conceded to be relatively weak, perhaps decrepit. A sense of community is fragile and is reflected in a kind of in-house socialism and search for parity. In such a college, it is recognized that there is a stiffer market in economics or computer science than in philosophy or the humanities generally, and that equity in salaries must give way in considerable measure to market forces. But there is great reluctance to allow the president to trade rank for stars.[12]

In contrast, the institution seeking to achieve an entirely new level of distinction with a wider orbit of potentially national visibility can to some extent leapfrog the stages of development, for example, by encouraging early and well-funded retirement for senior faculty making that choice, and by compensation that helps ease the discomfort many such faculty may feel as the institution jolts forward in the subspecialties of disciplines to which they became attached at an earlier point.

Trinity University illustrates the ability of a determined president to move an institution dramatically toward another level of selectivity for students and faculty members, while still maintaining some ties to the founding Presbyterian Church. Like Birmingham-Southern and Millsaps, but even more so, Trinity University has the advantage of location in a growing and increasingly attractive metropolis, a venue attractive to two-career families on the faculty and staff, and to students interested in internships or part-time work outside of the usual college work-study programs. Many of the liberal arts colleges at risk today outside the New England and mid-Atlantic area, and even there for the less eminent, are located in rural or small-town areas, which are not, in student parlance, where the action is. Even with generous scholarship aid, "buying" students rather than only athletes, it is nevertheless difficult for such an upwardly mobile college to develop a student culture which, in terms popularized years ago by Burton R. Clark and Martin Trow, is academic and nonconformist, in addition to having a general ambience of students who are academically capable and even hard-working, but whose interests are primarily in being certified for lucrative careers either on graduation or after attending business or law school, and on campus focus on social life and sports. Of course one will find students of this sort even in the most high-power and selective liberal arts colleges, but on the whole, the latter at their best engage students with faculty more intensely and the campus culture will have, in now outdated terminology, highbrow, middlebrow, and lowbrow segments with some parity of esteem.[13]

From the perspective of seeking or maintaining faculty cohesion, a metropolitan location has the drawback that faculty members themselves may live scattered all over the metropolitan area in contrast to the proximity characteristic of the liberal arts colleges located in Brunswick and Waterville, Maine; in Williamstown, Massachusetts; or Davidson, North Carolina; or the two colleges, St. Olaf and

Carleton, in Northfield, Minnesota; or Whitman College in Walla Walla, Washington.

Even in the best of circumstances today, for reasons widely understood, the "academic revolution" has meant that faculty members as they become more scholarly and research-minded are likely to move toward loyalty to their sub-discipline rather than to maintain ties beyond their departments to their colleges as a whole. What wise presidents of liberal arts colleges seek is a faculty that is at once "local" and "cosmopolitan," combining extramural orientations and connections with institutional loyalty. In the past and still to some extent today, this has been less difficult to accomplish if the "local" tie is supplemented by the maintenance of a religious affiliation; such affiliation raises questions when it extends to a religious test for faculty members (although it is still understood that presidents can be chosen from within the faith without running afoul of Affirmative Action). The presidents of some of these colleges, for example, Gordon Van Wylen at Hope College in Holland, Michigan, see their task as maintaining a delicate balance between a Christian (not necessarily Reformed Church) ethos and an ecumenical openness even for those faculty members, and of course students, without a religious tie. Holland, Michigan, with a population of 28,000, does not suffer from a geographically dispersed faculty, but like other colleges of its size and rural or small town location does face problems in maintaining disciplinary ties, especially in the more fast-moving fields of scholarship. Hope is one of the "research colleges" whose presidents met in June, 1985, at Oberlin College to make the case for 48 colleges of liberal arts and sciences as reservoirs of the future scientists of the country as a whole. In these colleges in the absence of graduate students, undergraduate majors in science are drawn into research with their professors, taken to scientific conferences with them, and publish papers jointly with them.[14]

The presidents who do focus on the academic climate, working with deans and departments at liberal arts colleges, are even in the case of excellent colleges such as Amherst, Grinnell, Wellesley, or Oberlin working with limited resources in terms of the specialties that there is room for in the fast-moving fields, and the kinds of facilities faculty members need, in terms of the level of state-of-the-art equipment faculty members must have to remain connected to research in their fields.[15] Some presidents of liberal arts colleges have come out of the natural sciences: Robert Gavin of Macalester, James Powell of Franklin & Marshall, and David Ellis of Lafayette all from chemistry; Gordon Van Wylen, already mentioned, from physics and engineering; David Fraser, M.D., from epidemiology.

That small number of presidents who seek to influence the choice of faculty and hence the long-run strength of their institutions, appear in my limited observation to rely primarily on their judgment of individual quality as an intelligent lay person would do. Their original training may give them self-confidence that no subject is so abstruse as to be impenetrable by assessors in neighboring fields. In some cases, in administration as well as in departmental matters, it may give them hubris, the belief that they unquestionably know what is good work in their own original fields and that they also can make a wholly independent judgment by reading a sampling of a prospective faculty member's scholarship. Some presidents of liberal arts colleges seek to read an article or bits of a dissertation of entry-level candidates in the humanities and the social sciences, and many of them can read work not only of course in English, but in at least one foreign language. Mainly, they will rely on departmental assessment, supplemented by the dean's judgment not only of the candidates for a position but of the departmental members themselves and the micro-politics of the department, whether or not that micro-politics is related to larger, extramural politics. Moreover, it is likely to become a political issue within a department and within an institution when it moves away from reliance primarily on good teaching, where scholarship is welcome but not requisite, to a situation where scholarship in the form of visible products is requisite, with teaching important but ancillary.[16] Only a small number of presidents can take the time to meet with entry-level candidates in all fields—and of course they cannot do so invariably, because their schedules too often take them away from campus and catch them up in some of the many non-academic issues that occupy the menu of their attention. They must rely on their judgment of the judgments of others, developing an increasingly detailed but inevitably sketchy map of the worlds of learning and craft, all the specialty shops that are to be found even in a small liberal arts college.

In some ways those presidents may be best off in this respect if they are not themselves planning to return, as insurance if not by choice, to their prior academic fields. Derek Bok, one of the considerable number of law school deans who have become college and university presidents, takes a topic for study every year in the program of further education for which he manages to find room while at the same time he has chosen a more active part in the problems of higher education nationally than when he, like other neophyte presidents, was learning on the job at the outset of his Presidency in 1971. Robert Edwards, also a lawyer who had worked for the State Department and for the Ford Foundation overseas, and then in the Ford Foundation headquarters before becoming President of Carleton in 1977, had no academic specialty to which to return, and used the time he could spare to read the books and articles his faculty wrote, something a few other presidents try to do, and in this fashion to develop his knowledge not only of their potential but of the fields they have partially colonized. Dan West, referred to earlier for his entrepreneurship, a Presbyterian minister with a Ph.D. in religion who is President of Arkansas College, a small liberal arts college in rural Arkansas, used his sabbatical year to complete a second doctorate at the Harvard Graduate School of Education, making higher education itself his specialty.

The instances just mentioned suggest that presidential involvement in academic affairs may raise difficult questions of timing. A first-time president, as all three are, must undergo a great deal of on-the-job training; even a seasoned president from another sort of institution must learn the culture of this particular place at this particular time. Hence their temptation will be to postpone involvement in recruitment and promotion of faculty, fearing to tread where even deans must be wary. However, if their non-involvement is seen as habitual, and if the faculty come to regard them, with the characteristic superciliousness of professors, as "mere" money-raisers, "mere" facilitators, they may find themselves estopped from later involvement as the faculty, the academic dean, the tenure and appointments committee, assume that the president's and the board's role will remain perfunctory.

Through campus visits, I have encountered many instances where presidents have sought to impose higher standards of integrity and have met resistance for interfering with faculty prerogatives. At one liberal arts college, the President denied tenure to a person who, it was conceded, had plagiarized much of the work he submitted to justify his promotion. This person was an outstandingly popular teacher and had won the student-awarded prize for best teacher the previous year. The case is now in litigation. But of course I am choosing instances of presidential leadership and the hazards such leadership invites when it goes into the academic and curricular arenas; there are many instances where it is faculty members who insist on standards and where the president may, for example, want to appoint a woman or minority person to satisfy expectations for Affirmative Action— expectations accepted by the faculty in principle, but not as a guide to a particular judgment. And of course there are worse motives all around, of political pressure or patronage, board interference, and so on. In this set of reflections I am making selective reference to particulars, to exceptional instances, from which it would be rash to draw great generalizations concerning the enormous diversity of some 700 liberal arts colleges—colleges which altogether enroll on the order of ten per cent of American undergraduates.

Many leading liberal arts colleges went through the faculty-student protests of the Sixties and early Seventies with their curricular requirements unimpaired, continuing, for example, to require courses in Western Civilization, mathematics and science, European and American history, a foreign language, and perhaps some work in the arts or art history. But in many instances, traditional curricular restraints were loosened, on the one hand in response to the cry for relevance and for a broadening beyond the Euro-American heritage, and quite as commonly in response to market pressure from student customers wanting a minimum of requirements for a multiplicity of reasons good and bad. A free curriculum, as at Brown, became itself invitational, allowing students advised but not required about what they should study to build their own often imaginative programs. More commonly, the result was to increase attraction for students wanting an undergraduate professional program in business and management, including accounting, and in health services, in addition to the traditional programs in education to prepare school teachers.[17]

Currently the fashions are changing again in many of the more visible institutions. Faculty are seeking to regain control by re-instituting or revising core curriculum requirements, rarely to create a common academic culture after the St. John's College and University of Chicago pattern, but rather to minimize pre-professionalism and see to it that all students are exposed to a variety of traditional liberal arts and sciences subjects and, in the going phrase, modes of inquiry. A number of presidents have taken leadership, in company with their deans of faculty, in this effort, supported as it has been by a congeries of reports from the Carnegie Foundation for the Advancement of Teaching and the Association of American Colleges, and from many leading educators.

However, it is important to resist the easy and prevalent assumption that liberal learning is the outcome of a liberal arts curriculum and the sometimes declared corollary that pre-professional learning is by definition illiberal. A large proportion of the education in the most selective liberal arts colleges can be termed pre-professional, in the sense that the college is the antechamber required by the prestige of medicine, law, and graduate programs in business and management, through which students must pass in order to become professionals at the postbaccalaureate level. Headed toward a narrow set of gates marked "Medical School," "Law School," "School of Business," their eyes are principally on grades, not on what they are supposed to be learning, some of which will be repeated later on in the professional schools.

Moreover, it is a self-serving mistake for professors, for example in the humanities, to see themselves as unequivocally providing a liberal education as distinct from disesteemed vocationalism. A musicologist, a philosopher, a sociologist who is seeking to re-create in his or her students a specialized professional scholar of his or her own "school" and subspecialty may be providing primarily vocational training. The reading list itself may encourage wider horizons, but the texts may be read in such a dehydrated way, with all the reductionist capabilities of renowned scholars, as to create in the undergraduate a perspective under which all other fields of knowledge are subsumed without having had actual experience with them. To put the issue differently, I believe that faculty members have an easier time teaching, let us say, anthropology in a liberating way than they might have teaching accounting, applied music, or engineering in a liberating way. In my own experience as an undergraduate much of the laboratory teaching of science was learning, in effect, how to cook over a Bunsen burner. Even so, I believe that teaching of crafts in and outside of the laboratory is important for its own sake, for their potential carryover to other fields, and for the virtues and understandings that can be cultivated if students are not too insistent that they learn only what is needed on the job, or rather, the first job, or first step toward graduate school, and nothing around or beyond that.

One task for the intellectually alert college president is to seek to understand the congruences, contradictions, and competitions within faculty members themselves and within and among departments, in terms of what is sought for in the long-run development of the student body. Several institutions which at the undergraduate level are primarily pre-professional seem to me to have done better in this respect than many of the liberal arts colleges. In a visit of a few days to Carnegie-Mellon University in 1981, I attended classes and talked with faculty in the College of Humanities and Social Science, a selection of whose courses are required for all CMU students in the Faculties of Engineering and Science, in Management and the Graduate School of Industrial Administration, and more recently in the School of Fine Arts. The University's selectivity and its demanding professionalism do not result in students' regarding the core curriculum courses in the humanities and the social sciences as cultural bull. In many engineering and other professional schools, those who are teaching the required courses in the humanities and social sciences frequently—like ever so many teachers in all levels of education—hold an unwilling student body by becoming entertaining, although in some contexts they seek to improve their self-respect at the cost of boring their students in order to maintain the level of ascetic rigor believed to exist in the natural sciences and in the professional programs. The CMU students were not of this persuasion. Although many of them are what Herbert Simon in an unpublished essay once referred to as "sociables," they conform to the general expectation that every course is to be taken seriously, in its own terms and as part of one's general academic formation. The institution's tradition, strongly sustained by President Richard Cyert, that it not do anything that it cannot do extremely well, seemed to carry over to the motivation of students in the required General Education program. If I am not misled by CMU's own bright self-image and my own of course limited observations combined with reading of much faculty self-criticism, Cyert's leadership has had an impact. Comparable efforts at Clarkson University (formerly, Clarkson Institute of Technology) and Worcester Polytechnic Institute, which I have studied more closely, seem to have met with considerable success.[18]

My own experience as a teacher of undergraduates at Chicago and Harvard and as an observer at many liberal arts colleges has been that able students in the natural sciences, though sometimes derided as science jocks or "nerds" (the term "jocks" suggesting that only in sports do students fully extend themselves!), have a much easier time crossing C.P. Snow's "two cultures" divide than students in the non-quantitative, non-spatial fields have moving in the opposite direction and gaining an appreciation for what doing science is like, and how science and technology influence each other in research and in society.[19] In our overwhelmingly coeducational patterns of schooling, girls and women more often than boys and men become intimidated in mathematics and in physics and other hard sciences— there is evidence they do somewhat better in single-sex settings, where they are not competing with boys and men on the latter's presumed turf. Sheila Tobias and others have developed programs to overcome "math anxiety," and "physics anxiety" and there is illustrative material in Sherry Turkle's *The Second Self: The Human Spirit in the Computer Age*, showing how the greater tendency of girls to see the computer as an instrument for interaction and of boys to see it as an instrument for mastery can be harnessed for pedagogic ends.[20]

These are the sorts of issues endemic to the educational process generally, which are significant for the intellectual and academic tone of a college and hence themes for potential presidential attention and incremental influence. It is not as if presidents did not have enough to do without daring to tackle the "two cultures" divide! But for some it will be occupational therapy for their many non-academic chores if their very distance from the immediacies of departmental and even decanal life can provide them with a focused perspective on how one might make the arts and sciences more liberal and more invitational, so that students would not automatically rule out, as an economic and also intellectual dead end, a career in academic life.

Acknowledgement

For support in preparing my essay, I am indebted to the Exxon Education Foundation, the Christian A. Johnson Endeavor Foundation, and to Douglass Carmichael's grant to the Project on Technology, Work, and Character.

Notes

[1] A report to the U.S. Department of Education, March 1986, Chapter 3.

[2] Such presidents have been delineated in the work of Ellen Chaffee or in the recently published collection edited by Janice Green and Arthur Levine, *Opportunity in Adversity: How Colleges Can Succeed in Hard Times* (Jossey-Bass, 1985).

[3] Befogged by what Michel Crozier has termed America's delirium of due process, honor codes can themselves make it as difficult for the person who reports an offense as it is for the victim—both are in effect on trial in the semi-judicial proceedings. See, e.g., my observations on the Wheaton (Massachusetts) honor code in "The Fear of Honor," a Convocation Address delivered at Wheaton College, 10 May 1984. For Crozier's view, see *The Trouble with America,* University of California Press, 1985.

[4] A good argument can be made that it is the scientists in the most liberal institutions such as MIT, Cornell, or the University of Illinois who should be permitted to do classified research because they would bring to it the wider understandings drawn from their colleagueship with critics, students as well as faculty, of the aims of that research. Prohibitions at the more liberal institutions—a judgment I have held also with respect of ROTC units—mean that such work is done only in institutions of less cosmopolitan and more provincial outlook, where American nationalism is more strident and unequivocal and where faculty members working on classified research neither learn from colleagues who think otherwise nor bring to the latter, outside of what is confidential, knowledge helpful to the understanding, for example, of the nature of arms races.

[5] For brief discussion of the problem of exchanges with the Soviet Union, whether by the International Physicians for the Prevention of Nuclear War or by scientific organizations, see Loren R. Graham, "Scientists, human rights, and the Soviet Union," *Bulletin of the Atomic Scientists* vol. 42, no. 4, April 1986, pp. 8-9.

[6] Cf. Martin Trow, "The Threat From Within: Academic Freedom and Negative Evidence," *Change,* vol. 17, September/October 1985, 8-9, 61-68.

[7] For limited discussion of this historical question, see Milton J. Rosenberg, Sidney Verba, and Philip E. Converse, *Vietnam and the Silent Majority: The Dove's Guide* (New York: Harper & Row, 1970), and my observations in Walter W. Powell and Richard Robbins, Eds., *Conflict and Consensus: A Festschrift in Honor of Lewis A. Coser,* Free Press, 1984, pp. 351-357.

[8] For fuller discussion see my introduction to Larry Litten, Daniel Sullivan, and David Brodigan, *Applying Market Research in College Admissions* (New York: College Board, 1983); also, Riesman, *On Higher Education: The Academic Enterprise in an Era of Rising Student Consumerism* (San Francisco: Jossey-Bass, 1980), passim.

[9] Diana B. Beaudoin, *Formal Procedures and Informal Influences: Assessing a College President's Performance,* unpublished doctoral dissertation, Harvard Graduate School of Education, 1986.

[10]See Clark Kerr and Marian Gade, *The Many Lives of Academic Presidents: Time, Place and Character.* Washington, D.C.: Association of Governing Boards of Universities and Colleges, 1986.

[11]For a graphic description of one president's diurnal rounds, based on a year's diary, see Richard Berendzen, *Is My Armor Straight?* (Adler & Adler, 1985). Berendzen is President of American University in Washington, D.C., a locale that makes such a life more readily accessible than if he headed, let us say, Willamette University in Salem, Oregon.

[12]For a cogent general overview, see Jack H. Schuster and Howard R. Bowen, "The Faculty at Risk," *Change*, vol. 17, no. 4, September/October 1985, pp. 13-21.

[13]For the Clark and Trow distinction, see Burton R. Clark, *Students and Colleges: Interaction and Change* (Berkeley: Center for Research and Development in Higher Education, 1972); also, Clark, *The Distinctive College: Antioch, Reed, and Swarthmore* (Chicago: Aldine, 1970).

[14]For the report released at Oberlin, see David Davis-Van Atta, Sam S. Carrier, and Frank Frankfort, "Educating America's Scientists: The Role of the Research Colleges," Oberlin College, 1985.

[15]Even scientists in major research universities must often travel to an astronomical observatory, a marine biology station, or a particle accelerator, but the chairmen and deans at such institutions can spare them for travel because they have fewer obligations as teachers and on college-wide committees.

[16]The elliptical remark in the text needs to be unpacked, but that would take us too far afield. I have known a few magnificent teachers who have stayed intellectually alive without external performance, whether in writing or in artistic production or in presentations to colleagues elsewhere, especially in academic settings where research is not the inescapable norm. In the topflight liberal arts college and in the research university, such individuals may become preoccupied with campus politics in an effort to establish a moral hegemony in the absence of an academic one. But in some cases they may happily continue in their roles as teachers and institutional loyalists, while keeping up with their fields and exhibiting a broad intellectual culture. However, I believe that administrators can rarely spot such people in advance, some of whom will claim to be interdisciplinary because they are undisciplined. See, e.g., Martin Trow, "On the Transition from College to Graduate or Professional School," in Papers Presented at the One Hundred and Twenty-Seventh Meeting of the Association of Colleges in New England, November 14 and 15, 1984, Tufts University, Medford, Massachusetts, pp. 11-17; and comments by Riesman, "Transitions and Way Stations," ibid., pp. 19-30.

[17]Some topflight liberal arts colleges and Ivy-type universities have minuscule programs, or occasionally departments of education, whose aim is to provide the course work and supervision requisite for certification to teach a particular subject in secondary school. Such programs often have simultaneously to combat the superciliousness of highbrow academia toward the subject of education and the constraints of state departments of education under the influence of the large undergraduate and graduate programs in education, with their ties to school systems and teacher unions.

[18]For further discussion, see Riesman, "Professional Education and Liberal Education: A False Dichotomy," in Joan Burstyn, ed. *Preparation for Life?* (London: The Falmer Press, 1986), pp. 35-37. Also Riesman, "A Conversation with Simmons College," transcription of meeting with the SPLICE Committee, Boston, Massachusetts, 24 June, 1974. Reprinted as "A Conversation with Simmons College," *Journal of General Education*, vol. 31, no. 2 (Summer 1979), pp. 79-108.

[19]In an elegant essay, Robert K. Merton concludes that his own mentor, one of the founding fathers of the history of science, George Sarton, had written about the two cultures divide along some of the lines C.P. Snow was later to take. See Merton, "George Sarton: Episodic Recollections by an Unruly Apprentice," *Isis*, 1985, 76: 470-486.

[20]New York: Simon & Schuster, 1984.

PART FOUR

Re-Imagining American Catholicism: The American Bishops and the Seamless Garment

Henry C. Kenski and
William Lockwood

"...religious experience in creatures who are intellect as well as imagination invariably leads to reflection, theology, philosophy, and creed. This is precisely because humans must examine their experiences and the images which resonate these experiences."

(Greeley, *Religious*, 3)

"We are living at a time in which we must re-imagine the Catholic Church. It isn't easy but it is necessary for every Catholic. We must examine our own moral convictions, work them through the light of the Gospel so that we hold them deeply for ourselves. In these pastoral letters, the bishops are not writing for political reasons, but to begin serious discussions on the major issues of our time."

(Bishop Rembert Weakland in Kennedy, 19)

The Bishops and National Politics: Historical Overview

Political activity by American Catholics is certainly not a new phenomenon, although the amount of time devoted to politics and the broad range of issues covered are unprecedented. Involvement of church leaders in politics was quite noticeable in the nineteenth century, for example, with Catholic bishops giving visible support to the newly emerging labor movement in the United States (Kennedy). Later, during the First World War, the Catholic bishops authorized the formation of a National Catholic War Council to assist the war effort. Afterwards the bishops met for the first time as a national body in 1919 and voted to transform the War Council into the National Catholic Welfare Council (NCWC) to coordinate church activities that were national in scope (Reichley). The NCWC had a rocky start, and was dissolved in 1922 due to papal opposition. At the request of a new pope, it was reconstituted and the word "council" was changed to "conference," as the former had connotations of substantive authority in Catholic canon law.

In 1966 the title was changed from the National Catholic Welfare Conference to the United States Catholic Conference, under which it continues to function as the "highest authority within the American church" (Reichley, 221).

The reconstitution created a dual structure. One part is the National Catholic Conference of Bishops (NCCB), a canonical body established by church law as a result of the decrees of Vatican II. It was designed to deal primarily with internal church questions such as worship and seminary education. The bishops constitute its membership and they meet annually, usually in Washington, D.C. (Kennedy).

The United States Catholic Conference (USCC) is the second component, and it is a counterpart civil organization through which public issues are addressed in a systematic way. Its members too are the bishops, but the structure also includes a staff of priests and religious and lay persons who possess policy expertise in various areas. Thus, the USCC provides much of the ideological underpinnings and policy orientation of the NCCB. The American bishops communicate officially in four ways: joint pastorals, formal statements, special messages, and resolutions and brief statements. A joint pastoral, such as the recent and famous one by the American bishops on the economy, can be issued only by the NCCB and requires the approval of two-thirds of the membership. The process is quite collegial in nature and reflects the vision posited by Vatican II (Kennedy).

The Political Arena as a Forum for Religious Imagination

Religious experience, as Andrew Greeley so aptly observes, originates in intellect and imagination (1981). For American Catholic bishops, this intellect and imagination has been focused increasingly on the public policy arena. The Second Vatican Council that convened in Rome in the 1960s did more than change the structural philosophy of the church as a religious institution. It created considerable dissent, change, and diversity that ultimately affected the approach of the Catholic bishops to national politics. Their annual meetings became forums for public policy as well as religious pronouncements. The Rev. J. Bryan Hehir, Secretary of the U.S. Catholic Conference's Department of Social Development and World Peace, has stated that "the agenda of the Catholic Church has become much broader" and that "the Church is both a community of the baptized and a social institution. In the bishops' minds, what they are trying to do is be teachers to get support and to shape it so that views are available in the wider civil community" (Cohen, 2082).

Thus the bishops have issued pastoral letters on the world food crisis (1974), race relations (1979), the role of the United States in Central America (1981), nuclear arms (1983), and the famous 1984 letter on the economy (Kenski, Reichley, and Kennedy). The third and final version of the letter called for the U.S. to do more for the poor and was endorsed 225 to 9 by the National Conference of Catholic Bishops in November of 1986 (Pear). It was in the context of the controversy surrounding this letter that Archbishop Weakland called for a re-imagination of the Catholic Church (Kennedy). Although he professed that the bishops are not writing for political reasons but to begin serious policy discussions, this letter, along with other pastorals, has promoted a lively political controversy both in the nation and within the Catholic community. The central purpose of this paper is to assess the extent to which the Catholic laity support the policy views of the bishops, particularly efforts of the latter to defuse political criticism by appealing to a policy linkage concept called "the seamless garment." An examination of it, however, first requires an identification of the broad positions of the Catholic bishops.

Public Policy Positions of American Catholic Bishops

Our policy analysis organizes the views of the bishops in three policy domains: social, economic, and foreign policy. Social is probably the most important, as it is the issue domain that has caused the most controversy and resulted in Catholic activists parting company "with their usual allies in Washington's liberal coalition" (Reichley, 290). The functioning of the NCCB and USCC in the 1960s and 1970s is documented and analyzed in Mary Hanna's excellent work *Catholics and American Politics*. She notes that their energy focused heavily on four issues: abortion, school aid, the Vietnam War, and assistance for the Spanish-speaking. Of these issues, abortion proved most salient. Long banned in church teaching, it became a primary political issue after several states enacted major changes and the Supreme Court legitimated the practice of abortion in 1973 in the case of *Roe v. Wade*. Hanna views it as the distinctive "Catholic" issue and notes that in her extensive interviews with institutional Church leaders "there was no other single issue on which they displayed the near unanimity they did on abortion." During the 1984 presidential election, several Catholic bishops were involved in harsh exchanges with vice-presidential candidate Geraldine Ferraro, a Catholic who supports a woman's right to have an abortion (Cohen).

Another salient social issue is capital punishment. The Catholic bishops made a definitive statement in 1980 urging its abolition. In November of that year the bishops voted 145 to 31, with 14 abstentions, to eliminate capital punishment as "a manifestation of our belief in the unique worth and dignity of each person from the moment of conception, a creature made in the image and likeness of God" (Hanson, 393).

On the economy, the bishops in 1986 have, as previously noted, endorsed the third and final version of their pastoral letter, first formulated in 1984. It emphasizes *employment generation*, stressing governmental responsibility for job creation, and a *preferential option for the poor*. It also endorses *economic help for developing countries* and *economic planning*. Building on this pastoral letter, the USCC in 1985-1986 issued public statements and testified before various committees on these topics, with a special emphasis on help for the poor from budget cuts, removing the tax burden on the poor, the need for public sector jobs, etc. (Heyer).

In the area of foreign policy, a major change has occurred in the Church. The strong emphasis on patriotism and anti-communism that characterized the Church from 1938 to 1967, the so-called period of "American Catholic nationalism," has been replaced by a very liberal one that questions nuclear deterrence and gives it only "conditional moral acceptance" (Reichley), calls for more foreign aid and trade with third-world countries, opposes military solutions to controversies because arms prolong conflicts, rejects Nicaraguan Contra aid, and calls for decreases in defense spending (Kenski). Reflecting this liberal orientation in March of 1985, U.S. Catholic Conference president Bishop James W. Malone sent a letter to every member of Congress, seeking to tip the balance against the MX missile. In doing so, he argued: "It is our considered judgment—not as strategists but as religious leaders—that sufficient evidence has been brought forward concerning the potential destabilizing impact which this weapons system may have on the arms race to support the conclusion that these funds ($1.5 billion) ought to be used to meet human needs" (*Washington Post*, A14).

The public positions of the bishops have stimulated political controversy within the Church and the nation. A seeming paradox and ongoing criticism of the position of the bishops is that they seem aligned with the most conservative segments of society on social issues like abortion, and yet are a key support group of the liberal coalition on economy and foreign policy issues. Part of the problem was that the bishops appeared to address policy issues in a piecemeal fashion, from capital punishment and abortion to nuclear weapons and governmental efforts to combat poverty (Heyer). An effort to resolve this problem in a larger political-religious context was made by Chicago's Cardinal Bernardin, who has sought to introduce "moral consistency" to Catholic positions by stressing that the "sanctity of life" is involved in such seemingly diverse issues as abortion, capital punishment, nuclear weapons, poverty, and human rights violations at home and abroad (Hanson, Bernardin, Heyer, and Briggs). His approach has been adopted by other bishops and it is referred to as the seamless garment.

The Seamless Garment

Although Cardinal Bernardin should be credited for his use of religious imagination and intellect and for his public advocacy of the seamless garment, some credit should also be given to Monsignor Francis Lally, director of the Department of Social Development and World Peace of the USCC. At his suggestion, the bishops issued a statement before the 1980 election urging "that voters . . . examine the position of the candidates on the full range of issues as well as the person's integrity, philosophy, and performance" (Reichley, 293-94). In 1982 Lally again reiterated that "there are many of us who are concerned about the phenomena of single-issue voting. We are making a strong effort to emphasize that Catholic teaching is concerned with the whole span of life, not just conception" (Reichley, 293).

In 1983 Cardinal Bernardin gave national visibility to this so-called "seamless garment approach" to issues. He had just succeeded New York's Cardinal Cooke as president of the Bishops' Pro-Life Committee, and "has tried to steer that organization to broader concerns than just abortion. Archbishop Roach made similar pleas to combine all pro-life issues while president of the NCCB" from 1980 to 1983 (Hanson, 180). During the heated 1984 presidential campaign, Bernardin again became chief spokesperson for the "seamless garment" approach to issues, both in a September column for the Chicago archdiocesan newspaper and in a speech at Georgetown University on October 25 (Hanson, Bernardin).

The column noted that the bishops "place special emphasis on abortion, in preventing nuclear war, and reversing the arms race and on programs which meet the needs of the poor" (Hanson, 188). His Georgetown speech consciously used parallel language on abortion and the arms race. Instead of demanding instant public acceptance of the church's position on abortion, Bernardin said:

I would not want a candidate for public office today to be complacent, passive, or satisfied with the level or the dynamic of the arms race or the defense budget of our nation. I would look for the person who says 'what we have is unacceptable, and I will work for change.' The process of change will surely not be simple, but the conscious choice and the willingness to change policy are the key. In the same vein, I would want candidates who are willing to say 'The fact of 1.5 million abortions a year is unacceptable and I will work for a change in the public policy which encourages or permits this practice.' In both areas—the arms race and abortion—it will take conscious decisions by citizens and public officials if we are to have deliberate policies which serve human life. ("Religion" 22-23).

Other bishops have also taken up Bernardin's refrain. At a meeting of the NCCB after the 1984 elections, the NCCB president Bishop James Malone called for cohesion behind the conference's "broad spectrum" of positions on nuclear arms, abortion, human rights, and poverty. "We oppose a 'single-issue' strategy," he said, "because only by addressing a broad spectrum of issues can we do justice to the moral tradition we possess as a church and thereby demonstrate the moral challenges we face as a nation" (Hanson, 189-190).

The position of the bishops is clear, but what about the Catholic laity? Do they agree with the bishops in each of these policy domains—social, economic, and foreign policy? Do they see the linkage between issues in various domains, the so-called seamless garment?

Current Social Science Research

Very little empirical research has been conducted on this topic, a shortcoming this article seeks to remedy. One book, however, that does address the topic is *The American Catholic People*, by Gallup, Jr. and Castelli. It offers a useful summary of various Gallup data, but is limited in two respects. First, no statistical tests on findings are presented, only descriptive summary tables of the position of the Catholic laity on various issues. Second, the authors overstate their findings, particularly their conclusion that "American Catholics are 'pro-life' but they do not blindly follow their bishops on issues and they are not single-issue voters; at the same time, they do seem to view life as a 'seamless garment' and a value to be protected" (Gallup and Castelli, 102). They are clearly correct in their emphasis on Catholic voters not blindly following the bishops or being single-issue voters, but they overstate the pro-life perspective and commitment to the seamless garment. Their own data on abortion and capital punishment do not support their claims. Moreover, Andrew Greeley notes that even in the early and mid-seventies Catholic attitudes on abortion "were at odds with the position of the official church" (*American*, 86). After an exhaustive analysis of National Opinion Research data, he concludes that today "American Catholics, at least under some circumstances, agree with the teaching authority of the church that abortion ought not to be available. However, they do not accept the official teaching, even on abortion" and "there has been no change since the early 1970s" (*American*, 87).

One other major work on the seamless garment is an interesting article by Cleghorn. Using NORC data from 1977-1978 and 1982-1983, he finds two dimensions underlying life issues: one dealing with personal liberties, and the other with defense of society. He finds mixed evidence on the seamless garment concept. The signs of the regression coefficients are correct for these tests, but they "also show that the effect of Catholic affiliation in a multivariate context is not significant for any of the dependent variables" (138). While conceding that the church has a unique role to play in the formation of a consistent life ethic, he also concludes that "there is a great deal of work to be done on convincing Catholics (and others) that the death penalty and nuclear armaments are immoral threats to life" (139). Moreover, he recommends that "from a policy standpoint, Bernardin and other church leaders must not assume widespread agreement or understanding on the sacredness of life" (139). While valuing Cleghorn's empirical efforts, we feel they are limited in two ways. First, he uses interval level statistical techniques on data that we believe should more appropriately be treated as nominal. Second, he reduces the three major policy arenas (social, economic, and foreign policy) into a single dimension called "defense of society," and uses only two variables—capital punishment and military spending—for this factor. It is our contention that multiple policy arenas and another statistical technique needs to be used to address this timely and important problem.

Data and Methods

To assess the effects of Catholic identification on those issues associated with the pro-life position of the bishops' "seamless garment" concept, we use the 1984 sample of the National Opinion Research Center's (NORC) General Social Survey (GSS). The GSS is an annual personal interview survey of a sample representing the total non-institutionalized population of the continental United States, 18 years of age or older. Surveys have been completed in every year from 1972 through 1987 except 1979 and 1981 and interviewing occurs in the months of February, March, and April. The 1984 sample has 1473 cases and was selected because it offered a wide variety of questionnaire items with which to investigate Catholic's support for the broad "consistent ethic of life" position. It also represents a point in time nearly a decade after the bishops' first "Pastoral Plan for Pro-Life Activities" statement, allowing sufficient time for even infrequent church attenders to be exposed to the Plan's message.

We utilize two general indicators of social policy issues, abortion and capital punishment. Attitudes toward abortion were actually surveyed across seven different circumstances with a general question worded "Please tell me whether or not you think it should be possible for a pregnant woman to obtain a legal abortion if..." The circumstances were "if there is a strong chance of serious defect in the baby?", "if she is married and does not want any more children?", "if the woman's health is seriously endangered by the pregnancy?", "if the family has a very low income and cannot afford any more children?", "if she became pregnant as the result of rape?", "if she is not married and does not want to marry the man?", and "if the woman wants it for any reason?" The capital punishment question read "Do you favor or oppose the death penalty for persons convicted of murder?"

Our indicators of foreign policy issues include questions about expenditures for national defense and foreign aid. These questions were prefaced by the interviewer with the statement "We are faced with many problems in this country, none of which can be solved easily or inexpensively." Respondents were then asked whether our country was spending "too much money, too little money, or about the right amount" on these issues. The 1984 GSS did not, unfortunately, include items about arms control or a nuclear freeze.

There were four questions that allow us to investigate Catholic support for policies reflecting a pro-economic justice orientation, including two items that deal with government policies for preferential treatment of the poor. One referred to welfare or assisting the poor and, like the foreign aid and national defense items described above, asked about the level of national expenditures on these problems. The other concerned income redistribution and was prefaced with the statement "Some people think that the government in Washington ought to reduce the income differences between the rich and the poor, perhaps by raising the taxes of wealthy families or by giving income assistance to the poor. Others think that the government should not concern itself with reducing this income difference between the rich and the poor." Respondents were given a card with a seven point scale and were told that the option "government should do something to reduce income differences between the rich and poor" was assigned point 1 on the scale while point 7 was used to represent the position that "government should not concern itself with income differences". They were then asked to circle the score between 1 and 7 which was closest to the way they felt.

Two economic policy questions had a broader focus than just on the poor. Respondents were presented with the statements "The government must see to it that everyone has a job and that prices are stable, even if the rights of businessmen have to be restricted" and "It is the responsibility of government to meet everyone's needs, even in case of sickness, poverty, unemployment, and old age." For both of the items, possible responses were strongly agree, somewhat agree, somewhat disagree, and strongly disagree.

In the cross-tabulations that provide the data for our analyses we contrast Catholics and Protestants, which make up 89.5 percent of the sample. The categories Jewish (1.8 percent), Other (1.4 percent), and None (7.3 percent) have too few cases for reliable parameter estimations when distributed across multiple categories of the response and control variables. Because the category Protestant includes such a large number of denominations (over 20 were listed by respondents in the 1984 GSS) it is unlikely that as a group Protestants would all share similar positions on our pro-life indicators. Indeed, the work of Reichley and Gallup, Jr. and Castelli underscore political attitudinal differences among various Protestant denominations. It is possible that differing views reflected by members of different denominations would be cancelled out when all Protestants are lumped together in our analyses.

But if Catholics could be shown to give greater support to the bishops' position than Protestants on most of the response variables, it would promote acceptance of the idea that there is a pro-life "seamless garment" among the Catholic populace.

If the Catholic populace is expected to share with the bishops the pro-life attitudes that make up the "seamless garment," they certainly need to be exposed to the bishops' positions. We suspect that more frequent exposure might lead to greater levels of acceptance so we control for church attendance in our analyses. Such measures of self-reported religious participation have also been used as indicators of religiosity since some theorists view church attendance as a crucial element in the development of religiosity (Finney, White). We also expect that more religious Catholics might have a greater level of acceptance for the teachings of the church. Finally, the inclusion of church attendance as a control is important for the contrasts we make between Catholics and Protestants because frequent attendance (at least weekly) is significantly higher for Catholics (Hout and Greeley). The variable is coded into a dichotomy that contrasts weekly with less frequent church attendance.

Another important control variable is race. In earlier research, race had been used particularly to isolate white Protestants (Greeley, "Catholics"), due to the fact that blacks were disproportionately Protestant and overwhelmingly liberal in their policy orientations. Thus, the inclusion of blacks in the Protestant category automatically dilutes the more conservative orientation of that group and tends to reduce Catholic-Protestant differences. Our basic intent is to identify white Protestants. We include black Catholics, although the number is very small (N 16) because the results were extremely consistent.

The data analysis technique we use is the fitting of standard hierarchical log-linear models (Goodman, Feinberg,), which assume that variables need only be measured nominally. Such qualitative data is certainly characteristic of the variables we have selected from the 1984 GSS. Log-linear models are described in terms of the combination of one-way (a single variable), two-way (the association between two variables), three-way (the interaction among three variables), or n-way (the interactions among n variables) marginals which most closely reproduce the observed cell frequencies in a n-way table. Each model produces "expected" or "fitted" cell frequencies which are compared to the observed frequencies with the likelihood-ratio chi-square statistic, L^2. The L^2 for a particular model is compared to the chi-square distribution for its appropriate degrees of freedom. A model is considered to "fit" the data if the probability of obtaining its L^2 is greater than .05. We refer to a "preferred" model as one which fits and, also, does not exclude any marginal relationships with L^2 probabilities less than .05.

Although log-linear models do not require that one variable be viewed as dependent while others are independent, it is convenient to present our findings in those terms. The indicators of pro-life attitudes outlined above are termed "response" variables. When discussing particular log-linear models we refer to the variables involved with bracketed letters. For example, if the letter "C" is assigned to race, "R" to religion, and "A" to an attitude question about, say, abortion, the model [CR] [CA] indicates that there is an association between race and religion and between race and response but religion and response are independent, given race. The model [CR] [CA] [RA] includes, in addition, an association between religion. The model [CRA] indicates that the three-way interaction is present.

The conventional way in which the relationships among variables under a preferred log-linear model are described is with the use of "odds" and "odds ratios" computed from the expected frequencies. Our results are presented with percentages instead of expected frequencies because our primary interest is determining to what extent Catholics support the position of their bishops' on various public policy issues. We believe it is easier for the reader to grasp the meaning of a statement like "under circumstance 'x' 75 percent of Catholics favor abortion" than "the odds for Catholics on favoring abortion under circumstance 'x' are 3.0"; although they are mathematically equivalent. The reader is cautioned, however, to avoid making comparisons between categories of one variable by calculating percentage-point differences across two or more categories of another variable. What could result is the appearance of a three-way interaction when the preferred model has no such interaction (Duncan and Duncan).

Findings

We hypothesized above that any relationships between religion and the indicators used to tap pro-life attitudes might vary by either religiosity or race. Unfortunately, the sample of individuals who make up the 1984 GSS are spread quite thin when four-way cross-classifications of religion by race by church attendance by response variable are created. The problem is especially acute for black Catholics who attend church at least weekly and most of the four-way tables we initially looked at had cells with zero observed cases. Although the expected frequencies under the preferred models from the hierarchical log-linear analyses of these four-way tables rarely yielded cells with zero cases, these "fitted" frequencies often were less than 1.0. Such a situation makes comparisons between categories of our background variables questionable.

The preferred models for these four-way tables rarely included any three-way interactions of race by attendance by religion or race by attendance by response variable, suggesting that including both control variables was unnecessary. We then proceeded with a parallel examination of three-way tables of religion by control variable by response variable for our two controls, religiosity and race. Our hypothesis that the relationship between religion and the various attitude questions that might tap a pro-life orientation might vary by level of religiosity was not supported by the data. Church attendance only had a significant effect on the abortion questions with weekly attenders more likely to support the bishops' position, and the foreign aid question where frequent attenders were slightly less likely to agree with the bishops that the nation was spending "too little." After controlling for church attendance, religion was found to have a significant effect only on attitude questions concerning guaranteed jobs and defense spending. Controlling for race, on the other hand, yielded significant religion by response associations on a number of the attitude questions. Therefore, the remainder of this section discusses results only from the three-way tables that include race.

Since the "seamless garment" concept initially grew out the Catholic bishops recognition that an opposition to abortion must be part of a broader pro-life orientation, we first investigate attitudes about legalized abortion. The top panel of Table 1 presents the observed percentages of respondents who share the position of the Catholic bishops' that abortion should not be legal under seven different circumstances. Among whites, the percentages of Catholics who feel that abortion should not be legal is three to six points greater than that of Protestants. The black Protestant percentages are from one to fifteen points higher than those of black Catholics. This suggests that three-way interactions of religion, race, and response might characterize the data.

This is not case as the bottom panel of Table 1 reveals. The preferred model for every abortion situation includes only two-way associations. Regardless of the circumstance, a higher percentage of blacks than whites are opposed to legalized abortion. Under four situations (families wanting no more children, poor families, single women, and abortion for any reason) a majority of Catholics do support the anti-abortion position of their bishops. But Protestants support that position by the same percentages as there is no effect of religion on responses to these four questions.

For the other three circumstances (possible birth defects, woman's health endangered, and rape) the majority of Catholics do support legalized abortion. The second of these situations involves two lives, that of the pregnant woman as well as the potential infant. Individual Catholics may still feel that the acceptance of abortion in this circumstance is pro-life. The other two situations may reveal that maintaining quality of life is as important to Catholics as sustaining human life. The preferred model for all three of these circumstances includes the religion by response association and a higher percentage of Catholic than Protestant respondents do support the position of the bishops. For the birth defect item, the partial association of religion by response was not statistically significant (L^2 = 3.34; d.f. = 1; p = .07) although the model without this association was not preferred since it did not fit the data (L^2 = 6.80; d.f. = 2;p less than .04). Overall, the response to these abortion questions provides weak evidence for the "seamless garment." Contrary to the teachings of the church, most of the Catholic populace does feel there are circumstances that abortion should be legal. In those situations when the majority of Catholics do support the bishops' position their attitudes are not different than those of Protestants.

The results from our analysis of the other indicator of the social policy component of the "seamless garment" are presented in Table 2. The hierarchical log-linear analysis of the capital punishment by religion by race cross-classification was the only one in which we were unable to reject the hypothesis of no three-way interaction. The observed frequencies indicate that a greater percentage of white Catholics than white Protestants support the bishops' opposition to capital punishment for persons convicted of murder while among blacks it is Protestants that show greater opposition. For the entire 1984 GSS sample 74.8 percent favor

TABLE 1. PERCENTAGE WHO AGREE WITH CATHOLIC BISHOPS' POSITION ON ABORTION BY RELIGION AND RACE, 1984[a]

		Should Abortion [A] Be Legal Under Following Circumstances?						
Race[C]	Religion[R]	Possible Birth Defects	Want No More Children	Woman's Health Endangered	Low Family Income	Rape	Not Married	Any Reason
Observed % Responding "No"								
White	Protestant	17.4	58.2	9.0	54.7	17.3	56.0	61.6
	Catholic	23.4	60.6	14.0	57.4	23.4	59.9	65.8
Black	Protestant	34.1	71.2	18.4	66.9	34.8	71.5	74.6
	Catholic	18.7	62.5	12.5	56.3	25.0	56.3	73.3
Expected % Responding "No" Under Preferred Model								
White	Protestant	17.8	58.9	9.3	55.6	17.6	57.2	62.9
	Catholic	22.5	58.9	13.4	55.6	22.7	57.2	62.9
Black	Protestant	31.7	70.3	17.1	65.8	33.0	69.9	74.5
	Catholic	38.3	70.3	23.9	65.8	40.3	69.9	74.5
Preferred Model		[CR][CA][RA]	[CR][RA]	[CR][CA][RA]	[CR][CA]	[CR][CA][RA]	[CR][CA][RA]	[CR][CA]
L^2		3.46	1.04	1.63	1.34	2.00	2.87	1.77
d.f.		1	2	1	2	1	2	2
p		.07	.59	.20	.51	.16	.24	.41

[a]See text for question wording and descriptions of preferred models.

capital punishment while 25.2 percent oppose it. It would appear that black Protestants have the greatest deviation from the overall distribution.

Although the model does not fit, it is useful to examine the expected percentages under the model of only two-way associations presented in the middle panel of Table 2. Here Catholics show slightly higher agreement with the bishops' position than do Protestants. It appears, however, that it is race rather than religion that has the greatest influence on capital punishment attitudes since the Catholic percentages on opposition are only about 4 points higher than Protestants while the black percentages on opposition are about 34 points higher than whites. The partial association of religion by response is not, in fact, statistically significant ($L^2 = 1.38$; d.f. = 1;p = .24) as can be seen when the fit of the model with the three two-way associations is compared with the fit of the model where the religion by response association is deleted (bottom panel). Notice how little the expected percentages change from the middle to the bottom panels. For the purposes of the present analysis, however, the most important finding concerning attitudes towards capital punishment is that Catholics do not support the bishops' position.

Table 2

Observed and Expected Percentages on Capital Punishment by Religion and Race, 1984*

	Race (C)	Religion (R)	Capital Punishment (U)	
			Favor	Oppose
Observed %	White	Protestant	80.8	19.2
		Catholic	75.5	24.5
	Black	Protestant	43.2	56.8
		Catholic	78.6	21.4
Expected % Under Model (CR) (CU) (RU)	White	Protestant	80.1	19.9
		Catholic	77.0	23.0
$L^2 = 9.06$ d.f = 1 p < .01	Black	Protestant	47.0	53.0
		Catholic	42.5	57.5
Expected % Under Model (CR) (CU)	White	Protestant	79.2	20.8
		Catholic	79.2	20.8
$L^2 = 10.44$ d.f. = 2 p < 0.1	Black	Protestant	46.6	53.4
		Catholic	46.6	53.4

* See text for question wording and descriptions of models.

We now turn to the indicators of the economic component of the "seamless garment" concept. Table 3 presents the expected percentages under the preferred model for the two general attitude questions about the government's responsibility for providing jobs and meeting basic human needs. The hierarchical log-linear analyses indicate a failure to reject the hypothesis of no three-way interaction between religion, race, and response for both questions. The fit of the preferred "jobs" question model [CR] [CJ] [RJ] is L^2 = 5.29, d.f. = 3, p= .15; while the fit of the preferred "meet needs" question model [CR] [CN] [RN] is L^2 = 1.79, d.f. = 3,p = .62. There is a strong race effect on response with about 65 percent of blacks agreeing with the "jobs" statement while only about 40 percent of whites agree and about 79 percent of blacks agree with the "meet needs" statement while only about 53 percent of whites agree. The religion effect is weaker with about 49 percent of Catholics agreeing with the "jobs" statement compared to about 42 percent of Protestants and about 61 percent of Catholics agree with the "meet needs" statement while only about 54 percent of Protestants agree.

Table 3

Expected Percentages on two Questions About the Role of Government by Religion and Race, 1984*

Race (C)	Religion (R)	Strongly Agree	Somewhat Agree	Somewhat Disagree	Strongly Disagree
Government Should Provide Guaranteed Jobs and Stable Prices (J)					
White	Protestant	10.7**	26.6	37.2	25.4
	Catholic	16.0	31.5	32.6	19.9
Black	Protestant	21.5	42.7	25.4	10.4
	Catholic	28.3	44.8	19.6	7.2
Government Should Meet Everyone's Needs (N)					
White	Protestant	15.6	34.0	32.7	17.7
	Catholic	20.3	39.5	28.5	11.7
Black	Protestant	42.5	35.9	16.8	4.8
	Catholic	48.1	36.4	12.7	2.7

* See text for question wording and descriptions of preferred models.
** Percentages add to 100 percent (with rounding error) across rows only.

Although Catholics are more likely than Protestants to support the "agree" position of the Catholic bishops on these two items, the fact that the majority of Catholics only support one item suggests that a broad acceptance of government programs that promote economic justice is not characteristic of Catholics. Additional lack of support among Catholics is evident from responses to the question concerning the government's role in reducing income differences between the rich and poor. Table 4 presents expected frequencies from the preferred model of the log-linear analysis of this item with religion and race. The preferred model [CR] [CI] excludes the religion by response association (L^2 = 13.89; d.f. = 12; p = .31). About 66 percent of blacks support government intervention (responses, 1, 2, and 3) while only about 46 percent of whites do. Overall, however, there is not strong support for government encouragement of income redistribution with only about 49 percent of both Catholics and Protestants thinking the government should act.

Table 4

Expected Percentages on Question Concerning Government's Role in Reducing Income Differences Between Rich and Poor (I)*

Race (C)	Religion (R)	Government Should Do Something To Reduce Income Differences Between Rich and Poor						Government Shouldn't Concern Itself With Income Difference
		1	2	3	4	5	6	7
White	Protestant	18.2	12.0	15.9	17.2	14.7	8.9	13.1
	Catholic	18.2	12.0	15.9	17.2	14.7	8.9	13.1
Black	Protestant	38.8	13.8	13.8	17.8	7.2	2.6	5.9
	Catholic	38.8	13.8	13.8	17.8	7.2	2.6	5.9

* See text for question wordking.
** Percentages add to 100 percent (with rounding error) across rows only.

Results from the log-linear analysis of the religion by race by "welfare" cross-classification shows the same weak support for economic justice among Catholics that we have seen above with two out of three indicators. The expected frequencies from the preferred model [CR] [CW] (L^2 = 7.02;d.f. = 4;p = .13) are presented in the top panel of Table 5. Again we find strong support among blacks for government promotion of programs designed to promote economic justice with over 77 percent believing that the government is spending "too little" on welfare compared to only about 48 percent of whites. There is no significant religion association with the "welfare" question. Thus, we see that only slightly more than half of Catholics and Protestants (about 52 percent) feel the government is spending "too little".

The middle and bottom panels of Table 5 present the expected frequencies under the preferred models when cross-classifications of religion, race, and foreign policy questions are analyzed. The preferred model for the "foreign aid" item [CR] [CF] excludes the religion by response association (L^2 = 2.16; d.f. = 4;p = .71). Blacks

Table 5

Expected Percentage on Three Questions Concerning The Level of Government Spending by Religion and Race, 1984*

| Race (C) | Religion (R) | Government Spending | | |
		Too Little	About Right	Too Much
Government Spending on Welfare (W)				
White	Protestant	48.1**	29.5	22.3
	Catholic	48.1	29.5	22.3
Black	Protestant	77.5	14.4	8.1
	Catholic	77.5	14.4	8.1
Government Spending on Foreign Aid (F)				
White	Protestant	3.2	19.9	76.9
	Catholic	3.2	19.9	76.9
Black	Protestant	8.2	19.7	72.1
	Catholic	8.2	19.7	72.1
Government Spending on Defense (D)				
White	Protestant	22.6	45.5	31.8
	Catholic	15.2	39.3	45.5
Black	Protestant	20.3	37.1	42.6
	Catholic	12.7	30.0	57.3

* See text for question wording and descriptions of preferred models.
** Percentages add to 100 percent (with rounding error) across rows only.

are slightly more likely to feel that "too little" is spent on foreign aid, however, the most notable finding is the overwhelming belief, contrary to the Catholic bishops' position, that "too much" is being spent. If this question were viewed as belonging with other indicators of attitudes about "economic justice" then Catholics clearly do not have a consistent pro-life ethic.

Government spending on defense is the final indicator we use in our attempt to tap whether the Catholic populace shares their bishops' "seamless garment." The preferred model [CR] [CD] [RD] includes all three two-way associations (L^2 = 0.51; d.f. = 2; p = .77). Here the bishops' position is that "too much money" is being spent and, again, blacks are more likely that whites to agree with that position. Catholic support is stronger than that of Protestants (46 percent versus 34 percent) but less than a majority agree with their bishops.

The welfare, foreign aid, and defense items were part of experiments conducted by NORC to test differences in the wording of questions. The GSS used three forms in 1984, each with about 490 respondents. While the prefatory remarks for these three items on all three forms were the same, the subject probe varied. The three probes for the welfare item were "welfare", "assistance to the poor", and "caring for the poor." For the foreign aid question probes were "foreign aid", "assistance to other countries," and "helping other countries." "The military, armaments and defense," "national defense," and "strengthening national defense" were the defense item probes. Responses were treated above as if the question wording was the same on all three forms in order to have a sufficient number of cases for the statistical analysis of cross-tabulations of these items with religion and other variables.

It is important, however, to investigate to what extent the results presented above could be affected by the wording of the questions. We feel confident that our results concerning the "welfare" item are reliable since the preferred model for the cross-classifications of religion by race by response were the same for each wording variation as we found for the aggregated question. When "foreign aid" was the question probe we obtained the same results as discussed above but with the probes "assistance to other countries" and "helping other countries" the preferred model no longer included an association between race and response. As the findings with respect to Catholics were not changed (no effect of religion on response) our conclusion that Catholics do not support preferential treatment for the poor of other countries need not be modified.

The preferred models for the three wording variants of the "defense" item were all different than that of the aggregated item (which included all two-way associations) and, also, different than each other. When the question probe was worded "the military, armaments and defense" the preferred model included a religion effect (Catholics were more likely than Protestants to feel that "too much" was being spent) but no effect of race on response. For the question worded "national defense" the preferred model was a three-way interaction, although the partial association of religion and response was not statistically significant. The preferred model when the probe was worded "strengthening national defense" included an effect of race on response but no effect of religion on response. These findings suggest that the religion effect on the "defense" item we presented above is likely to be an artifact of question wording rather than a real difference between Catholics and Protestants. If our hunch is correct it indicates even less support among Catholics for the position of their bishops.

Conclusions

The Catholic Church and the bishops indeed have a unique and continuing role to play in the formation of a consistent life ethic, the so-called seamless garment. Such an ethic is clearly a desirable goal, but considerable work must be done to promote its acceptance by the laity.

Descriptive data analysis will indicate support by the Catholic laity for the position of the bishops on some issues, sometimes by a majority and sometimes by a plurality. The introduction of race as a control variable, however, frequently erodes both the overall percentage of support by Catholics as well as Protestants. Controlling for church attendance, on the other hand, had little effect on political attitudes, with the exception of guaranteed jobs and cuts in defense spending.

Our use of log-linear models on the 1984 National Opinion Research Center (NORC) General Social Survey (GSS) data set uncovered little support for the bishops' positions by the Catholic laity, particularly if one insists on statistical significance. In the social policy arena, there is mixed support at best for the position of the bishops on abortion, and in three specific circumstances a majority of Catholics support legalized abortion (possible birth defects, woman's health endangered, and rape). Race proves to be a more salient variable than religion, with a higher percentage of blacks than whites opposed to legalized abortion regardless of circumstance. On capital punishment, white Catholics show slightly higher agreement with the bishops' position than do Protestants, but with a strong majority of Catholics not supporting the bishops' position. Again, race rather than religion has greater influence, with blacks considerably more opposed to capital punishment than whites.

In the economic realm, race again proved more potent than religion. Similarly, Catholics were more likely to support the bishops' views than are Protestants, but with only 49 percent of Catholics favoring guaranteed jobs and 61 percent supporting the view of government meeting everyone's needs. Support for this latter item must be tempered by the finding of additional lack of support among Catholics with respect to the government's role in reducing income differences between the rich and the poor, and spending on welfare. Race is clearly a more salient factor.

In the foreign policy arena, a solid majority of Catholics are at odds with the bishops on foreign aid, with minimal racial difference. On defense spending, Catholic support is stronger (46 percent) than Protestant support (34 percent) for the bishops' position that "too much money" is spent on defense, but even here less than a majority agree with the bishops. Finally, we stress that findings on the defense questions is affected by questioning wording.

Overall, we conclude that systematic social science research on the seamless garment underscores weak support by the Catholic laity for the bishops' views. Much toil must be done in the religious vineyard before it is accepted by the laity. At present, pastoral letters and exhortations about re-imagining the church are not enough.

References

Bernardin, J.C. "Call for a Consistent Ethic of Life," *Origins* 13.29 (1983): 491-494.
_____"Religion and Politics: Stating the Principles and Sharpening the Issues." Paper presented at the Woodstock Forum, Georgetown University, Washington, D.C. 1984.

Briggs, K. "Bernardin Asks Catholics to Fight Both Nuclear Arms and Abortion," *New York Times*, 7 Dec. 1983.

"Catholic Bishops Urge Congress to Reject MX." Washington Post, 16 Mar. 1986.

Cleghorn, J.S. "Respect for Life: Research Notes on Cardinal Bernardin's 'Seamless Garment'." *Review of Religious Research* 28 (1986): 129-141.

Cohen, R.E. "Getting Religion," *National Journal* 17 (1985): 2080-2084.

Duncan, B. and O.D. Duncan. *Sex Typing and Social Roles: A Research Report*. New York: Academic Press, 1978.

Feinberg, S.E. *The Analysis of Cross-Classified Categorical Data*. 2nd ed. Cambridge: MIT Press, 1980.

Finney, J.M. "A Theory of Religious Commitment." *Sociological Analysis* 39.1 (1978): 19-35.

Gallup, G. Jr. and J. Castelli. *The American Catholic People*. New York: Doubleday and Co., 1987.

Goodman, L.A. 1970. "The Multivariate Analysis of Qualitative Data: Interactions Among Multiple Classifications." *Journal of the American Statistical Association*. 65 (1970): 226-56.

———— "A General Model for the Analysis of Surveys." *American Journal of Sociology* 77 (1972): 1035-86.

Greeley, A.M. "Catholics and Coalition: Where Should They Go?" In S.M. Lipset (ed.) *Emerging Coalitions in American Politics*. San Francisco: Institute for Contemporary Studies, 1978.

———— *The Religious Imagination*. Los Angeles: Sadlier, 1981.

———— *American Catholics Since the Council*. Chicago: Thomas Moore Press, 1985.

Hanna, M.T. *Catholics and American Politics*. Cambridge: Harvard UP, 1979.

Hanson, E. O. *The Catholic Church in World Politics*. Princeton: Princeton UP, 1987.

Heyer, M. "Bernardin Views Pro-Life Issues as 'Seamless Garment'," *Washington Post*, 10 Dec. 1983.

———— "Bishops Urge U.S. to Shield Poor," *Washington Post*, 29 Mar. 1986.

Hout, M. and A.M. Greeley. "The Center Doesn't Hold: Church Attendance in the United States, 1940-1984." *American Sociological Review* 52 (1987): 325-45.

Kennedy, E. *Re-imagining American Catholicism*. New York: Vintage Books, 1985.

Kenski, H.C. "Religion and the Public Square: The Case of American Catholics." Presented at the Annual Meeting of the American Political Science Association, Washington, D.C. 1986.

Pear, R. "Catholic Bishops Say U.S. Must Do More for the Poor," *New York Times*, 14 Nov. 1986.

Reichley, A.J. *Religion in American Public Life*. Washington D.C.: The Brookings Institution, 1985.

White, R.C. "Toward A Theory of Religious Influence." *Pacific Sociological Review* 11 (1968): 23-8.

The American Bishops and Catholic Women: The Failure of Political Imagination

Margaret Corgan Kenski

"When we speak of the commerce with our colonies, fiction lags after truth, invention is unfruitful, and imagination cold and barren."—Edmund Burke, Speech on Conciliation with America, 22 March, 1775.

Two hundred years and more after Burke indicted the British government for its failure of imagination in dealing with its colonies, America's Catholic bishops (beneficiaries of those same colonies' revolt against Britain) are displaying a similar unfruitful invention and cold, barren imagination in their attitudes toward Catholic women. Using the political symbolism derived from America's liberal tradition, the bishops through highly publicized pastoral letters have urged acceptance of a more extensive welfare state (1984), expressed grave reservations about development of nuclear arms (1983), and pressed for improved race relations (1979). Where they have parted company from their usual allies in the Washington liberal coalition is the point at which an extension of orthodox liberal thinking would force a reexamination of their historical position on matters affecting gender and the family (Reichley). Refusal to deal creatively with the problem will not make it go away. As Andrew Greeley has recently written of the American Catholic church: "The 'woman' problem is serious, very serious indeed. And one cannot imagine a way in which it is not going to get even more serious in the years ahead." (192).

This article examines the seriousness of the "woman" problem within the American Catholic Church from the perspective of political science, with an overt bias toward a greater role for women within the Church. (The bias, however, appears to be a preference shared by increasing numbers of American Catholics as verified by the survey data cited below). We begin by exploring briefly the current conflict over women within the American Catholic church, and then proceed to the American hierarchy's response to date, and the current state of Catholic public opinion on the role of women. The second section highlights a failure of political imagination by the American bishops in their response to their female constituency, namely their failure to recognize that the political attitudes of American Catholic women are closer to the views in the bishops' recent pastoral letters than are the political

105

attitudes of American Catholic men. Survey data from several sources will show that appeals to Catholic women to support the bishops' programs are more likely to be effective than appeals to Catholic men—provided that the bishops' leadership credibility is not damaged by their attitudes toward the very women who could be a natural political constituency and power base for social and economic reform.

1. The "Woman" Problem Is the Problem with Men

For feminist Catholics, the "woman" problem within the Church is really a "man" problem—i.e., the major power holders are males unwilling for doctrinal, political or psychological reasons to share power with one-half of the Church's members. No longer content to accept salvation without representation, feminist Catholics, many of whom are members of religious orders, have begun to challenge vigorously the Church's exclusion of women from official decision making positions (Friedrich). Media coverage of the rise of Catholic feminism tends to focus on such newsworthy items as a 12-year old's exclusion from parochial school for refusing to recant her pro-abortion views (McLoughlin); the Rev. Terrance A. Sweeney's resignation from the Jesuit order rather than obey his superior's order to suppress the results of a survey of the American bishops on celibacy and ordination of women (Goldman); and the Vatican's order to religious signers of a statement in the *New York Times* declaring "a diversity of opinions regarding abortion among committed Catholics" to recant or be disciplined (Dionne "Determined").

Less dramatic than these events, but essential in the conflict between the Church hierarchy and activist women is the root issue of ordination of women. In the words of Mary Gordon, "It is the central issue because without it, there is no route to power within the Church." (Friedrich). There is little doubt, however, that Pope John Paul II will continue to affirm the traditional ban on ordination of women. From his dismissal of the 1979 challenge by Sister M. Theresa Kane, President of the Leadership Conference of Women Religious, to be open to "the possibility of women as persons being included in all ministries of our church," (Hanson) to his recent letter to Archbishop of Canterbury Runcie warning that Anglican ordination of women posed a "serious obstacle" to Anglican-Roman Catholic reunion, there has been little change in the Pope's view of the role of women in the Church (Dionne "Pope").

Caught between Catholic feminist demands and the papal reluctance to discuss enlarging the role of women, the American bishops, operating through the National Conference of Catholic Bishops, have staked out an ambiguous position that is notably less liberal than their positions on race or the economy. While an NCCB report in 1985 called for a larger role for women in the Church, it also "advised against priesthood." (Greer). The statement by an American bishop after a visit with the Pope that he "is vehement on this particular question and would eliminate any candidate for the bishopric who has ever entertained even the possibility of a woman's becoming a priest" (Kennedy, 168-169) would dampen enthusiasm for an independent course of action in any event. That the bishops personally tend to support the Pope's views on the role of women can be seen in the results of the Rev. Sweeney's study. Of the 142 bishops who responded, only 8 percent approved of ordination of women and 28 percent of women as deacons. (Goldman).

Cross-pressure on the American bishops to make some concessions to women in the Church comes from a number of sources. The same bishops who have espoused liberal American values in calling for aid for the poor and equality for minorities cannot be totally blind to the contradiction involved in denying equality and access to women in the Church. If philosophical consistency were not a sufficient inducement, practical considerations would have an effect. As Eugene Kennedy has said, "A fair argument could be made that the Catholic Church in this country is what it is because of women... So if you lose women, you sustain a loss that you can't make up." (Friedrich). In a Church wounded by a decline in religious vocations since the 1960s, 83% of the parish leadership positions have been filled by laity, 58% of whom are women (Leege). Although the Church has historically "depended on a subordinate sisterhood" (Dionne, "Determined"), it is unlikely that Catholic women who are increasingly well educated will continue to provide services without a voice in policymaking.

Moreover, public opinion among the Catholic laity has moved to majority support for the ordination of women. As Andrew Greeley has noted, there has been considerable change in a short period of time "in the teeth of repeated statements from Church authority that the ordination of women is an impossibility" (Greeley 182). From 29% approval of ordination of women in 1974, American Catholic opinion moved to 44% approval in 1982 (Greeley) and reached majority support in a 1985 CBS/New York Times poll at 52% (Goldman). Hoge's study with polling by Gallup in June 1985 showed overall approval of women's ordination at 47% with sharp differences among age groups. Catholics aged 21 to 30 approved by 65%, a figure that dropped consistently with age to a low of 19% for Catholics aged 61 or older (Hoge). Clearly the opinion trend among Catholic laity runs counter to the pope's explicit and the bishops' more muted opposition to inclusion of women in the priesthood.

2. The Failure of Imagination

The bishops' reluctance to support equality and access within the Church stands in sharp contrast to their positions expressed in recent pastoral letters on aid to the poor and minorities, the use of nuclear deterrents, and U.S. military involvement in Central America. As Eric O. Hanson has described so well, the American bishops' condemnation in 1971 of continued American military operations in Southeast Asia constituted a repudiation of the American Catholic nationalism which had characterized the political and religious values fostered by the hierarchy since the 1830s. (Hanson). After 1971, the American bishops saw their role defined by Vatican II as compelling collegial deliberation on major problems. Archbishop Rembert Weakland, chairman of the bishops' committee that wrote "Catholic Social Teaching and the U.S. Economy," declares that "...we must reimagine the Catholic church. It isn't easy but it is necessary for every Catholic... In these pastoral letters, the bishops are not writing for political reasons but to begin serious discussions on the major issues of our time." (Kennedy, 19).

Thus far the re-imagining has not reached to equality for women within the Church. And in one sense this is a political failure for the American bishops. For Catholic women are more likely than Catholic men to take seriously the bishops' pastorals on current issues—many have arrived at several of the same judgments themselves. It is only in the area of abortion among major social and political issues of the day, that Catholic men are more in agreement with the bishops than are Catholic women.

The existence of an American gender gap on political issues was first seriously discussed during the 1980 presidential season, and has been a feature of political calculation and analysis ever since (Kenski, Klein). That women are somewhat more liberal and Democratic than males can be demonstrated from even a cursory inspection of the data in major survey research collections. The national gender gap in attitudes also permeates into the American religious subcultures, including Catholics. To demonstrate that American Catholic females are more attuned to the policy views of their bishops than are Catholic males, the bishops' views in areas of economic, social, and foreign/defense policy are contrasted with public opinion findings on questions relating to those issues.

The first area is economic policy. The bishops' 1984 pastoral letter on "Catholic Social Teaching and the U.S. Economy" called for government aid to help minorities and the poor and for government guarantees of employment. Tables 1A and 1B below compare the responses of all adults or voters, Catholic females, and Catholic males to questions dealing with these issues. On all three questions, Catholic females score higher than males on the liberal side of the issue. For example, in Table 1A, on the seven point scale on aid to minorities with a score of 1 the most liberal response of government responsibility and 7 the most conservative response of minorities' being responsible for themselves, Catholic women showed slightly more liberal than Catholic males (3.918 to 4.014) in 1984 and 1982 (4.342 to 4.569). The differences are not significant but the direction is correct for our purposes. A more general economic question uses a scale where 1 = government job guarantees and 7 = government noninvolvement. Catholic women in both 1984 and 1982 were more liberal than Catholic males with the difference in 1982 being statistically significant. In Table 1B's responses to a 1984 question on whether federal aid to the poor should be increased, kept the same or decreased, Catholic female voters were again more liberal than males with 49.3% wishing to increase federal aid, compared to 46.0% for Catholic males. A consistent pattern emerges across all three sets of responses, making future exploration a worthwhile endeavor.

Table 2 takes a simple question on capital punishment, denounced by the bishops in 1980 (Goodman), and two on abortion (consistently and adamantly opposed by the Church) as indicators for proximity to the bishops' views on social issues. On capital punishment, Catholic women are strikingly closer than males to the bishops, although both sexes disagree with the view of the bishops. While both males and females voice majority approval, the percentage of Catholic females who favor capital punishment at 69.9% is closer by 13.5% than males. Abortion is the one area in which Catholic women appear to be farther than males from the bishops. While only 14% of both males and females would ban all abortions

Table 1A:

Gender Differences Between Catholics on Aid to Minorities and Guaranteed Jobs: Mean Scores on 7-Point Interval Scales

Issues and End Point Positions on a 7-Point Scale	Year	All Adults	Catholic Females	Catholic Males
Aid to Minorities: 1= Gov't Should Help Minority Groups to 7= Minority Groups Should Help Themselves	1984	4.081	3.918	4.104
	1982	4.409	4.342	4.569
Guaranteed Jobs: 1=Gov't Should See to a Job and Good Standard of Living to 7=Gov't Should Let Each Person Get Ahead On His Own	1984	4.132	3.967	4.237
	1982	4.336	3.894	4.667*

* Indicates that the difference between the mean scores is significant at p <.05.
SOURCE: American National Election Studies for 1982 and 1984, Center for Political Studies, University of Michigan.

Table 1B:

Gender Differences Between Catholics on Federal Aid for the Poor: 1984 Voters (%)

Percent Who Believe That Federal Spending on the Poor Should be:	All Voters	Catholic Females	Catholic Males
Increased	43.5	49.3	46.0
Kept Where It Is Now	41.3	40.4	40.4
Decreased	15.2	10.4	13.6

SOURCE: CBS/*New York Times* Election Survey, 1984.

Table 2:

Gender Differences Between Catholics on Social Issues: Capital Punishment and Abortion (%)

Item	National	Catholic Females	Catholic Males	Difference Females Minus Males
Death Penalty for Murder— NORCa				
Favor	74.8	69.9	83.4	-13.5
Oppose	25.2	30.1	16.6	+13.5
Views on Abortion—ANESb				
Never Permit	13.2	14.3	14.6	-0.3
Permit for Rape, Incest or				
to Save Life	30.1	31.1	36.1	-5.0
Permit for a Clear Need	19.8	15.5	17.2	-1.7
Matter of Personal Choice	36.1	37.8	31.8	+6.0
Other	0.8	1.2	0.4	+0.8
Should Abortion Be Legal?— CBSc				
Yes, as It Is Now	44.0	39.7	35.8	+3.9
Only in Extreme				
Circumstances	29.3	30.6	30.0	+0.6
No	26.7	29.7	34.2	-4.5

a National Opinion Research Center, General Social Survey, 1984.
b American National Election Study 1984, Center for Political Studies, University of Michigan.
c CBS/*New York Times* Election Study 1984.

(the bishops' view), Catholic women are 6% more likely than Catholic males to see abortion as a matter of personal choice. Close to 40% of Catholic females agree that abortion should be legal as it is now, compared to 36% of Catholic males. On foreign policy issues, however, Catholic women resume the pattern of higher agreement with the bishops on specific issues. The Catholic bishops have called for a nuclear freeze (1983), reduced defense spending (1985) and advised against military solutions in Central America. Again using 7-point scale questions in Table 3A, American Catholic women (at 4.888) were significantly closer than Catholic males (4.544) to the view that the U.S. should become much *less* involved in the

Table 3A:

Gender Differences Between Catholics on Involvement in Central America and Defense Spending: Mean Scores on 7-Point Interval Scales

Issues and End Point Positions on a 7-Point Scale	Year	All Adults	Catholic Females	Catholic Males
U.S. Involvement in Central America: 1=U.S. Should Become *Much More* Involved to 7=U.S. Should Become *Much Less* Involved	1984	4.376	4.888	4.544*
Change in Level of Defense Spending: 1=Defense Spending Should be Greatly *Decreased* to 7=Defense Spending Should Be Greatly Increased	1984 1982	3.991 3.859	3.860 3.500	4.104 4.103*

* Indicates that the difference between mean scores is significant at $p < .05$.

SOURCE: American National Election Studies for 1982 and 1984, Center for Political Studies, University of Michigan.

internal affairs of Central American countries. In both 1982 and 1984 Catholic women were closer than Catholic males to the view that defense spending should be decreased. Similarly, Catholic females as seen in Table 3B were nearly 9% more in favor of a nuclear freeze than males, 8% more in favor of negotiating a freeze first, and nearly 10% were opposed to U.S. military involvement in Central America.

While the bishops do not endorse either political party as they explore social, economic and foreign policy issues, it is certainly fair to say that their recent economic and foreign policy views come closer to those of Democratic than Republican Party activists. Table 4 indicates that Catholic female voters appear to find Democratic Party candidates more compatible with their views than do Catholic males. Catholic females in 1984 gave the Democratic presidential candidate a support level 6.9% higher than did Catholic males, Democratic Senate contenders an 8.6% higher vote, and Democratic House candidates a 6.7% higher support.

Table 3B:

Gender Differences Between Catholics on U.S. Military Forces in Central America and the Nuclear Freeze: 1982 and 1984 Voters (%)

Item	National	Catholic Females	Catholic Males	Difference Females-Minus/Males
A Nuclear Arms Freeze With the Soviet Union: (1982)				
Favor	67.0	76.8	68.0	+8.6
Oppose	33.0	23.2	32.0	-8.6
What U.S. Should Do First: (1984)				
Negotiate Freeze with USSR	49.6	59.7	51.5	+8.2
Strengthen Defenses Before Negotiating	50.4	40.3	48.5	-8.2
Is Communist Threat in Central America Serious Enough to Justify Having U.S. Military Forces there?				
Yes	56.0	49.1	59.0	-9.9
No	44.0	50.9	41.0	+9.9

SOURCE: CBS/*New York Times* Election Studies 1982 and 1984.
S OURCE: CBS/*New York Times* Election Studies 1982 and 1984.

This overall pattern of Catholic females having greater potential as a support group for the bishops' views is likely to continue in the future—except for the issues of abortion, birth control, capital punishment and ordination. As the data in Table 5 indicate, the gender gap is alive and well among Catholics under 30. While Catholic females aged 18 to 29 are more likely to oppose the bishops on abortion, this same group is more liberal by far than their male counterparts. As the table shows, the gender gap appears to be wider for young Catholics on every indicator except Senate Democratic support. If the bishops are serious about affecting social and economic change; younger Catholic females might well be the strongest bloc in their coalition.

Table 4:

Gender Differences Between Catholics on Major Party Support Scores: 1984 Voters

Office	National	Catholic Females	Catholic Males	Differences (Females-Minus/Males
Presidency				
Democratic	40.8	48.6	41.7	+6.9
Republican	59.2	51.4	58.3	-6.9
U.S. Senate				
Democratic	46.4	56.8	48.0	+8.6
Republican	53.6	43.2	52.0	-8.6
U.S. House				
Democratic	48.9	59.5	52.8	+6.7
Republican	51.1	40.5	47.2	-6.7

SOURCE: CBS/*New York Times* Election Study 1984

Table 5:

Support Among Catholics For "Liberal" Positions on Select Issues in 1984 by Age and Gender (%)

Issue Position		Catholic Females	Catholic Males	Gender Gap
Favor Legal Abortion—	All	39.7	35.8	3.9
Current Law	Under 30	56.5	46.1	10.4
Favor Negotiating a Freeze	All	59.7	51.5	8.2
With U.S.S.R.	Under 30	65.8	52.4	13.4
Favor Increased Federal	All	49.3	46.0	3.3
Spending on the Poor	Under 30	45.9	37.8	8.1
Oppose U.S. Military Forces	All	50.9	41.0	9.9
In Central America	Under 30	51.8	39.0	12.8
Voted Democratic for	All	48.6	41.7	6.9
Presidency	Under 30	43.2	34.3	8.9
Voted Democratic for	All	56.8	48.0	8.8
U.S. Senate	Under 30	53.4	47.9	7.5
Voted Democratic for	All	59.5	52.8	6.7
U.S. House	Under 30	57.1	45.1	12.0

Gender Gap: Percentage Catholic Females minus percentage Catholic Males.

SOURCE: CBS/*New York Times* Election Studies. 1982 and 1984.

Catholicism has always been a syncretic religion, surviving and adapting its images and practices to the local cultures in which it grew. The very organismic images (seed, body, etc.) of the Church and its relationships to peoples around the world signify the potential for growth and change. (O'Neil,). The American bishops may not be willing or able to move unilaterally toward ordination of women. What they could do is press the case harder at the Vatican while recognizing women's contributions to vigorous parish life and encouraging greater local decisionmaking power for women. It would take only a mild exercise in political reimaging for the bishops to do so, as our data suggest that Catholic women are more politically compatible with the hierarchy than are Catholic males. Failure to reimagine the role of women in the Church may ultimately place the bishops in the same sad position as the British government of Burke's day—watching the colonies that could have been an invigorating partner slip away on their own path.

References

Dionne, E.J. "Determined to Lead." *New York Times*, 12 May 1985.
_____ "Pope Tells Runcie He Objects to the Ordination of Women. *New York Times*, 1 Jul. 1986.
Friedrich, O. "Women: Second Class Citizens." *Time*, 4 Feb. 1985.
Goldman, A.L. "Catholicism, Democracy, and the Case of Father Curran." *New York Times*, 24 Aug. 1986.
Goodman, W. "Religious Alliance Against Execution Grows." *New York Times*, 7 Dec. 1983.
Greeley, A.M. *American Catholic Since the Council: An Unauthorized Report*. Chicago: Thomas More Press, 1985.
Greer, W. "Catholic Bishops Say Women's Role Should Be Larger: Priesthood Not Advised." *New York Times*, 16 Sep. 1985.
Hanson, E.O. *The Catholic Church in World Politics:* Princeton: Princeton UP, 1987.
Hoge, D.R. *Trends in Catholic Lay Attitudes Since Vatican II on Church Life and Leadership.* Study of Future Church Leaderships, No. 5 D.C.: Catholic University of America, 1986.
Kennedy, Eugene. *Reimagining American Catholicism*, New York: Vintage Books, 1985.
Kenski, H.C. "Gender Gap: Myth or Reality." In *Politics of the Gender Gap*, ed. Carol Mueller. Beverly Hills: Sage, 1987.
Klein, E. *Gender Politics:* Cambridge: Harvard UP, 1984.
Leege, D.C. *Parish Life Among the Leaders, No. 9* Notre Dame: Study of Catholic Parish Life, 1986.
McLoughlin, M. "The Pope Gets Tough." *U.S. News and World Report*, 17 Nov. 1986.
O'Neil, D.J. "The Secularisation of Religious Symbolism: The Case of Ireland." *The International Journal of Social Economics.* xiv (1986): 3-24.
Reichley, A.J. *Religion in American Public Life*. D.C.: Brookings, 1985.

PART FIVE

A Tale of Two Values:
Cents and Sense

Albert Bergesen

These are the best of times, these are the worst of times. Best because there is a flowering of cultural analysis, from studies of language and myth to discourse and mentalities, as structuralism/post-structuralism has affected the study of history (Foucault), psychoanalysis (Lacan), Marxism (Althusser), anthropology (Levi-Strauss), literary criticism (Derrida) and practically all areas of the social sciences. The place of signs, symbols, and semiotic value in social theory is at a high point. But these are also the worst of times, for this analysis, by and large, treats cultural objects from art to ideology as an autonomous domain of social existence, self-generative and self-transformative.

The basic theoretical assumption underlying much of this linguistic based cultural analysis remains that of Saussure, who saw linguistic meaning as a product of the positional opposition of signs within a self contained system of signs and not their reference to things out there in the real world. While this made a great deal of sense for understanding some of the vexing peculiarities of linguistic structure, it proved fatal when applied to other meaning systems besides language proper. Now everything from primitive myths through class ideologies are understood as autonomously structured meanings devoid of determinate ties to the material world of concrete economic relations. With symbolic systems self-determining, economic factors, external to culture, are now eliminated from theories of culture. The economic and the cultural are increasingly seen as having their own separate logics, captured in the notion of the "autonomy" and "relative autonomy" of the superstructural or cultural sphere.

One by-product of this has been a general split in thinking about the origins of the market or economic value in art versus its more purely aesthetic or semiotic value. Put another way, there are two approaches to the question of the value of art. First, there is a painting's market value, worth, or significance. Its exchange value expressed in money. Second, there is it's more aesthetic or semiotic significance, where the painting is more a sign vehicle. Importantly, any concrete object of art signifies both kinds of value at the same time. It has meaning in market terms and in more symbolic or semiotic terms. Accordingly there have been studies of the economics of art (Baxandall, 1972, Becker, 1982) and linguistic based studies of the more symbolic significance of art (Foucault, 1983, Bryson, 1983, Clignet, 1985, Bourdieu, 1984, Matejka and Titunik, 1984). The important point is that the theoretical logic of the economic and semiotic rarely lead to the other. My question is how do these two values of art systematically interact: how does sense produce cents and cents produce sense.

I begin this analysis with a commonplace observation. When an art movement receives a certain degree of critical and commercial success, or at least popularity with patrons in earlier centuries, this is often thought to produce inflated artistic egos, laziness, and a general stagnation or complacency in stylistic development. Styles rigidify. Success, it is warned, can be dangerous to the creative process. To explore this idea from a more sociological perspective I will propose a preliminary model of the interaction between changes in economic value (market success) and resultant changes in semiotic value (altered styles). In this process market and semiotic value mutually affect each other. When viewed over time there is an identifiable pattern of interaction: the very market success of a style plants the seeds for a later stagnation in stylistic development which in turn sets off mechanisms that lead to new styles and increased marketability.

This cyclical process will be explicated with ideas from the sociolinguistic study of the coded structure of language. Here I will assume that art can reasonably be conceived as a kind of language (Bergesen, 1984; 1987), a sign system that communicates and signifies meaning. The concrete example of art history through which these ideas will be explicated is the change in styles of New York based modern art since the 1940s. The unit of analysis will be at the level of styles of art in general, not individual artists. The interest here is in the sequence of styles from Abstract Expressionism through Minimalism and Conceptualism, ending in the Neo-Realism/Neo-Expressionism of the 1980s. If the dependent variable is social—styles in general—so is the independent variable. I am dealing with large groupings of artists and the network relations both among them and from them to the larger world.

Style as Linguistic Code

A style will be defined as the crystallization of the formal elements of painterly discourse, the organization of art's vocabulary and syntax, the structuring of line, form, color, and shape. Identifiable styles, then, are kinds of linguistic codes, particular structural forms through which individual expression occurs.

Where different speech codes have been found to be affected by changes in the density of community network relations (Bernstein, 1975), I propose that art codes (styles) should also vary with changes in the network relations of the art world. More specifically, close knit in group communities with dense social networks will produce more restricted codes, whether as speech, art, or music (Bergesen, 1984). Modes of Communication (linguistic codes) reflect the social bonds and networks of the community in which they are produced. When network ties are dense and the sense of community solidarity high there is less need to spell out intentions in as much detail as when ties are weak and solidarity low. More is simply known by the members of the community, resulting in a more minimal form of communication. In these situations taken-for-granted assumptions of the community are higher and less elaborated linguistic expression is required to convey the same amount of information that could be conveyed by a more detailed specification, that is by a more spelled out elaborated code. What people don't know, or cannot assume, has, by necessity, to be spelled out in detail, hence the elaboration of the code. In more general terms what I am referring to is the tendency of groups as they become more self conscious and inbred to express themselves in ever more in-group jargon and slang.

The important dimension of linguistic organization defining these codes are (1) vocabulary pool—larger to smaller—and (2) syntax—flexible and supple at one end, stiff, rigid, mechanical, and simplified at the other. More elaborated codes are comprised of a wider pool of vocabulary and a more open, supple and complex set of syntactical rules. More restricted codes comprise a smaller vocabulary pool from which painterly acts are constructed and a more limited and rigid set of syntactical alternatives, or artistic conventions, such as color combinations, rules of perspective, and drawing techniques.

The more abstract the art, then, the more it acts as a restricted mode of artistic communication. In effect, abstraction hints at, or presents a blueprint of what could in principle be spelled out in more detail, that is in a more elaborated format. More elaborated artistic codes tend toward realism, where things are spelled out in actual detail and where the signification process extends beyond the formal structure of the painting proper to more generalized meanings in the larger society. Realistic paintings of nature, people, historical events, or urban landscapes all involve things and meanings that are identifiable by a public larger than the immediate network of artists. More abstract, minimalist, and conceptual art has meanings that are largely limited to the in-group culture of the more immediate art world. The stylistic progression over time from Abstract Expressionism (1940s-1950s) through Minimalism (1960s) to Conceptualism (1970s) involved a continuous restriction in meaning to ever smaller social networks. The meaning system is so constricted with conceptual art that the piece is often accompanied with some form of documentation to explain what the art means. In general, the more restricted the code of artistic expression, the more supplemental information is required to explain the meaning of these simplified artistic gestures.

Self Referential Codes

Restricted codes can also be examined in terms of the semiotic distinction between the signifier (here the art object) and the signified (the meaning or referent of that sign). In the case of realist painting, the signifier as, say, a vase of flowers, portrait, or landscape, specifically refers to flowers, persons, and the larger environment. While it is certainly true that realist paintings can have added or ulterior meaning, the point here is that the first step of meaning, the simple matching of the painted figuration with a cultural category—this is a tree that a vase—can be automatically accomplished with realism but not with nonrepresentational abstraction. What is a drip of pigment or just a straight line? The important point is that these kinds of signs, these signifiers, signify many possible things. They may signify a tree, but it is not apparent from the formal pictorial structure of the painting itself. For that signification to occur (line=tree) some extra-painterly information is required to make the linkage. In conceptual art where the object is so abstract, or minimal, almost every piece is accompanied by some form of documentation to provide extra-art interpretation. Often this is of the most fundamental sort to simply designate the object as art and not an element in the non-art environment.

Thus, the more minimal or severe the abstraction the more it acts as a self-referential sign system, and the more its form becomes its content. It is important to realize that this self-referentiality is also a property of restricted codes. When we speak of a dense cryptic code whose meaning is largely limited to an immediate group, we are also speaking of a form of language that has a high degree of self-referentiality about it. This is important for it allows us to link the socio-linguistics of codes with the semiotics of signs. If groups with dense network ties and high degrees of solidarity produce restricted codes that means they also produce self-referential sign systems.

The Economic-Semiotic Cycle

This brings us to a more systematic exposition of the interaction of the economic and the linguistic. The process will be broadly conceptualized using the imagery of economic or business cycles of a Schumpeterian type, where there is an A-Phase of expansion and upturn followed by a B-Phase of contraction and stagnation. These two phases are interconnected. The A-Phase of expansion plants the seeds for the later B-Phase of contraction. In terms of art, the commercial success of an art style plants the seeds for its later commercial failure. The cyclical process begins with an A-Phase in which an art movement, like the emerging abstraction in New York, is becoming a commercial success. The market value of art is increasing. But this very market success sets in motion important social processes that will alter that initial style, resulting in a modified style that will be much less marketable. The A-Phase of success will lead to a B-Phase of failure, through the sociolinguistic mechanism of style changes.

The process works as follows. Market success generally involves a growing number of and increased density in social network relations between artists and the larger world. Galleries expand, museums increase contact with artists, and critics popularize and analyze the emerging style. The isolation of the artist and art community generally declines. In the case of New York art this was seen in the gradual acceptance of abstraction and the move away from the more isolated Bohemia of the 1940s and 1950s toward the highly visible 1960s where sales boomed, and artists, galleries, and dealers became media figures. The New York art world became a very self conscious social "scene," replete with rites of self dramatization and adulation, from "happenings" and loft parties to the celebratory self consciousness of Pop art. Tremendous attention was focused upon the art world. Network ties with the larger world and consuming public increased, and with all this interest and discussion of artists and their work, the level of taken for granted assumptions concerning the history and meaning of modern art increased. The distinctly corporate existence of New York art as both community and style was captured in the emerging collective designation, the New York School.

What is important about these changes is that they provided the social conditions that produced a more restricted code of painterly expression. That is, the more gestural expressive abstraction of the 1940s and 1950s was transformed into the more minimal, sparce, and hard edge simplified geometric abstraction that came to be called Minimalism in the 1960s. Here a more elaborated code of art was becoming more minimal and restricted. The growing self referentiality of pictorial discourse did not cease with the simplified schemes of 1960s. Into the 1970s the restriction process continued such that the art object was virtually restricted out of existence in a mode of expression called Conceptualism, where the art was now idea, not painted pigment.

This altered style created problems for its economic value. Conceptual art, no longer an object to be purchased was, to put it mildly, difficult to sell or hang on walls. The problem went deeper though, for there was written and photographic documentation available of earth and conceptual art that could in theory be bought and sold. (Although a polaroid of Robert Smithson's Spiral Jetty sticking out into the Great Salt Lake is not exactly the same as owning the tons of rock deposited by huge earthy moving trucks.) There was a more semiotic crisis linked to the ever more abstract painting.

The Semiotic Crisis

As mentioned earlier, when the art object, as signifier, becomes ever more restricted and minimal the external meanings it could possibly signify automatically increase. For instance, who knows what a few drops of paint signify? This, that, what? What is being signified now becomes more and more open ended and non-determined by the values of the sign itself. The signification being done by the art object is now insufficient to point toward much else other than itself, so that abstract art came more and more to signify only the vocabulary and syntax of art. Art for art's sake. Modern art came to be understood as only concerned with the formal techniques of painting, not the content those techniques could signify. In this process form was becoming content.

What is interesting in retrospect is that the idea that painting is about painting was not seen as a problem or crisis of modern art, but hailed in the most prominent art criticism of the day as the liberating characteristic of this new American mode of expression. For example, the theories of Clement Greenberg legitimated the ever more sparce and abstract tendencies of American art. He argued modernism involved purity of expression best attained through utilizing those techniques unique to each of the arts, that is, unique to literature, sculpture, drama, poetry, etc.. From this point of view the more painting was about painting the more pure it became, making the task of painting painting.

The task of self-criticism became to eliminate from the effects of each art any and every effect that might conceivably be borrowed from or by the medium of any other art. Thereby each art would be rendered 'pure,' and in its 'purity' find the guarantee of its standards of quality as well as of its independence. Purity meant self-definition... (Greenberg, 1983: 6)

For painting the removal of the effects of other arts involved eliminating realism, the illusion of three dimensional space, effects derived from the physicality of sculpture or the situation of literature.

Realistic, illusionist art had dissembled the medium, using art to conceal art. Modernism used art to call attention to art. The limitations that constitute the medium of painting— the flat surface, the shape of the support, the properties of pigment—were treated by the Old Masters as negative factors that could be acknowledged only implicitly or indirectly. Modernist painting has come to regard these same limitations as positive factors there to be acknowledged openly. (Greenberg 1983: 6)

Or, in the argument being put forward here, the Old Masters used the vocabulary and syntax of painting, the form, to express a different content (love, drama, heroism, nature, etc.), whereas modern abstraction uses the form to express the form. The content conveyed by line, color, shape, pigment, is now line, color, shape, and pigment.

It is important to understand Greenberg's theories as part and parcel of the times, not an account above the transformations of the art world. Sociologically, it makes sense that there would appear a theoretical legitimation (Harold Rosenberg, C. Greenberg) of the emerging abstract pictorial discourse in good part because the very restrictedness of the art required some additional extra-painterly meaning to fill it out. If the signifier (abstract art) can no longer point toward a specific signification then the appearance of bodies of theoretical discourse function to link the restricted abstract signifier with a concrete signification. If there is uncertainty what the splashes and drips of Jackson Pollock signify the theory of Greenberg points the way. The expressive daps of color that was Abstract Expressionism is, through these theories, understood as part of the modernist experiment, whether the ideas come from Alfred H. Barr (1974) who linked the growth of abstraction to the more general trend of modernist experimentation or Greenberg's theory that this new abstraction is a move toward artistic purification, hence a more advanced form of painterly expression than the simple depiction of reality found in the Old Masters. From a broader sociological point of view we should expect all movements of more highly in-coded group artistic expression to be accompanied by such theoretical documents to fill in, or out, the meanings that are assumed in these restricted codes. That there were various manifestos accompanying movements such as Dada and Surrealism—whose codes of expression were very much ingroup and almost secret language—is an example of the very point being made here.

There is one other point. From the perspective of group formation and cohesion, artists who work in a similar style are symbolically linked through the common artistic conventions that comprise their particular style. Further, when an art movement emphasizes the more formal elements of style—questions of line, form, shape, thickness of pigment, etc.—it can be seen from a sociologist's point of view as a form of heightened group consciousness. Individuals emphasizing the core conventions they share, rather than expressing their individual differences, reflect a condition where the solidity of the group is strong. In general, then, when the group is accentuated or there is a high degree of self consciousness and collective concerns, one would expect the artistic discourse (styles) to emphasize the more technical aspects of the art over questions of content. That is, the old question of form and content should be viewed as a variable that varies over time depending upon changes in the solidity and network relations of the art community.

Where network ties are weak and group solidarity low one would expect more of an emphasis upon realism, upon the content of the art and not upon the forms of expression. Conversely, when network ties are stronger/denser and solidarity higher one would expect more emphasis upon the vocabulary and syntax of the style, that is a move toward abstraction and an emphasis upon form over content. Consequently, the more inbred or ingroup that collectivity of artists becomes the more emphasis there should be upon those common artistic conventions that in a very real sense is their group reality as a school or movement. These ideas shed some light on the observation that artists outside densely concentrated groups of artists—typically outside New York—tend to paint in more realistic modes. While there is a certain New York bias that these forms are less "advanced" means of expression it may very well reflect differences in social density of artists and not sensibility. Or, more advanced art may be done in New York, but that may be a product of network density and not cosmopolitan sensibility, unless density is what one wants to mean by cosmopolitanism. Alone, without a surrounding community of artists to share common assumptions, the singular artist must spell out intentions in more detail to insure their understanding, that is, be more of a realist, whereas artists nested in a dense community can speak in a restricted code assuming that the others will understand. More isolated artists simply do not have the social network ties, and their styles may reflect their social situation, not the fact that outside purportedly cosmopolitan centers there is less advanced art. In effect, put Jackson Pollock back in Wyoming and who knows what he would paint. Or, what would happen to Andrew Wyeth's realism if he was a permanent member of the Manhattan art world?

The B-Phase

Where sales had led to a more restricted style, now that restrictedness was leading back to a decrease in saleability. The narrowed intelligibility of self-referentiality had a direct economic complement. Little understood—or even recognized as art— conceptualism, the end point of ever more pure abstraction, was not something that was readily bought and sold. Its meaning was increasingly the possession of a smaller and smaller community of knowledgeable people, which narrows the market field, reducing sales, and thereby changing market value. Where market value altered style, now, on the downside, the process repeats itself. This time it is a lack of market success that acts to transform the means of artistic expression and push for new styles that are more spelled out, more elaborated, more realistic, and more capable of being understood by a wider range of consumers.

As the A-Phase of market success led to the B-Phase of market crisis, the B-Phase now leads back to success, for with declining popularity, sales, and attention, the social process producing restricted ingroup styles now works in the opposite direction. The esoterica of conceptualism leads to less attention and less sales, which results in looser ties with the broader art consuming public. These altered economic conditions now favor looser network ties with less common group solidarity, which in turn, through the sociolinguistic mechanism, leads to the emergence of a more elaborated form of expression. The B-Phase of conceptualism now leads to more content oriented art, seen in the new figuration and realism of the late 1970s and 1980s. This figurative art establishes broader networks of intelligibility than the earlier conceptualism and provides an important foundation for an increase in sales. There is also a return to the canvas, to the commodifiable object and a move away from the general outdoor nature of much conceptualism.

Summary

Increases in market value set off the sociological mechanism of denser network ties and a growing self consciousness among the art community, which in turn directly affects the pictorial structure of art: it becomes more restricted which means it is understandable to a smaller and smaller network of people, which means it is less and less usable as a market commodity, which means, as in conceptualism, it has less and less market value. The art simply becomes too esoteric. Too much artists just talking to themselves, which is exactly what is meant by ingroup codes of discourse. Now this change acts back out upon the art's economic value: sales diminish, which sets off the sociological mechanism as the community has difficulty supporting itself on the sales of conceptual art alone. This in turn results in a transformation of the code of artistic expression toward a more elaborated format, with more emphasis on content over form. This change in semiotic value now affects economic value as the web of cognitive relations of intelligibility is broadened which qualifies a wider network for purchasing art and the cycle begins once again.

References

Barr, Alfred H. *Cubism and Abstract Art.* New York: Museum of Modern Art, 1974.
Baxandall, Michael. *Painting and Experience in Fifteenth Century Italy.* New York: Oxford UP, 1972.
Becker, Howard S. *The Art World.* Berkeley: University of California. Press, 1982.
Bergesen, Albert. "Spirituals, Jazz, Blues, and Soul Music: The Role of Elaborated and Restricted Codes in the Maintenance of Social Solidarity." In Robert Wuthnow (ed.) *New Directions in the Empirical Study of Religion.* New York: Academic Press, 1979. 333-350.
_____ "The Semantic Equation: A Theory of the Social Origins of Art Styles." In *Sociological Theory 1984*, Randall Collins, (ed.) San Francisco: Jossey-Bass, 1984. 187-221.
_____ "The Decline of American Art." In Terry Boswell and Albert Bergesen (eds.) *America's Changing Role in the World-System* 1987. 221-232.

Bernstein, Basil. *Class, Codes, and Control.* New York: Schocken Books, 1975.

Bourdieu, Pierre. *Distinction: A Social Critique of the Judgement of Taste.* Cambridge: Harvard UP, 1984.

Bryson, Norman. *Vision and Painting.* New Haven: Yale UP, 1983.

Clignet, Remi. *The Structure of Artistic Revolutions.* Philadelphia: Univ. of Penn. Press, 1985.

Foucault, Michel. *This is Not a Pipe.* Berkeley: University of California Press, 1983.

Greenberg, Clement. "Modernist Painting" in *Modern Art and Modernism*, Francis Frascina and Charles Harrison (eds.), New York: Harper and Row, 1983. 1-10.

Matejka, Ladislav and Irwin R. Titunik (eds.) *Semiotics of Art.* Cambridge: MIT Press, 1984.

Saussure, Ferdinand de *Course in General Linguistics.* New York: Philosophical library, 1959.

The Garden of Love:
Heaven-on-Earth in Baroque Art

Charles Scribner III

In the last decade of his life Rubens painted one of his noblest, and most personal, celebrations of life and love: the *Garden of Love* (fig. 1) which hangs today in the Prado, Madrid, the brightest star in that celebrated galaxy of Rubens paintings. It is one of those rare masterpieces that may be fully appreciated on its own terms, a work that truly speaks for itself. Unlike Rubens's altarpieces, historical epics, or classical mythologies it requires no learned interpretation. Just as in Mozart's *Marriage of Figaro* we need not understand the Italian libretto in order to experience the emotions translated into the language of music, so it is in Rubens's sublime painting. These figural variations on a theme—the theme being the cultivation of love—are played out in harmony with the idyllic landscape, the architectural cadences, the sculptural counterpoints, and even the hovering *putti*, those airborne cherubs and cupids, the painter's version of so many grace notes and flourishes. And yet, probably no single painting by Rubens has evoked so many conflicting scholarly explanations: I am reminded of Shakespeare's sonnets and the shelves of scholarship—and sometimes fantasy—they have inspired. We seem to be on much firmer ground in Rubens's religious and mythological scenes. Poetic fantasias about love, on the other hand, tend to invite a scholars' free-for-all. What is this painting really about? Whom is it about?

The range of interpretations so far has run from the autobiographical to the arcane, from slice-of-life genre painting to the most complex allegory.[1] To some the picture simply illustrates a garden party around Rubens and his recent bride, Helena Fourment, complete with sisters-in-law and brothers-in-law.[2] To another it represents an intricate neo-platonic allegory of love personified by the three seated ladies—sensual, celestial, and earthly love: a cinematic progression, so to speak, through love's initiation, maturation, and culmination in matrimony.[3]

Is the figure at the left really the elderly Rubens rejuvenated by love with his wife Helena, as one scholar has suggested?[4] Or is Helena to be found seated in the middle—or standing at the right?[5] Do the three seated ladies, all notably without escorts, represent three allegorical stages of love; or perhaps the Three Graces, fleshly counterparts to their statue in the grotto above and behind them? Or are they personifications of sight, hearing, and touch?[6]

Fig. 1 Peter Paul Rubens, *Garden of Love* (Prado, Madrid).

Sifting through the reams of scholarship on the subject, I felt I had stumbled on the ultimate multiple-choice, college board question: A,B,C, all of the above, none of the above? One recent interpretation is based on the painting's earliest recorded Flemish title, *Conversatie à la Mode* (a social gathering, in vogue), as a work extolling social gallantry, fashion, and aristocratic courtship mirrored in the English cavalier poetry and French "how to" manuals of the day.[7] Our present, brief survey here will not permit excursions through such Baroque mazes. Instead, we must return to the evidence within the painting itself, as seen against the background of the artist's life and works and the broader artistic landscape in which this Garden of Love was planted.

First of all, Rubens painted his *Garden of Love* sometime within two or three years immediately following his marriage to Helena Fourment in 1630: she was a girl of sixteen, he a widower of fifty-three. Describing his reasons for the marriage, four years later in a letter to his friend and correspondent Nicolas-Claude Fabri de Peiresc, Rubens wrote: "I made up my mind to marry again, since I was not yet inclined to live the abstinent life of the celibate, thinking that if we must give the first place to continence, we may enjoy licit pleasures with thankfulness. I have taken a young wife of honest but middle-class family, although everyone tried to persuade me to make a Court marriage. But I feared pride, that inherent vice of the nobility, particularly in that sex, and that is why I chose one who would not blush to see me take my brushes in hand."[8]

It was a blissful and fruitful marriage, to say the least: their fifth child was born eight months after Rubens's death in 1640. During this twilight decade Rubens painted a number of portraits of Helena, such as the famous *Het Pelsken* ("The Fur") in Vienna, where she is portrayed as the classical *Venus Pudica*—"in the flesh," so to speak. Among the family portraits, his *Walk in the Garden* (Alte Pinakothek, Munich, fig. 2) describes a garden of love, but here an actual and thoroughly domesticated one, the artist's own. Rubens walks arm-in-arm with Helena toward the sculpture pavilion, his son Nicolaas a few steps behind. In the background stands a cupid-and-dolphin fountain (symbolizing love's swiftness); in the foreground, the dog and peacocks (emblems of fidelity and marriage) underscore the theme of conjugal harmony. The Munich panel foreshadows Rubens's late self-portrait with Helena and their youngest son, Peter Paul, also set in a garden, now preserved in the Metropolitan Museum, New York.[9]

So much for the happy home front, the spirit of which clearly permeates its imaginary, allegorized reflection in the Prado—"imaginary" because Rubens's *Garden of Love* is surely not lifted from the artist's family album. Rather it derives from a formal tradition of love gardens which he infused with personal feeling and significance.

During the 1630s, Rubens retired from his active diplomatic career and devoted more time than ever to painting for his own personal pleasure—landscapes, portraits, genre subjects. In his famous *Kermesse* in the Louvre, Rubens offered his version of a Pieter Bruegel, of the Flemish pictorial tradition of peasants at play. At the other end of the scale, but clearly related in its accelerating rhythms, is his *Feast of Venus* (Kunsthistorisches Museum, Vienna), a full-bodied, Baroque revival of

Fig. 2 Peter Paul Rubens, *Walk in the Garden* (Alte Pinakothek, Munich).

Fig. 3 Peter Paul Rubens, *Couples Playing Near a Castle* (Kunsthistorisches Museum, Vienna).

a classical Bacchanal. Somewhere in between we find the *Dance of Peasants* (Italian peasants this time) in the Prado and *Couples Playing Near a Castle* (Kunsthistorisches Museum, Vienna, fig. 3), recalling Rubens's purchase in 1635 of the Castle of Steen, his beloved country retreat where he spent his final years as Lord of Steen. The couples are now Flemish, well-to-do, *haut bourgeois,* and somewhat tempered, but hardly restrained, in their amorous pursuits. We begin to approach the Garden.

The tradition of love gardens goes back to medieval art where it was often associated with matrimony, as we find in the illuminated month of April in the *Très Riches Heures du Duc de Berry* by the Limbourg Brothers, illustrating a betrothal in a castle garden (fig. 4). Sometimes the theme was treated satirically, as in the anonymous Flemish *Geuchmatt* ("Fool's Meadow," fig. 5), where erstwhile fickle men have their wings clipped and their ankles ensnared, their spouses holding them on very short leashes. (Perhaps, I am tempted to suggest, it was painted to adorn a wedding chest.) The recently auctioned Flemish *Love Garden* of around 1600, attributed to Louis de Caullery (fig. 6), may be seen as a more immediate precedent for Rubens's treatment with corresponding musician, walled garden, couples strolling and dallying, a dog (faithfulness), peacocks (sacred to Juno, symbolizing marriage), but notably without any mythological sculpture or invasive putti. This is a simple, conventional *Conversatie à la Mode.*

What transforms Rubens's version into something more resonant, into a metaphorical *Garden of Love,* are the sculptural additions, like so many iconographic footnotes, and the flying putti bearing emblems of love. Rubens's invented sculpture always conveys a specific meaning: here it is the goddess Venus presiding over her realm. She is literally *expressive,* her breasts functioning as fountains, recalling Rubens's fertile fountain of "Mother Earth"*(Gaia),* the mother of Erichthonius, from the earlier *Discovery of Erichthonius* in the Liechtenstein Collection. We are reminded that Venus—like Rubens's Venus/Helena of *Het Pelsken*—is also a mother: she is the mother of Cupid, the god of love, who prompts the couple entering at the left. (Cupid's paternity is doubtful: Mars, Jupiter and Mercury have variously been given the honor; some ancient Greek writers thought his father was Chaos— "like father, like son.")

In the pavilion, hidden water jets surprise the cavorting couples. A popular sixteenth-century Italian garden amusement, it is more clearly visible in the woodcut by Christoffel Jegher, based on Rubens's drawing in the Metropolitan Museum (fig. 7).[10] The rusticated façade derives from Rubens's own architectural contributions to his Antwerp house and garden. A true Renaissance man, Rubens practised architecture as well as invented sculpture. Within the pavilion a sculpture of the Three Graces denotes the prevailing civility of this highly cultured garden. But, above all, the flying cupids provide the key to the nature of the love here celebrated: the flaming torch, the turtle doves, the floral crown, and finally the yoke are all marriage symbols.[11] This is not "free love," but *conjugal* love being fostered by Venus and her minions. (The yoke refers to the Latin *coniungere,* "to yoke together," from which we get the word conjugal—as well as that sobering image, the yoke of wedlock.) In this way the picture celebrates Rubens's own recent marriage, here reflected by analogy and allegory rather than specified by anecdotal

Fig. 4 The Limbourg Brothers, *April*, illumination from the *Très Riches Heures du Duc de Berry* (Musée Condé, Chantilly).

Fig. 5 Anonymous Flemish painter, *Geuchmatt* ("Fools' Meadow," collection unknown).

Fig. 6. Attributed to Louis de Caullery, *Love Garden* (Auction: Sotheby's, New York).

Fig. 7 Peter Paul Rubens, drawing for woodcut of *Garden of Love* (Metropolitan Museum of Art, New York).

portraiture. Rubens has thoroughly transformed the pictorial tradition of the Garden of Love, recasting it in his High Baroque style, infusing it with psychological depth, and raising it to a new poetic plane. Among seventeenth-century love gardens it stands apart, unrivaled in its appeal. For its true artistic descendents, we must look to the next century, to the *fêtes galantes* of Antoine Watteau.[12]

A Fleming by birth (from Valenciennes, formerly part of Flanders), Watteau appeared in Paris just as the long drawn-out battle in the French Academy between the Poussinistes and Rubénistes—the classicizing defenders of line versus the Baroque proponents of color—was turning in Rubens's favor. One of Watteau's early masters, the decorative painter Claude Audran, was also the curator (*"concierge"*) of the Luxembourg Palace; he had the key to the gallery of Rubens's celebrated Medici cycle, and the hours Watteau spent studying and sketching these monumental Flemish Baroque canvases were ultimately to transform the future of French Rococo painting.

Watteau's translation of his Flemish heritage into a Parisian idiom is typified by his drawing of a dancing peasant couple from Rubens's *Kermesse* and their transference to a far more rarefied setting in Watteau's *La Surprise*.[13] The banded columns of Watteau's *Music Party* (Wallace Collection, London) have their architectural roots in Rubens's *Garden of Love*. But his true debt to Rubens is far less specific and far more pervasive. Watteau's *fêtes galantes* (virtually untranslatable: something between "gallant festivals" and "merry parties"), a new genre and category devised especially for him by the French Academy, owe to Rubens's *Garden of Love* not only their subject matter and Rubéniste stylistic values, but also the repeated inclusion of invented statues of Venus to sound, as it were, the appropriate keynotes.

Their pitch and tone are distinctly mellower than in Rubens. Watteau strikes a melancholy note within the gaiety. His lovers are tentative where Rubens's were exuberant. His sculptured Venus is usually languid as in *Fêtes Vénitiennes* (National Gallery of Scotland, Edinburgh), sometimes even asleep, where Rubens's was demonstrative and assertive. In his *Champs Elysées* (Wallace Collection, London fig. 8) Watteau translates into stone his flesh-and-blood sleeping Antiope, painted five years earlier (*Jupiter and Antiope*, Louvre, Paris), which in turn is a quotation from a Hellenistic bronze of a sleeping cupid (Metropolitan Museum, New York)— an artistic metamorphosis from sculpture, through flesh, back to sculpture.[14] Watteau's statues seem in fact to hover on the boundary of stone and flesh, of art and life, of what is real and what is imagined, like the statue of Hermione stepping down from her pedestal at the end of Shakespeare's *The Winter's Tale*.

So, too, Watteau's lovers seem at times to hover between theatre and life, between the play and—to quote the Broadway title—"The Real Thing." In his *Mezzetin* (Metropolitan Museum, New York, fig. 9), for example, Watteau presents an actor from the *Commedia dell' arte* plaintively serenading his inamorata. We can almost hear Don Giovanni's *"Deh, vieni alla finestra"* ("come to the window"). She— off stage, off canvas—remains unseen, but her response may be inferred in the cold shoulder of the female statue turning its back on poor Mezzetin: despite his good voice, this stock character was ever hapless in love.

There is a melancholy strain that runs throughout the lightness and gaiety

Fig. 8 Antoine Watteau, *Les Champs Elysées* (Wallace Collection, London).

Fig. 9 Antoine Watteau, *Le Mezzetin* (Metropolitan Museum of Art, New York).

of Watteau's *fêtes galantes* like the poignant counterthemes woven through some of Mozart's brightest movements: a sense of the ephemeral, of the transitory nature of these visions of love and happiness. The yearning for permanence within the Garden of Love is tempered by the realisation that, like Watteau's perfectly poised dancer in *L'Indifferent* (Louvre, Paris),the magical equilibrium is but momentary. Mozart evokes it in music; T.S. Eliot, in our own century, in one of his *Four Quartets:*

At the still point of the turning world. Neither flesh nor fleshless;
Neither from nor towards; at the still point, there the dance is,
But neither arrest nor movement. And do not call it fixity,
Where past and future are gathered. Neither movement from nor towards,
Neither ascent nor decline. Except for the point, the still point,
There would be no dance, and there is only the dance."[15]

This theme is fully played out in Watteau's consummate Garden of Love—we might say his Sacred Grove of Love—the so-called *Pilgrimage to Cythera* (Louvre, Paris, fig. 10), the official painting submitted for his admission into the French Academy in 1717. I say "so-called" because, despite some recent muddying of the scholarly waters, it is now generally accepted that Watteau chose to depict the lovers about to *depart* from Cythera, Venus's sacred island, the ultimate goal of these amorous pilgrims, complete with festive pilgrims' staffs.[16]

The statue of Venus, an antique "term" marking the boundary of her realm, has been adorned with roses; at its base hang a bow and quiver full of arrows, the weapons of love. Golden rays of twilight suffuse the background as the lovers, their quest fulfilled, proceed to reboard the vessel to return home to the mainland.

Watteau's unusual choice of subject—specifically, his poignant sense of timing—is underscored by comparison with his earlier, overtly theatrical version of *L'Isle de Cythère* in Frankfurt (1709)—representing an outdoor performance of a play—and by a contemporary print by Claude Duflos (c. 1708). Both leave no doubt that in his Academy piece Watteau chose to depict the departure, not the setting out. The couples are clearly already on Cythera, not in some mythological Battery Park waiting for the ferry! A popular novel at the time was entitled *The Return from the Isle of Love*; the theme was clearly in the air. Lest there be any doubt, Watteau's second version, in Berlin (Charlottenburg Castle, c. 1717-1719, fig. 11), introduces several telling details: the foreground couple already fulfilled in love; the gathering of flowers ("to flirt" derives from the Old French *fleureter*, "to talk flowers"); the cupid about to shoot a lover with an arrow *reversed*, feathers first, to cancel love;[17] and the animated statue of Venus. Significantly she is here shown withholding the quiver from cupid: the time for love, we are to understand, is past. At the base of the statue lie trophies of military armor and the arts (music, literature) as offerings having been placed before the goddess of love: *Omnia vincit Amor.*

Rubens's *Garden of Love* expresses a gathering crescendo; Watteau's, a graceful diminuendo. Rubens's lovers approach conjugal fulfillment; Watteau's already begin to withdraw from transitory bliss. Rubens spent the last decade of his long productive career rejuvenated by marriage. Watteau remained a bachelor, always something

Fig. 10 Antoine Watteau, *The Departure from Cythera* (Louvre, Paris).

of an outsider despite his fame, his promising career cut tragically short by tuberculosis. Yet almost singlehandedly he created a new, typically French Rococo tradition of the love garden. Tended by Watteau's followers Jean-Baptiste Pater and Nicolas Lancret, it achieved its final flowering in the art of Jean-Honoré Fragonard. (I pass over Fragonard's master François Boucher on thematic, not art-historical, grounds: with Boucher the garden was for one thing only, and to label it love, well....)

Now Fragonard admittedly was not the first to introduce the "swinging lady" into love's gardens—she already made a cameo appearance in Watteau's *The Shepherds* (Charlottenburg Castle, Berlin)—but Fragonard, without doubt, swept her to unprecedented heights.[18] In what is surely the world's most famous *Swing* (Wallace Collection, London, 1767, fig. 12) she is propelled higher and higher by, some say, a bishop; others, her unsuspecting husband or elderly suitor, until her secret lover gains the optimum view of her legs—and perhaps more. He lies sprawled appropriately in a bed of roses (an obvious visual pun) as she flings off her shoe, a popular eighteenth-century motif symbolising the casting off of virtue. The sculpture of Cupid by Falconet admonishes silence while, in the background, two putti riding a dolphin symbolise the swift surge of love's pleasures. These sculptural glosses clearly maintain their iconographic function as established by Rubens and followed by Watteau. For Fragonard, as well, they play far more than a merely decorative role, as we shall see in his consummate masterpiece at the Frick Collection in New York, *The Progress of Love*.

A garden of love in four acts, so to speak, the series was commissioned by King Louis XV's last mistress, Madame du Barry (who ultimately lost her head on the guillotine for royal love) for her country pavilion at Louveciennes. Fragonard painted the four large canvases between 1771 and 1773: they represent his most important commission and grandiose cycle of paintings. But already at their completion they had outlived their times. Neo-classicism *à la grecque* was already on the horizon. The more austere style of Joseph-Marie Vien was coming into vogue and would, quite literally, displace Fragonard. After a mere few weeks on view, Fragonard's masterpieces were returned to the artist, who eventually took them back home to Grasse.[19] (The over-abundance of fragrant flowers in these scenes—especially roses—reminds us that Fragonard came from the heart of France's perfume industry.) There, installed in his cousin's house, the series was supplemented by ten additional canvases. The paintings crossed the Atlantic in 1915 and eventually settled at the Frick, where they have been recently cleaned and together create the most perfect French eighteenth-century room—and "garden"—in the New World.

We shall here confine ourselves to the original four narrative scenes. Their sequential order has been the subject of much scholarly debate: in addition to the three different sequences heretofore proposed, one critic reads them as two complementary pairs, another as having no intended narrative sequence at all. I am inclined to follow Donald Posner's suggested order because it corresponds to the documented installation of the paintings in Grasse and to the sequence of Vien's neo-classical series which replaced Fragonard's at Louveciennes—and, above all, because it tells a good story and rings true.[20] Still, I recognize that the pursuit

Fig. 11 Antoine Watteau, *The Departure from Cythera* (Charlottenburg Castle, Berlin).

of love, almost by definition, admits alternative approaches! It has been claimed (in the Frick's own catalogue) that Fragonard's prominent statues have only the most generalized anecdotal connection with his foreground subject.[21] This I cannot accept. In my view, they provide precise and equally witty iconographic commentaries on the meaning of each scene, symbolic touchstones of love's progress.

In the opening *Surprise* (fig. 13) the aspiring lover has scaled the wall of the garden of love, startling the unprepared and visibly alarmed young lady who has been reading a letter—we may guess whose: its seal, like the gentleman's jacket, is red. Between and above them, we find the now-familiar statue of Venus withholding the quiver from Cupid. We may recall the same statue in Watteau's second *Departure from Cythera* and, with closer application to the present scene, in his *Garden Party* in Dresden: the time for love's fulfillment, it reveals, has not yet come. The green pitcher on the ground is as yet unbroken, an emblematic footnote to our heroine's virtue which likewise remains intact.

And so we proceed to *The Pursuit* (fig. 14), where the tempo, *allegro con brio*, is marked by the sculpture of cupids riding a dolphin, recalling those in Fragonard's *Swing* and the familiar fountain motif in Rubens's mythologies. The maiden's precarious footing, as she flees, suggests an imminent fall—in love, "*tomber amoureux.*"

The next scene (fig. 15) used to be called *Love Letters* but, based on Sauerländer's correct identification of the allegorical statue of *Amicitia*, is better titled *Love and Friendship*. The pair are now shown reading together—at least *she's* reading— with the dog of faithfulness at their feet. The love letters bear the familiar red seal. The merging cloudlike foliage above seems to embrace, mirroring the figures below. It has been proposed that this subject should come last, illustrating Madame de Pompadour's motto that "love passes but friendship endures."[22] A touching thought. But it is hard to reconcile such sentiments with either Fragonard or the new royal mistress, Madame du Barry, who unlike her predecessor, the aging La Pompadour, had no physical infirmity requiring her to fall back on such a consoling philosophy.

Finally in *The Lover Crowned* (fig. 16), the traditional symbols of the love garden (music, garlands, floral crown) appear as well as the artist himself sketching this happy conclusion. Once again, the soft foliage and counterpointed, calligraphic branch reflect the lovers below. And what of little Cupid? He is now asleep: his job done, he has earned his nap.

If nature plays a supporting dramatic role in this cycle, in the late Fragonard *fêtes* it truly dominates. The figures recede in importance, enveloped by the sensuous and overblown foliage foreshadowing the landscape fantasies of Hubert Robert and early Romanticism—for example, in Fragonard's *Swing* in Washington or *Fête at Rambouillet* (Gulbenkian Foundation, Oeiras, fig. 17): a Watteau minuet has, in effect, been re-orchestrated as a symphony. The trees themselves now seem to embody the pent-up forces of nature, like gathering thunderstorm clouds about to break at any moment.

Fragonard outlived the Rococo. He personally survived the French Revolution, but his style did not. For the finale of the Garden of Love we must look to another

Fig. 12 Jean-Honoré Fragonard, *The Swing* (Wallace Collection, London).

Fig. 13 Jean-Honoré Fragonard, *The Surprise* (The Frick Collection, New York).

Fig. 14 Jean-Honoré Fragonard, *The Pursuit* (The Frick Collection, New York).

Fig. 15 Jean-Honoré Fragonard, *Love and Friendship* (The Frick Collection, New York).

Fig. 16 Jean-Honoré Fragonard, *The Lover Crowned* (The Frick Collection, New York).

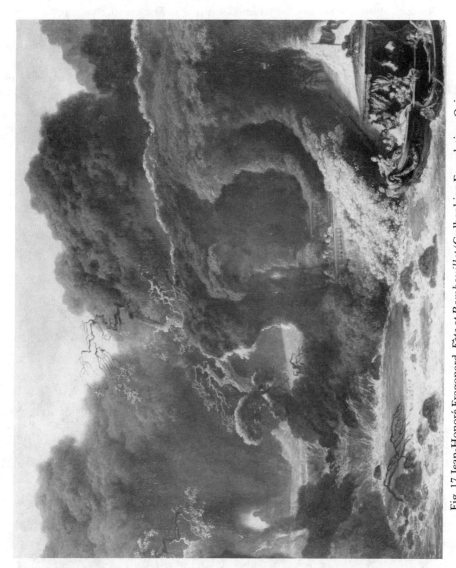

Fig. 17 Jean-Honoré Fragonard, *Fête at Rambouillet* (Gulbenkian Foundation, Oeiras, Portugal).

medium, to the last act of Mozart's *Marriage of Figaro:* if only Fragonard had designed the backdrops! (Jean-Pierre Ponnelle's new sets at the Metropolitan Opera suggest, by contrast, a "petrified garden" and seem to derive from Piranesi engravings, overshadowed as they are by gray crumbling architecture). Someone at London Records, at least, has sensed the natural affinity with Fragonard, choosing the artist's bi-level *capriccio* in his *Gardens of the Villa d'Este at Tivoli* (fig. 18, Wallace Collection, London) to illustrate this opera about "upstairs/downstairs" in the Garden of Love.

In Mozart's fourth and final act, the garden becomes the scene of amorous pursuits, disguised rendezvous, intrigues, infidelities and entrapment. Then, through the perfect fusion of Mozart's music and Da Ponte's libretto, it is transformed into a place of grace and redemption, as the Countess suddenly reveals her true identity

Fig. 18 Jean-Honoré Fragonard, *Gardens of the Villa d'Este at Tivoli* (Wallace Collection, London), as backdrop to Mozart's *Marriage of Figaro* (London Records).

to the wayward Count, who has just finished accusing her of unfaithfulness. Caught in his infidelity and now thoroughly chagrined, he begs for her pardon. "I am kinder and say yes" (*"Più docile io sono, e dico di si"*) replies the forgiving Countess in the most heavenly absolution ever pronounced through music.

It has been said that the ultimate goal of art is to reconcile us to life. If so, then nowhere is that reconciliation more inviting or more assured than in these ever-refreshing Gardens of Love by Rubens, Watteau and Fragonard. In these worldly, secular, and overtly sensual settings, we are offered glimpses—as in the novels of Andrew Greeley—into Eden redeemed, heaven-on-earth, where divine and erotic love, *Agape* and *Eros*, are revealed to be but two reflections of the same Face.

Notes

[1]For a review of previous interpretations, see J.S. Held, *Rubens Selected Drawings* (New York, 1986) 151. See also, E. Goodman, " *Rubens's Conversatie à la Mode:* Garden of Leisure, Fashion, and Gallantry," *Art Bulletin*, LXIV (1982) 247-248.

[2]G. Glück, "Rubens Liebesgarten," *Jahrbuch der Kunsthistorischen Sammlungen in Wien*, XXXV, (1920-21): 7-98.

[3]A. Glang-Süberkrüb, *"Der Liebesgarten: eine Untersuchung über die Bedeutung der Konfiguration für das Bildthema im Spätwerk des Peter Paul Rubens* (Bern, 1975), 13-35.

[4]Leo Steinberg, in public lecture at Columbia University, November 1977.

[5]J.S. Held, *The Oil Sketches of Peter Paul Rubens*, (Princeton, 1980) 400-401.

[6]H.G. Evers, *Peter Paul Rubens*, (Munich, 1942) 339-348.

[7]Goodman 247 ff.

[8]Letter to Nicolas-Claude Fabri de Peiresc, dated 18 December 1634; see R.S. Magurn (ed.), *The Letters of Peter Paul Rubens (Cambridge, 1955)*, 393.

[9]See W. Liedtke, *Flemish Painting in the Metropolitan Museum of Art*, (New York, 1984) 176-187. Cf. my review in *Burlington Magazine* (July 1986) 515-516.

[10]J.S. Held, *Rubens Selected Drawings* (New York, 1986) 151.

[11]Held 151.

[12]See O. Banks, *Watteau and the North: Studies in the Dutch and Flemish Influences on French Rococo Painting* (New York, 1977).

[13]D. Posner, *Antoine Watteau* (Ithaca, 1984), 69.

[14]Posner, 79-80.

[15]From T.S. Eliot, "Burnt Norton," stanza II, lines 16-22.

[16]M. Levey, "The Real Theme of Watteau's *Embarkation for Cythera*," *Burlington Magazine*, CIII (1961): 180-185. Cf. D. Posner's recent—and unconvincing—revision of Levey's thesis, in *Watteau*, 188-195.

[17]This detail is crucial to Levey's interpretation: M. Levey, 185.

[18]See D. Posner, "The Swinging Women of Watteau and Fragonard," *Art Bulletin*, LXIV (1982): 75ff.

[19]*The Frick Collection, an Illustrated Catalogue*, II, New York, 1968, New York 114.

[20]D. Posner, "The True Path of Fragonard's 'Progress of Love'," *Burlington Magazine*, CXIV (1972): 528 ff. Cf. sequences proposed by F. Biebel, "Fragonard and Madame du Barry," *Gazette des beaux-arts*, LVI (1960): 207 ff; and W. Sauerländer, "Über die Ursprüngliche Reihenfolge von Fragonards 'Amours des Bergers'," *Münchner Jahrbuch der Bildenden Kunst*, XIX (1968) 127 ff.

[21]The Frick Collection 114.

[22]W. Sauerländer 143 ff. Cf. D. Posner, "True Path," 529.

PART SIX

Chin Music:
Popular Storytelling As The
New Oral Tradition

Michael T. Marsden

"Storytellers make us remember what mankind would have been like, had not fear, and the failing will and the laws of nature tripped up its heels."
—William Butler Yeats

Few areas of human endeavor have been as misunderstood or maligned as the popular storytelling process. Yet few such areas of artistic effort have reached more people than the simple but complex art form of popular storytelling. In the minds of too many literary critics popular storytelling is located somewhere between "folklore" and "literature", with uncertitude about its location resulting in its being assigned to the scrap heap reserved for those activities deemed crass commercialism. It fails as "literature", they say, because it is not stylistically sophisticated. It fails as "folklore", they add, because it exists in the commercial world of paperback publishing. Making chin music for the mass audience is considered unartistic, pandering craftwork. No wordsmiths these scribbling entrepreneurs. The purpose of this essay is to inquire into the nature of the popular storytelling process and to assess its value for contemporary society.

One of my basic theories about popular storytelling is that the more "literary" a popular writer becomes, the more that removes the writer from the audience being served. In fact, the popular storyteller is successful in direct proportion to the closeness maintained with the oral tradition, not the literary tradition. The model is that of a dedicated popular writer "speaking" his stories to a group of interested listeners. Given the economic realities of reaching a significantly large audience to earn a living, the storyteller working in the print medium keeps the focus on the oral stories as the model, not the stylized narratives of the printed page. The result is that those storytellers who succeed in the mass marketplace are those who keep true to the rhythms, tones, and structures of the oral tale. Literary critics approaching popular literature have for the most part been using the wrong tools.

The basic image which emerges from the story of any successful popular writer is that of a storyteller sharing a deeply felt tale with a friendly and willing audience. Most popular writers I have researched maintain a strong personal correspondence with a good number of their readers because they are truly interested in the exchange and because that very exchange informs their writing. They also appear on talk shows to further encourage this audience identification. In effect, they have learned to carry on a continuing conversation with their readers by using and sometimes redirecting the mass media. They make their own rules because continuing conversations with their readers demand it.

Popular narratives exist primarily in the world of feeling. This is not to suggest they are devoid of intellectual content. Rather, they are emotional renderings of complex human experiences and not intellectual articulations of unknowable realities. They exist to "move" people out of self-isolation and back into the warmth of human interconnectiveness.

Popular storytellers happily work within genres which are continuing, unfinished narratives. As genre theorists note, the genre story is not complete in itself; it is a gradually unfolding story which because of complexity of the telling is never complete. Each version reveals both the past tellings of the tale and adds to those to help complete an epic narrative. The process requires constant interaction between artist, artifact and audience, resulting in a co-creative process unmatched in the so-called "high" arts.

The popularity of certain genre stories can be explained, as John Cawelti has noted, by the fact that they seem to fulfill more social and psychological needs than do other story forms. But that does not explain their origin. Evidence is strong for the proposition that genre stories are the result of collective audience sentiment and that popular storytellers are those who can interpret the pressing societal concerns and values and present them within the most effective narrative structure. Genre stories have a very special function in society because they have been developed to allow a society to "escape into" its problems by restructuring them so they can be dealt with in an acceptable and non-threatening manner. Good wordsmiths structure their tales according to culturally preconceived patterns. (A most perceptive student pointed out to me a few years ago how the structure of UFO captivity narratives was essentially the same as that used for many of the early Indian captivity narratives).

The popular storytelling process rekindles our sense of belonging to the human condition and helps to protect against the isolation of the study which occurred following the introduction of the printing press into Western culture. Popular storytelling is a counteractive force against the separateness print brought into the world when it allowed the speaker to become physically separated from the listener. The rise of individualism in Western culture clearly parallels the rise of print. The law becomes distant and impersonal as it relies upon the written record and not the spoken tradition. Neither an isolated figure "experiencing" literature nor a passive escapist, the reader of popular literature is a caring, feeling and thoughtful member of a large audience who knows a good story and a good storyteller when presented with them, and who is humble enough to allow the chin music to work its magic now and then. Instead of trying to condemn popular storytellers for what they are not and what they do not do, we should be preparing an ode to those who assist in reuniting readers in both a secular and a sacred way with the human community.

The popular storyteller is more like the anonymous folk artist than the contemporary writer of "literature" who mails off his interpretations of life to the world from the confines of a hidden study. It has always been interesting to me to find out how approachable most popular writers are; they welcome contact with their readers as they strive to perfect their craft and strengthen their perceptions of the world they and their readers inhabit. Popular storytellers have learned the ultimate discipline—that of sublimating their private imaginations to the needs of the public imagination. It is, of course, the force of their private imaginations struggling for expression under the strength of inherited story traditions which gives their stories "fire." Their role as public figures is one of arbitrator and encourager. They serve to broadcast consensus values and attitudes while also narrowcasting a vision of future possibilities.

The "fire" which drives a popular storyteller is an interesting force. It is my theory that the popular storyteller's fire, which is the major tie to the oral tradition, is diminished in direct proportion to the writer's emphasis on stylistics. It is the "fire" of a popular storyteller which the readers most readily respond to as they seek out voices for their longings among the many offered on the paperback racks.

This is certainly a different perspective on the popular storytelling process than that promulgated in most literary circles. Large portions of popular literature are ignored by the literary critics and scholars because they are seen as damnably formulaic. The problem is one of not perceiving subtle but crucial dissimilarities between individual examples of a particular story form. The trained student of popular literature can perceive and assess significant differences between two examples of a particular genre. But for the untrained, prejudiced observer, it is impossible to entertain the possibility that a formulaic piece of literature could have distinctive qualities which allow it to both contribute to the further development of a genre story form while at the same time reinforcing previous story patterns. The apparent and remarkable paradox of the popular narrative is that the very constraints it operates under provide it with remarkable freedom. An individual example of a genre story assumes that the reader is familiar with an elaborate story tradition and then can build upon that tradition. What is seen by most literary critics as artistic limitation in the genre story form is in fact a liberating process for the storyteller who wishes to work new magic within the context of a well defined tradition. The formulaic writer of genre stories is thus the freest of all writers because of the rich tradition within which he/she operates.

It can be argued that because of its well established traditions which can win and hold a large audience, the popular story form is actually able to take bolder steps towards narrative innovation than the less conventional story form which has to spend a good deal of time and space establishing the reference points for writer and reader. Where an individual example of a genre story takes them depends upon the mutual understandings and agreements of storyteller and audience. Popular stories do as much to expand our understandings as they do to confirm our prior experiences. They become part of the cultural glue which binds the audience to the human community.

It is interesting how often a popular storyteller will in conversation convey the experience of the story actually taking control at a certain point in the creative process. It is almost as if the author is a conduit and not the true source of the energy. Seemingly having a life force of its own, the popular story begins and ends with the audience; the popular storyteller apparently mediates between the worlds of the collective imagination and the particular set of circumstances which define the story.

As noted by Jeff Okkonen, a reviewer of a new edition of Cree Indian tales, the Cree Indians believed a story lives for a time in this world and then inhabits a person. When the story is retold by that person, it again lives. So with the popular story which lives for a time in the world, inhabits a popular storyteller, and through his/her artistry is again given life.

Popular narratives do not move people through a single experience. Rather they move people slowly through time and circumstances into a new awareness of their collective reality. There is an essential conservatism about the popular storytelling process since its main purpose is to socialize people into the shared traditions and values of the society, to make them aware of the cares and concerns, hopes and dreams, fears and nightmares of a people, not just an individual. The role of the popular storyteller is to be a friendly voice telling the audience what they already half-know. The popular storyteller provides a reasonable shape and structure for unreasonable truths. Providing linkages between our several worlds of experience, the popular storyteller brings the audience back to the communal hearth with tales which reach into the human mind and heart. No mean vocation this sacred role of human reintegration.

In addition to shoring up traditional attitudes and values, the popular storytelling process can, as several theorists have pointed out, function as a way of confronting changes in society and assisting the audience in coping with them. The fear of change is thus reduced because the change itself is presented within the context of a familiar story which seems ever so slightly new. Whether set in the past, present or future, the popular narrative can also examine less acknowledged and often hidden areas of human experience in a way which provides the audience with a surrogate experience minus the risk which would otherwise be involved.

An often misunderstood aspect of the popular storytelling process is the necessary balance which the storyteller must strike between conventional elements and inventional elements. Certainly no one has commented more fully on this topic than John Cawelti. But it is useful to review and expand upon his analysis. Every popular artist utilizes conventional elements with which the audience is familiar. But the popular artist must also utilize inventional elements to provide the necessary challenges the audience needs to maintain interest. The artistry occurs in the balance between the "old friends" and the "new acquaintances" each storyteller strikes in the narrative. The metaphor which seems to work best at explaining this balance is that of meeting an old friend. We revel, at least temporarily, in reliving past, shared experiences with our old friend. But we also eagerly await the "new news" we expect the old friend to share with us about life between visits. A friendship can only be based on a constant balance of old understandings and new awarenesses if it is to thrive. Formulaic conventions, like old experiences, can be retold in a creative manner; often it is the juxtaposition of conventional elements in a narrative which can be highly creative and challenging for an audience. The fact that certain forms of artistic expression have a higher frequency of "invention" while others tend to be characterized by the presence of "convention" speaks not to the artistic merit of the individual works, but to the relationships between artist and the audience.

It is most unfortunate many of those in literary circles insist on suggesting that popular writers are not "serious" writers; popular storytellers could not be more serious about their vocation. And although the audience is certainly seeking entertainment, they are equally serious about the quality of their fictional lives. There is, without question, a complicated, sophisticated conversation occurring between popular storytellers and their grateful audiences. Unfortunately, not many literary critics actually listen to the conversation.

In formula stories characters tend to become personifications because they represent forces not individuals. This particular fictional quality of the popular narrative has led many critics to condemn the world of popular fiction as inferior when in fact it is a world operating out of a different literary mode and aesthetic dimension. These "felt experiences" the popular storytellers weave are very often attempts to stretch the confines of a genre form in order to challenge the audience into new understandings in a non-threatening manner.

As most theorists on popular story genres would agree, they are above all else, "paradigms of ritual and order" which seek to provide important linkages between the experienced world, the felt world and the understood world. Popular storytelling has replaced traditional oral folk culture in the sense that it now conveys the shared traditions of a people who read rather than share spoken stories. The function remains the same—bringing people into the warm circle of the communal hearth.

Theorist Leo Braudy has noted that genre should be understood to function in the same way for the popular arts that tradition has for the classical arts. Formulaic genre stories can, in fact, be perceived as necessary constraints for the artist, lest the function and purpose of popular storytelling be forgotten. One of the truly useful lines in contemporary American film occurs when Dirty Harry near the end of *Magnum Force* says to the antagonist: "A man has got to know his limitations." And why? So they can be acknowledged and exceeded. Only then can the popular storyteller lead the audience forward to new understandings and appreciations of the human struggle.

This then is an attempt to describe and define the popular storytelling process which because it serves a bardic function in contemporary society has endeared itself to many millions of readers. The relationship between the writer and the reader is a sacred one, for it involves the soul as much as the emotions or the intellect. That the process engage the intellect and the emotions is important; but that the process move people from a state of relative isolation into the larger community of human concern and understanding is more important. The popular storyteller has been embraced by everyone but the literary critics who have consistently failed to understand the popular storytelling process and its functions in society. Lavishing praise on highly stylized narratives with little story content, these same critics have long since moved away from the warmth of the communal hearth and into the solitary forests beyond where shadows are often mistaken for life forms. Meanwhile, people are learning, loving and laughing as the wordsmith works the magic of the popular story.

Author's Note: I would like to thank the several enlightened theorists who have directly or indirectly influenced my own thinking on the popular storytelling process. I would also like to thank Madonna Coughlin Marsden, my wife, for sharing her insights into popular storytelling with me over the years.

The American Religious Imagination and Three Contemporary Imaginers: A Look at Mary Gordon, Tom McHale and Andre Dubus[1]

Joseph J. Feeney, S.J.

Some months ago, without ever quite planning to do so, Andrew Greeley and John Updike fell into a dispute about the religious imagination. It began in September, 1986, when both novelists addressed a *New York Times* literary brunch in Manhattan. Fr. Greeley, in explaining why a priest would become a storyteller and popular novelist, said that "the world [is] a metaphor for God" and that "God is radically present in the world." Stories and novels, then, are ways of telling God's love without trying to educate or indoctrinate. Even his novels' "mildly erotic" scenes, he continued, express God's love, for "sex...is a metaphor for God's passion" and a woman's gentle, attracting tenderness expresses the tenderness of God.[2]

These comments somehow disturbed John Updike, and two weeks later in a *Washington Post* interview he questioned Fr. Greeley's views. Greeley, he told the interviewer, had "talked of Catholicism as a kind of pantheism, as God in the moonlight and sunlight." He contrasted Greeley's "warm and present Catholic God" with his own "cold and distant one." Then Updike, an Episcopalian with a Lutheran background, clarified his own view of God—a view, he admitted, greatly influenced by Karl Barth. "All Christian religions claim that God is the creator," he said, "and so to that extent for all of us He's in the moonlight and sunlight." "But," Updike added, "He's also in the tiger's jump and the parasite that eats out your insides, and the AIDS virus and the wave that drowns you, so I'm not sure that... [Greeley's] particular formulation solves the problem of evil."[3]

Between the brunch and the interview, it seems, Updike's mind and imagination had refashioned Greeley's comments to the point of serious misquotation, and on reading Updike's comments Fr. Greeley was himself disturbed. The comments, he wrote, "bore little resemblance to what I said" for he did not "advocate pantheism" nor "talk of God as being in the moonlight or the sunlight." Rather, he was "merely describing in more popular language David Tracy's theory of the analogical imagination." Updike, he concluded, "has the right to his religious sensibility (and Karl Barth's world is bleak indeed)" but should not distort Greeley's own perspective or tradition."[4]

It is not my concern here to adjudicate this dispute between Greeley and Updike. Rather, I use their disagreement to raise the larger question of the religious imagination. In arguing about how to visualize and imagine God, Andrew Greeley and John Updike are, in reality, discussing the Christian imagination and its modes and varieties. How, they ask, should God be imagined: as warm or cold, near or remote, lover or ruler? Should God's action in the world be imagined through a process of analogy or through a sterner approach which finds God remote from his creation? And of course, though Greeley and Updike appeal respectively to a medieval and a Reformation perspective, both novelists, quintessentially American, are thinking and imagining and talking and disagreeing as Americans in an American context.

The American religious imagination is complex. How, one might ask, do Americans imagine religion? As people saunter along the street, what religious images float around in their heads? Are some imaginations totally secularized? When religious images appear in memory or consciousness, what are these images—a dark church, a walk by the ocean, the smell of incense, or a sermon on money? What sights, smells, sounds, feels, and tastes epitomize religion? Is religious music Mozart's "Ave Verum," or a Black Baptist hymn, or a guitar group? Is God "cold" or "warm," a lover or a judge? Is God a "he" or a "she"?

On a larger, comparative scale other questions arise. In America, what are the differences between a Lutheran imagination and a Baptist one, between an Episcopalian imagination and a Catholic one? Among a group of—say, Catholics— how differently do Tom from Chicago, Heather from Boston, and Ida Mae from Arkansas see, smell, and hear their religious experience? What about the immigrant Gelsamina, Ivan, Pierre, or lovely Bao-Nga from Vietnam? Or, how does an American religious imagination in 1660 differ from the romantic one of 1860—Increase Mather's from Ralph Waldo Emerson's? For a Catholic, how does a pre-Vatican II imagination differ from a younger one? Or consider a novelist, a theologian, a female C.E.O., and an archbishop: what are *their* different images and views of God and religion? How does the religious imagination change from the age of 8 to 16 to 40 to 87? Such questions go far beyond the disagreement of Andrew Greeley and John Updike, and lead to a new, vast, fascinating, and uncharted territory.

Some few mapmakers have investigated this land. Twenty-five years ago the late William F. Lynch, S.J., developed a theology of the imagination in his book *Christ and Apollo*.[5] During the last ten years John Shea, John Navone, S.J., and Thomas Cooper have written on the theology of story, and Andrew Greeley, writing as a sociologist, has done both a book called *The Religious Imagination* and a study of religious imagery as a "predictor variable" for political and social attitudes.[6] In 1985 Jaroslav Pelikan, struck by how the portrayals of Jesus in painting and general culture differed from era to era, published *Jesus through the Centuries: His Place in the History of Culture*.[7] More recently, the British journal *The Way* devoted its October, 1986, issue to "Images of God."

The religious imagination, however, still needs exploration, for much territory is uncharted. In this essay, of course, I cannot engage in major explorations or draw all the maps. Rather, I choose as my limits the United States, the contemporary era, and the Catholic imagination—a large enough land in itself. I will look, first, at some images of religion in America today, second, offer a definition of the religious imagination, and third, explore the religious imaginations of three contemporary novelists, Mary Gordon, Tom McHale, and Andre Dubus.

Defining: What Is the Religious Imagination

The wise definer, especially in dealing with the imagination, begins with examples. And so do I, going from the individual to the group. My definition of "imagination," though, will be broad: it will emphasize images, but also include the attitudes, values, and concepts associated with these images.

For examples I look first to my university, Saint Joseph's in Philadelphia, where I twice conducted an honors seminar on the literary imagination. For their final paper I asked my students to do an autobiography of their religious imaginations, a task they found puzzling and fascinating. One response, from a woman who was a physics major, was typical: "My inability to define...the nature of my religious imagination both troubles and astonishes me. I never realized that...my experience of religion was so real and important to me, yet so complex and difficult to articulate."[8] But articulate she did, as did her fellow seminarists.

The results were diverse. The students found some religious images universally appealing: a large church with pillars, incense-smell, and a great organ. Bible stories, especially of Mary and Joseph, affected their childhood imaginations, and one man remembered a grammar-school film about a prehistoric boy named "Kree" searching for a pre-Hebrew God. Some sacramental rituals stayed vivid: the Mass (they don't use the words "liturgy" or "Eucharist"), First Communion (its clothes and its kids in line), and Confirmation (his archbishop, one man noted, "put oil on my forehead, called me by my confirmation name, and hit me. I haven't liked him since"). Christmas and Easter affected them, and one woman had a supremely vivid memory of Christmas Mass: "That the feel of mink is a 'touch' of Christmas is due to my childhood experiences at Midnight Mass. As a child I used to wearily snuggle next to Mom (and her mink!) as I sat in church. I had no idea what could be as cozy as sitting in Mass, enveloped in mink, surrounded by song, and overflowing with joy. To me, the touch of mink, and the emotions it revives, is Christmas."

For one student eight years of public grammar school were imageless years, and C.C.D. was dull and hated. The group did not like Mass in a gym with folding chairs, and they gave mixed reviews to nuns and priests—some affection but memories of harshness. Grandparents were important; one grandmother's room "was always dotted with beatific portraits of Jesus." Since both she and Jesus had serene, glowing faces, her grandson "used to think in a vague sort of way that the two of them were related. She was a sort of sacred figure to me." Family deaths and cemeteries also touched their imaginations, and they continued to maintain contact with the dead: one woman, just accepted to medical school, drove to the cemetery to tell the news to her grandfather—"Poppop." She found her grandmother already there, also to give him the good news.

High school and college brought new images, and some students stopped visualizing God and turned to the human Christ for images. One man wrote that for him "God always wears jeans." A woman realized to her dismay that her religious images were increasingly supplied by TV. Interestingly, only one student mentioned the devil, whose image went from the "traditional ugly humanoid with the horns," to a dragon, to "God's pet monster," to a "dark and sinister...monstrous figure" who inhabited places like bedroom closets, and finally to the recognition of evil in the world. Such examples could go on, for this assignment opened floodgates to the students' past. But, as I work towards a definition, I look to the broader adult population and try to describe some—just a few—of the varieties of the American Catholic imagination.

One day in the summer of 1986 I informally jotted down some types of the adult Catholic imagination and, having suddenly become a taxonomist, I had a collection of fifty-five modes. I have since added to the list. Here, to indicate my approach, I briefly describe four varieties, or modes, of the religious imagination. Each mode offers a way of representing God and religion, and each mode operates regularly in many Americans. An individual, I believe, usually mixes together several modes of religious imagination, with two or three predominating in each person. As examples, I offer four modes, and I name them (1) the esthetic mode, (2) the financial mode, (3) the ritual mode, and (4) the athletic mode. Each mode—including the financial and athletic varieties—is truly imaginative and creative, a personal way of visualizing and humanizing God. Every individual believer has, consciously or not, developed an individualized way of imagining God and religious experience.

(1) The esthetic mode approaches religion in terms of sensual beauty. Religious experience is characterized by sweet incense, Bach preludes, brocaded vestments, and soaring dark churches with lace altar cloths and multiple candelabra. Such Americans prefer to worship in tasteful cathedrals or exquisite convent chapels, and on a European vacation they find bliss in Vienna (in the Hofburg chapel with the Vienna Choir Boys) or in a solemn papal Mass at St. Peter's in Rome. Religion and God are best celebrated through beauty and spectacle, done supremely well. This esthetic mode, at its best, is a way of contacting God through beauty. It has inspired Chartres, the *Sainte Chapelle* in Paris, the York Minster, Gregorian Chant, and Beethoven's *Missa Solemnis*.

(2) The financial mode applies to religious experience a secular imagination which is filled with images of money, investment, or trade. Priests of this mode often talk about "paying off the debt," prefer to be pastors in a wealthy suburb, and rank parishes by their Sunday collections. Parishioners see the pastor as the "money-man," and the more cynical (or realistic?) remember Sunday Mass as the time for sermons on money. Financial exchanges loom large: bingo, Mass cards, letters of appeal with prayers promised in return. Such a mode involves a *quid-pro-quo* mentality: prayers buy a successful exam; a statue on the windowsill buys good weather; a man prays, "If you cure my wife's cancer, I'll never drink again." This mode also affects theology, for the concept of "redemption"—"buying-back"—

grew from the image of ransoming a person or buying a thing back for a price. By way of variation, a Deuteronomic editor both accepts this mode and plays against it: "Yahweh has brought you into the land...[which has] great and prosperous cities not of your building, houses full of good things not furnished by you, wells you did not dig, vineyards and olives you did not plant." Surely, he argues, Yahweh's action was generous. But then he calls in the debt: "When you have eaten these and had your fill, then take care you do not forget Yahweh.... You must fear Yahweh your God, you must serve him."[9] And the Gospels speak of Christ using this mode of imagination when, for example, he talks of "the hundredfold."

(3) The ritual mode delights in formal services and in the sacraments, whether or not the ceremony is esthetically pleasing. (This mode, I might note, differs from the esthetic mode. Here the appeal is ceremony and form; for the esthete, it is beauty.) This ritual mode esteems ashes, blessed palms, holy water, novenas, signs of the cross, First Communions, May Processions, and Midnight Mass at Christmas. At worst this mode produces superstition—some repeated fixation. But at the best and deepest level God is contacted through ritual, and the ritual is a sacrament— an encounter with Christ and a means of grace. Through a ritual such people link their own experience with that of Christ and interpret their experience in terms of God's action as reenacted in the ritual.[10] On a larger scale this ritual mode—and its deeper aspect, the sacramental imagination—affect whole communities when on major feasts a people's religious past and present belief are reenacted in rituals which bring a renewal of hope for the whole community.

(4) The athletic mode is usually a male phenomenon, and is very American. Such a mode sees God as the Great Coach and life as an important game (football, somehow, is the customary game). The trophy, of course, is heaven. Superbowl Americans love this appeal; it fits our religio-political need to win, to say "We're Number One." (I might note how hierarchical, power-oriented, and success-conscious is this mode of the religious imagination.) Sermons or invocations based on this model are particularly fervent—even obsessed—and in one of his novels Tom McHale parodies a sermon on God as the "Great Coach." St. Paul, interestingly, exemplifies this athletic mode when he tells the Corinthians, "All the runners at the stadium are trying to win, but only one of them gets the prize.... All the fighters at the games go into strict training.... That is how I run, intent on winning; that is how I fight, not beating the air." Paul's favorite sports, it seems, are racing and boxing.[11]

Such are four varieties of the religious imagination. Many others could be added: the ethnic (Irish *or* Italian *or* Polish, etc.) mode, the moralistic mode, the peace-movement mode,[12] the power mode, the profanity mode (an occasional "Jesus Christ" or "By God"), the erotic mode as in the "Song of Songs," or that last vestige of the religious imagination which reduces belief to place names: San Francisco, Santa Barbara, Mission Dolores.

Clearly, the religious imagination is multiple and varied; my examples have ranged from college-students' remembrances to California place names. But before examining three specific varieties—the imaginations of Mary Gordon, Tom McHale, and Andre Dubus—I should define the phrase "religious imagination" as I understand it. By "religious," I mean "pertaining to the divine and to those beliefs and observances which deal with the divine."[13] In using the word "imagination" I stress images but do not limit the word to them; while emphasizing the physicality of sight, smell, touch, taste, and hearing, I include also the ideas, views, attitudes, and affections attached to or associated with such sensations. (In an individual, "imagination" is more internal than "sensibility" and more ordered than "consciousness.") Thus, adapting the first part of my definition from Coleridge and I.A. Richards, I use the word "imagination" to mean the following: (1) the production or memory of vivid images, (2) the inventive faculty which brings together elements not ordinarily connected,[14] (3) the resulting patterns of related images, and (4) the attitudes, values, and concepts associated with these images and image-patterns.[15] I offer one illustration: when I write of the religious imagination as "financial," I stress images of money, but I also include love of money, and some knowledge of finance; such images, attitudes and concepts, by the creative process, become linked with religion, so that when such a person talks about religion his images, metaphors, and even language are drawn from money and business.

One final preliminary note: to have a religious imagination does not require religious belief. An atheist can imagine religion equally well in terms of Beethoven's *Missa Solemnis* or in terms of a grasping pastor. Again, as perhaps in the case of James Joyce, a religious imagination can be a remnant of lost belief without any metaphysical or religious significance.[16]

Three American Imaginations

A surprising number of American fiction-writers, whatever their current beliefs, stand in or come from the Catholic tradition. The dean of such writers is surely Walker Percy, but contemporary "Catholic" writers (i.e., those born in the past seventy-five years) range from Mary McCarthy through Jack Kerouac to Donald Barthelme and Don DeLillo. They include such writers as Flannery O'Connor, J.F. Powers, William Kennedy, John Gregory Dunne, Elizabeth Cullinan and David Plante. I count about thirty novelists of the Catholic tradition, and for this study of the American Catholic religious imagination I select the fictions of three, Mary Gordon, Tom McHale, and Andre Dubus.

Mary Gordon, born in 1949 and a feminist, is best known for her three novels, *Final Payments* (1978), *The Company of Women* (1980), and *Men and Angels* (1985). She has also published stories, essays, and reviews, and has collected twenty of her stories (dating back to 1975) in *Temporary Shelter: Short Stories* (1987).

Gordon's three novels instantly show her religious imagination, for each has an aggressively religious opening. *Final Payments* begins, "My father's funeral was full of priests. Our house had always been full of priests."[17] *The Company of Women*'s initial sentence is equally churchy: "Felicitas Maria Taylor was called after the one virgin martyr whose name contained some hope for ordinary human happiness."[18] *Men and Angels*, finally, begins with a woman opening her Bible and reading Isaiah. Each opening, by happy chance, indicates a major mode of

Gordon's imagination—an imagination which is clerical, steeped in the Catholic subculture, and scriptural.

Priests abound in Gordon's first two novels. In *Final Payments* her heroine, daughter of a widowed college professor, grows up with priests around the house; they are always "talking to my father, asking his advice, spending the night or the week, leaving their black shaving kits on top of the toilet tank, expecting linen towels for their hands" (p. 1). They argue about theology, tell in-house jokes, and ignore women; with a barb Isabel Moore remembers how "they determined the precise nature of Transubstantiation, fumbling for my name as I freshened their drinks" (p.1). Later, as a grown and rebellious woman of the late 1960s, Isabel is still clerical: she describes Fr. Daniel Berrigan as "the priest we yearned to seduce" (p. 14). She also maintains affection for an old alcoholic parish priest, Fr. Mulcahy, and flees to him in a crisis. And in Gordon's next book the conservative and stern Fr. Cyprian is a central character who brings unity and focus to the "company" of six diverse women. With so much attention paid to priests, Gordon's imagination is surely clerical.

Her imagination also focuses on a priest's normal *locus*, the parish, and on the Catholic subculture of neighborhood, school, and intellectual milieu. In *Final Payments* Gordon recreates a Catholic ghetto in Queens before Vatican II, where people read *The Sacred Heart Messenger* and talk about the Holy Name Society, the Rosary Society, the Catholic Daughters, and the parish nuns. Young girls clap their hands like nuns and listen to a radio program called "Sister Says." A woman's important friends are made through the church—at a Catholic private school or at Fr. Cyprian's annual retreat. Even the catty remark is Catholic: "Look at the shoes on the wife. Do you believe it? Bows. Manhattanville 1962. I bet she has a miraculous medal pinned to her bra" (*FP*, p. 23).

The bright people are no less ghettoized in their Catholic and parish cultures. When Professor Moore, a medievalist, speaks of "Western Civilization" he means "the Church." He is "the neighborhood intellectual" who spurns the larger Manhattan world of museum, opera, or the ballet, publishes only in Catholic periodicals, and is confident that he has "the truth" (*FP*, pp. 9, 40). Even the pictures in his home are religious: Holbein's St. Thomas More and Dürer's engraving of St. Jerome and the lion. To be sure, Isabel Moore reacts against the smallness of this world, but when Isabel and her friends leave the Catholic world and Catholic morals, they still miss the old *sureness*, the certainty, of their Catholic subculture. And that culture lives on in their memories, their conversations, and their imaginations.

A third mode of Gordon's imagination is its emphasis on scripture. While drinking coffee Isabel Moore reflects on St. Paul. Walking up a flight of steps she remembers the anointing of Christ's feet and reflects that previously "it was a passage I had not understood" (*FP*, p. 298). Again, spurned by her lover, she compares him to Moses and remembers his back as "an Old Testament back, a punishing back" (*FP*, p. 209). In *The Company of Women* a character interprets an insult in terms of Christ's suffering in the Garden. Most scriptural, however, is the novel *Men and Angels* in which a main character, Laura Post, reads the

Bible regularly, both to plan her actions and interpret their results. A religious fundamentalist, Laura had the Spirit come to her when she was 17 and is convinced that, in her words, "I am the chosen of the Lord." She even *thinks* in Biblical words and concepts: "She would be as wise as serpents," "It would be more terrible for them than for Sodom and Gomorrah," "It was the Spirit of the Lord inside her."[19] However Mary Gordon's characters deal with scripture, the novelist's imagination teems with images and stories and texts of the Bible.

One final mode of Gordon's religious imagination needs comment: its strongly moral dimension, often communicated in radical either-or terms. In *Final Payments* Isabel Moore must choose between total self-giving or self-enjoyment. One option, nursing her paralyzed father and caring for a former housekeeper, is heroic but involves inhabiting a dark house, smelling the sickbed, and growing fat. The other option brings a private apartment, chic wool skirts, a white-and-blue French coffee mug, and a protective lover. In *A Company of Women* young Felicitas must also make a disjunctive moral choice: on one hand, church pamphlets, holy water, and Fr. Cyprian's words, "You must hate the world and love God" (*CW*, pp. 45, 72); on the other, a gold-wrapped novel of Jane Austen, a handsome young professor at Columbia, and a young baby to love. In these two novels the choice is stark: heroic generosity *vs.* freedom and sense-pleasure, or bodiless spirituality *vs.* individuality and love. In *Men and Angels* the choice is, perhaps, easier: religious fanaticism *vs.* the joy of family, art, and beauty. In each novel the restraints— usually male and usually religious—are thrown off in favor of a new feminist freedom to love and to enjoy artistic and bodily pleasure. But in Gordon's disjunctive morality, religious belief and practice stand opposed to freedom and pleasure. Her heroines do not integrate religion and the world—a sign, perhaps, of a disjunctive spirituality underlying her imagination.

Though Mary Gordon still describes her religious life as going on in a Catholic framework, her Catholic images are disappearing. The "old" church, though secure, confident, and tasteful, is seen as cold and confining, and her characters rarely make contact with the "new" church; when they do, they find trendiness and poor taste.[20] Most of Gordon's early, abundant religious images come from her Catholic past; her recent religious imagination grows increasingly more secular. Her imagination, it seems, is gradually casting off the images and references of Catholicism.[21]

As novelist, Tom McHale inhabits a different world—a world of males, murders, and black comedy. Born in 1941, he won a certain notoriety through the wild humor of his first two novels, *Principato* (1970) and *Farragan's Retreat* (1971). Eleven years, four novels, and a few short pieces later, he died in Miami, a suicide. McHale's imagination is by far the most bizarre of our three writers, with its wild parodies of religious rituals and people. In his religious imagination, which like Gordon's grows more secular as his career progresses, four modes prevail: ritual, clerical, ethnic, and—encompassing all of these—wildly humorous.

In his early writings—a high-school sketch and a story in *McCall's*—McHale treats religious experience seriously and respectfully. By 1970, though, he begins to show both his quirky humor and his fascination with ritual. In "Why We Gave up Kidnapping"[22] McHale writes about a skid-row drunk whom a Scranton family hosts for Christmas-Eve Mass and Christmas dinner. The drunk enjoys Christmas Eve—glimmering tree, hearty dinner, and Midnight Mass with the family. But during the night he dies, his system shocked by lack of alcohol. In what was to become a typical McHale scene, Christmas dinner becomes a ritual of simultaneous merrymaking and death. At this stage, though, the religious rituals—Midnight Mass and the drunk's funeral Mass—are still solemn and straight.

McHale's tone soon changes. Some appalling action takes place during a religious ritual, and the contrast produces black comedy. At a wedding in *Principato*, for example, the groom's father, refusing to attend the wedding Mass because he hates priests, interrupts the ceremony with blaring car horns. In *Farragan's Retreat* the hero plots a murder during Sunday Mass in Philadelphia's Cathedral, and a few chapters later two Knights of Columbus, wearing plumes and swords for an honor-guard, start a duel in a church sacristy. *School Spirit* has a marriage scene where a Mafia don dies in church; at his death the bride's and groom's families fight before the altar for the privilege of removing the corpse. And in *The Lady from Boston* a bride is shot on the church steps. The wedding reception, however, still goes on; one character comments, "It was a dignified and marvelously upbeat kind of mourning. We went right on with the wedding reception as if the bride and groom were there with us. Drinks, food, and dancing to two bands." The groom "couldn't talk..., but he sure did dance.... Everyone stood around laughing and clapping with tears streaming down their faces."[23] Rituals—Masses, weddings, funerals, even a wake with food, drink, and laughter around the casket—offer McHale the perfect setting for a comedy absurdly mixing laughter, solemnity, and death.

McHale's imagination is also clerical, and he makes fun of clergymen and nuns. Irish-American priests are stiff, formal, and dull. One Jesuit, a Fr. Corrigan who teaches theology at Gonzola University, gives passing grades to dumb students who date his ugly niece. On the other hand, Italian-American priests are venal, passionate—and also hypocritical. Monsignor Allergucci, pastor of St. Igitur's parish, drives a sleek convertible, wears clerical-black swimming trunks, hears confessions by telephone, and works with a birth-control group. In *School Spirit* a group of teaching brothers cover up a murder at their boarding school. Nuns, too, are duplicitous, for a Sister Veronica gets engaged before she leaves the convent, and a Sister Winifred assaults visitors to her hospital for the crippled. Even the miracles of Lourdes are parodied, when Sister Winifred receives a pious postcard from a cripple on pilgrimage: "Today a man across from me got a very strange look in his eyes, unbuckled his leg braces, and stood up from his wheelchair. I think it was a miracle." The alleged "pilgrim" later tells his brother the full story: the man really did stand up but then "he fell flat on his ass."[24]

It is interesting to watch how McHale's religious—and ethnic—modes begin to disappear. In *Principato* the hero's dying father tells his son, "I think when you get your life rearranged, you aren't going to need the old Church as much as you used to. It'll be good to get rid of that crutch if you can" (*P*, p. 226). McHale's own religious imagination changes in the same way; the process becomes clear in his treatment of ethnic Catholics and (once again) of rituals.

In his first two novels, *Principato* and *Farragan's Retreat*, almost all the characters are Catholics of Irish or Italian background. The Irish are cold, selfish, and sexually frigid; the Italians are warm, familial, and passionate. The Corrigans and the Principatos illustrate the difference; Fr. Corrigan, S.J., and Monsignor Allergucci confirm it. Then in McHale's next two novels, *Alinsky's Diamond* (1974) and *School Spirit* (1976), his ethnic world expands. McHale keeps his Irish and Italians, but adds some American Jews and an occasional American of German, Polish or Scandinavian background. He even introduces some few French citizens and British subjects. But his last novels, *The Lady from Boston* (1978) and *Dear Friends* (1982), show a different McHale, for they are set in New England and have WASP heroes named Dwight David Aldrich and James Sutherland. Some minor characters are still ethnic and Catholic: Pasquale Mugiani, a detective, or Catherine McGivern, a maid whose breath smells of tea and stale cauliflower. In *Dear Friends* he even creates Mike Mallory, an Irishman from South Boston, who first wants to be a "philosopher-priest,"[25] later becomes a good cop, and finally dies a suicide. A few religious references also remain: Midnight Mass (on television), the mention of "a penitential season." Yet these last novels—and McHale's imagination—focus on a culture which is secular, Waspish, Bostonian. His humor is less wild, his despair closer to the surface. Interestingly, McHale's love of ritual endures this loss of interest in religion, and the rituals themselves become secular: a mythic Indian burial, a Christmas dinner, a formal dance of death under the New Hampshire sky. McHale still loves a ritual, but his ritual mode has become secular.

Tom McHale had one of the strangest Catholic imaginations in America, and critics called it fecund, "prodigal," and "spendthrift."[26] It was also irreverent, quirky, inventive. Perhaps his religious imagination never totally outgrew adolescence, as it bizarrely mixed religion, food, sex, and death. His imagination, as it were, liked to laugh in church. Focusing on rituals and ethnic groups, it highlighted the human gargoyles that Catholic practice had wrought.

The imagination of Andre Dubus is radically different in both development and content. Dubus, born in 1936, has published nine books of fiction, mostly short stories and novellas. Two of his finest works are *We Don't Live Here Anymore* (1984), made up of four interlinked novellas, and the short novel (or novella) *Voices from the Moon* (1984).

Dubus's imagination, unlike those of Gordon and McHale, grows more religious as his career progresses. His first novel, *The Lieutenant* (1967), though demonstrating a passion for truth, justice, and fidelity, has few specifically religious touches other than an occasional "my God" or "Jesus Christ." But his later work, dealing with marriages and families and loneliness, manifests a strong religious consciousness in both adults and children. His religious imagination might best be described as moral, ritual, and sacramental. His characters, in other words, often think in moral terms and see rituals and sacraments as points of contact with God rather than empty ceremonies.

In his novellas and stories Dubus frequently places his events in a complex moral context, though he deftly—and appropriately—avoids didacticism. Young people lose their virginity, and their parents fall into adultery. Genteel Southerners insult Blacks. Men and women sin against truth, fidelity, and justice. To be sure, Dubus's moral universe is not simple or simplistic as he probes motives and consequences. He is deeply compassionate to his characters and usually forgiving, yet can also write clearly that a woman "had committed herself to sin."[27] A young boy can *know* that God didn't want him to strangle a cat and yet strangle it, and a father can repeatedly dream about his aborted baby, pink and tender, lying next to him on a beach. Or again: after oral sex a high-school girl can feel her soul "recoil" and conclude that "If doing that isn't wrong, then I do not know what is."[28] In Dubus's fiction the actions are often vivid or shocking, but the framework is moral.

Dubus, too, occasionally makes more general moral statements. In "Rose" his narrator pointedly distinguishes two varieties of Catholics—those who understand Catholicism as the imitation of Christ and those who define it as avoiding birth control—and in another spot he offers a poignant and telling definition of damnation: "If there is damnation, and a place for the damned, it must be a quiet place, where spirits turn away from each other and stand in solitude and gaze haplessly at eternity. For it must be crowded with the passive: those people whose presence in life was a paradox;... [who] witnessed evil and lifted neither an arm nor a voice to stop it, as they witnessed joy and neither sang nor clapped their hands" (*LWE*, pp. 194-95).

Besides his sense of sin, Dubus also has a strong sense of the sacraments as both rituals and encounters with God. Many of his characters habitually go to Mass—to folk Masses, big parish Masses, quiet weekday Masses, Midnight Mass at Christmas. For one person, the Eucharist is a way to avoid loneliness; for another, a way to praise God; for a third, a sacrament of love during five years of a bad marriage. One character even interprets his lovemaking in sacramental terms: "With all his heart he believed in [love], saw it as a microcosm of the Eucharist which in turn was a microcosm of the earth-rooted love he must feel for God in order to live with certainty as a man" (*AOC*, p. 169). In such words, dense as they are, Dubus shows that even in writing fiction he can be a theologian of the Eucharist.

He is also, in his way, a wise commentator on the Mass as ritual. For Dubus the Eucharist is not just a formal action or, as for McHale, a good setting for black humor. Rather, Dubus sees the Mass as a means of coming in contact with, and communicating with, God. In one story he explains its function *as ritual* through an eloquent metaphor: "Ritual," he writes, "allows those who cannot will themselves out of the secular to perform the spiritual, just as dancing allows the tongue-tied man a ceremony of love."[29] In *Voices from the Moon* Dubus probes even more deeply into the Eucharist through the character of Richie Stowe, twelve years old. Receiving Communion, Richie "felt that he embraced the universe." Later, he even interprets his own experience in a Gospel perspective, understanding his father's and his own tears in terms of St. Peter crying after the cock-crow and Christ weeping over Jerusalem.[30] In confession, too, Richie links his own sufferings with those of Christ as he comes to forgive his parents for their divorce: "Everyone had to bear a cross as Christ did,...but he saw now that...he had already borne the one for his childhood.... Two years ago his mother moved out and then they were divorced and he carried that one, got himself nailed to it,...and something in him died—he did not know what—but afterward, like Christ on Easter, he rose again, could love his days again, and the people in them, and he forgave his parents, and himself too for having despaired of them" (*VM*, p. 88). Such a personal identification with Christ, as communicated through the sacraments, shows the profound possibilities *in fiction* of what I call a sacramental imagination.

Like Mary Gordon and Tom McHale, Dubus shows other modes of the religious imagination. He can use religion in story-titles: "Contrition," "Bless Me Father," "Sorrowful Mysteries." He can (like Tom McHale) use certain religious phrases: "consecrated hands," "Holy Saturday," "state of grace." His characters can pray, or say grace before meals, or wear a religious medal, or even describe naval uniforms as "white as altar cloths" (*LWE*, p. 25). But Andrew Dubus is most distinctive, I think, since amid his powerful, compassionate, sexual, and ever believable storytelling, he both communicates a strong moral sense and expresses the human and religious power of a sacrament.

Much earlier, I used the metaphor of mapmaking to explain this study of the American religious imagination. The map I have offered is at best a quick land-survey, sketched with a broad pencil. Some hills and rivers have been noted, some plains and valleys drawn. The map is rough, with tentative boundaries and uncharted territory. But some patterns still appear.

The American religious imagination, first, teems with variety: the imagination— or, more accurately, modes of the imagination—can be clerical, ethnic, ritual, parochial, sacramental, financial, scriptural, athletic, and so on and on and on. Furthermore, the religious imagination of a person (and of a writer) shows itself to be dominated by several characteristic modes; for a novelist, these modes even serve as an internal signature for his or her work. A person's religious imagination, thirdly, is frequently—perhaps always?—in process of change; Gordon and McHale grow more secular, Dubus becomes more religious and sacramental.

Every man's or woman's religious imagination is immensely important, I believe, since it offers contact with God and myth and primal experience. Everyone's religious imagination, furthermore, is worthy of study as both a personal and a social phenomenon; even more worthy, perhaps, is the study of a writer's religious imagination since the poet or novelist or playwright is, by virtue of talent and craft, uncommonly conscious of imagery. If this imagination is studied biographically, the results will surely tell much about the images and experiences of a person's childhood and youth and adulthood. Finally, if the religious imagination is studied and understood in a social and cultural context—say, for example, through a study of the imaginations of Mary Gordon, Tom McHale, and Andre Dubus—, the results should offer insight into both religion and religious faith, and into both believer and belief, as they are found, alive and changing, in today's America.

Notes

[1]This essay, in shorter and somewhat different form, was the Jesuit Chair Lecture, 1986-1987, at Georgetown University. It was delivered there on March 30, 1987, under

the title, "Imagining Religion in America: Three Contemporary Novelists." It has also appeared, in shorter and different form, in *The Critic*.

[2]"Why a Priest Story Teller," ms. of a talk to the *New York Times* Literary Brunch, Plaza Hotel, September, 14, 1986, n.p.

[3]Mary Battiata, "John Updike, In Restless Pursuit," *The Washington Post*, September 30, 1986, p. D-9.

[4]Letter of Andrew M. Greeley to author, March 20, 1987.

[5]*Christ and Apollo: The Dimensions of the Literary Imagination* (New York: Sheed and Ward, 1960).

[6]See John Shea, *Stories of God: An Unauthorized Biography* (Chicago: Thomas More, 1978); John Navone, S.J., and Fr. Thomas Cooper, *Tellers of the Word* (New York: Le Jacq, 1981); and Andrew M. Greeley, *The Religious Imagination* (New York: Sadlier, 1981) and "Religious Imagery as a Predictor Variable in the General Social Survey," Plenary Session of Society for Scientific Study of Religion, October 26, 1984. For Greeley's reflections as a novelist, see "The Making of a Storyteller," *Thought*, 59 (1984), 391-401.

[7](New Haven: Yale Univ. Press, 1985).

[8]I here express gratitude to my seminar students, in 1982 and 1985, who have contributed to my thinking on the religious imagination. I offer special thanks to those whose work I have quoted: David Burns, John P. Lamond, Juliet A. Marciano, Gregory P. Plociennik, and Dr. Lisa M. Sheppard.

[9]Deut. 6: 10-13, tr. from *The Jerusalem Bible* (New York: Doubleday, 1966).

[10]An interesting example from the Southern Baptist tradition is Dilsey's deep identification with Christ during the Easter celebration in the last section of William Faulkner's *The Sound and the Fury*.

[11]1 Cor 9: 24-26. On boxing and racing see also Gal 2:2, 5:7; Phm 2:16, 3:12-14; 2 Tm 4:7.

[12]For examples of this perhaps uncommon imagination see William C. Spohn, S.J., "The Biblical Theology of the Pastoral Letter and Ignatian Contemplation," in "Jesuits and Peacemaking: A Symposium," ed. W.C. Spohn, S.J., *Studies in the Spirituality of Jesuits*, 17 (September, 1985), 8-10; and Denise Priestley, *Bringing Forth in Hope* (New York: Paulist, 1983).

[13]Adapted from *Webster's Seventh New Collegiate Dictionary* (Springfield, Mass.: Merriam, 1965).

[14]Denis Donoghue, *The Sovereign Ghost: Studies in Imagination* (Berkeley: Univ. of California Press, 1976), pp. 1-33, esp. p. 2; see I.A. Richards, *Principles of Literary Criticism*, 2nd ed. (London: Routledge and Kegan Paul, 1926), pp. 239-43.

[15]For the philosophy of the imagination which underlies this essay see Arthur Koestler, *The Act of Creation* (London: Pan, 1975), and specifically his theory of "bisociation."

[16]My wording here is taken in part from Thomas Dilworth, "David Jones and Gerard Manley Hopkins," in *Hopkins among the Poets: Studies in Modern Responses to Gerard Manley Hopkins*, ed. Richard F. Giles (Hamilton, Ontario: International Hopkins Association, 1985), p. 53. The full passage adds further clarity: "For Jones as for Hopkins, the Catholic faith is a medium of feeling and perception. It is not—as, for example, in the writing of Joyce—merely a residue of cultural symbolism devoid of metaphysical significance."

[17](New York: Ballantine, 1979), p. 1. Further references, using the abbreviation *FP*, will be included in the text.

[18](New York: Ballantine, 1982), p. 3. Further references (*CW*) in text.

[19]*Men and Angels* (New York: Ballantine, 1985), pp. 8, 9, 54.

[20]Carol Iannone, "The Secret of Mary Gordon's Success," *Commentary*, 79 (June, 1985): 62-3.

[21]For a similar judgment, see Ann-Janine Morey, "Beyond Updike: Incarnated Love in the Novels of Mary Gordon," *The Christian Century*, 102 (November 20, 1985): 1059-63, esp. p. 1062.

[22]*McCall's* 98 (December, 1970): 40, 120.

[23](Garden City, N.Y.: Doubleday, 1978), pp. 140-41.

[24]*Principato* (New York: Viking, 1970), pp. 36-37. Further references (*P*) in text.

[25](Garden City, N.Y.: Doubleday, 1982), p. 376.

[26]Richard Freedman, "Trouble in Memphis and Boston," rev. of *The Lady from Boston, New York Times Book Review*, March 5, 1978, p. 37; Mark Taylor, "McHale's Retreat," rev. of *Alinsky's Diamond, Commonweal*, 101 (March 14, 1975): 462; Paul Gray, "Mutual Loathing," rev. of *The Lady from Boston, Time*, Feb. 6, 1978, p. 91.

[27]*Adultery and Other Choices* (Boston: Godine, 1977), p. 153. Further references (*AOC*) in text.

[28]*The Last Worthless Evening: Four Novellas and Two Stories* (Boston: Godine, 1986), pp. 144, 152. Further references (*LWE*) in text.

[29]*The Times Are Never So Bad* (Boston: Godine, 1983), p. 165.

[30](Boston: Godine, 1984), pp. 10, 41-43. Further references (*VM*) in text.

Death And Revery in James T. Farrell's O'Neill–O'Flaherty Novels

Charles Fanning

James T. Farrell was born in 1904 and raised in a South-Side Chicago neighborhood that became the setting for much of his remarkable body of fiction. Filling to date some fifty volumes, this work includes hundreds of stories and four large fictional cycles: the Studs Lonigan trilogy, the O'Neill-O'Flaherty pentalogy, the Bernard Carr trilogy, and the Universe of Time sequence, of which nine volumes were published before Farrell's death in 1979. The first two groups, the three Lonigan and five O'Neill novels, share a setting (the South-Side neighborhood around Washington Park where Farrell himself grew up), a time frame (roughly, 1900 to 1930), and several characters. I believe that these eight "Washington Park" novels should be seen as comprising one grand design, with two contrasting movements: the downward, negative alternative embodied in Studs Lonigan, who dies pointlessly, and the upward, positive possibility embodied in Danny O'Neill, who lives to become a writer. The tragedy of the wholly inadequate critical response to Farrell's work is that *Studs Lonigan* has been seen as the whole story, when, in fact, it isn't even half of the story about Washington Park.[1]

With a wisdom uncommon in beginning writers, Farrell knew that before he could tell the second part of the story, so much closer to his own experience than Studs's, he had first to deal with an attitude that, had it been applied to autobiographical materials, would have negated his aim of objectivity: that is, the young artist's exaggerated hatred and rejection of his background. In part, *Studs Lonigan* is the exorcism desired by young Danny O'Neill when, in the middle of the Lonigan trilogy, in which he is a minor figure, he vows that "Some day, he would drive this neighborhood and all his memories of it out of his consciousness with a book."[2] Instead of the tight, fatalistic narrative drive of the Lonigan trilogy, the five O'Neill-O'Flaherty novels are diffused and episodic, and in this looser structure is embodied a broader, more open-ended, but still unsentimentalized view of urban society. Moreover, in his complex creation of the interrelated lives of the O'Neills and O'Flahertys, Farrell has provided the most thoroughly realized embodiment in American literature of three generations of Irish American life. The novels are as follows: *A World I Never Made* (1936), *No Star is Lost* (1938), *Father and Son* (1940), *My Days of Anger* (1943), and *The Face of Time* (1953).[3] Taken

170

together, they are a great achievement in characterization, setting, and structure, one that has not been sufficiently acknowledged.

The portraits of three generations of Irish Americans, from a nineteenth-century immigrant laborer to a twentieth-century intellectual and artist, are compelling in their fullness and definition. A strong-willed immigrant matriarch, Mary O'Flaherty dominates the early novels. An aging, retired teamster, her husband Tom is a quiet man who comes to life only in the concluding volume *The Face of Time*. Their children live out a range of responses to the second-generation ethnic dilemma at the turn of the century: cut off from faith in their parents' culture by shame and pressure to assimilate, they have had to make sense of the world on their own. Shoe-salesman Al O'Flaherty embraces Horatio Alger's dream of success by hard work and self-education. His brother Ned puts his faith in the simplistic anaesthesia of a hazy, pop philosophy, "the power of the wish." Margaret O'Flaherty is caught painfully between her Catholic training in the neighborhood and the jazzy hedonism of the Loop, where she works as a hotel cashier. Her sister Lizz, married to poorly paid teamster Jim O'Neill with a new child every year, retreats into a concentrated piety that insulates her from the constant crises of her daily life. A decent, pragmatic working man, Jim O'Neill fights tough odds to make a better life for his children, and loses to three paralyzing strokes. In *Father and Son*, he faces uselessness, boredom, and death with heroic courage and dignity.

In the third generation, the main character is Lizz and Jim's son, Danny O'Neill, a slightly younger South-Side contemporary of Studs Lonigan who takes another road—out of Chicago and toward understanding and control of his life. Danny's environment is less stable than Studs's—the O'Flahertys are raising him because the O'Neills are so poor—but he is more intelligent than Studs, and he is driven by a persistent dream of accomplishment that crystallizes into the desire to be a writer. His story is the first American portrait of the artist in which the young man emerges from the Catholic working class.

As to setting, Farrell's characters exist in a place as fully and vividly presented as any in fiction. These books tell us in concrete detail what it looked, sounded, smelled, and felt like to live in Chicago apartment-house neighborhoods, what areas such as Washington Park provided and lacked for working and lower-middle-class urban Americans, and how this world changed over time, specifically from the late nineteenth century to the summer of 1927.

The concern of this paper will be the third, and least critically recognized, element of Farrell's achievement in the O'Neill-O'Flaherty series: its thematic structure. I believe that, without impeding its realistic narrative flow, Farrell has made this 2500-page sequence a single, coherent work of art by means of his brilliant organization of the material around two powerful themes. Two streams of experience mingle in these pages: the outer stream of social life, a chronicle of the works and days of three generations of Chicagoans, and the inner stream of consciousness, the perceptions of that chronicle and of themselves in the minds of the individuals living it. Throughout the series, the same two watershed experiences recur, always embodying major themes. These are death and illuminating revery. Deaths in the family constitute the central events of the outer stream and emphasize the most important social theme of the series, what Farrell has called "the tragedy of the worker, the central social tragedy of our times."⁴ Solitary reveries are the central events of the individual inner streams of consciousness in the series, and these emphasize what I take to be the most important internal, or psychological theme, the inability of these people to articulate to one another their real perceptions, insights, and feelings. Clarifications of life and honest self-assessment come only in dreams and daydreams, and they are never shared. I believe that Farrell's juxtaposition of these two themes conveys a central fact of life for the Irish American generations in his chronicle. The grim experience of unremitting physical labor beat something out of the American Irish—the gift and luxury of sincere verbal self-expression. Farrell was the first to recognize and to measure this loss. These themes gather force in the three last volumes of the series, in which three major characters die without having spoken their minds to anyone. Danny O'Neill is the exception here. He comes to understand the social tragedy of his family's thwarted lives and the psychological tragedy of their failure to communicate. Furthermore, his development suggests a third important theme of the series: with understanding comes the resolution to act; in Danny's case, to use art as a weapon against both tragedies. This essay will concentrate on the last three novels, but I want to begin by pointing out the importance of dreaming and death in the first two.

A World I Never Made opens in August, 1911, in seven-year-old Danny's mind, and finds him preoccupied immediately with death and revery.⁵ He thinks about dying and imagines what Hell would be like. (It's Sunday morning and he's worried about the consequences of missing Mass.) He also thinks about his Aunt Louise, "who had gone to Heaven only a little while ago," and imagines playing Buffalo Bill and "saving her from the savage Indians who wanted to tomahawk her." He also asks his Aunt Margaret to "read me about Danny Dreamer in the funny papers," and he imagines himself as Billy Sullivan, the White Sox catcher, warming up Big Ed Walsh for a game with the Philadelphia Athletics (3-8).

Constant through the novel, Danny's dreaming is both isolating—he is often alone and lonely—and predictive of his artistic career. The association with baseball is also important, and there is a larger pattern here that I want to mention in passing, one that connects the O'Neill-O'Flaherty series with the preceding *Studs Lonigan* trilogy. The Street and the Park emerge in the eight Washington Park novels as archetypal opposing options for the city child. Each represents a possible way of growing up, with its own pantheon of heroes. The choice of Studs Lonigan, the Street is the destructive element, characterized by gang life with its brutalization of finer instincts by pressures to conform: to fight, drink, dissipate energy and time, all in the service of an ideal of being "tough and the real stuff." The center of street life in Washington Park is Charley Bathcellar's poolroom on Fifty-eighth Street near the El station; its heroes are the gamblers, drinkers, and loafers who congregate there. The Park, on the other hand, is the creative and liberating element, the setting for a pastoral dream of release from the disorder of the streets and the claustrophobia of apartment living. The center of park life is the athletic field, a lined-out grassy place where rules are clear and enforced and success and failure are unambiguous. Its heroes are sports figures, from park league stars to the Chicago White Sox, the pride of the South Side.

Danny O'Neill's most vivid childhood memory involves having watched a no-hitter pitched by Chicago's Ed Walsh on the Sunday afternoon when *A World I Never Made* opens. This thing of athletic beauty is his first exposure to art, and it sinks in. Danny chooses the Park and practices baseball by the hour through his childhood years, mostly alone with a rubber ball and his imagination. Baseball is at once the most beautiful sport to watch and the least team-oriented of team sports, so it is not surprising that it fascinates this lonely, sensitive child. It is no more surprising that Studs Lonigan chooses the Street. A normally inquisitive boy, he shows signs of intelligence, even imagination, in early scenes of *Young Lonigan*. And yet he is weak-willed and easily led, and he assumes the facile and corrupting "tough guy" values of the street-corner society to which he is drawn after graduation from eighth grade. He joins the Fifty-eighth Street Gang and takes his models from the poolroom and the silver-screen gangsters at the Michigan Theater. It is significant that the recurrent, ever-receding dream of Studs's short, unhappy adulthood is of his one afternoon in the Park with Lucy Scanlan during their eighth-grade summer. So the twig is bent for both boys, and the opposition of Street and Park is central to Farrell's delineation of the complex mixture of character and environment that brings Danny to his vocation as an artist and Studs to his grave at twenty-nine.

To return to the themes being treated here, *A World I Never Made* ends for Danny, still seven at Christmas time, 1911, with two important, related imaginative experiences—a daydream of art and a nightmare of death. The first occurs on his way to the Loop with Aunt Margaret to see Santa Claus:

The telephone poles and buildings passed him like sixty. He saw himself as two Danny O'Neills. One of him was sitting in the elevated train that was going along, swish, zish. The other of him was outside, running, going just as fast as the train was, jumping from roof to roof, leaping all the way across the streets that the train passed, going on jumping and leaping and keeping right up with the train....

Away, right over another street, and wasn't that a jump, down over a street and over one two three four back yards onto a barn, and then, without stopping or falling, or getting wet by snow, springing right up onto the roof of a building bigger than the tracks, then down again about four stories onto a back fence. Boy, didn't he wish he could really make jumps like that, instead of just pretending that he was making them! (457-58)

This is an artist's dream of doubleness and control—to be able to step outside the self and walk easily through a recognizable world.

The second experience occurs on Christmas Eve, when Danny dreams of hissing snakes and "a boy as big as Mother, with a beard like a dwarf and a black suit like the Devil," come to carry him off and kill him (494-96). The connection between these two dreams is not forged until the fourth volume, *My Days of Anger*, where the use of art to counter death becomes an article of faith at the beginning of Danny's life as a writer. Indeed, the early memory of "two deaths in the family this year" (11), Old Tom O'Flaherty of stomach cancer and twenty-one-year-old

Louise of consumption, infuses *A World I Never Made*, and it rounds out the concluding description of "our first Christmas without poor Father and Louise" (502). Here Margaret, Al, and Mrs. O'Flaherty are left in the parlor, soothed by "Kathleen Mavourneen" on the new victrola. The tableau is not entirely comforting, however. They are all in the same room, but each is alone in the private dream that music evokes.

Death and dreams continue to be important in the second volume, *No Star Is Lost*, which, although it has the most beautiful title, is the bleakest of the O'Neill-O'Flaherty novels.[6] Its two most powerful sequences of events are Arty O'Neill's death from diptheria (compounded by poverty) and Margaret O'Flaherty's self-destructive drinking bout of several weeks.

Two-year-old Arty's death is a focal point for the social tragedy theme in the series, which follows the O'Neill family's painful struggle toward a better life. In 1914 and 1915, the time of *No Star Is Lost*, the O'Neills are living in a small cramped cottage at 45th and Wells, and on cold days the children "take turns sticking their feet in the oven." Jim O'Neill is working a back-breaking six-day week as a poorly paid teamster for Continental Express. After Arty gets sick, the doctor (a friend of Al O'Flaherty's) ignores several phone calls from the O'Neills, and the infant dies unattended. Nor will a priest come from St. Martha's, just across the street. "There's only one crime in this world, Lizz," says the heartsick Jim, "to be a poor man" (602). As Lizz is about to give birth to another child, Jim buries Arty with only little Catherine attending, and on the way back to the city from Calvary Cemetery, he sees middle-class homes and thinks, "In these homes the kids were happy and well-fed and had the care of a doctor when they were sick. And in these homes, the kids were alive" (620). That same day, the rest of the children are packed off to a public hospital (they all have diptheria), and Lizz bears a stillborn son. An agonized Jim asks, "Do I have to bury this? Two in one day?" (629), but the doctor calls an ambulance. At the end of the novel, Jim is sitting alone in the darkened cottage, watching "the first gray streaks of dawn through the window" (629).

Margaret is the most insecure, troubled, and unhappy of the O'Flaherty children. An affair with Lorry Robinson, a wealthy married man, increases her confusion, and she storms through a frenetic and tortured young womanhood, marked by excessive drinking and paranoid delusions of persecution. When Lorry breaks off their relationship, she goes on a terrifying drunk, a protracted psychological suicide attempt that nearly tears her family apart.

Throughout this period, Margaret and her mother engage in verbal battles of epic proportion and harrowing fierceness, most of them observed by Danny O'Neill, who turns eleven in the middle of all the trouble. To an extent, these fights are cathartic, for Margaret and Mrs. O'Flaherty articulate and thus somewhat exorcise their worst fears and criticisms of each other: ungrateful, immoral prostitute/daughter vs. overbearing, ignorant, greenhorn/mother. The sad part is that invective seems the only form of communication in this family where vestiges of eloquence remain, and this irony is a part of their larger tragedy. The O'Flahertys can articulate their anger, but not their love.

When a briefly sober Margaret comes begging forgiveness, her mother refuses to listen: "Tell your sorrow to Satan and the tinkers" (374). This rebuff sends Margaret off again, and she ultimately reels home comatose, incontinent, and hounded with DT's so horrifying that she tries suicide by turning on the gas. Vividly described in the novel, Margaret's Bosch-like delirium features snakes and devils, waiters pouring gin from phallic-shaped bottles, hideous animals, mud, slime, and excrement. Unfortunately, this nightmare vision is her only contribution to the pentalogy's catalog of dreams. In *My Days of Anger* Margaret reaches the age of forty, chastened and defeated, locked into a boring daily round, and convinced that she has been cheated out of her chance at life.

Farrell's most effective technique for revealing these characters, all of whom have such trouble expressing their deepest affections and motives aloud, is a kind of daydream-soliloquy. For example, in *No Star Is Lost*, Mary O'Flaherty has a fine long chat out in Calvary Cemetery with her husband, who has been dead five years. Recalling Ireland, the Mullingar Fair where they met, their first hard years in America, and the death of their first son, Mary realizes that this gravesite is "the only plot of ground that they had ever owned in America" (135). Suddenly Old Tom seems to be standing there with her, "a small old man in a white nightgown, with a slightly drooping gray mustache," and Mary begins to complain about Peg's drinking and running around: "She's a child of Satan himself, she is." She goes on to admit what she would never say to a living soul: she is sad because "I'll never be seein' the old country and me people again." Finally she reverts to her everyday self by administering a typical scolding to poor Tom, for whom even the grave is no protection. Having been annoyed several times by Lizz O'Neill's reports that her dead father has been speaking to her, Mary sets her husband straight one more time:

And Tom, don't you be going and giving all these visions to me daughter, Lizz, that she does tell me about. If you have messages, you give them to me. It's me that should get them, and not her. Don't you be giving your visions to her. If you acted like that when you were here with me on earth, I would have skinned you alive. I'm a hard woman when I'm crossed, Tom, a hard woman, and I'll make you toe the mark, dead or alive. You be comin' to me with your words and your messages. You're my man. When Lizz's man dies, let him come to her. (142-43)

Two more of Danny's dreams are related as well in *No Star Is Lost*. In one, he has another vision of being dead and in Hell. His "black" and "white" angels read off his debits and credits to the Devil, and just as he is plunged into the fire, he hears the black angel challenging the white to "Go back and be a guardian angel to the White Sox" (243). In the other, Danny's commitment to art is again suggested. He is grown up, "a man so big he could almost touch the ceiling," and walking with his grandmother through the neighborhood. "It seemed suddenly," in this dream, "as if there were a wind that cried like somebody he knew, a wind that cried like a voice" (269).

Having dealt briefly with the introduction of these themes in the first two novels, I want now to examine at greater length Farrell's presentation of failed communication through the conjunction of revery and death in the three later novels. Also to be traced is the major contrasting theme of Danny O'Neill's growth toward articulation through art.

In *Father and Son* Jim and Danny O'Neill are living only a block apart: Jim, with Lizz and their other children in their best apartment ever, at Fifty-eighth and Calumet, and Danny, with his grandmother at 5816 1/2 South Park Avenue. Here Danny gropes toward maturity. He goes through St. Stanislaus High School, graduating in 1923, and begins to take pre-legal courses at the night school of St. Vincent's College in the Loop. Finally, he enrolls at the University of Chicago, just across Washington Park but an intellectual world away from South Park Avenue, where he is encouraged to write in an advanced composition course. These steps parallel Farrell's own attendance at St. Cyril's (later renamed Mt. Carmel High School) at 64th and Dante Avenue, the night school at De Paul University, and the University of Chicago. During these years, Danny also holds down his first full-time jobs—at the Express Company where his father worked and as a gas station attendant. And most important for his growth, he experiences the deaths of his father in 1923 and his grandmother Mary O'Flaherty in 1927. Although the O'Neills seem finally to be out of the woods, thanks to Jim's promotion to dispatcher and their new apartment, their luck does not hold. In a matter of months, three crippling strokes, the legacy of his years of bone-wearying labor, render Jim O'Neill unemployed and helpless. As presented in this, the central novel of the pentalogy, Jim's life and death embody both the social "tragedy of the worker" and the psychological tragedy of failed communication.[7]

In the middle (exactly, p. 308 of 616) of *Father and Son*, Jim attends Anna McCormack's wake and is deeply frustrated by his inability to communicate with her grieving husband:

Aware of how deeply he sympathized with Old Mike, he couldn't think of anything worth saying that would express his feelings. When you most wanted to tell another man something, you were least able to do so. Jim felt a sudden and profound loneliness. He felt himself all alone in a world of men. The words he could say to another man, they did not get him closer to that man. Even with Lizz, he was still alone with himself, alone in the world.

All through the series, and especially as he feels death approaching, Jim struggles to express himself to his family.

His wife's often hysterical religiosity is a constant bone of contention. Lizz O'Neill stakes everything on the positive nature of suffering on earth as test and preparation for the afterlife, and her fatalism clashes with Jim's pragmatic, "God helps those who help themselves" approach to life. They often fight bitterly about her incessant visits and donations to the Church, which come at the expense of personal hygiene, housekeeping and sometimes meat for the table. Lizz walks the world in a dirty-faced daze, seeing visions of dead relatives and Satan under the bed, wishing that she had become a nun, and facing every exigency with blind faith in "God's will." Jim periodically cleans their apartment, only to find it dirty again within hours. The last time he does this, during his vacation after his first stroke, he becomes exhausted by the effort, has to take a nap, and dreams of sweeping and sweeping the floor with a new broom and never getting it clean.

Jim's other great frustration is Danny, whom he sees turning into a "dude," and forgetting that he comes "from poor people." One of Jim's greatest sorrows comes from sensing that, after the strokes have rendered him helpless and shambling, Danny is ashamed to walk down the street with him. Jim blames the O'Flahertys in part, but also himself, for having lost his son to his wife's family. Father and son try unsuccessfully to talk throughout this novel, but their only close moment comes when Jim asks Danny to recite Polonius's speech to Laertes. Shakespeare's words briefly bridge the gap between them, as Jim declares, "I'm your father, and I couldn't give you any better advice" (485).

Shakespeare, in fact, is Jim's companion and consolation. After his first stroke, he often sits up late alone, reading *Julius Caesar* and *Hamlet,* and struggling to understand his life and approaching death. The dignity and courage of his solitary questioning make him one of the most memorable characters in Farrell's fiction. Jim's thoughts range widely. He meditates on the mystery of having children, and on the teachings of his Church: "He liked to think that Christ was born in a poor man's home, and never in His life was He rich. ... A lot of people ought never to forget that." Feeling that "There wasn't a great deal of justice in the world," he tries anyway to tell his children to live right, all the time asking, "would doing right get them anywhere?" When the last stroke sends him permanently home from work, he knows he will never get better, and feels "that others didn't understand life and that he did. *Vanity, all is vanity.*" And when his doctor dies suddenly of heart failure, Jim's own situation comes clear:

Before this last stroke, he had feared death for what he would be leaving behind. Now he was ready to die, ready to face his God. His family would be better off without him. He was just a helpless old man taking bread from the mouths of his children, whose lives were ahead of them, while his was over with (514-15).

Jim's last weeks are filled with petty indignities. Another of his children, the third, is sent away to the O'Flahertys. Lizz suggests that he put himself in a public hospital. His son Bill takes over as head of the house, and contradicts him on a point of discipline regarding the younger children. He is shamed by a Christmas basket from a Protestant charity which the family is unable to refuse. He has to make an X to get money at the bank, and he loses a five-dollar bill in the street. People on the El think he's drunk, kids mock and mimic his limp, and an apartment-house janitor chases him away as a loiterer. But worse than any of these is the fact that he has no one to talk to. All of his thinking is done in silent revery by the parlor window. He is unable to share his struggle for meaning with another living soul.

Jim's last day, like Iván Ilých's in the novel's epigraph, is "most simple and most ordinary and therefore most terrible." At lunch, Lizz is full of Mrs. Muldoon's wake, where she stayed all night "because my heart bled with pity for her." When two of his children start arguing over the last bran muffin, Jim lashes out at the whole family: "You don't care about anyone else. You don't care about anything but gorging yourselves. All of you. What if your father is sick? What if your brothers work and put the bread in your mouths, none of you care" (592). Pointing an accusing finger at Lizz ("It's your doing"), Jim leaves the room to lie down, "too tired even to be angry at what had happened." These bitter words are his last. He lapses into coma and dies the next afternoon without regaining consciousness.

Father and Son also records Danny O'Neill's frustrated first attempts to articulate his thoughts. He fails with his father, of course, but also with his peers, most of whom continue to regard him as an odd-ball, a "goof." Danny is unable to tell a girl who is going to a different high school that he will miss her: "He couldn't say the words" (125). Nor is he able to talk honestly to himself, failing three times in junior high and high school to start a diary of his "real feelings." There are, however, some signs of improvement. With an O'Flaherty family fight raging around him, Danny is able to finish a story that he knows is good enough for the high school literary magazine. Also, Danny's reaction to his father's death is a climactic encouraging sign. At first, he is troubled because "he felt empty more than he felt anything." And yet he does recognize immediately two facts that restate the novel's main themes of social and psychological tragedy. First, he sees that "there was something tragic about his father. He told himself that his father was a man who'd never had a chance. His father had been a strong man, and a proud man, and he had seen that pride broken." Second, he sees that "he had never really known his father, and his father had never really known him" (601, 599).

These ending revelations mark the beginning of Danny's coming of age, which is completed in the fourth novel, *My Days of Anger*. Having crossed Washington Park to attend the University of Chicago, he is at once stimulated by new friends and the world of ideas. He writes his first honest diary entries and goes on from there to produce a torrent of fiction in an advanced composition course. He loses his faith, at first in a dream, and wakes up a non-believer, "free of lies" (215). Other liberating rejections follow: of a pseudo-Nietzchean friend, Ed Lanson, of the university, and of Chicago itself. At the same time, and gradually through the novel, Danny's "days of anger" (again the phrase is from Baudelaire) and confusion slowly evolve toward understanding of his family.[8] In this process, his grandmother's death in the spring of 1927 is the crucial event.

Mary O'Flaherty's death, like that of Jim O'Neill, also embodies a statement of the tragedy of failed communication. Throughout the series, Mary has been a classic immigrant matriarch, holding her family together by sheer force of will. She often describes herself as "a hard woman from a hard country." But the other side of the coin is that the hard years have left her unable to express love and sympathy to those in the family who are most in need: Margaret in her emotional crises, Lizz swamped by the demands of her own large family, and Old Tom O'Flaherty on his death bed. Nor has she shared her own fears and sorrows with anyone. As she approaches death in *My Days of Anger*—she is just back from the hospital with a broken hip, thinner than ever, and eighty-six years old—a last extended daydream (all of chapter 26, pp. 362-71) provides a summation of her character and concerns.

As memories of Ireland and her parents' generation flood back, Mary admits the pain of emigration that she has kept to herself for sixty years: "And, sure, wouldn't I be giving me right arm to be seeing the steeple of Athlone in the sunshine, ah, but it was beautiful and wasn't it tall? Indeed it was." Of course, she was saddened and frustrated by the news of her mother's death, "and there I was in Green Bay, Wisconsin, not knowing if me father had the money to give her a decent burial," and by the death of her own first child: "we christened him, the little angel, and he died, and what Christian name did we give him? And here I am forgetting the name of me own son, John...and his headstone is sinking into the ground."

There is a refrain running through Mary's mind in this lovely, lyrical chapter—the one word, "Soon." She knows her death is near: "I do see the old men with death in their eyes. Nobody fools me. I won't be long here." She can see the circle of her life closing: "The strength is gone out of me bones. here I am, and they take care of me just like I took care of them, and they carry me around like a baby." In a typical paradox, Mary now reveals that she has been kept going all these years by both love and love of a fight. "Last Sunday at dinner," she happily recalls, "I put me two cents in to keep them fighting away. And then I told me grandson, I told him, Son, I'm only fooling, and sure it's the fun of it I like. So I kept them at it for all they were worth." At the same time, she acknowledges her love and compassion for her family: for her husband—"Me poor Tom, your Mary that could run swift as the wind and sang you the songs that day of the Mullingar Fair is coming to you," for "me beautiful virgin daughter Louise...out with Tom in Calvary Cemetery," for "me poor son Al, carrying those heavy grips to pay all the bills," for "Lizz, me darling Lizz, the poor woman with all of those children, and one coming after the other," and even for Margaret, "wearing her hands to the bone caring for me and bathing and washing me, and cooking and caring for me and emptying me pots, the poor girl." And she also declares what Danny O'Neill has meant to her: "Me grandson, he's me son. Doesn't he call me Mother?... What's kept me alive, with me family raised all these years, but me grandson?" "I'm no scholar but I met the scholars," says Mary, and she is proud of her grandson's chosen vocation: "and sure it's the poet and scholar he'll be, and don't I know that they'll be saying what a fine man he is, and it's poems he'll write."

In the middle of this chapter, Mary is carried to the bathroom by Danny, who then returns to his typewriter and the book, his first novel, on which he is working. here the point of view shifts for the only time in the chapter, and the focus on Mary's consciousness is interrupted briefly by the thoughts of her grandson:

He wanted to finish this book before she died.
If he did and it were published, he'd dedicate
it to her. But she couldn't read.
    What was she thinking of by the window?
What went on in her mind?

Imagining answers to these questions is going to be Danny O'Neill's lifework.

Danny learns several important lessons from his grandmother's death a few days later. He is struck immediately by the incalculable value of time: "This life which he had been so spendthrift of, how precious it was." His youthful rebellion, especially against the Church, is tempered by understanding that "The sorrows of death remained, remained in the hearts of the living. ... He understood now why people did what he could not do, what he could never do—pray" (393, 392). Another sign here is that, on the morning of his grandmother's death, Danny kneels down, blesses himself, and pretends to pray with his family. This negates his earlier contention among his University of Chicago friends that he agrees with Stephen Dedalus' refusing to pray at his dying mother's bedside in *Ulysses:* "What has kindness got to do with conviction?" says Danny. "I won't bend my knees" (377). Even his belief that "it was unmanly to cry," gives way to the release of real emotion, and he sobs and calls out his grandmother's name.

Danny's part in the O'Neill-O'Flaherty series leads ultimately to the summer day in 1927, a month after his grandmother's death, on which he prepares to leave Chicago for New York and a new life as a writer. Walking home down Fifty-eighth Street from the El, perhaps for the last time, he feels the weight of Washington Park as "a world in itself...a world in which another Danny O'Neill had lived." Feeling that he has "finally taken off a way of life,...as if it were a worn-out suit of clothes," Danny now has confidence in the "weapons" of his writer's trade: "now he was leaving and he was fully armed." (In this, he echoes Stephen Dedalus, leaving Dublin for Paris in 1902 with his own "weapons" of "silence, exile, and cunning.") Danny now also has a mature understanding of his position as an artist in relation to his family:

His people had not been fulfilled. He had not understood them all these years. He would do no penance now for these; he would do something surpassing penance. There was a loyalty to the dead, a loyalty beyond penance and regret. He would do battle so that others did not remain unfulfilled as he and his family had been....

...Yes, he was the first of his family who could go forth fully armed and ready to fight. (401-02)

The last pages of *My Days of Anger* are a kind of litany to this place and this family, for the weight of both is embedded in Danny's consciousness, even as he leaves them behind. From the street, he turns to "the stones, the buildings" of the old neighborhood. He enters "the alley that he had known since he was a boy," pushes open "the broken backyard gate," and climbs the stairs into the O'Flaherty kitchen. Looking into his grandmother's room, he sees, along with her clothes still hanging in the closet, pictures of Christ and the Sacred Heart, a crucifix, a holy-water fount, and rosary beads—the symbols of her life-long Catholicism, which he has also left behind, but which he no longer scorns. Then Danny walks to the parlor in the front of the apartment to sit "brooding over his plans," and his mind here at the end of the novel comes to rest where his dreams have always been centered: "He listened to the summer wind in the trees across the street in

Washington Park." As a devoted reader of W.B. Yeats, Farrell may be making the connection so common to that Irish poet's work between the wind and artistic inspiration.

The first of the novels chronologically and the last to be written, *The Face of Time* is a perfect coda for the O'Neill-O'Flaherty series.[9] Opening in the summer of 1909, it brings the series full circle to the deaths of Old Tom O'Flaherty and his daughter Louise, the memory of which hangs over *A World I Never Made*. Also, in its rendering of Tom and Mary O'Flaherty's memories of Ireland and their early years in America, the novel returns to the very beginning of this family's story. The result is one of the finest American novels dealing with the felt experience of emigration from Ireland. In addition, the theme of failed communication gets its fullest statement here, in the characterization of Old Tom, who lives out a restless retirement, alternately bored and harassed, and dies of a painful stomach cancer. Feeling useless and used up, Tom submits quietly to his wife's nagging, admitting only to himself that "he loved his Mary but he didn't love her tongue" (14). It is clear here that coming out to America has affected the O'Flahertys differently. Tom seems not to have recovered from the early humiliations, while Mary has emerged stronger, though not always in attractive ways. In fact, her dominance has turned Tom into the forgotten man of the family. When a shared can of beer makes both of them melancholy, she stares across the kitchen table at him and asks, "What have I got but me grandson and me son Al?" Tom refrains from asking "if she didn't have him, too," because "living all these years with Mary, he had learned that many a thing was better not said to her" (34). When a family fight erupts, Tom makes no impression on anyone, and is ordered by his son Al to "get the hell out of here" (42). Even five-year-old Danny O'Neill is affected by his grandfather's lack of status at home. he wakes up one night frightened to find that his grandmother has gone out and left him alone in the apartment, and when she returns and reminds him that "your grandfather was here," Danny thinks, "He hadn't thought of calling Father. Why hadn't he thought of Father?" (134). And after Tom has been taken to the hospital, Mary remarks to Al that "Ah, Pa was no trouble. You'd hardly know he was in the house" (318).

At the end of the novel, the inability to communicate becomes pervasive. On the day of his hospitalization, Tom's voice fails and he is unable to say goodbye to Danny. Her voice "breaking," Mary tells her family to "let me be," and that night they eat dinner "in silence" (312-16). The old man doesn't live on for long in the hospital, and in a last daydream-soliloquy, he reveals all the sad secrets that he has never articulated: he has never felt at home in America, he is puzzled and embittered at having worked so hard and ended up with so little, and he wishes he could die in Ireland. Here is some of his final revery:

He'd wanted to tell Mary that he was afraid of America, afraid of it here in America, and, sure, if he told her that, what kind of a man would she be thinking him to be? Ah, she was a woman with nary a fear in her, not Mary. It was a source of wonderment to him that she had nary a fear in her heart, and the two of them, greenhorns if you like it, greenhorns in America in Brooklyn, New York, and Green Bay, Wisconsin, and

Chicago. The strange people he'd seen and they were Americans and not his own people....

Lying here in his hospital bed, when the pains weren't on him, he would think of all this, and think of what he came out here for. Sure, wasn't it to make money and marry Mary? Devil a lot of money he made, and until the children grew up it had been all they could do to keep body and soul together and put food in their mouths. And how would the children know what was in him and the work he had done, the saving of money for his own horse and wagon and for the plot of burial ground in Calvary Cemetery?

*   *   *

He furrowed his brows as he heard footsteps in the hall. Sure, when he first came to America, he would look at the people in New York and Brooklyn, New York with wonder in his eyes because they were Americans and he was in America. And not a soul on this earth knew how he was always wanting to go back and wishing he had never come out, and himself driving the horse and wagon and not knowing the names of the streets and wanting to ask this man and that for directions and not always asking because of his brogue and his not wanting it thought he was a greenhorn, and getting lost and not knowing where he was and wanting to go home to Ireland. (334-35)

After Old Tom's death in December, 1910, and before the August, 1911, opening of *A World I Never Made*, twenty-one-year-old Louise O'Flaherty dies of tuberculosis. Throughout *The Face of Time*, her pain and bewilderment mirror her father's. Her childish dreams of a romantic Ireland and love with "Prince Charming" go unshared, as do the shame she feels at having contracted "consumption" and her fear of dying. She is equally frustrated at not being able to talk honestly with the family, and especially her father: "she was afraid that maybe he would die before she said something to him that she ought to say, only she didn't exactly know how to put it into words. It was that she loved him and wanted him to know that she loved him, only she couldn't say that" (164).

The Face of Time closes with three final echoes of its major theme. During his family's last visit to his bedside, Tom can hear Mary and Margaret discussing his imminent death, but he is unable to speak. When the hospital calls with the news of Tom's death, Mary leaves the family and shuts herself away in her bedroom, to grieve and pray alone. Standing before his grandfather's casket in the parlor, six-year-old Danny O'Neill thinks, "There was Father. He couldn't talk. He was Father all right, and he wasn't Father." Then the novel (and the series as well) ends with a dying fall of incoherent sound, as Danny hears "whispering voices in the dining room, the low agonized sobs of his Aunt Margaret, and then the noise of a streetcar going by on Indiana Avenue" (366).

Through these five novels, a few large themes build to powerful, cumulative statement. Of central importance in that process are the clarifying but unshared reveries and unprotesting deaths of Jim O'Neill, Mary O'Flaherty and Tom O'Flaherty. Danny O'Neill's opposing movement in the direction of art provides effective counterpoint, but does not mitigate the force of the presentation of his family's tragedies. In fact, Danny's isolated battling toward significant speech serves, by its uniqueness, rather to underscore the problems—some internal, some imposed from without—of the culture in which he grows up. Moving, in *The Face of Time*, toward the end of her own short, lonely life, Louise O'Flaherty asks the largest question: "And was this the end of love, one going, dying, the way her father was dying? Must you, in the end, always be alone?" (321).

Thoroughly grounded in American, urban, and ethnic realities, the themes of Farrell's fiction emerge naturally from the context of a fully realized narrative world. He perfected an urban American plain style as the fitting mode for registering the thoughts and speech of ordinary people for whom self-expression came hard. (I would further suggest that for this prodigiously gifted intellectual, encyclopedically well-read and fiercely committed to the life of the mind, the forging of that style was a heroic effort of will.) The reward for Farrell's scrupulous adherence to the plain style is that in his best work an authentic, minimal eloquence wells up in the death-bed reveries of Jim O'Neill at his window on Calumet, Mary O'Flaherty looking out over the Park, and Old Tom O'Flaherty in Mercy Hospital. The results are consistent with what James T. Farrell saw as "my constant and major aim as a writer—to write so that life may speak for itself."[10]

Notes

[1]Recently, the critical tide has begun to turn. Excellent essays published in the past few years include the following: Ann Douglas, "*Studs Lonigan* and the Failure of History in Mass Society: A Study in Claustrophobia," *American Quarterly*, XXIX: 5 (Winter 1977): 487-505; Ann Douglas, "James T. Farrell, The Artist Militant," *Dissent* (Spring, 1980): 214-16; Robert James Butler, "Christian and Pragmatic Visions of Time in the Lonigan Trilogy, *Thought*, 55 (December 1980): 461-75; Robert James Butler, "The Christian Roots of Farrell's O'Neill and Carr Novels," *Renascence*, XXXIV (1982): 81-97. Farrell's thinking about Irish history and literature has been collected in James T. Farrell, *On Irish Themes* (Philadelphia: Univ. of Pennsylvania Press, 1982), edited with a brilliant introduction by Dennis Flynn. Most of the earlier, relevant criticism of the O'Neill-O'Flaherty series has tended to focus on two subjects, Farrell's development of characters and the contribution of the novels to the social history of the American city. This work includes the following books and essays: Nelson M. Blake, *Novelists' America, Fiction as History*, 1910-1940 (Syracuse: Syracuse UP 1969), 195-225; Edgar M. Branch, *James T. Farrell*, Univ. of Minnesota Pamphlets on American Writers, no. 29 (Minneapolis: Univ. of Minnesota Press, 1963); Edgar M. Branch, *James T. Farrell*, Twayne's U.S. Authors Series, no. 185 (New York: Twayne Publishers, 1971); Charles Fanning and Ellen Skerrett, "James T. Farrell and Washington Park," *Chicago History*, VII: (Summer 1979): 80-91; Blanche Gelfant *The American City Novel* (Norman: Univ. of Oklahoma Press, 1954), 175-227; Horace Gregory, "*James T. Farrell:* Beyond the Provinces of Art," *New World Writing: Fifth Mentor Selection* (New York: New American Library, 1954), 52-64; Alan M. Wald, James T. Farrell: *The Revolutionary Socialist Years* (New York: New York UP, 1978).

[2]*Studs Lonigan: A Trilogy* (New York: The Modern Library, 1938), 372.

[3]All were published in New York by the Vanguard Press. It is an American publishing scandal that none of these five novels is currently in print. All page references to these novels will be made in the text.

[4]James T. Farrell, "Introduction" to *Father and Son* (Cleveland and New York: World Publishing Co., 1947), xi.

[5]The novel's title and epigraph are from a poem by A.E. Housman: "I, a stranger and afraid,/In a world I never made."

[6]Again, the title and epigraph are from Housman:

Stars, I have seen them fall,
  But when they drop and die
No star is lost at all
  From all the star-sown sky,
The toil of all that be
  Helps not the primal fault;
It rains into the sea
  And still the sea is salt.

[7]Farrell's epigraphs succinctly gloss what will be the major concerns of *Father and Son*. Jim O'Neill's tragedy is set beside that of Tolstoi's hapless burgher: "Iván Ilých's life had been most simple and most ordinary and therefore most terrible." Danny's growth toward an artist's understanding is compared to Baudelaire's: "—Ah! Seigneur! donnez moi la force et le courage/De contempler mon coeur et mon corps sans dégoût!"

[8]Taken from Baudelaire's *Intimate Journals*, one of the novel's epigraphs reads: "Nevertheless, I will let these pages stand—since I wish to record my days of anger." The second epigraph, from a poem by James Joyce, pays homage to the Irish writer whom Danny takes as one of his models:

"Ah star of evil! star of pain!
Highhearted youth comes not again.

Nor old heart's wisdom yet to know
The signs that mock me as I go."

[9]The title and epigraph are taken from Yeats's "Lamentation of the Old Pensioner," which ends with a kind of artistic credo for Farrell's fiction:

There's not a woman turns her face
Upon a broken tree,
And yet the beauties that I loved
Are in my memory;
I spit into the face of Time
That has transfigured me.

[10]"How *The Face of Time* Was Written," in *Reflections at Fifty and Other Essays* (New York: Vanguard Press, 1954), 41.

Faulkner's Religious Sensibility

Joseph Blotner

One of the most touching scenes in the Yoknapatawpha saga comes at the end of *The Reivers*, when Lucius Priest returns home, ready to accept the punishment from his father that will permit him to atone for his transgressions in the preceding six days which have seen his passage from innocence to experience. But even as they descend the steps to the cellar, he and Maury Priest both know that a razor strop will be an inadequate instrument to conclude such a *rite du passage*. It is the grandfather, old Boss Priest, with the wisdom of age, who sees that the answer is not mere physical punishment. It is acknowledgement and acceptance. He tells his weeping grandson that he must live with his sins of commission and his sins of omission. "A gentleman can live through anything," he tells the eleven-year-old boy. "He faces anything. A gentleman accepts the responsibility of his actions and bears the burden of their consequences, even when he did not himself instigate them but only acquiesced to them, didn't say No though he knew he should."[1] This little homily is couched in moral rather than religious terms, but its ultimate basis lies in the Judaeo-Christian value system acknowledged by the South of Faulkner's ancestors, no matter how it might sometimes be more honored in the breach than the observance, as in the actions of Col. William Charles Falkner. *The Reivers* is the most overtly autobiographical of William Cuthbert Faulkner's novels. The part of it which I have just described can, I think, offer a good point of entry into that private area, Faulkner's religious sensibility.

What was the atmosphere into which he was born, in those last years of the nineteenth century? True to the Scottish inheritance, Col. Falkner was a Presbyterian. Ripley, Mississippi, the seat of Tippah County, was known as a "temperance town," and Falkner was an influential member of the local chapter of an organization called the Knights of Temperance. One spring day in 1849 Robert Hindman confronted Falkner with the accusation that he had blackballed him for admission. An argument ensued and Hindman pulled a gun. It misfired three times, and Falkner drew a knife and killed Hindman. Apparently Falkner continued a Knight in good standing, however, until he was murdered forty years later by another prominent citizen of the town.

Falkner's only child by his first marriage was John Wesley Thompson Falkner. Three weeks after Hindman's attempt on Falkner's life, Holland Pearce Falkner died of consumption. Falkner took their motherless son to his aunt, Justiania, and

185

she and her husband, John Wesley Thompson, agreed to adopt the child if Falkner agreed not to take him back if he remarried. They raised the boy as a Methodist. In 1859 John Wesley Thompson paid a hundred dollars as a shareholder in the Book and Tract Society of the Memphis Conference of the Methodist Church, South. One of the perquisites was a massive Bible with hundreds of pages of blank genealogical tables bound in between the Old and New Testaments. He gave it to his wife with the stipulation that after his death it should go to their adoptive son and after that to the oldest son of each succeeding generation. Seventy-three years later William Faulkner would receive it and eventually write new entries in the table in his turn.

In describing the churches of Tippah County in the middle and later years of the nineteenth century, county historian Andrew Brown wrote that "The Methodists were most numerous, accounting for probably half the church membership in the country before the War Between the States. The next largest denomination was the Baptist, followed by the Cumberland Presbyterian and 'Old Line' Presbyterian faiths."[2] As in other frontier areas, the churches of Tippah County held a central place in that society. Moreover, as Brown writes, "Under the hard and often turbulent conditions of a century ago, churches felt impelled to keep a close watch on the lives and morals of their members. In the Methodist Church the duty of 'laboring privately with members for public offenses' rested largely upon the pastor, in the Presbyterian Church on the pastor and the Elders. . . . Under the congregational system of government of the Baptist Church, however, offenders were brought before the entire congregation." In these Baptist church courts, "Such sins as drunkenness, gossiping, theft, lying and immoral conduct—which at times was stretched to include such venial sins as card-playing and 'dancing and fiddling'— were made the subject of searching investigations, and unless the offender acknowledged his guilt and promised to do better (as he usually did), his punishment might be anything up to and including excommunication from the church."[3] As far as I know, there had been no Baptists among the Faulkners. But then, in the fall of 1896, J.W.T. Falkner's oldest son, Murry C. Falkner, married an Arkansas girl named Maud Butler. Her mother, whose grandchildren would call her "Damuddy," was a devout Baptist all her life. One of her grandsons, William Faulkner, watching a church league baseball game as a young man, would say to a companion, "I don't know what church God belongs to, but I know he isn't a Baptist because he permits the other sects to exist."[4]

Murry and Maud Falkner were living in New Albany, in Union County, just south of Tippah County, where their first son was born and baptised William Cuthbert Falkner by the local Methodist minister. A few months later, they moved to Ripley. By that time, J.W.T. Falkner and his wife, Sallie Murry, had been living in Oxford, to the west, for more than a dozen years. But the numerous Murry family lived in and near Ripley, and the Falkners must have seen them almost every day during their residence there over the next five years. Sallie Murry's father, John Young Murry, was as able a man as Col. William C. Falkner in many ways, if not as spectacular and notorious. A graduate of Philadelphia's Jefferson Medical College, he was elected county Sheriff and County Treasurer before serving in the war as Captain and Assistant Surgeon of the Tippah Rangers (later the 34th Mississippi Infantry), after which he was county Health Officer for many years. He was also a Mason who served for two years as Grand Master of the Mississippi Lodge, and he found time after that to serve for two years in the Mississippi Legislature.[5] He was also an Elder and a Deacon in the Presbyterian Church and a faithful attender of Sunday School conventions. A tall, thin white-bearded patriarch who dressed in black, he made house calls on horseback during most of the sixty-six years he practiced medicine. William Faulkner would later say, "My Great-Grandfather Murry was a kind and gentle man, to us children anyway. That is, although he was a Scot, he was (to us) neither especially pious nor stern either: he was simply a man of inflexible principles. One of them was, everybody, children on up through all adults present, had to have a verse from the Bible ready and glib at tongue tip...if you didn't have your scripture verse ready, you didn't have any breakfast, you would be excused long enough to leave the room and swot one up.... It had to be an authentic, correct verse. While we were little it could be the same one, once you had it down good, morning after morning, until you got a little older and bigger, when one morning (by this time you would be pretty glib at it, galloping through without even listening to yourself....) you would suddenly find his eyes on you—very blue, very kind and gentle, and even now not stern so much as inflexible; and next morning you had a new verse. In a way, that was when you discovered that your childhood was over; you had outgrown it and entered the world."[6]

The *rite du passage* Faulkner describes here probably took place during one of the many visits to Ripley his family made after they had moved to Oxford when he was five. There in Oxford he did not lack for religious instruction and supervision. (A religious census conducted two years after their arrival revealed that "there were only 180 unconverted persons in the community, 2/3 of this number being under the age of 12 years.")[7] Not only was his grandmother, Sallie Murry Falkner, an ardent temperance worker, it was said that she and "Miss Rosie" Stone, the mother of Faulkner's friend-to-be Phil Stone, "ran" the Methodist Church. He went to its Sunday School. Damuddy lived with his family, and her piety was so strong that it was probably instrumental in Murry Falkner's abjuring swearing on Sunday and refusing to touch a playing card on that day, even to build a card house for the children. Sometimes Damuddy took Billy with her to the Baptist Church. One Sunday she became so engrossed in the sermon that she failed to notice what her grandson was doing. He was drawing a picture of a train in one of the hymnals.

There were other signs. Every summer brought the Camp Meeting, with as many as half a dozen ministers, some from Water Valley, Holly Springs, and even Memphis. Families would put up substantial tents around the tabernacle for the several days the meeting would last. Maud Falkner faithfully took her children, and they would stay in J.W.T. Falkner's roomy tent. Murry Falkner somehow managed to be excused from this devotional exercise. He preferred the hunting camp atmosphere of the Tallahatchie "Club House," as they called it (a big two-room cabin a dozen miles northeast of town at the mouth of the Tippah River where it flowed into the Tallahatchie). So did his oldest son. One of his perquisites as oldest son—as with Lucius Priest—was to spend a good deal of time in his father's livery stable. He found that atmosphere congenial too. Somehow, in the face of all the collective family piety, he managed, by the time he had passed his twelfth birthday, to stop going to Sunday School.

Many years later he would say, about certain kinds of imagery in his work, "the Christian legend is part of any Christian's background, especially the background of a country boy, a Southern boy. My life was passed, my childhood, in a very small Mississippi town, and that was a part of my background. I grew up with that. I assimilated that, took that in without even knowing it. It's just there. It has nothing to do with how much of it I might believe or disbelieve— it's just there."[8]

But something of which he was quite conscious was happening as he moved into adolescence. "At the age of sixteen," he would write, looking back a dozen years later, "I discovered Swinburne. Or rather, Swinburne discovered me, springing from some tortured undergrowth of my adolescence, like a highwayman, making me his slave."[9] It is likely that he found appealing not only Swinburne's poetical devices (which he imitated in many poems of his own) but also a sensibility that found a deep appeal in things pastoral and Greek but also embodied a rejection of things Christian. One sees this in Swinburne's "Hymn to Proserpine," subtitled "After the Proclamation in Rome of the Christian Faith," in lines such as

Thou has conquered, O pale Galilean; the world has grown gray from thy breath;
We have drunken of things Lethean, and fed of the fullness of death.

That period of his life, Faulkner said, closed with the discovery of Housman's *A Shropshire Lad.* Forty years later, he would still know by heart a poem that reasonated deeply with some of his fundamental feelings. It was poem XLVIII from that volume, the one which began,

Be still, my soul, the arms you bear are brittle,
Earth and high heaven are fixt of old,

and which ended,

Oh why did I awake? When shall I sleep again.?

But he was by no means finished with Christianity.

He would use it again, in a number of ways. When he and Phil Stone made plans in 1918 to enlist in the British armed forces, they believed not only that they would have to pass at least as British "territorials" if not Englishmen, but also that they would require references. And so they wrote them themselves, Stone said. In one, the Reverend Mr. Edward Twimberly-Thorndike called them "god-fearing young Christian gentlemen." They mailed these testimonials to London whence they were posted to British recruitment offices in New York. Faulkner went further than that in Toronto when he supplied information for his RAF Certificate of Service. He informed the clerk that he had been born in Finchley, Middlesex, England, and that he belonged to the Church of England. There is no record, however, of his attendance during these years at any of its services.

*   *   *

A few years later, after returning home a gallantly uniformed RAF pilot, he settled in New Orleans as a bohemian author. There one summer day he stood to one side with a young woman he liked, watching a group of seemingly carefree swimmers. Then he turned to her suddenly, without preamble, and said "Margery, we believe in God, don't we." She could not tell in which God he believed, and it would never be easy for anyone to tell.

He was then just beginning to sell sketches and stories to The New Orleans *Times-Picayune*. The I-narrator in several of them was clearly modeled on Faulkner. In one of the earliest, he got his sketch under way and then stopped to describe a certain capacity his protagonist had. It was the same one, he said, that produced Jesus of Nazareth and "a fairy tale that has conquered the whole Western earth...."[10] It was by no means the last time he would use a term such as "fairy tale" in such a context. Half a dozen years later, in his full maturity as a novelist, he would write in *Light in August* about a character named Joe Christmas. Many years after that, when he was asked if he intended "any Christ symbolism," he denied it. There were so few plots, he said, that sooner or later the writer would use one that someone else had used, and the "Christ story is one of the best stories that man has invented, assuming that he did invent that story...."[11] Some of his hearers might have been excused if they found his answer disingenuous, but that is not the point here. It is the idea expressed that the central truth of Christianity is a fairy tale, a madeup story, a fable. Nearly fifteen years after *Light in August*, he was at work on a novel which, he told his literary agent, would continue on "through the Three Temptations, the Crucifixion, and the Resurrection." He told his publisher, "The argument is...in the middle of that war, Christ (some movement in mankind which wished to stop war forever) reappeared and was crucified again."[12]

In *A Fable* he was working primarily from The New Testament, but that was not his favorite part of the Bible. "To me," he said, "the New Testament is full of ideas and I don't know much about ideas. The Old Testament is full of people, perfectly ordinary normal heroes and blackguards just like everybody else nowadays, and I like to read the Old Testament because it's full of people, not ideas. It's people all trying to get something for nothing or...to be braver than they are— just ordinary everyday folks, people, that's why I like to read that. That's apart from the fine poetry of the prose."[13] He liked it enough so that when he was on his first Hollywood assignment, in 1932, when he was by no means affluent, one of the few purchases he made there was a second-hand twelve-volume Cambridge edition of *The Holy Bible*. His work would of course be saturated with Christian imagery and allusions. (If he invoked one Saint more than any other, it was probably St. Francis, though in a subtle way he was associated more with death than spiritual life or life everlasting.)

The Scriptures were one thing, but the clergy was another. In his mid-twenties he had devotedly served as Scoutmaster for a troop sponsored by the Presbyterian Church. A few years later, however, under a new minister, he was removed as unfit for the job because of his drinking—which had never interfered with the performance of his duties. Twenty-five years later he was outraged once more when all of Oxford's clergymen except the Catholic and Anglican priests confederated in an election campaign to keep beer illegal in oxford. At his own expense he had a broadside printed and distributed to counteract what he called false propaganda. When the other side won, he composed an ironic public letter. His major objection, he wrote, was "to a priest so insulting the intelligence of his hearers as to assume that he can make any statement, regardless of its falsity, and because of respect for his cloth, not one of them will try or dare to check up on it." But most of all, he wrote, "I object to ministers of God violating the canons and ethics of their sacred and holy avocation by using, either openly or underhand, the weight and power of their office to try to influence a civil election."[14] Some of his readers might have wondered if the phrase "sacred and holy" was written out of conviction or rhetoric.

In the latter part of his career, the appearance of *A Fable*, and before it, *Requiem for a Nun*, served to focus interest on the religious component in his work and thought. Though the reception of the former was quite mixed, there seemed to be a consensus on one thing: it was no orthodox use for the purposes of fiction of Christ's passion and death. If anything, it was rather the use of religious material for secular, or humanistic, purposes. And the operation of sin, guilt, faith, atonement, and redemption in the latter was perceived by most readers as difficult if not muddy and obscure. It is challenging to try to determine what Faulkner's private and personal beliefs now were.

When Jill Faulkner was a child, her parents would sometimes take her to the Christmas Eve service at St. Peter's Episcopal Church. Apart from those occasions, however, she went with her friends to their churches. Later on, parishioners would occasionally see William Faulkner escorting his wife down the main aisle to a pew near the front. Once seated, he appeared to look straight ahead for the whole service. It was not surprising that he should have chosen to go, on the rare occasions when he did, to the Episcopal Church. That was Estelle Faulkner's church (though they had not been permitted to marry in it because she was divorced) and their daughter had been married in it. For another thing, it probably fit better into Faulkner's pattern of Anglophilia, ever since his RAF days, in spite of his strong sense of his Scots ancestry and the Presbyterian affiliations of that part of his family. (One thinks here of two other novelists who went to church in their later years: James Joyce, who said he went on certain Holy Days to hear the music performed at certain masses, and Thomas Hardy, who said that he too went to hear the music, and that his attendance was sentimental rather than devotional). It seems likely that Faulkner's attendance sprang from similar non-religious, or at least heterodox, feelings. There was another form which he observed. One night when my wife and I were the Faulkners' only dinner guests, Estelle said, "Bill, will you say the blessing?" He rose from his place, bowed his head, and said a short rapid, conventional grace. I wondered if he thought then of his Great-Grandfather Murry.

Two tenets which must have been articles of faith with John Young Murry his great-great grandson completely rejected: the idea of a personal God and the conviction of life after death. When a student asked William Faulkner if there was one character in all his work who had been saved by grace, he answered, "Well, I have always thought of God as being in the wholesale rather than the retail business." His views became firmer with the passing years. When Caroline Barr, the black woman who had helped raise him, died at one hundred or thereabouts, her body lay in state in his parlor. He had a choir in from her church to sing spirituals, and he gave the eulogy, as she had asked him to do. He paid tribute to her precepts, her service, and her love. Then he concluded, "She was born and lived and served, and died and now is mourned; if there is a heaven, she has gone there."[15] Ten years later, accepting an award, he recalled the time, in his fiftieth year, when he had looked back over all his work and "decided that it was all pretty good—and then in the same instant I realised that that was the worst of all since that meant only that a little nearer now was the moment, instant, night: dark: sleep: when I would put it all away forever that I anguished and sweated over, and it would never trouble me anymore."[16] Half a dozen years later, he would say that the writer "knows he has a short span of life, that the day will come when he must pass through the wall of oblivion, and he wants to leave a scratch on that wall—Kilroy was here—that somebody a hundred, a thousand years later will see."[17] The figure of speech would vary—he might call it "Supreme Obliteration"—but it would recur many times. One day over coffee I was carried away beyond our usual casual or topical conversation and picked up something Faulkner had just said in a class and pursued it to a point that implied the possibility of some mode of experience beyond this life. Faulkner looked at me, almost impatiently. Then he began, "As we've said, we have to pass through the wall of oblivion..." I can't remember what he said then, but I remember how that first phrase, as he spoke it, was quite chilling. Later I would think of Wallace Stevens' phrase in "Sunday Morning": "sure obliteration."

But Faulkner felt some of the same immortal longings that troubled Stevens's woman in the peignoir, and they appear to have gotten into the fiction. Harry Wilbourne in *The Wild Palms*, says *"between grief and nothing I will* take grief."[18] Faulkner repeated that line, appropriated it for himself so many times, in letters and in conversation, that it lived in his life as well as his fiction. McCaslin Edmonds says it in *Go Down, Moses*. "Think of all that has happened here, on this earth," he tells his nephew. "All the blood hot and strong for living, pleasuring, that has soaked back into it.... And even suffering and grieving is better than nothing.... But you can't be alive forever, and you always wear out life long before you have exhausted the possibilities of living. And all that must be somewhere; all that could not have been invented and created just to be thrown away."[19]

How could Faulkner reconcile the antithetical wish and conviction? He tried during the last two decades of his life. His most sustained effort to explain his thought was made in 1952 to a young Frenchman who told him, in speaking about the influence of Sartre and Camus, that many young people were substituting faith in man for faith in God. Faulkner thought that was wrong. "God is," he told him, in a phrase that might have come out of Genesis. "It is He who created man.... You question God, and then you begin to doubt...and God fades away by the very act of your doubting him." By now, thought the interviewer, Faulkner was absorbed in what he was saying, developing his thought. "Naturally," he said, "I'm not talking about a personified or a mechanical God, but a God who is the most complete expression of mankind, a God who rests in both eternity and in the now." The young man asked if Faulkner was thinking of the God of Bergson. "Yes," he answered, "a deity very close to Bergson's." Then, as he developed his argument further, he took the line he would use increasingly, in which art and religion, God and the artist, began to merge. "Art is not only man's most supreme expression;" he said, "it is also the salvation of mankind." Three years later a young Japanese asked him if he believed in Christianity. "Well," he said, "I believe in God. Sometimes Christianity gets pretty debased, but I do believe in God, yes. I believe that man has a soul that aspires towards what we call God, what we mean by God." A few days later he told another Japanese questioner, "To me, a proof of God is in the firmament, the stars. To me, a proof of man's immortality, that his conception that there could be a God, that the idea of a God is valuable, is in the fact that he writes the books and composes the music and paints the pictures. They are the firmament of mankind. They are the proof that if there is a God and he wants us to see something that proves to him that mankind exists, that would be proof." Then, in the next question, he returned to his formulation about the artist's leaving his sign, "Kilroy was here" on the wall of oblivion.[20]

If he was certain how the artist should use his gifts, he was sometimes uncertain about their source. The two artists of his time he praised most highly were Thomas Mann and James Joyce, but the techniques of *Ulysses* and *Finnegans Wake* troubled him. "He had more talent than he could control," he said. "That was the case of a genius who was electrocuted by the divine fire."[21] Speaking of his own gift, he told a young writer, "I don't know where it came from. I don't know why God or gods or whoever it was, selected me to be the vessel."[22] But he also told the same young woman not to be afraid, "because there is a God that looks after the true artist because there is nothing as important as that and He knows it."[23]

His idea of God and the artist produced some interesting and curious comments when he used it to measure some of his contemporaries. His tribute to Albert Camus was a curious one, especially in the light of his own repeated references to the wall of oblivion. Faulkner wrote, "He said, 'I do not like to believe that death opens upon another life. To me, it is a door that shuts.' That is, he tried to believe that. But he failed. Despite himself, as all artists are, he spent that life searching himself and demanding of himself answers which only God could know; when he became the Nobel laureate of his year, I wired him 'on salut l'ame qui constamment se cherche et se demande'; why did he not quit then, if he did not want to believe in God?"[24] Faulkner had referred to Camus's view that man was born into an absurd world, and he himself had spoken about man's problems living in what he called a ramshackle universe held together by electricity. He praised Ernest Hemingway's

The Old Man and the Sea because in that book, he said, Hemingway "discovered God, a Creator," writing about "something somewhere that made them all: the old man who had to catch the fish and then lose it, the fish that had to be caught and then lost, the sharks which had to rob the old man of his fish; made them all and pitied them all."[25] It was a review to make a reader think of Emerson or Wordsworth, or perhaps Coleridge at the instant when his Ancient Mariner blessed the water snakes and the Albatross fell from around his neck.

John Dos Passos would say of Faulkner, "His stories are full of the knowledge of death."[26] There was much in his life to supply that knowledge. He mourned his grandparents, and then, much later, when he was in his early sixties his long-lived mother began to fail. He told one friend that she knew she was going to die "So I created a fairy tale for her. I would tell her about Heaven and what it was going to be like, how nice it was going to be and how she would like it." After one of his descriptions of the joys of the Blessed, she said she just didn't know how she would stand those robes all the time. Then she asked him a direct question. "Will I have to see your father there?" she asked.

"No," he said, "not if you don't want to."

"That's good," she said. "I never did like him."

*   *   *

Not too many years before this, in a period of depression, he had written one of his most powerful and poignant stories, another recollection by an I-narrator, entitled "Sepulture South: Gaslight." He recalled his grandfather's funeral and his own horrified rejection of the idea of death: "So they in the hearse could not be dead: it must be something like sleep: a trick played on people. . . tricked into that helpless coma for some dreadful and inscrutable joke until the dirt was packed down, to strain and thrash and cry in the airless dark, to no escape forever. So that night I had something very like hysterics, clinging to Sarah's legs and panting: 'I won't die! I won't! Never!' " At the end of the story, anticipating the day when he would be the eldest surviving male, he wrote about the cemetery and its statuary. "And three or four times a year I would come back, I would not know why, alone to look at them, not just at Grandfather and Grandmother but at all of them looming among the lush green of summer and the regal blaze of fall and the rain and ruin of winter before spring would bloom again, stained now, a little darkened by time and weather and endurance but still serene, impervious, remote, gazing at nothing, not like sentinels, not defending the living from the dead by means of their vast ton-measured weight and mass, but rather the dead from the living; shielding instead the vacant and dissolving bones, the harmless and defenseless dust, from the anguish and grief and inhumanity of mankind."[27]

Not long before this story, in a foreword to a collection of his work, he had written again about why the artist writes, but the odor of mortality hung over it more heavily than ever before. The artist wrote, he said, to partake of immortality. "Some day he will be no more, which will not matter then, because isolated and itself invulnerable in the cold print remains that which is capable of engendering still the old deathless excitement in hearts and glands whose owners and custodians are generations from even the air he breathed and anguished in; if it was capable once, he knows that it will be capable and potent still long after there remains of him only a dead and fading name."[28]

When he knew he was going to enter a hospital, William Faulkner would take with him his standard hospital reading. It consisted of four books. One was The Bible. Two others, Estelle Faulkner said, were The Rule and Exercises of Holy Living and The Rule and Exercises of Holy Dying, by Anglican Bishop Jeremy Taylor. Chaplain to Charles I, apostle of toleration and opponent of Presbyterians, he was called "the Shakespeare and the Spenser of the pulpit, the English Chrysostom and the most eloquent of theologians." A close observer both of man and nature, he has also been praised as "as a prose poet, and as a poet...closely a kin to the great Elizabethans."[29] (Once when I went with Estelle Faulkner to help in the process of Faulkner's being discharged from the hospital, sure enough, there they were on his night table. He had once asked me to see if I could get him seventeenth century editions of the two books and I had ordered them from London.) I do not know what parts of Bishop Taylor's books he read. If not the chapter entitled "Christian Sobriety," perhaps the one entitled "Of Christian Justice." If not the chapter entitled "The Practice of Preparation for a Holy and Blessed Death," perhaps the one entitled "The Practice of Those Graces Belonging to the State of Sickness Which a Sick Man May Practice Alone." Actually, I suspect he read these books as he did the other old favorites to which he returned, skipping about and reading in them, rather than systematically reading through them in a devotional exercise. And I suspect that he liked these books for some of the same reasons that he said he liked the Bible. Lest the readers think that this small library excessively pious, the fourth book was Boccaccio's Decameron.

When Estelle Faulkner and her nephew Jimmy took William Faulkner to Wright's Sanitarium on July 5, 1962, they did not take the books with them, and he was in no condition then to read them anyway. His hospitalization had been precipitated by a series of painful injuries, falls from horses, and their aftermath. One day he had walked down the road to the nearby home of Felix Linder, a childhood playmate, now a retired orthopedist who had treated him from time to time. He walked gingerly and it was obvious that he was in pain. He spoke directly. "Felix," he said, "I don't want to die." Felix looked at him, troubled. He could not take on a case like this. "I could give you something to keep you from suffering," he said. "I could do that. I'll be glad to."

"That ain't what I want," Faulkner replied, and left.[30] In A Fable the old general had said, "Nothing—nor power nor glory nor wealth nor pleasure nor even freedom from pain, is as valuable as simple breathing, simply being alive even with all the regret of having to remember and the anguish of an irreparable worn-out body."[31] Felix Linder could not know that Bill Faulkner had apparently seen, suddenly and close-up, that wall of oblivion he had so often mentioned.

He was buried according to the rites of the Episcopal Church. The minister read from the Order for the Burial of the Dead, intoning the words of the Forty-sixth Psalm and St. Paul to the Romans.

His tombstone would bear the words, selected by his wife, "Beloved, Go with God." It might equally well have born the words, coming from another tradition, which he himself had written those long years ago when he read the poems of Swinburne and Housman which had lasted him all his life, words he had called "My Epitaph":

If there be grief, let it be the rain
And this but silver grief, for grieving's sake,
And these green woods be dreaming here to wake
Within my heart, if I should rouse again.

But I shall sleep, for where is any death
While in these blue hills slumbrous overhead
I'm rooted like a tree? Though I be dead
This soil that holds me fast will find me breath.[32]

Notes

[1]*The Reivers* (New York: Random House, 1961) 302.

[2]Andrew Brown, *History of Tippah County, Mississippi: The First Century* (Ripley, Miss.: The Tippah County Historical and Genealogical Society, Inc., 1976) 53.

[3]Brown, A. 57.

[4]Calvin S. Brown Jr., in *William Faulkner of Oxford*, eds. James W. Webb and A. Wigfall Green, (Baton Rouge: Louisiana State UP 1965) 46.

[5]Brown, A., 239.

[6]Jean Stein, in *Lion in the Garden: Interviews with William Faulkner, 1926-1962*, eds. James B. Meriwether and Michael Millgate (New York: Random House, 1968) 250.

[7]The Oxford *Eagle*, 24 Oct. 1907.

[8]Frederick L. Gwynn and Joseph L. Blotner, eds. *Faulkner in the University*, (Charlottesville: The Univ. of Virginia Press, 1959) 86.

[9]Carvel Collins, ed. "Verse Old Nascent: A Pilgrimage," repr. in *William Faulkner: Early Prose and Poetry* (Boston: Atlantic Monthly Press, 1962) 114.

[10]Carvel Collins, ed. "Mirrors of Chartres Street," reprinted in *William Faulkner: New Orleans Sketches*, (New York: Random House, 1968) 16.

[11]Gwynn and Blotner, 117.

[12]Joseph Blotner, *Selected Letters of William Faulkner*, (New York: Random House, 1977) 179-180.

[13]Gwynn and Blotner 169.

[14]James B. Meriwether, Repr. in *Essays Speeches & Public Letters* (New York: Random House, 1965) 209-210.

[15]Meriwether 118.

[16]Meriwether 206.

[17]Gwynn & Blotner 61.

[18]*The Wild Palms* (New York: Random House, 1939) 324.

[19]*Go Down, Moses* (New York: Modern Library Fiction, 1955) 186.

[20]*Lion in the Garden* 70, 71, 100, 103.

[21]Gwynn and Blotner 53, 280.

[22]Blotner, *Selected Letters* 348.

[23]Joseph Blotner, *Faulkner: a Biography*, (New York: Random House, 1974) 1437.

[24]Meriwether 113.

[25]Meriwether 193.

[26]"Faulkner," *The National Review*, January 15, 1963.

[27]Joseph Blotner, ed. *Uncollected Stories of William Faulkner* (New York: Random House, 1979) 452, 455.

[28]*The Faulkner Reader* (New York: Random House, 1954) ix,.

[29]Emile Legouis and Louis Cazamian, *A History of English Literature* (New York: The Macmillan Company 1935) 545-546.

[30]Webb and Green 173.

[31]*A Fable* 350.

[32]*The Marble Faun and A Green Bough* (New York: Random House, 1965) 67.

PART SEVEN

Story-Telling and the Incarnation of God In Formative Judaism

Jacob Neusner

Among the diverse Judaisms that flourished in ancient times, one emerged paramount and became normative. It is the Judaism of the dual Torah, oral and written. Specifically, the Judaism of the dual Torah appealed to the story that, at Sinai, God revealed the Torah—revelation—to Moses not only in writing but also through oral formulation and oral transmission, that is, through processes of memory. The written Torah of that Judaism corresponds, over all, to the Hebrew Bible or "Old Testament." The oral Torah, this same Judaism maintains, was transmitted through memory from Sinai onward to the early centuries of the Common or Christian era, when it was written down. That oral Torah of the Judaism of the dual Torah reached its initial formulation in the Mishnah, a philosophical law-code redacted at about A.D. 200, and came to its ultimate statement in the Bavli, in English, the Talmud of Babylonia, a systematic commentary to both Scripture and the Mishnah, that is, both parts of the one whole Torah revealed to Moses, called our rabbi, of ca. A.D. 600. In between a variety of exegetical works took shape around the Mishnah, on the one side, and Scripture, on the other.

The character of divinity in the Judaism of the dual Torah underwent diverse changes between the Mishnah and the Bavli. In the earlier stages in the unfolding of the Judaism of the dual Torah, from the Mishnah forward, God serves as premise of all being, sometimes takes the role of a presence, called Shekhinah, ordinarily translated Divine Presence, and even becomes a person, that is, a "you," in particular in liturgical settings, as in "Blessed are you, Lord our God, king of the world, who...." But it is only in the latest stages in the unfolding of the Judaism of the dual Torah that God regains that rich and protean personality that, to begin with, the written Torah, or Scripture, imputes to God. The statement of God as not merely premise, presence, and person, but fully exposed personality—hence the process of the incarnation of God in the model of the human being—comes to complete expression only in the Bavli. And it takes the form in particular of stories. Since the honoree of this volume has shown the power of narrative, storytelling in particular, to bring to expression the full meaning, for his Church in the present age, of the belief that Jesus Christ worked and walked among humanity as God incarnate, it is an appropriate tribute to show how, in the Judaism that took shape in the period in which Christianity came into being, the great Judaic sages resorted to narrative, in particular, story, to state their encounter with God in human form, in our image and after our likeness, much as did the writers of the Gospels, much as does Andrew Greeley in our own time.

I

No Narrative, No Personality
God in the Mishnah as Premise, Presence, and Person

We shall see as truly remarkable the Bavli's authorship's resort to narrative in the presentation of the incarnation of God only when we have a clear picture of the alternative. In the Mishnah God never forms the center of a story, and God also never appears as having a fully formed personality, on the one side, or as an incarnate being, on the other. A rapid review of the Mishnah's statement of the character of divinity, the initial one in the canon of the Judaism of the dual Torah, will place into the appropriate context the later survey of the Bavli's amazing restatement of matters.

1. God as Premise in the Mishnah

Let us start with a specific case and move to the more general principle. The premise that God has imposed requirements upon humanity in general, and Israel in particular, encompasses the entirety of the corpus of commandments presented in the Torah and the Mishnah sets forth the rules governing observance of those commandments. From that fact it must follow that God forms the principal premise of all Mishnaic discourse. That is moreover a statement not of theory but of everyday fact. If one violates the law of the Torah, as set forth in the Mishnah, one transgresses the expressed will of God. One explicit statement of that view is as follows:

Those [who practice usury] transgress a negative commandment: the one who lends at usury, the one who borrows, the one who guarantees the loan, and the witnesses. Sages say, "Also the scribe."
They transgress the commandments, "Thou shall not give him your money upon usury" (Lev. 25-27), "You shall not take usury from him" (Lev. 25:36), "You shall not be to him as a creditor" (Ex. 22:25), "Nor shall you lay upon him usury" (Ex. 22:25), "You shall not put a stumbling block before the blind, but you shall fear your God. I am the Lord" (Lev. 19:14).

(M. Baba Mesia 5:11)

Here is an explicit statement, among many, that God through the Torah stands behind the laws of the Mishnah, and that those who violate the laws offend God, those who keep them please God. Here we find no characterization of God in terms we can call incarnational. It is simply a different mode of description of the divinity. The premise of the Mishnah's authorities is that God revealed the Torah at Sinai, and that the Torah represents God's will for Israel. The Mishnah's "Israel" is holy because of that fact. To be sure, the authorship of the Mishnah, excluding that of tractate Avot, never tells us the basis on which they in particular exercise authority and therefore are able to declare that matters are to be done in one way rather than in some other. Nonetheless, the document in some passages explicitly appeals to the authority of the written Torah—therefore to the will of God—and in many more does so implicitly. Of the latter fact we may be certain for two reasons. The first is that vast stretches of the Mishnah propose to spell out in detail the way in which to carry out the requirements of the law of the Torah. Consequently, the Mishnah's authorship clearly proposed to perform a secondary act of explication, depending upon the primary authority of the Torah. Such tractates as Yebamot, Pesahim, and Yoma, for a few obvious instances, specify in rich detail the ways in which the Torah's laws are to be observed and applied. While the authorship at hand only rarely cites verses of Scripture, seeing no need for proof-texts, that same authorship has as a principal task the application of the Torah's laws to everyday situations. The authority behind Scripture, which is God's revelation to Moses at Sinai, therefore stands behind the Mishnah, and, it follows, the presence of God's will and word forms the paramount fact of the Mishnah.

2. God as Presence in the Mishnah

It is one thing to find God as premise of the law. It is quite another to find God as a presence within the processes of exposition and—more important—application of the law. The Hebrew word generally translated Presence, *Shekhinah*, does occur in the Mishnah, if in only one passage:

Said R. Meir, "When a human being is in distress, as to the Presence of God, what does [its] tongue say...?"

M. San. 6:5

The premise is that God suffers along with human beings. It follows that, in general, God is understood not merely as a philosophical premise, a source of authority, but also as a presence. But the picture in general leaves a quite different impression.

Like eighteenth century Deists, the Mishnah's philosophers focus upon the government by rule and law that God has set forth in the Torah, taking slight, and then merely episodic, interest in God's particular and ad hoc intervention into the smooth application of the now-paramount regularities of the law. That sort of intervention by God is invoked only in one instance known to me, as I shall suggest in a moment. The Mishnah's authorship rarely decides a rule or a case by appealing to God's presence and choice particular to that rule or case. That is to say, God does not very often play an everyday and active role in the Mishnah's processes and system. To take two stunning examples, in the entire division of Purities, which encompasses more than a quarter of the Mishnah in volume, I cannot point to a single passage in which God's presence forms a consideration, one way or the other, in the statement or application of a rule (excluding the tacked-on conclusion at M. Uqsin 3:12). The rules of susceptibility to and contracting of uncleanness, as well as those of removing that uncleanness work themselves out with appeal to God's will or person. That is the case, even though the division attends to laws meant by the account of the priestly authorship of Leviticus and Numbers to protect the cult from the danger of uncleanness. A survey of the civil code presented in the tractates Baba Qama, Baba Mesia, and Baba Batra, covering the transactions of commerce, real estate, torts, damages, labor law, and the like, that, in the aggregate, correspond to civil law in our own society, yields not a single appeal to God's presence or God's *ad hoc* intervention into a case. All things are governed by regularities and norms, such that God has no place in the everyday world of mortals' exchanges and interchanges. While God forms the prevailing premise of discourse, that fact makes slight difference in what is said. The Mishnah's is a God of the philosophers.[1] God's presence in the system of the Mishnah, while everywhere a premise and an implicit fact, plays only a limited, and, on the whole, a passive or inert role. Quite to the contrary, it is the will and intention of the human being—not those of God—that form the variable. God is the norm and the given, God's will and law, revealed in the Torah, the ubiquitous fact. For the philosophers behind the Mishnah, therefore, God's presence forms part of the guaranteed and reliable structure of existence. It is the human will that is unpredictable—and that imparts to the Mishnah's system its movement, energy, dynamism.

Still, God forms a ubiquitous presence throughout the Mishnah's system. God's presence is signified by awareness of the character of the occasion as well, e.g., the number and splendor of those present. Rules covering the recitation of prayers took account of the size and importance of those present on the occasion. If three are present, for the Grace after Meals one begins, "Bless the one of whose bounty we have partaken," if there are ten, "Bless our God...," and onward up to ten thousand: "We will bless the Lord our God, the God of Israel, the God of hosts, who sits between the Cherubim, for the food we have eaten..." (M. Ber. 7:3). But this is a minor point. The main consideration is that God responds to the human will and expression of human intentionality. That becomes especially blatant when we turn to how God hears statements of what a human being wishes, or does not wish, joined to an act of consecration or sanctification through human words: vows, oaths, statements of sanctification and dedication, and the like. Here is where God's and the human person's encounter takes place—which is to say, at the human being's action and volition.

3. God as Person in the Mishnah

God as a person whom one might envisage and even see formed the subject of interpretation of Ezekiel's vision of the Chariot (Ez. 1:4), but the framers of the Mishnah merely allude to that fact (M. Hag. 2:1) and do not tell us the substance of the vision of God as a physical person.[2] But, we must again emphasize, God's person, not merely presence, forms the presupposition of all acts of the recitation of prayer, which take for granted that God not only hears prayer but also cares what the human being requests. One example, among many, is the prayer of the high priest on the Day of Atonement: "O God, your people, the house of Israel, have committed iniquity, transgressed and sinned before you. O God, forgive the iniquities and transgressions and sins which your people, the house of Israel, have committed...as it is written in the Torah of your servant, Moses, 'For on this day shall atonement be made for you to clean you, from all your sins shall you be clean before the Lord (Lev. 16:30)' " (M. Yoma. 6:2). God is everywhere a "you," and therefore a person. Not only so, but, as a person, God is assumed to respond to words and to events pretty much as human beings do. For example, when the community suffers from drought and prays for rain, God is not only asked to act as God had done in times past, "May the one who answered our ancestors at the Red Sea answer you" (M. Ta. 2:4), but the acts of self-mortification and deprivation are meant to impress God and to win sympathy, much as they would (it was assumed) from a mortal ruler. The one who represents the community in prayer therefore was to be an elder, who had children for whom to worry and a house empty of food (M. Ta. 2:2); such a one would then be wholehearted in the prayer. God would discern the sincerity and respond with sympathy. Hence God was understood as a person, in whose model the human being had been made, and human beings, searching their own hearts, could understand God's.

While, throughout the Mishnah we find the datum that God hears and answers prayer, for example, "When I enter [the house of study], I pray that no offense will take place on my account, and when I leave, I give thanks for my lot" (M. Ber. 4:2), that is not the end of the matter. Of still greater interest, God is assumed to take the form of a person, in the model of a heavenly monarch or emperor. For example, when one is reciting the Prayer, one is assumed to stand before the King and that location, in God's presence, requires appropriate probity: "Even if the king greets a person, one is not to reply, and even if a snake wrapped itself around one's heel, one is not to interrupt" (M. Ber. 5:1). The response to the recitation of prayer derives not from concrete personal engagement by God; there is no story in the Mishnah that suggests anyone believed God talked back to the one who says the prayer. But there are explicit statements that God heard and answered prayer and so indicated on the spot:

If one who recites the Prayer makes an error, it is a bad omen for that person, and if that person recited the Prayer in behalf of the entire community, it is a bad omen for those who assigned the task to that person.

They said of R. Hanina that, when he would say a prayer over the sick, he would say, "This one will live," or, "That one will die."

They said to him, "How do you know?"

He said to them, "If my prayer flows easily in my mouth, I know that it is accepted, and if not, I know that it is rejected."

M. Ber. 5:5

God as "you" occurs not only in liturgy, but also in legal formulas recited upon specified occasions. Here, to be sure, the context is defined by Scripture:

"...I have removed...according to all your commandment which you have commanded me..."[Deut. 26:13ff.]...

"Look down from your holy habitation from heaven:" We have done what you have decreed concerning us, now you do what you have promised to us....

M.M.S. 5:10-13

The transaction is between two persons, each bound by the same rule as governs the other.

But the person-hood of God as a "you" plays a role principally in the address of prayer. Scripture's portrait of God as an active personality finds no counterpart whatsoever in the Mishnah. That fact may be seen in a simple observation. The majestic presence of God in the unfolding of events, which forms the great theme of the scriptural narratives of ancient Israel's history, may define a premise of the Mishnah's world-view. But at no passage in the Mishnah does an action of God serve to explain an event, nor do we find lessons drawn, as to God's purpose or will, from events. Events take place, truths endure, but the two form a merely assumed and implicit relationship.

4. God as Personality in the Mishnah

If God is conceived as not merely a person but possessed of specific traits of personality, the Mishnah hardly contains evidence that its authorship could specify what those personal traits might be. True enough, one may infer from the rules that the Mishnah contains the attitudes of mind and preferences of personality of the God who stands behind the Mishnah as premise, who even is invoked in the rules of the Mishnah as presence. For instance, God is assumed to favor deeds of lovingkindness and study of the Torah; honoring of parents; making peace among people. Accordingly, God may be assumed, as a personality, to be generous, studious, respectful, and ironic, a picture explicitly limned in tractate Avot. But no stories portray God in one way, rather than in some other. Later on, we shall see precisely how traits of a theological character are restated as characteristics of a personality— and that is through the medium of story-telling. While for the authorship of the Mishnah we may impute such traits and others to the God that serves as premise and even presence, the authorship of the Mishnah, unlike the diverse scriptural writers, does not portray God as a personality. Nor, apart form liturgical settings, does that translate its fixed premise of God as giver of the Torah into the notion of the active presence of God in the everyday and the here and now. God hears and answers prayers of the individual—setting aside the general rules of being when God chooses to do so. The way in which an authorship among the canonical documents of the Judaism of the dual Torah does portray the personality of God will show us, in due course, what has not been done in the Mishnah. What we find in later documents but not here is a drastic shift in the modes of discourse concerning God.

Narrative in general finds more than slight place in the Mishnah, since the entire account of the Temple and its cult, the rites of the altar, the priesthood and their activities, is presented in essentially narrative form.[3] But narrative never in the Mishnah serves as a vehicle for discussing either the personality or activity of God. Indeed, even when the opportunity to do so presents itself, the authorship of the Mishnah does not respond. The occasions that in Scripture commonly provoke God's anger—hence portraying God's personality in concrete terms—involve idolatry, generating God's jealousy. The counterpart discourse in the Mishnah deals with worship of alien gods, Abodah Zarah. No passage in that tractate refers to God's anger with idols or jealousy when Israelites worship idols. It is simply not a component of discourse on the subject. In the Mishnah's treatment of the matter, what is at stake is the relationship between Israelites and gentiles, not between Israel and God, and the purpose of the law is to define permissible and impermissible transactions with gentiles on the occasion of their celebration of their idolgods. Secondary issues, e.g., use of foods prepared by gentiles, disposition of pieces of idols, and the like, do not change the picture of an authorship interested in outlining the boundaries between holy Israel and the gentile world.

II

The Incarnation of God

The conception that God may take human form, of course, derives from Scripture and formed a commonplace among both Judaisms and nascent Christianities of late antiquity. The incarnation of God will have surprised few Jews or Christians. The full statement of that conception in the Judaism under study, however, makes its appearance only in the later stages of the formation of the canon of that Judaism, in the fifth and sixth century compilations. The fundamental theory that sages may perceive an incarnation of God first occurs, so far as I can discern, in two fifth-century compilations of exegeses of Scripture. The first is Genesis Rabbah, compiled at ca. A.D. 400, as part of a vast response on the part of the Judaic sages to the conversion of the Roman Empire to Christianity and the establishment of the Church as the religion of the state. A systematic commentary to the book of Genesis, the compilation, Genesis Rabbah, rereads the lives of the patriarchs and matriarchs as a foretelling of the history of their children after the flesh, Israel, in the here and the now of a world just short of redemption. In that compilation we find the following:

> 1. A. Said R. Hoshaiah, "When the Holy One, blessed be he, came to create the first man, the ministering angels mistook him [for God, since man was in God's image,] and wanted to say before him, 'Holy, [holy, holy is the Lord of hosts].'
> B. "To what may the matter be compared? To the case of a king and a governor who were set in a chariot, and the provincials wanted to greet the king, 'Sovereign!' But they did not know which one of them was which. What did the king do? He turned the governor out and put him away from the chariot, so that people would know who was king."
> C. "So too when the Holy One, blessed be he, created the first man, the angels mistook him [for God]. What did the Holy One, blessed be he, do? He put him to sleep, so everyone knew that he was a mere man."
> D. "That is in line with the following verse of Scripture: 'Cease you from man, in whose nostrils is a breath, for how little is he to be accounted' (Is. 2:22)."

> Genesis Rabbah VIII:X⁴

A view such as the present one invites precisely the development fully exposed in the pages of the Talmud of Babylonia. There we see in a variety of dimensions the single characterization of God as incarnate. The incarnation moreover was not merely a matter of pointing to spiritual or other non-material traits shared by God and humanity. God's physical traits and attributes are represented as identical to those of a human being. That is why the character of the divinity in the later documents of the canon of the Judaism of the dual Torah may accurately be represented as incarnational: God in the flesh, God represented as a person consubstantial in indicative physical traits with the human being.

A somewhat later compilation of scriptural-exegeses, organized not around a book of Scripture but rather around the order of synagogue lections, Pesiqta deRab Kahana, stated the matter in still greater detail:

6. A. Because the Holy One, blessed be he, had appeared to them at the sea like a heroic soldier, doing battle, appeared to them at Sinai like a teacher, teaching the repetition [of traditions], appeared to them in the time of Daniel like a sage, teaching Torah, appeared to them in the time of Solomon like a younger man,

B. [it was necessary for] the Holy One, blessed be he, to say to them, "You see me in many forms. But I am the same one who was at the sea, I am the same one who was at Sinai, *I [anokhi] am the Lord your God who brought you out of the land of Egypt* (Ex. 20:2)."

7. A. Said R. Hiyya the Elder, "It is because through every manner of deed and every condition he had appeared to them [that he made that statement namely:]

B. "he had appeared to them at the sea as a heroic soldier, carrying out battles in behalf of Israel,

C. "he had appeared to them at Sinai in the form of a teacher who was teaching Torah and standing in awe,

D. "he had appeared to them in the time of Daniel as an elder, teaching Torah, for it is appropriate for Torah to go forth from the mouth of sages,

E. "he had appeared to them in the time of Solomon as a youth, in accord with the practices of that generation: *His aspect is like Lebanon, young as the cedars* (Song 5:15),

F. 'so at Sinai he appeared to them as a teacher, teaching Torah: *I am the Lord your God who brought you out of the land of Egypt* (Ex. 20:2).

Pesiqta deRab Kahana XII:XXIV

From the position outlined here, which makes ample provision for the conception of an incarnation of God, to the detailed account of what God as a human being looks like and what God as a human being says and does, we have to turn to the Bavli. There we find a reversion to the Scripture's richly incarnational portrait of God, and, it follows we may expect to see what in the Judaism of the dual Torah God incarnate says and does. Not surprisingly, as we shall see, that God forms the model of the sage, that is, the Talmudic authority in particular.

III

The Centrality of Narrative in the Bavli's
Characterization of Divinity

Telling stories provides the means by which theological traits are portrayed as personalities of God who is like a human being. Specifically, the specification of an attribute of God, such as being long-suffering, is restated in the following by means of narrative. God then emerges not as an abstract entity with theological traits but as a fully exposed incarnate person, a personality. God is portrayed as engaged in conversation with human beings because God and humanity can understand one another within the same rules of discourse. When we speak of the incarnation of God, we shall see, traits of a corporeal, emotional, and social character form the repertoire of appropriate characteristics. To begin with, we consider the particular means by which, in the pages of the Talmud of Babylonia or Bavli, in particular, these traits are set forth. The following story shows us the movement from the abstract and theological to the concrete and narrative mode of discourse about God:

> A. "And Moses made haste and bowed his head toward the earth and worshipped: (Ex. 34:8):
>
> B. What did Moses see?
>
> C. R. Hanina b. Gamula said, "He saw [God's attribute of] being long-suffering [Ex. 34:7]."
>
> D. Rabbis say, "He saw [the attribute of] truth [Ex. 34:7]. "It has been taught on Tannaite authority in accord with him who has said, "He saw God's attribute of being long-suffering."
>
> E. For it has been taught on Tannaite authority:
>
> F. When Moses went up on high, he found the Holy One, blessed be he, sitting and writing, "Long-suffering."
>
> G. He said before him, "Lord of the world, "Long-suffering for the righteous?"
>
> H. He said to him, "Also for the wicked."
>
> I. [Moses] said to him. "Let the wicked perish."
>
> J. He said to him, "Now you will see what you want."
>
> K. When the Israelites sinned, he said to him, "Did I not say to you, 'Long suffering for the righteous'?"
>
> L. [111B] He said to him, "Lord of the world, did I not say to you, 'Also for the wicked'?"
>
> M. That is in line with what is written, "And now I beseech you, let the power of my Lord be great, according as you have spoken, saying" (Num. 14:17). [Freedman, *The Babylonian Talmud. Sanhedrin*, p. 764, n. 7: What called forth Moses' worship of God when Israel sinned through the Golden Calf was his vision of the Almighty as long-suffering.]
>
> B San 111 a-b, VI

The statement at the outset, A-D, is repeated in narrative form at Fff. Once we are told that God is long-suffering, then it is in particular, narrative form that trait is given definition. God then emerges as a personality, specifically because Moses engages in argument with God. He reproaches God, questions God's actions and judgments, holds God to a standard of consistency—and receives appropriate responses. God in heaven does not argue with humanity on earth. God in heaven issues decrees, forms the premise of the earthly rules, constitutes a presence, may even take the form of a "you" for hearing and answering prayers. But all of this is in accord with established reasons and laws. When God argues, discusses, defends and explains actions, emerges as a personality etched in words, then God attains that incarnation that imparts to God the status of a being consubstantial with humanity. It is in particular through narrative that transformation of God from person to personality takes place.

IV

Incarnation: The Physical Attributes of God

The claim that the character of God is shaped in the model of a human being requires substantiation, first of all, in quite physical traits, such as are taken for granted in the passage just now cited. Incarnation means precisely that: representation of God in the flesh, as a human being, in the present context, as a man. We begin with a clear statement that has God represented as a man, seen in the interpretation of the vision of the prophet Zechariah:

A. And said R. Yohanan, "What is the meaning of the verse of Scripture, 'I saw by night, and behold a man riding upon a red horse, and he stood among the myrtle trees that were in the bottom' (Zech. 1:8)?

B. "What is the meaning of, 'I saw by night'?

C. "The Holy One blessed be he, sought to turn the entire world into night.

C. " 'And behold, a man riding'—'man' refers only to the Holy One, blessed be he, as it is said, 'The Lord is a man of war, the Lord is his name' (Ex. 15:3).

E. " 'On a red horse'—the Holy One, blessed be he, sought to turn the entire world to blood.

F. "When, however, he saw Hananiah, Mishael, and Azariah, he cooled off, as it is said, 'And he stood among the myrtle trees that were in the deep.'

B. Sanhedrin 1:1 XLII [93A]

The passage in Pesiqta deRab Kahana, cited above, has prepared us for the citation of Ex. 15:3 as proof that God makes the appearance of a human being. Scripture of course knows that God has a face, upon which human beings are not permitted to gaze. But that face was understood in a physical way, and that God enjoyed other physical characteristics, emerges entirely clearly in the following:

A. "And he said, 'You cannot see my face' " (Ex. 33:20).

B. It was taught on Tannaite authority in the name of R. Joshua b. Qorha, "This is what the Holy One, blessed be he, said to Moses:

C. " 'When I wanted [you to see my face], you did not want to, now that you want to see my face, I do not want you to.' "

D. This differs from what R. Samuel bar Nahmani said R. Jonathan said.

E. For R. Samuel bar Nahmani said R. Jonathan said, "As a reward for three things he received the merit of three things.

F. "As a reward for: 'And Moses hid his face,' (Ex. 3:6), he had the merit of having a glistening face.

G. "As a reward for: 'Because he was afraid to' (Ex. 3:6), he had the merit that 'They were afraid to come near him' (Ex. 34:30).

H. "As a reward for: 'To look upon God' (Ex. 3:6), he had the merit: 'The similitude of the Lord does he behold' (Num. 12:8)."

A. "And I shall remove my hand and you shall see my back" (Ex. 33:23)

B. Said R. Hana bar Bizna said R. Simeon the Pious, "This teaches that the Holy One, blessed be he, showed Moses [how to tie] the knot of the phylacteries."

B. Ber. 7A, LVI

That God is able to tie the knot indicates that God has fingers and other physical gifts. God furthermore is portrayed as wearing phylacteries as well. There is no element of a figurative reading of the indicated traits. That is why, when God is further represented as having eyes and teeth, we have no reason to assign that picture to the status of (mere) poetry:

A. "His eyes shall be red with wine, and his teeth white with milk" (Gen. 49:12):

B. R. Dimi, when he came, interpreted the verse in this way: "The congregation of Israel said to the Holy One, blessed be he, 'Lord of the Universe, wink to me with your eyes, which gesture will be sweeter than wine, and show me your teeth, which gesture will be sweeter than milk.'"

b. Ket. 111b

The attribution of physical traits is explicit and no longer general or possibly figurative. Another such representation assigns to God cheeks:

A. R. Joshua b. Levi, "What is the meaning of the verse, 'His cheeks are as a bed of spices' (Song 5:13)?

B. "At every act of speech which went forth from the mouth of the Holy One, blessed be he, the entire world was filled with the fragrance of spices."

C. But since at the first act of speech, the world was filled, where did the second act of speech go?

D. The Holy One, blessed be he, took from his treasures a strong wind, which removed the first draft of fragrance in sequence."

B. Shab. 88b

Joining speech, which is not material, to fragrance, cheeks, and the like, will not have surprised the authorship of Pesiqta deRab Kahana, as we have already noted. From eyes and teeth and cheeks, we move on to the physical attributes of having arms and the like. In the following passage, God is given hands and palms:

E. Further, [the congregation of Israel] made its request in an improper manner, "O God, set me as a seal on your heart, as a seal on your arm" (Song 8:6).

F. [But the Holy One, blessed be he, responded in a proper way.] Said the Holy One, blessed be he, to [the congregation of Israel,] "My daughter, now you are asking for something which sometimes can be seen and sometimes cannot be seen. But I shall give you something which can always be seen."

G. "For it is said, 'Behold, I have graven you on the palms of my hands' (Is. 49:16) [and the palms are always visible, in a way in which the heart and arm are not]."

b Ta. 4a

Hands are attached to arms, and it is implicit that God has arms as well. That God has arms again is shown by the claim that God puts on phylacteries just as Moses does:

A. Said R. Abin bar Ada said R. Isaac, "How do we know on the basis of Scripture that the Holy One, blessed be he, puts on phylacteries? As it is said, 'The Lord has sworn by his right hand, and by the arm of his strength' (Is. 62:8).

B. " 'By his right hand' refers to Torah, as it is said, 'At his right hand was a fiery law for them' (Deut. 33:2).

C. " 'And by the arm of his strength' refers to phylacteries, as it is said, 'The Lord will give strength to his people' (Ps. 29:11).

D. "And how do we know that phylacteries are a strength for Israel? For it is written, 'And all the peoples of the earth shall see that the name of the Lord is called upon you and they shall be afraid of you' (Deut. 28:10)."

E. And it has been taught on Tannaite authority:

F. R. Eliezer the Great says, "This [Deut. 28:10] refers to the phylacteries that are put on the head."

B. Ber. 6A, XXXVIII

Once more we find clear evidence of a corporeal conception of God. We have no basis on which to assume the authorship at hand meant a (merely) poetic characterization, or, indeed, what such a more spiritual interpretation would have required. Assuming that the words mean precisely what they say, we have to conclude that God is here portrayed as incarnate. Later on we shall be told what passages of Scripture are written in the phylacteries that God puts onto his right arm and forehead.

God not only looks like a human being but also does the acts that human beings do. For example, God spends the day much as does a mortal ruler of Israel, at least as sages imagine such a figure. That is, he studies the Torah, makes practical decisions, and sustains the world (meaning, administers public funds for public needs)—just as (in sages' picture of themselves) sages do. What gives us a deeply human God is that for the final part of the day, God plays with his pet, leviathan. Some correct that view and hold that God spends the rest of the day teaching youngsters. In passages such as these we therefore see the concrete expression of a process of the incarnation of God:

> A. Said R. Judah said Rab, "The day is twelve hours long. During the first three, the Holy One, blessed be he, is engaged in the study of the Torah.
>
> B. "During the next three God sits in judgment on the world and when he sees the world sufficiently guilty to deserve destruction, he moves from the seat of justice to the seat of mercy.
>
> C. "During the third he feeds the whole world, from the horned buffalo to vermin.
>
> D. "During the fourth he plays with the leviathan, as it is said, "There is leviathan, whom you have made to play with' (Ps. 104:26).''
>
> E. [Another authority denies this final point and says,] 'What then does God do in the fourth quarter of the day?
>
> F. "He sits and teaches school children, as it is said, 'Whom shall one teach knowledge, and whom shall one make to understand the message? Those who are weaned from milk' (Is. 28-9)."
>
> G. And what does God do by night?
>
> H. If you like, I shall propose that he does what he does in daytime.
>
> I. Or if you prefer: he rides a light cherub and floats in eighteen thousand worlds...
>
> J. Or if you prefer: he sits and listens to the song of the heavenly creatures, as it is said, "By the day the Lord will command his lovingkindness and in the night his song shall be with me (Ps. 42:9).''
>
> b. A.Z. 3b

Other actions of God that presuppose a physical capacity are indicated in the following, although the picture is not so clearly one of concrete physical actions as in the earlier instances:

> A. Said R. Judah said Rab, "Everything that Abraham personally did for the ministering angels the Holy One, blessed be he, personally did for his children, and everything that Abraham did through servants the Holy One, blessed be he, carried out also through ministering angels.
>
> B. " 'And Abraham ran to the herd' (Gen. 18:7), 'And a wind went forth from the Lord' (Num. 11:31).
>
> C. " 'And he took butter and milk' (Gen. 18:8). 'Behold, I will rain bread from heaven for you' (Ex. 16:4).
>
> D. " 'And he stood by them under the tree' (Gen. 18:8). 'Behold, I will stand before you there upon the rock' (Ex. 17:6).
>
> B.B.M. 86b

The passage proceeds to point out further examples of the same parallels. The various actions of God in favor of Israel correspond to the concrete actions of Abraham for God or the angels. The comparison of Abraham's actions to those of God invites the notion that God is represented as incarnate. But in this instance we are not compelled to a reading of God as an essentially corporeal being. The actions God does can be accomplished in some less material or physical way.

V
Incarnation: The Emotions and Attitudes of God

The incarnation of God encompassed not only physical, but also emotional or attitudinal traits. In the final stage of the Judaism of the dual Torah God emerged as a fully-exposed personality. The character of divinity, therefore, encompassed God's virtue, the specific traits of character and personality that God exhibited above and here below. Above all, humility, the virtue sages most often asked of themselves, characterized the divinity. God wanted people to be humble, and God therefore showed humility.

> A. Said R. Joshua b. Levi, "When Moses came down from before the Holy One, blessed be he, Satan came and asked [God], " 'Lord of the world, Where is the Torah?' "
> B. "He said to him, 'I have given it to the earth...' [Satan ultimately was told by God to look for the Torah by finding the son of Amram.]
> C. "He went to Moses and asked him, 'Where is the Torah which the Holy One, blessed be he, gave you?'
> D. "He said to him, 'Who am I that the Holy One, blessed be he, should give me the Torah?'
> E. "Said the Holy One, blessed be he, to Moses, 'Moses, you are a liar!'
> F. "He said to him, 'Lord of the world, you have a treasure in store which you have enjoyed every day. Shall I keep it to myself?'
> G. "He said to him, 'Moses, since you have acted with humility, it will bear your name: "Remember the Torah of Moses, my servant" (Mal. 3:22).' "
>
> b. Shab 89a

God here is represented as favoring humility and rewarding the humble with honor. What is important is that God does not here cite Scripture or merely paraphrase it; the conversation is an exchange between two vivid personalities. True enough, Moses, not God, is the hero. But the personality of God emerges in a vivid way. The following passage shows how traits imputed to God also define proper conduct for sages, not to mention other human beings. At issue once again is humility, and as we see, arrogance—the opposite—is treated as denial of God, humility, the imitation of God:

> P. And R. Yohanan said in the name of R. Simeon b. Yohai, "Whoever is arrogant is as if he worships idolatry.
> Q. "Here it is written, 'Everyone who is arrogant in heart is an abomination to the Lord," (Prov. 16:5), and elsewhere it is written, 'You will not bring an abomination into your house' (Deut. 7:26)."
> R. And R. Yohanan on his own account said, "He is as if he denied the very Principle [of the world],
> S. "as it is said, 'Your heart will be lifted up and you will forget the Lord your God' (Deut. 8:14)."
> T. R. Hama bar Hanina said, "He is as if he had sexual relations with all of those women forbidden to him on the laws of incest.

U. "Here it is written, 'Everyone who is arrogant in heart is an abomination to the Lord' (Prov. 16:5), and elsewhere it is written, 'For all these abominations...' (Lev. 18:27)."

V. Ulla said, "It is as if he built a high place,

W. "as it is said, 'Cease you from man, whose breath is in his nostrils, for wherein is he to be accounted of' (Is. 2:22).

X "Do not read, 'wherein,' but rather, 'high place.' "

b. Sot. 5b, XVI

A. Whence [in Scripture] do we derive an admonition against the arrogant?

B. Said Raba said Zeiri, " 'Listen and give ear, do not be proud' (Jer. 13:15)."

C. R. Nahman bar Isaac said, "From the following: 'Your heart will be lifted up, and you will forget the Lord your God' (Deut. 8:14).

D. "And it is written, 'Beware, lest you forget the Lord your God' (Deut. 8:11)."

E. And that accords with what R. Abin said R. Ilaa said.

F. For R. Abin said R. Ilaa said, "In every place in which it is said, 'Beware lest...that you not...,' the meaning is only to lay down a negative commandment [so that one who does such a thing violates a negative admonition]."

b. Sot. 5b, XVIII

A. "With him also who is of a contrite and humble spirit" (Is. 57:15).

B. R. Huna and R. Hisda:

C. One said, "I [God] am with the contrite."

D. The other said, "I [God] am the contrite."

E. Logic favors the view of him who has said, "I [God] am with the contrite," for lo, the Holy One, blessed be he, neglected all mountains and heights and brought his Presence to rest on Mount Sinai,

F. and he did not raise Mount Sinai upward [to himself].

G. R. Joseph said, "A person should always learn from the attitude of his Creator, for lo, the Holy One, blessed be he, neglected all mountains and heights and brought his Presence to rest on Mount Sinai,

H. "and he neglected all valuable trees and brought his Presence to rest in the bush."

b. Sot. 5b. XX

A. Said R. Eleazar, "Whoever is arrogant is worthy of being cut down like an asherah [a tree that is worshipped].

B. "Here it is written, 'The high ones of stature shall be cut down' (Is. 10:33),

C. "and elsewhere it is written, 'And you shall hew down their Asherim' (Deut. 7:5)."

D. And R. Eleazar said, "Whoever is arrogant—his dust will not be stirred up [in the resurrection of the dead].

E. "For it is said, 'Awake and sing, you that dwell in the dust' (Is. 26:19).

F. "It is stated not 'you who lie in the dust' but 'you who dwell in the dust,' meaning, one who has become a neighbor to the dust [by constant humility] even in his lifetime."

G. And R. Eleazar said, "For whoever is arrogant the Presence of God laments,

H. "as it is said, 'But the haughty he knows from afar' (Ps. 138:6)."

b. Sot. 5b XXI

A. R. Avira expounded, and some say it was R. Eleazar, "Come and take note of the fact that not like the trait of the Holy One, blessed be he, is the trait of flesh and blood.

B. "The trait of flesh and blood is that those who are high take note of those who are high, but the one who is high does not take note of the one who is low.

C. "But the trait of the Holy One, blessed be he, is not that way. He is high, but he takes note of the low,

D. "as it is said, 'For though the Lord is high, yet he takes note of the low' (Ps. 138-6)."

b. Sot. 5b. XXII

A. Said R. Hisda, and some say it was Mar Uqba, "Concerning whoever is arrogant said the Holy One, blessed be he, he and I cannot live in the same world,

B. "as it is said, 'Whoever slanders his neighbor in secret—him will I destroy; him who has a haughty look and a proud heart I will not endure' (Ps. 101:5).

C. "Do not read, 'him [I cannot endure]' but 'with him [I cannot endure].'"

D. There are those who apply the foregoing teaching to those who slander, as it is said, "Whoever slanders his neighbor in secret—him will I destroy" (Ps. 101:5).

b. Sot. 5b XXIII

A. Said R. Joshua b. Levi, "Come and take note of how great are the humble in the sight of the Holy One, blessed be he.

B. "For when the sanctuary stood, a person would bring a burnt-offering, gaining thereby the reward for bringing a burnt-offering, or a meal-offering, and gaining the reward for a meal offering.

C. "But a person who is genuinely humble does Scripture treat as if he had made offerings of all the sacrifices,

D. "as it is said, 'The sacrifices [plural] of God are a broken spirit' (Ps. 51:19).

E. "And not only so, but his prayer is not rejected, as it is said, 'A broken and contrite heart, O God, you will not despise' (Ps. 51: 19)."

b Sot. 5b XXIX

The repertoire shows clearly that sages impute to God those traits of personality that are recommended and claim that God favors personalities like God's own. The clear implication is that God and the human being are consubstantial as to attitudes, emotions, and other aspects of virtue.

God laughs just as does a human being. The attribution to God of a sense of humor portrays the divinity once more as incarnate, the model by which the human being was made not only in physical form, but also in personality traits.

A. [In a dispute between R. Eliezer and R. Joshua, a heavenly voice stated, "Why do you argue with R. Eliezer, since in all matters, the law is in accord with his position." R. Joshua stood and exclaimed, " 'It is not in heaven' (Deut. 30:12), [meaning that decisions of the law are made by sages and not by divine intervention]. R. Nathan met Elijah and asked him, "What did the Holy One, blessed be he, do then?"

B He said to him, "He laughed out loud, saying, 'My children have won over me, my children have won over me.' "

b. B.M. 59b

God's laughter is not only because of delight. It may also take on a sardonic character, for instance, as ridicule:

A. Said R. Yose, "In the age to come idolaters will come and convert [to Judaism]...and will put phylacteries on their foreheads and arms, place show-fringes on their garments and a *mezuzah* on their doorposts. When, however, the battle of Gog and Magog takes place, they will be asked, 'Why have you come?'

B. "They will reply, 'Against God and his anointed...'(Ps. 2:1).

C. "Then each of the converts will toss off the religious emblems and leave...and the Holy One, blessed be he, will sit and laugh,

D. "as it is said, 'He who sits in heaven laughs...'(Ps. 2:4)."

The repertoire of God's emotions encompasses not only desirable, but also undesirable traits. God not only exhibits and favors humility and has the capacity to laugh out of both joy and ridicule. God also becomes angry and performs acts that express that anger:

A. And said R. Yohanan in the name of R. Yose, "How do we know that one should not placate a person when he is angry?

B. "It is in line with the following verse of Scripture: 'My face will go and then I will give you rest' (Ex. 33:14)

C. "Said the Holy One, blessed be he, to Moses, 'Wait until my angry countenance passes, and then I shall give you rest.' "

D. But does the Holy One, blessed be he, get angry?

E. Indeed so.

F. For it has been taught on Tannaite authority:

G. "A God that is angry every day" (Ps. 7:12).

H. And how long is this anger going to last?

I. A moment.

J. And how long is a moment?

K. It is one fifty-eight thousand eight hundred and eighty-eighth part of an hour.

L. And no creature except for the wicked Balaam has ever been able to fix the moment exactly.

M. For concerning him it has been written, "He knows the knowledge of the Most High" (Num. 24:16).

N. Now if Balaam did not even know what his beast was thinking, was he likely to know what the Most High is thinking?

O. But this teaches that he knew exactly how to reckon the very moment that the Holy One, blessed be he, would be angry.

P. That is in line with what the prophet said to Israel, "O my people, remember now what Balak, king of Moab, devised, and what Balaam, son of Beor, answered him...that you may know the righteous acts of the Lord" (Mic. 6:5).

Q. Said R. Eleazar, "The Holy One, blessed be he, said to Israel, 'Know that I did any number of acts of righteousness with you, for I did not get angry in the time of the wicked Balaam. For had I gotten angry, not one of (the enemies of) Israel would have survived, not a remnant.'

R. "That is in line with what Balaam said to Balak, 'How shall I curse whom God has not cursed, and how shall I execrate whom the Lord has not execrated?' (Num. 23:8).

S. "This teaches that for that entire time [God] did not get mad."

T. And how long is God's anger?

U. It is a moment.

V. And how long is a moment?

W. Said R. Abin, and some say, R. Abina, "A moment lasts as long as it takes to say 'a moment.' "

X. And how do we know that a moment is how long God is angry?

Y. For it is said, "For his anger is but for a moment, his favor is for a lifetime" (Ps. 30:6).

Z. If you like, you may derive the lesson from the following: "Hide yourself for a little while until the anger be past" (Is. 26:20).

AA. And when is God angry?

BB. Said Abayye, "It is during the first three hours of the day, when the comb of the cock is white, and it stands on one foot."

CC. But it stands on one foot every hour.

DD. To be sure, it stands on its foot every hour, but in all the others it has red streaks, and in the moment at hand there are no red streaks [in the comb of the cock].

b. Ber. 7A, LI

What is striking in this sizable account is the characterization of God's anger in entirely corporeal terms. God not only becomes angry, God also acts in anger. For one example, in anger God also loses his temper:

A. Said R. Judah said Rab, "When the Holy One, blessed be he, proposed to create the world, he said to the angeic prince of the sea, 'Open your mouth and swallow all the water in the world.'

B. "He said to him, 'Lord of the world, it is quite sufficient if I stick with what I already have.'

C. "Forthwith he kicked him with his foot and killed him.

D. "For it is written, 'He stirs up the sea with his power, and by his understanding he smites through Rahab' (Job 26:12)."

b. B.B. 74b

Like a human being, God thus can lose his temper. God's anger derives not only from ill-temper but deeper causes. God is dissatisfied with the world as it is and so expresses anger with the present condition of humanity, on account of Israel:

F. For it has been taught on Tannaite authority:

G. R. Eliezer says, "The night is divided into three watches, and [in heaven] over each watch the Holy One, blessed be he, sits and roars like a lion,

H. "as it is said, 'The Lord roars from on high and raises his voice from his holy habitation, roaring he does roar because of his fold' (Jer. 25:30).

I. "The indication of each watch is as follows: at the first watch, an ass brays, at the second, dogs yelp, at the third, an infant sucks at its mother's breast or a woman whispers to her husband."

b. Ber. 3a, VI

A. Said R. Isaac bar Samuel in the name of Rab, "The night is divided into three watches, and over each watch, the Holy One, blessed be he, sits and roars like a lion.

B. "He says, 'Woe to the children, on account of whose sins I have wiped out my house and burned my palace, and whom I have exiled among the nations of the world. ' "

b. Ber. 3a, VII

A. It has been taught on Tannaite authority:

B. Said R. Yose, "Once I was going along the way, and I went into one of the ruins of Jerusalem to pray. Elijah, of blessed memory, came and watched over me at the door until I had finished my prayer. After I had finished my prayer, he said to me, 'Peace be to you, my lord.'

C. "And I said to him, 'Peace be to you, my lord and teacher.'

D. "And he said to me, 'My son, on what account did you go into this ruin?'

E. "And I said to him, 'To pray.'

F. "And he said to me, 'You would have done better to pray on the road.'...

J. "And he said to me, 'My son, what sound did you hear in this ruin?'

K. "I said to him, 'I heard the sound of an echo moaning like a pigeon and saying, "Woe to the children, on account of whose sins I have wiped out my house and burned my palace and whom I have exiled among the nations of the world.' "

L. "He said to me. 'By your life and the life of your head, it is not only at this moment that the echo speaks in such a way, but three times daily, it says the same thing.

M. " 'And not only so, but when Israelites go into synagogues and schoolhouses and respond, "May the great name be blessed," the Holy One shakes his head and says, "Happy is the king, whom they praise in his house in such a way! What does a father have, who has exiled his children? And woe to the children who are exiled from their father's table!' ""

b. Ber. 3a, VIII

God's anger and mourning form emotions identical to those of human beings, as is made explicit. Israel are God's children, and God mourns for them as a parent mourns for children who have suffered. The incarnation of God therefore takes the form of representing God's attitudes as the same as those of human beings, though of a cosmic order. But God's anger derives from broader causes than Israel's current condition.

VI

Incarnation: The Social Attributes of God

The humanity of God emerges in yet another way. God enters into transactions with human beings and accords with the rules that govern those relationships. So God exhibits precisely the social attributes that human beings do. A number of stories, rather protracted and detailed, tell the story of God as a social being, living among and doing business with mortals. These stories provide extended portraits of God's relationships in particular arguments, with important figures, such as angelic figures, as well as Moses, David, and Hosea. In them God negotiates, persuades, teaches, argues, exchanges reasons. The incarnation of God therefore comes to expression in a variety of portraits of how God will engage in arguments with men and angels, and so enters into the existence of ordinary people. These disputes, negotiations, transactions yield a portrait of God who is reasonable and capable of give and take, as in the following:

> F. Rabbah bar Mari said, "What is the meaning of this verse: 'But they were rebellious at the sea, even at the Red Sea; nonetheless he saved them for his name's sake' (Ps. 106:7)?
> G. "This teaches that the Israelites were rebellious at that time, saying, 'Just as we will go up on this side, so the Egyptians will go up on the other side.' Said the Holy One, blessed be he, to the angelic prince who reigns over the sea, 'Cast them [the Israelites] out on dry land.'
> H. "He said before him, 'Lord of the world, is there any case of a slave [namely, myself] to whom his master [you] gives a gift [the Israelites], and then the master goes and takes [the gift] away again? [You gave me the Israelites, now you want to take them away and place them on dry land.]'
> I. He said to him, 'I'll give you one and a half times their number.'
> J. "He said before him, 'Lord of the world, is there a possibility that a slave can claim anything against his master? [How do I know that you will really do it?]'
> K. "He said to him, 'The Kishon brook will be my pledge [that I shall carry out my word. Nine hundred chariots at the brook were sunk, (Jud. 3:23) while Pharaoh at the sea had only six hundred, thus a pledge one and half times greater than the sum at issue.]'
> L. "Forthwith [the angelic prince of the sea] spit them out onto dry land, for it is written, 'And the Israelites saw the Egyptians dead on the sea shore' (Ex. 14:30)."
>
> B. Ar. 15A-B

God is willing to give a pledge to guarantee his word. He furthermore sees the right claim of the counterpart actor in the story. Hence we see how God obeys precisely the same social laws of exchange and reason that govern other incarnate beings.

Still more interesting is the picture of God's argument with Abraham. God is represented as accepting accountability, by the standards of humanity, for what God does.

A. Said R. Isaac, "When the temple was destroyed, the Holy One, blessed be he, found Abraham standing in the Temple. He said to him, 'What is my beloved doing in my house?'

B. "He said to him, 'I have come because of what is going on with my children.'

C. "He said to him, 'Your children sinned and have been sent into exile.'

D. "He said to him, 'But wasn't it by mistake that they sinned?'

E. "He said to him, 'She has wrought lewdness' (Jer. 11:15).

F. "He said to him, 'But wasn't it just a minority of them that did it?'

G. "He said to him, 'It was a majority' (Jer. 11:15).

H. "He said to him, 'You should at least have taken account of the covenant of circumcision [which should have secured forgiveness despite their sin]!'

I. "He said to him, 'The holy flesh is passed from you' (Jer. 11:15).

J. "And if you had waited for them, they might have repented!

K. "He said to him, 'When you do evil, then you are happy' (Jer. 11:15).

L. "He said to him, 'He put his hands on his head, crying out and weeping, saying to them, 'God forbid! Perhaps they have no remedy at all!'

M. "A heavenly voice came forth and said, 'The Lord called you "a leafy olive tree, fair with excellent fruit' " (Jer. 11:16).

N. " 'Just as in the case of an olive tree, its future comes only at the end [that is, it is only after a long while that it attains its best fruit], so in the case of Israel, their future comes at the end of their time.' "

b. Men. 53b

God relates to Abraham as to an equal. That is shown by God's implicit agreement that he is answerable to Abraham for what has taken place with the destruction of the Temple. God does not impose on Abraham silence, saying that is a decree not to be contested but only accepted. God as a social being accepts that he must provide sound reasons for his actions, as must any other reasonable person in a world governed by rules applicable to everyone. Abraham is a fine choice for the protagonist, since he engaged in the argument concerning Sodom. His complaint is expressed at B: God is now called to explain himself. At each point then Abraham offers arguments in behalf of sinning Israel, and God responds, item by item. The climax of course has God promising Israel a future worth having. God emerges as both just and merciful, reasonable but sympathetic. The transaction attests to God's conformity to rules of reasoned transactions in a coherent society.

The same picture is drawn in still greater detail when God engages Hosea in discussion. Here, however, Hosea complains against Israel, and God takes the part of Abraham in the earlier account. God's social role is defined in the model of the sage or master, a role we shall presently find prominent in the repertoire of portraits of incarnation. God teaches Hosea by providing an analogy, for Hosea, of what Hosea proposes that God do.

> I.A. Said the Holy One, blessed be he, to Hosea, "Your children have sinned."
>
> B. He should have said to him, "They are your children, children of those to whom you have shown grace, children of Abraham, Isaac, and Jacob. Send your mercy to them."
>
> C. It is not enough that he did not say the right thing, but he said to him, "Lord of the world, the entire world is yours. Trade them in for some other nation."
>
> D. Said the Holy One, blessed be he, "What shall I then do with that elder? I shall tell him, 'Go, marry a whore and have children of prostitution.' Then I'll tell him, 'Divorce her.' If he can send her away, then I'll send away Israel."
>
> E. For it is said, "And the Lord said to Hosea, Go, take a whore and have children of prostitution" (Hos. 1:1).

> II.A. After he had two sons and a daughter, the Holy One, blessed be he, said to Hosea, "Should you not have learned the lesson of your master, Moses? Once I had entered into discourse with him, he separated from his wife. So you too, take your leave of her."
>
> B. He said to him, "Lord of the world, I have children from her, and I simply cannot drive her out or divorce her."
>
> C. Said to him the Holy One, blessed be he, "Now if you, married to a whore, with children of prostitution, and you don't even know whether they're yours or whether they come from some other fathers, are in such a state, as to Israel, who are my children, children of those whom I have tested, the children of Abraham, Isaac and Jacob...
>
> D. "...how can you say to me, 'Trade them in for some other nation'?"
>
> E. When [Hosea] realized that he had sinned, he arose to seek mercy for himself. Said the Holy One, blessed be he, to him, "Instead of seeking mercy for yourself, seek mercy for Israel, against whom I have on your account issued three decrees [exile, rejection, and without compassion, reflecting the names of his children]."
>
> F. He went and sought mercy and [God] annulled [the decrees] and gave them this blessing: "Yet the number of the children of Israel shall be as the sand of the sea...and instead of being called 'You are not my people.' they will be called 'You are the children of the living God.' And the children of Judah and the children of Israel shall be gathered together. ...And I will sow her to me in the land, and have compassion on her who was not treated with compassion and say to those who were not my people, 'You are my people' (Hos. 2:1-2, 25)."

B Pes 87a

Hosea negotiates with God, proposing that God reject Israel for some other nation. God's reply is that of an experienced teacher. He puts the disciple through a concrete lesson, which imparts to the disciple the desired experience and leads to the disciple's drawing the right conclusion. The social transaction then is worked out in accord with rules of reason. Just as experience teaches Hosea the lesson that one does not reject, but forgives, sinful relations, so Hosea draws the correct conclusion.

The story then portrays God in a social transaction that is governed by accepted laws of orderly conduct.

God's relationships with David, a paramount theme in the story of David's sin with Bath Sheba, yield the picture of how God responds in a reasonable way to a reasonable proposal. Then, to be sure, God teaches a lesson of right conduct. But, throughout, God's role remains the same: a social and rational being, like mortals. What is important for my argument is the representation of God as engaged in negotiation in accord with rules that apply to heaven and earth alike. God then enters into society as a full participant in the world of humanity and plays a role that forms the counterpart to that of any just person. The incarnation of God here takes the now-well-established form of God as fully engaged in social transactions with counterparts on earth. We consider only those portions of the story that pertain to our topic:

A. Said R. Judah said Rab, "One should never put himself to the test, for lo, David, king of Israel, put himself to the test and he stumbled.

B. "He said before him, 'Lord of the world, on what account do people say, "God of Abraham, God of Isaac, and God of Jacob, "but they do not say, "God of David"?'

C. "He said to him, 'They endured a test for me, while you have not endured a test for me.'

D. "He said before him, 'Lord of the world, here I am. Test me.'

E. "For it is said, 'Examine me, O Lord, and try me' (Ps. 26:1).

F. "He said to him, 'I shall test you, and I shall do for you something that I did not do for them. I did not inform them [what I was doing], while I shall tell you what I am going to do. I shall try you with a matter having to do with sexual relations.'

G. "Forthwith: 'And it came to pass in an eventide that David arose from off his bed' (2 Sam. 11:2)."

The opening passage represents God in conversation with David and responsive to David's reasoning. This is more than the presence of God familiar in the earliest strata of the canon, and God in conversation with David forms a personality, not the mere "you" of prayer familiar in the initial writings of the Judaism of the dual Torah. Where God cites Scripture, it is not merely to prove a point but to make a statement particular to the exchange at hand. So it is not a conventional portrait of God's serving as the voice of an established text. It is, to the contrary, the picture of God engaged in a social transaction with a sentiment being.

We skip the description of David's relationship with Bath Sheba and move directly to David's plea of forgiveness. In the passages that follow, God serves merely as audience for David's statements:

A. Raba interpreted Scripture, asking, "What is the meaning of the following verse: 'To the chief musician, a Psalm of David. In the Lord I put my trust, how do you say to my soul, Flee as a bird to your mountain?' (Ps. 11:1)?

B. "Said David before the Holy One, blessed be he, 'Lord of the world, Forgive me for that sin, so that people should not say, "The mountain that is among you [that is, your king] has been driven off by a bird.' ""

C. Raba interpreted Scripture, asking, "What is the meaning of the following verse: 'Against you, you alone, have I sinned, and done this evil in your sight, that you might be justified when you speak and be clear when you judge' (Ps. 11:1)?

D. "Said David before the Holy One, blessed be he, 'Lord of the world. It is perfectly clear to you that if I had wanted to overcome my impulse to do evil, I should have done so. But I had in mind that people not say, "The slave has conquered the Master [God, and should then be included as 'God of David'].' "

E. Raba interpreted Scripture, asking, "What is the meaning of the following verse: 'For I am ready to halt and my sorrow is continually before me' (Ps. 38:18)?

F. "Bath Sheba, daughter of Eliam, was designated for David from the six days of creation, but she came to him through anguish."

G. And so did a Tannaite authority of the house of R. Ishmael [teach], "Bath Sheba, daughter of Eliam, was designated for David, but he 'ate' her while she was yet unripe."

H. Raba interpreted Scripture, asking, "What is the meaning of the following verse: 'But in my adversity they rejoiced and gathered themselves together, yes, the abjects gathered themselves together against me and I did not know it, they tore me and did not cease' (Ps. 35:15)?

I. "Said David before the Holy One, blessed be he, 'Lord of the world, it is perfectly clear to you that if they had torn my flesh, my blood would not have flowed [because I was so embarrassed].

J. "Not only so, but when they take up the four modes of execution inflicted by a court, they interrupt their Mishnah-study and say to me, "David, he who has sexual relations with a married woman—how is he put to death?"

K. " 'I say to them, "He who has sexual relations with a married woman is put to death through strangulation, but he has a share in the world to come," while he who humiliates his fellow in public has no share in the world to come.' ""

Now God emerges once more and plays the role of antagonist to David's protagonist:

A. R. Dosetai of Biri interpreted Scripture, "To what may David be likened? To a gentile merchant.

B. "Said David before the Holy One, blessed be he, 'Lord of the world, Who can understand his errors?' (Ps. 19:13).

C. "He said to him, 'They are remitted for you.'

D. " 'Cleanse me of hidden faults" (Ps. 19:13).'

E. " 'They are remitted to you.'

F. " 'Keep back your servant also from presumptuous sins" (Ps. 19:13).'

G. " 'They are remitted to you.'

H. " 'Let them not have dominion over me, then I shall be upright" (Ps. 19:13), so that the rabbis will not hold me up as an example.'

I. " 'They are remitted to you.'

J. " 'And I shall be innocent of great transgression" (Ps. 19:13), so that they will not write down my ruin.'

K. "He said to him, 'That is not possible. Now if the Y that I took away from the name of Sarah [changing it from Sarah to Sarah] stood crying for so many years until Joshua came and I added the Y [removed from Sarah's name] to his name, as it is said, "And Moses called Oshea, the son of Nun, Jehoshua" (Num. 13:16), how much the more will a complete passage of Scripture [cry out if I remove that passage from its rightful place]!' "

God once more emerges as a fully formed personality. For God's role here is not merely to cite Scripture. K forms the centerpiece. God can do just so much, but no more, and this detail is the contribution not of Scripture but of the story-teller. The incarnation of God once more takes shape in the notion of God as bound by rules of procedure and conduct. God enters into civil and rational transactions with human beings and conforms to the same rules with the result that is expressed here.

A. "And I shall be innocent from great transgression: (Ps. 19:13):
B. He said before him, "Lord of the world, forgive me for the whole of that sin [as though I had never done it]."
C. He said to him, "Solomon, your son, even now is destined to say in his wisdom, 'Can a man take fire in his bosom, and his clothes not be burned? Can one go upon hot coals, and his feet not be burned? So he who goes in to his neighbor's wife, whoever touches her shall not be innocent' (Prov. 6:27-29)."
D. He said to him, "Will I be so deeply troubled?"
E. He said to him, "Accept suffering [as atonement]."
F. He accepted the suffering.

A. Said R. Judah said Rab, "For six months David was afflicted with *saraat*, and the Presence of God left him, and the sanhedrin abandoned him.
B. "He was afflicted with *saraat*, as it is written, 'Purge me with hyssop and I shall be clean, wash me and I shall be whiter than snow; (Ps. 51:9).
C. "The Presence of God left him, as it is written, 'Restore to me the joy of your salvation and uphold me with your free spirit' (Ps. 51:14).
D. "The sanhedrin abandoned him, as it is written, 'Let those who fear you turn to me and those who have known your testimonies' (Ps. 119:79).
E. "How do we know that this lasted for six months? As it is written, 'And the days that David rules over Israel were forty years: [107B] Seven years he reigned in Hebron, and thirty-three years he reigned in Jerusalem' (I Kgs. 2:11).
F. "Elsewhere it is written, 'In Hebron he reigned over Judah seven years and six months' (2 Sam. 5:5).
G. "So the six months were not taken into account. Accordingly, he was afflicted with saraat [for such a one is regarded as a corpse].
H. "He said before him, 'Lord of the world, forgive me for that sin.'
I. " 'It is forgiven to you.'

J. " 'Then show me a token for good, that they who hate me may see it and be ashamed, because you, Lord, have helped me and comforted me' (Ps. 86:17).

K. "He said to him, 'While you are alive, I shall not reveal [the fact that you are forgiven], but I shall reveal it in the lifetime of your son, Solomon.'

L. "When Solomon had built the house of the sanctuary, he tried to bring the ark into the house of the Holy of Holies. The gates cleaved to one another. He recited twenty-four prayers [Freedman, p. 734, n. 4: in 2 Chr. 6 words for prayer, supplication and hymn occur twenty-four times], but was not answered.

M. "He said, 'Lift up your head, O you gates, and be lifted up, you everlasting doors, and the King of glory shall come in. Who is this King of glory? The Lord strong and might, the Lord mighty in battle' (Ps. 24:7ff).

N. "And it is further said, 'Lift up your heads, O you gates even lift them up, you everlasting doors/ (Ps. 24:7).

O. "But he was not answered.

P. "When he said, 'Lord God, turn not away the face of your anointed, remember the mercies of David, your servant' (2 Chr. 6:42), forthwith he was answered.

Q. "At that moment the faces of David's enemies turned as black as the bottom of a pot, for all Israel knew that the Holy One, blessed be he, had forgiven him for that sin."

b. San. 106b-107a, CCXLVI-CCLI

As we see, our hero is not God but David. Nonetheless, the portrayal of God justifies the claim that we have here an incarnate God, consubstantial with humanity not only in physical and emotional traits, but also, and especially, in the conformity to the social laws of correct transactions that, in theory at least, make society possible.

VII

God as Sage

Among the available models for the incarnation of God, such as those introduced in Pesiqta de Rab Kahana's authorships' repertoire—warrior, teacher, young man— the one that predominated entailed representation of God as sage. We recall that God is represented as a school master:

F. "He sits and teaches school children, as it is said, 'Whom shall one teach knowledge, and whom shall one make to understand the message? Those who are weaned from milk' (Is. 28:9)."

b. A.Z. 3b

But this is not the same thing as God as a master-sage teaching mature disciples, that is, God as rabbi and sage. That representation emerges in a variety of ways and proves the single most important mode of the incarnation of God. God's personality merged throughout with the Bavli's authorships' representation of the personality of the ideal master or sage. That representation in the Bavli proved detailed and specific. A sage's life—Torah learned, then taught, through discipleship—encompassed both the correct modes of discourse and ritual argument, on the one side, and the recasting of all relationships in accord with received convention of courtesy and subservience. God then is represented in both dimensions, as a master requiring correct conduct of his disciples, and as a teacher able to hold his own in arguments conducted in accord with the prevailing ritual. For one example, a master had the right to demand an appropriate greeting, and God, not receiving that greeting, asked why:

> A. Said R. Joshua b. Levi, "When Moses came up on high, he found the Holy One, blessed be he, tying crowns onto the letters of the Torah. He said to him, 'Moses, don't people say hello in your town?'
> B. "He said to him,'Does a servant greet his master [first]?'
> C. "He said to him, 'You should have helped me [at least by greeting me and wishing me success].'
> D. "He said to him, " 'Now I pray you let the power of the Lord be great, just as you have said" (Num. 14:17).' "
>
> b. Shab. 89a

Moses here plays the role of disciple to God the teacher, a persistent pattern throughout. Not having offered the appropriate greeting, the hapless disciple is instructed on the matter. Part of the ritual of "being a sage" thus comes to expression. Yet another detail of that same ritual taught how to make a request—and how not to do so. A request offered in humility is proper; one made in an arrogant or demanding spirit is not. Knowing what to ask is as important as knowing how. The congregation of Israel shows how not to do so, and God shows, nonetheless, the right mode of response, in the following:

> A. The congregation of Israel made its request in an improper way, but the Holy One, blessed be he, responded in a proper way.
> B. For it is said, [the congregation of Israel said to God.] "And let us know, eagerly strive to know, the Lord, the Lord's going forth is sure as the morning, and the Lord shall come to us as the rain" (Hos. 6:3).
> C. Said the Holy One, blessed be he, to [the congregation of Israel,] "My daughter, now you are asking for something which sometimes is wanted and sometimes is not really wanted. But I shall give you something which is always wanted.
> D. "For is is said, 'I will be as dew to Israel' (Hos. 14:6)."
> E. Further, [the congregation of Israel] made its request in an improper manner, "O God, set me as a seal on your heart, as a seal on your arm" (Song 8:6).
> F. [But the Holy One, blessed be he, responded in a proper way.] Said the Holy One, blessed be he, to [the congregation of Israel,] "My daughter, now you are asking for something which sometimes can be seen and sometimes cannot be seen. But I shall give you something which can always be seen.
> G. "For it is said, 'Behold, I have graven you on the palms of my hands' (Is. 49:16) [and the palms are always visible, in a way in which the heart and arm are not]."
>
> b. Ta. 4a

Dew is always wanted, rain not. To be a seal on the heart or arm is to be displayed only occasionally. But the hands are always visible. Consequently, God as sage teaches Israel as disciple how to make a proper request.

The status of sage, expressed in rituals of proper conduct, is attained through knowing how to participate in argument about matters of the Torah, particularly the law. Indeed, what makes a sage an authority is knowledge of details of the law. Consequently, my claim that God is represented as a particular sort of human being, namely, as a sage, requires evidence that God not only follows the arguments (as above, "My sons have conquered me!") and even has opinions which he proposes to interject, but also himself participates in debates on the law. Ability to follow those debates and forcefully to contribute to them forms the chief indicator. That ability joins some men to God is furthermore explicit. So the arguments in the academy in heaven, over which God presides, form the exact counterpart to the arguments on earth, with the result that God emerges as precisely consubstantial, physically and intellectually, with the particular configuration of the sage:

> A. In the session in the firmament, people were debating this question: if the bright spot came before the white hair, the person is unclean. If the white hair came before the bright spot, he is clean. What about as case of doubt?
> B. The Holy One, blessed be he, said, "Clean."
> C. And the rest of the fellowship of the firmament said, "Unclean."
> D. They said, "Who will settle the matter?"
> E. It should be Rabbah b. Nahmani, for he is the one who said, "I am an expert in the laws of plagues and in the effects of contamination through the overshadowing of a corpse."...
> F. A letter fell down from the sky to Pumbedita" "Rabbah b. Nahmani has been called up by the academy of the firmament..."
>
> b. B.M. 86a

Part of a much longer account attached to the academy of Pumbedita of how Rabbah b. Nahmani was taken up to heaven, the story shows us how God is represented in a heavenly session of the heavenly academy studying precisely those details of the Torah, here Leviticus Chapter Thirteen as restated in Mishnah-tractate Negaim, as were mastered by the great sages of the day. That the rest of the heavenly court would disagree forms an essential detail, because it verifies the picture and validates the claim, to come, that heaven required the knowledge of the heroic sage. That is the point of B-C-D. Then Rabbah b. Nahmani is called to heaven—that is, killed and transported upward—to make the required ruling. God is not the centerpiece of the story. The detail that a letter was sent from the heavenly academy to the one on earth, at Pumbedita, then restates the basic point of the story, the correspondence of earth to heaven on just this matter.

Though in the image of the sage, God towers over other sages, disposes of their lives and determines their destinies. Portraying God as sage allowed the story-tellers to state in vivid way convictions on the disparity between sages' great intellectual achievements and their this-worldly standing and fate. But God remains within the model of other sages, takes up the rulings, follows the arguments, participates in the sessions, that distinguish sages and mark them off from all other people:

> A. Said R. Judah said Rab, "When Moses went up to the height, he found the Holy One, blessed be he, sitting and tying crowns to the letters [of the Torah].
> B. "He said to him, 'Lord of the universe, why is this necessary?'
> C. "He said to him, 'There is a certain man who is going to come into being at the end of some generations, by the name of Aqiba b. Joseph. He is going to find expositions to attach mounds and mounds of laws to each point [of a crown].'
> D. "He said to him, 'Lord of the universe, show him to me.'
> E. "He said to him, 'Turn around.'
> F. "[Moses] went and took his seat at the end of eight rows, but he could not understand what the people were saying. He felt weak. When discourse came to a certain matter, one of [Aqiba's] disciples said to him, 'My lord, how do you know this?'
> G. "He said to him, 'It is a law revealed by God to Moses at Mount Sinai.'
> H. "Moses' spirits were restored.
> I. "He turned back and returned to the Holy One, blessed be he. He said to him, 'Lord of the universe, now if you have such a man available, how can you give the Torah through me?'
> J. "He said to him, 'Be silent. That is how I have decided matters.'
> K. "He said to him, 'Lord of the universe, you have now shown me his mastery of the Torah. Now show me his reward.'
> L. "He said to him, 'Turn around.'
> M. "He turned around and saw people weighing out his flesh in the butcher-shop.
> N. "He said to him, 'Lord of the universe, such is his mastery of Torah, and such is his reward?'
> O. "He said to him, 'Be silent. That is how I have decided matters.' "
>
> B. Men. 29b

God's role in the story finds definition as hero and principal actor. He is no longer the mere interlocutor, nor does he simply answer questions of the principal voice by citing Scripture. Quite to the contrary, God makes all the decisions and guides the unfolding of the story. Moses then appears as the straight-man. He asks the questions that permit God to make the stunning replies. Why do you need crowns on the letters of the Torah? Aqiba will explain them, by tying laws to these trivial and opaque details. What are these laws? I cannot follow them. Aqiba will nonetheless attribute them to you. Why then give the Torah through me instead of him, since he understands it and I do not? It is my decree. Finally, comes the climax: what will this man's reward be? His flesh will be weighed out in butcher shops. The response remains the same. Moses does not understand. God tells him to shut up and accept his decree. God does what he likes, with whom he likes. Perhaps the story-teller had in mind a polemic against rebellious brilliance, as against dumb subservience. But that does not seem to me the urgent message, which rather requires acceptance of God's decrees, whatever they are, when the undeserving receive glory, when the accomplished come to nothing. That God emerges as a fully formed personality—the model for the sage—hardly requires restatement.

VIII
Incarnation in Heaven and on Earth: God and Israel

The paramount trait of the sage in the Bavli is his profound engagement with the life of Israel, God's people. The sage conducts an on-going love-affair with Israel, just as does God, caring for everything that Jews say and do, the sanctity of their community, the holiness of their homes. Israel, unique among nations and holy to God, form on earth a society that corresponds to the retinue and court of God in heaven. No surprise, then, that, just as Israel glorifies God, so God responds and celebrates Israel. In the passages at hand the complete incarnation of God, in physical, emotional, and social traits, comes to expression. God wears phylacteries, an indication of a corporeal sort. God further forms the correct attitude toward Israel, which is one of love, an indication of an attitude on the part of divinity corresponding to right attitudes on the part of human beings. Finally, to close the circle, just as there is a "you" to whom humanity prays, so God too says prayers—to God, and the point of these prayers is that God should elicit from himself forgiveness for Israel:

> A. Said R. Nahman bar Isaac to R. Hiyya bar Abin, "As to the phylacteries of the Lord of the world, what is written in them?"
> B. He said to him, " 'And who is like your people Israel, a singular nation on earth' (1 Chr. 17:21)."
> C. "And does the Holy One, blessed be he, sing praises for Israel?"
> D. "Yes, for it is written, 'You have avouched the Lord this day...and the Lord has avouched you this day' (Deut. 26:17, 18).
> E. "Said the Holy One, blessed be he, to Israel, 'You have made me a singular entity in the world, and I shall make you a singular entity in the world.
> F. " 'You have made me a singular entity in the world,' as it is said, 'Hear O Israel, the Lord, our God, the Lord is one' (Deut. 6:4).
> G. " 'And I shall make you a singular entity in the world,' as it is said, 'And who is like your people, Israel, a singular nation in the earth' (1 Chr. 17:21)."
> H. Said R. Aha, son of Raba to R. Ashi, "That takes care of one of the four subdivisions of the phylactery. What is written in the others?"
> I. He said to him, " 'For what great nation is there.... And what great nation is there....' (Deut. 4:7, 8), 'Happy are you, O Israel...' (Deut. 33:29), 'Or has God tried...,' (Deut. 4:34). And 'to make you high above all nations' (Deut. 26:19)."
> J. "If so, there are too many boxes!
> K. "But the verses, 'For what great nation is there' and 'And what great nation is there,' which are equivalent, are in one box, and 'Happy are you, O Israel' and 'Who is like your people Israel' are in one box, and 'Or has God tried...,' in one box, and 'To make you high' in one box.

L. "And all of them are written in the phylactery that is on the arm."

B. Ber. 6a-b XXXIX

A. Said R. Yohanan in the name of R. Yose, "How do we know that the Holy One, blessed be he, says prayers?

B. "Since it is said, 'Even them will I bring to my holy mountain and make them joyful in my house of prayer' (Is. 56:7).

C. " 'Their house of prayer' is not stated, but rather, 'my house of prayer.'

D. "On the basis of that usage we see that the Holy One, blessed be he, says prayers."

E. What prayers does he say?

F. Said R. Zutra bar Tobiah said Rab, " 'May it be my will that my mercy overcome my anger, and that my mercy prevail over my attributes, so that I may treat my children in accord with the trait of mercy and in their regard go beyond the strict measure of the law.' "

B. Ber. 7A, XLIX

A. It has been taught on Tannaite authority:

B. Said R. Ishmael b. Elisha, "One time I went in to offer up incense on the innermost altar, and I saw the Crown of the Lord, enthroned on the highest throne, and he said to me, 'Ishmael, my son, bless me.'

C. "I said to him, 'May it be your will that your mercy overcome your anger, and that your mercy prevail over your attributes, so that you treat your children in accord with the trait of mercy and in their regard go beyond the strict measure of the law.'

D. "And he nodded his head to me."

E. And from that story we learn that the blessing of a common person should not be negligible in your view.

B. Ber. 7a. L.

The corporal side to the incarnation of God is clear at the outset, God's wearing phylacteries. The consubstantial traits of attitude and feeling—just as humanity feels joy, so does God, just as humanity celebrates God, so does God celebrate Israel—are made explicit. The social transactions of incarnation are specified as well. Just as Israel declares God to be unique, so God declares Israel to be unique. And just as Israel prays to God, so God says prayers. What God asks of himself is that he transcend himself—which is what, in prayer, humanity asks for as well. The process of the incarnation of God which we have traced item by item culminates in the portrait of God as Israel's counterpart, trait by trait, and in all relationships: God unique in heaven, Israel unique on earth, the one like the other and matched only by the other—and both finding ultimate embodiment in the sage.

IX
The Centrality of Narrative in the Incarnation of God

We have noted the predominance of narrative in the characterization of the divinity in incarnational terms. Nearly every account of God as a human being, bearing human traits of body, mind, and soul, engaging in transactions with other persons in accord with a single set of rules governing both divinity and humanity, reaches expression in the form of stories of one sort or another. When we reviewed the representation of God in an other-than-incarnational theology, such as we found, for one important example, in the Mishnah, we realized the difference. A different mode of describing the divinity, one in which God appears as premise, presence, and person, but not as a fully exposed personality, predominates. And when a document's authorship proposes to characterize God through other than narrative means, then God emerges in an other-than incarnational portrait.

I may conclude by pointing to an obvious fact. The contrast between the pictures of God emerging in the letters of the apostle, Paul, and the Gospels of the several Evangelists, tells a not dissimilar story. When the founding intellects of both Judaism and Christianity wished to explore the meaning of the notion (in Christian language) of the word become flesh, they resorted to stories to say just what that could mean. So too, in the final and authoritative statement of the Judaism of the dual Torah, such as the Talmud of Babylonia presented for all time, God in whose image, after whose likeness, we are formed, comes to us principally through accounts of a narrative character concerning what God says and does. In the two great religions of the West, Andrew Greeley may claim to find rich precedents for his theological adventure in fiction.

Notes

[1]The contrast will underline the validity of that statement. Tractate Avot presents us with a divine Presence whenever two people sit and exchange Torah-teachings, for example. The Tosefta's conception of God's presence is treated presently.

[2]God when appearing as a personality in the canonical writings of the Judaism of the dual Torah is represented as a man, never as a woman. My translations may reflect that fact, but in the body of my text, I mean to avoid inappropriate usages.

[3]I cite the pertinent passages in my *Judaism: The Evidence of the Mishnah* (Chicago, 1981: University of Chicago Press), pp. 000-000.

[4]All translations are my own.

The Symbolism of the Song of Songs

Roland E. Murphy, O. Carm.

Symbolism, and not least of all sexual symbolism, has played a large role in the writings of the man this *Festschrift* honors. Hence it is appropriate to explore, however briefly, the symbolism of the Song of Songs. We will proceed by examining certain individual symbols within the Song, and finally the symbolism of the book as a whole.[1]

1. Symbols Within the Song

It would be difficult and perhaps unnecessary to attempt to classify the individual symbols. The most prominent category is the *wasf*, or description of the physical charms of the beloved, in which various parts of the body are singled out and praised. Much more resistant to classification is the atmosphere that the language exudes by the use of the names of animals, flowers, places, etc.

The initial reaction to the *wasf* is sheer puzzlement in many cases. How can the hair of the woman be compared to "a flock of goats that stream down Mount Gilead" (4:1; 6:5)? And her neck is "like David's tower, built in rows; a thousand shields hang upon it, all the weapons of warriors" (4:4), and also "like a tower of ivory" (7:5). Her nose "is like the tower of Lebanon looking toward Damascus" (7:5). Finally, she states "I am a wall, and my breasts like towers" (8:10).

These apparently extravagant metaphors have proved enigmatic to scholars as well as to the average reader. One solution has been to deny the representational quality and to regard them as merely evocative of a sensation. R. Soulen[2] has argued that such images convey the delight of the beholder, without intending any comparison. But this view is hardly adequate. There seems to be clear representational intent in such metaphors as the image of a scarlet thread for the mouth (4:3), or "two fawns, the twins of a gazelle" for the two breasts (4:5; 7:4). Even though the precise representation is difficult to pin down, the metaphors are more than merely evocative of a subjective feeling. The problem is to capture the nuance of the symbol, if at all possible.

One scholar suggests that we should recognize the incongruities and tensions that exist in metaphorical language. Michael Fox writes that "a metaphor depends for its meaning—its full contextual meaning with its new and unparaphrasable connotations—not only on the extent of the common ground but also on the 'metaphoric distance' between image and referent: that is, the degree of

229

unexpectedness or incongruity between the juxtaposed elements and the magnitude of the dissonance it produces."[3] This is a delicate judgment. Metaphoric distance can be stimulating, but if the distance becomes too great (Fox instances the absurdity of "your teeth are like leafy boughs"—of course this does not occur in the Song), the impact of the metaphor can be lost.

While "metaphoric distance" has a certain validity, one may also ask if the distance between image and referent is due more to our inability to understand the world view of the ancient writer. In this respect the iconographic studies of O. Keel have been fruitful.[4] He starts with the premise that dynamics, not form, is the prominent feature of the ancient biblical symbol. That is to say, the point of the comparison lies not in form or shape so much as in the function and power of the symbol. For example, there is the well known biblical idiom, in which 'ap ("nose") symbolizes anger; 'ayin ("eye") has to do with a glance (cf. 5:9), rather than the shape of the physical organ. Keel goes on to discuss the difficult symbols which have already been mentioned. Thus, with respect to the comparison to a tower he asks what is its function? It suggests protection, due to its firmness, height and inaccessibility. It is not surprising then that these aspects of the woman be celebrated by this metaphor. Iconography of the ancient Near East sheds light on the "shields" (4:4), for there are representations of women with necklaces in the form of rows of beads, suggesting a certain majesty and pride. Women are also depicted with a diadem in the form of a wall with towers. Hence to compare the neck to David's tower is to suggest the pride and majesty of the woman, who is also as inaccessible as David's tower.

In 4:8 the man invites his beloved,

"With me from Lebanon, O bride,
  with me from Lebanon shall you come!
Come down from the top of Amanah,
  from the top of Senir and Hermon,
From dens of lions,
  from ramparts of leopards."

In context he has just finished a description of her physical charms, and now he appears to be addressing her as if she were in some mountain fastness (cf. also 2:14) surrounded by wild animals. What does this picture suggest? Keel illustrates it with ancient art that portrays goddesses enthroned on mountains with lions and other types of animals. Again, the effect is to underscore the inaccessible character of the woman.

A common comparison in the Song, and apparently the simplest, is the association of eyes with doves (in the case of the woman, 1:15; 4:1, and of the man, 5:12). Interpreters have gone in several different directions with this comparison, mainly in terms of shape and color. However, Keel has recourse to the dynamic use of "eye" as in Prov. 23:31, where the "eye" of the wine refers to its sparkle, or in Ezek 1:7 where the "eye" of bronze represents its gleam or luster. Hence the reference is rather to the glance, than to the physical organ of the eye. What is the point scored by the mention of doves? Keel points out that in the ancient

Levant the white dove is associated with the goddess of love as a love messenger. Hence he paraphrases "your eyes are doves" as "your glances are messengers of love."

The speed with which the lover comes to the beloved seems to be the reason why she compares him to "a gazelle or a young stag" in 8-9, and in an inclusio at the end of the reminiscence in 2:8-17 she invites him to be "like a gazelle or a young stag upon the mountains of Bether," a reference that can mean only her own person, just as in 8:14 she invites him to be "like a gazelle or a young stag upon the mountains of spices," i.e., herself. The metaphor has moved from the speed of the animal to its roaming in favorite haunts.

Some metaphors deserve delicate treatment, such as the comparison of female breasts to "two fawns, twins of a gazelle, browsing among the lilies" (4:5; in 7:4 the browsing is omitted). The reader can be spared the odd interpretations that have accumulated over the centuries. Even in recent times there have been clumsy references by insensitive commentators (e.g., the breasts compared to a static vision of the backsides of fawns nuzzling among flowers). M. Pope thinks that "the youth of the fawns bespeak the youthful freshness and small size of the mammary orbs." But he interprets the woman's words in 8:10 as referring to her "towering *mammae*."[5] It is a mistake to take size as the key to the passage. More imaginatively, Keel suggests that the playful motion and mobility of the breasts are suggested by the grace of these animals. He has also pointed out the association of gazelles and goats with the lotus (the "lilies" in the Song of Songs) in Egypt and Palestine.

If there is a climax in the Song, it may be seen in the superlative lines of 8:6,

Place me as a seal on your heart,
  as a seal on your arm.
Strong as Death is love,
  intense as Sheol is ardor;
Its shafts are shafts of fire,
  a flame of Yah.

This is obviously intended as a compliment to love, but what is the point of the comparison of love/ardor to Death/Sheol? The Hebrew understanding of Death and the nether world supplies the answer. Israel's understanding of death was influenced by the Ugaritic deity, Mot (Death). Although Death was not divine for the Israelite, it was felt to be a dynamic, not a static power. It was pictured as pursuing a human being through life. Its presence was particularly felt when any degree of non-life (pain, distress, hostility, etc.) afflicted a person. Thus the psalmist cries out in gratitude to the Lord, "You brought me up from Sheol" (Ps. 30:4). Metaphorically, the psalmist was in the grip of the power of Death, but now he experiences restoration (not resuscitation). And Sheol/Death is the great enemy who will eventually claim one's life. But love, too, can make its own claims.

2. The Song as Symbol

What is the symbolism of a love poem? By itself does love poetry mean more than its fruity lines, and express an idea or vision that transcends itself? I think that a case can be made that the love poetry of Israel aspires to more than it directly says. Expressions of love can be merely self-centered, but at their best they express some degree of commitment and mutuality, as the Song certainly does. The role of the self is inescapable, but it is redeemed by concentration on the beloved. And here what is left unsaid or even unfathomed is part of the outreach of the poem itself. The beloved does not hear or read love poetry as though it were an encyclopedia. The experience of being in love is the atmosphere of the poem. In the case of the Song one might claim that there is nothing unusual in its celebration of human love. But the history of the interpretation of the Song suggests that in itself this love poem is a symbol of another love.

The striking fact is that the two communities of faith that preserved and read the Song understood it on a level different from human sexual love. Centuries of Jewish and Christian tradition have rarely given such an example of a unified understanding of a book of the Hebrew Bible. Both traditions, as far back as evidence will lead us, interpreted the Song as dealing with God and God's People. Divine/human love, not human sexual love, is the referent of the Song. Of course, significant variations immediately occur. In the Jewish tradition the Song reflects the tortuous but blessed relationship between God and Israel (in the Targum, from the Exodus to the messianic eschaton). In Christian tradition the Song was understood in the light of Christ and the Church, God and the individual soul. It was Origen (d. *ca.* 253) who was the lodestar for Christian interpreters. A genre of spiritual/mystical commentary was born and nourished, especially in the monasteries. It has been noted that in the 12th century some thirty commentaries on the song appeared—more than for any other biblical book. The trend came to a climax in the 86 "sermons" which Bernard of Clairvaux wrote for his Cistercian brothers—and he never got beyond the first two chapters! The influence of this heritage can be seen in the famous "Cantico Espiritual" of San Juan de la Cruz, and in recent times in the writings of Paul Claudel.[6]

Is all this tradition just a brilliant mistake? One can point out at least two reasons that justify the traditional interpretation as a valid meaning. The first is the bold fact that Israel made human love the symbol of the mutual love of her Lord and herself. One need only recall Hosea 1-3, and this theme appears consistently in other prophets (Isa 1:21; Jer 3:1, etc). True, it occurs more often in the context of Israel's infidelity. But the ideal remained, as Isa 62:5 testifies:

As a young man marries a virgin,
  your Builder shall marry you;
And as a bridegroom rejoices in his bride
  so shall your God rejoice in you.

The covenant formula, "you shall be my people and I shall be your God" was understood as more than a binding legal agreement. It was a marriage. As Deuteronomy put it, "It was not because you are the largest of all nations that the Lord set his heart on you and chose you, for you are really the smallest of all nations. It was because the Lord loved you..." (Deut 7: 7-8). Hence the protestation in the Song was heard by Israel and eventually by the Church on a deeper level: "My lover belongs to me and I to him" (2:16; 6:3; 7:11).

Perhaps a serious reservation about the traditional meaning as it developed in the communities of faith should be expressed here. The allegorical method of interpreting the text is not essential for the validity of the traditional meaning. Symbolism is involved in the allegorical process, but unless a poem is written precisely in the allegorical mode (as, for example, Ezek 17: Eccles 12: 2-6), allegorical method is subject to arbitrary *ad hoc* interpretations that detract from the vitality of the traditional meaning.

The second reason in favor of the traditional interpretation is a hint contained within the Song itself in 8:6, where the shafts of love (already compared for its power to Death/Sheol, as seen above) are described as "fiery shafts, a flame of Yah." It is grammatically justifiable to translate the Hebrew *šalhebetyah* (literally, "Yah [weh] flame") as "a most vehement flame" (so the RSV, and similarly many other translations, such as the New Jewish Version). In this case, the short form of the divine name, *yah*, is taken as a kind of superlative (divine, mighty, etc.). But a literal translation is "flame of Yah," rendered emphatically in the New Jerusalem Bible as "a flame of Yahweh himself." It is frequently said that the divine name is absent from the Bible only in the books of Esther and the Song of Songs; much depends on the rendering of 8:6.

If one adopts this possible translation, there is a clear affirmation that sexual love as described in the Song is somehow associated with the Lord. That association is left unspecified, but it should not go unmentioned. It is part of the symbolism of human love. Human love suggests an outreach to (an origin from, or a participation in?) the God who is described as love (1 John 4:8).

The validity of the traditional meaning is to be affirmed on the basis of the symbolism of human love. A misfortune of history has been the fact that the traditional meaning was allowed to snuff out the literal historical meaning which expressed love between the sexes. The Christian attitude to sex suffered from this impoverishment. It should not have been so, and it remains for the communities of faith which accept the Song as canonical to nourish themselves in the inner symbolism of human love which the poetry breathes, as well as the outreach to the divine which it provides.

In his exciting study of Mesopotamian religion Thorkild Jacobsen singled out central religious metaphors which he detected in the culture. Among them is a view of the gods as parents, and also as providers. Analogously we want to claim that one religious metaphor in Israel is God as lover. This is unmistakably shown in the prophetic writings, and it is rooted in the Song of Songs as well. As Jacobsen remarks, "a religious metaphor is not truly understood until it is experienced as a means of suggesting the Numinous."[7]

Notes

[1]This is not the place to expand on a philosophy of symbolism. The prejudices of the writer will doubtless be apparent to the reader, who may be referred to the helpful treatment of Avery Dulles in *Models of Revelation* (Doubleday, 1983), esp. 131-54.

[2]Cf. R. Soulen, "The Wasfs of the Song of Songs and Hermeneutic," *Journal of Biblical Literature* 96 (1967): 183-90.

[3]M. Fox, *The Song of Songs and the Ancient Egyptian Love Songs* (University of Wisconsin Press, 1985) 276.

[4]O. Keel, *Deine Blicke sind Tauben. Zur Metaphorik des Hohen Liedes* (Stuttgarter Bibelstudien 114/115; Katholisches Bibelwerk, 1984).

[5]M. Pope, *Song of Songs* (Anchor Bible 7C; Doubleday, 1977) 470; 683.

[6]The works of Origen, St. Bernard, and St. John of the Cross are easily available in translation. For Claudel, see his *Paul Claudel interroge le Cantique des cantiques* (Paris, 1948).

[7]Cf. T. Jacobsen, *The Treasures of Darkness* (Yale UP, 1976) esp. 3-5, 20-21, the quotation is from p. 5. In the case of Mesopotamia one is of course working with another set of symbols; Israel worshipped a lover, but not a fertility god.

PART EIGHT

Theology and the Symbolic Imagination: A Tribute to Andrew Greeley

David Tracy

In the course of his remarkable intellectual career, Andrew Greeley has illuminated the pervasiveness of symbols in our social and personal, our secular and religious lives. As one who shares that belief, I will use the welcome occasion of this *Festschrift* to reflect on the reality and permanence of symbol in theology.

Indeed, a distinguishing characteristic of the contemporary period in religious studies and theology is the continuing recovery of the symbolic imagination. As represented, for example, by those several theologies which employ story, metaphor, image, symbol, myth and ritual as their central categories, the emergence of the centrality of the imagination for the study of religion, and thereby of fundamentally aesthetic criteria[1] for interpreting and appropriating the symbolic possibilities of our several religious traditions seems a legitimate inference. Sometimes this concern is articulated by the imaginative genius of a genuine story-teller with a theological bent as with Elie Wiesel or Walker Percy or John Updike or Andrew Greeley or by artists of drama, dance, music who employ their art forms in strikingly contemporary-i.e. both aesthetically satisfying and religiously compelling forms of worship. More often constructive theologians are concerned not to develop new rituals and symbols but to appropriate an analysis of symbol and imagination into more familiar forms of theological argument. In brief, basically theological-aesthetic criteria have joined more familiar philosophical, ethical, and historical criteria as relevant to the theologian's task.

Amidst the conflict of interpretations on the exact meaning of symbol, theologians from several traditions now unite to urge a critical reappropriation of the enriching possibilities for our present situation provided by the central stories, myths, symbols and rituals of our Western religious traditions. There is every good reason for all those in the liberal traditions in theology to affirm and to aid this new resource. Indeed, there seem good reasons to believe that only those theologians formed by both a religious and aesthetic sensibility and by a critical attitude in theology can achieve the kind of aesthetic and religious 'second naiveté'[2] towards the symbolic resources of the religious traditions which these sometimes rather disparate theologies of symbol and these new attempts at worship really represent. To be sure, it does seem to be the case that we now live in what has often been named a post-modern period of life and reflection.[3] Yet another truism also remains the case: post-modern need not mean a retreat to that kind of obscurantism which masks an intellectual failure of nerve reveling in the present, real dilemmas of liberalism and sometimes meretriciously wishing to impose a merely conservative first-naiveté on our present situation. Rather, for those who have truly appropriated the modern, critical tradition, the term 'post-modern' implies that the modern tradition should remain firm in its basic belief in the need for continued critical fidelity to the best of both contemporary experience and the best of the tradition. Only such firmness will assure the success of a move forward into a situation wherein the richness of the tradition, including its traditional forms of worship, can now be restructured and reappropriated by a fuller and critical concentration upon the emancipatory possibilities of the major symbolic expressions of the religious imagination encapsulated in the images of its communal life, in the metaphors, stories, and myths of its writings, in the rituals of its forms of worship, in the analogies of its theologies.[4] Yet that very reappropriation of the symbolic imagination, I believe, will probably prove fruitful only in the context of the continuing critical reexamination of the modern heritage, viz. tradition and critique.

II. Context of the Discussion: Tradition and Critique

As Hans-Georg Gadamer, perhaps more than any other modern thinker, has insisted, the concept 'tradition', so suspect by Enlightenment thinkers, may bear a fully positive meaning.[5] To be sure, the merely authoritarian concept of tradition was correctly challenged by Enlightenment thinkers in favor of a model of critical autonomy. That latter model, incorporated both personally and communally in the various reformed and modern traditions in contemporary religious life, has surely proved one of the important and, one hopes, enduring characteristics of the modern period.[6] Unhappily, as Gadamer persuasively argues in philosophical terms, this modern achievement often became the occasion for a dangerously naive rejection of the very realities of tradition and thereby symbol itself. Naive, because we can deny in theory but cannot really reject in fact the radical historicity of our social selves. Dangerously naive, because by their own partial failures at appropriation of symbolic reality, many liberals in effect handed over the authentic symbolic resources of the tradition to those least able to appreciate them: those once embattled but now reinvigorated opponents of modernity in every tradition— those Pope John XXIII labelled the dark prophets of gloom in our culture; those whose voice, if not whose arguments, so pervade our present moment in history.

Neither a romantic—today we say nostalgic—explosion of praise for the tradition nor a merely hostile hermeneutics of suspicion upon the very concepts and reality of tradition and its central component, the symbolic imagination, seems an appropriate response to the present situation.[7] Indeed, the vanishing art of the old scholastic distinction seems in order here. If one means by tradition simply to accept without question the *tradita* (i.e. the handed-down and unexamined conclusions of any intellectual or religious heritage), then, with our Enlightenment forebears, one must, in conscience, simply say *nego*. If, however, one really means tradition as *traditio* (i.e. the living, liberating, and resourceful modes of inquiry, sensibility and imagination of any intellectual or religious heritage), then every critical inquirer can applaud the continuing fruitfulness of critical inquiry and retrieval of all the major traditions, rituals, and symbols of our history.[8]

Precisely this post-modern concept of tradition as *traditio* seems the driving intellectual force behind the contemporary theological reexamination of the resources of the several possible modes-of-being-in-the-world disclosed by such expressions of the traditional religious imagination as story, symbol, myth, ritual, metaphor, and analogy. Yet the question recurs: how can one assure that even this notion of tradition does not become the occasion to disown the need for critical inquiry into all claims to truth, to disclosure, to emancipation: does not, for example, simply become the occasion to insist upon worship-services untouched by contemporary concerns for authentic reappropriation not mere repetition: for a second, not a lost first naiveté? In the midst of a revival of interest in symbolic forms, how can one avoid the kind of historical romanticism that has clouded many a liturgical renewal?[9] How can one assure that spirit of the examined life—including our lives at worship—which still defines the genuinely emancipatory character of the reformed and liberal religious and theological traditions?

In one sense, of course, the question is a self-answering one. For insofar as one really means tradition as *traditio*, not *tradita*, one affirms the route taken by so many in our period: a return to symbol, but *only* by means of the mediation of critical inquiry; a continued recognition, for example, that a first naiveté in worship seems forever lost to us; a continued search to see whether a second naiveté is indeed an authentic possibility, not a strategy of desperation. Only a genuinely critical attitude, I suggest, now directed to aesthetic and religious criteria for assuring a second naiveté will allow that possibility. For only a continued fidelity to critical inquiry seems to allow an ethical way of retrieving the enriching disclosures upon our common lives of traditional expressions and rituals of the religious imagination. As a consequence, far more than was previously the case, most modern theologians now seem more willing to admit that tradition and symbol, like their ethical correlates loyalty, fidelity, patriotism, are too rich in reality, too disclosive in possibility, to be handed over to the purveyors of sterile condemnations of modern innovation and autonomy.

In another sense, the question of a proper attitude to a revival of interest in symbol is not self-answering at all. For the post-modern theologian is faced with the further and familiar dilemma that the Enlightenment notion of critical reason, once so liberating, now seems too often in practice a narrowing of possibilities. Rather the contemporary situation, as those revisionist Marxists known as the Frankfurt School among others have argued,[10] now seems one where reason itself may too often become merely technical reason; where the finest expression of autonomous human inquiry, scientific reason, can result in the mere fetish of scientism and expertise; where concepts too often seem not to bear the emancipatory power of truly critical reason. More to our present point, as Ernst Bloch observes, a merely technical reason can misunderstand itself as critical reason and thereby disallow symbol, ritual and imagination as emancipating possibilities. A merely technical reason can reify reality and serve merely to legitimate the prevailing status quo. It can disown the symbolic needs of the human spirit and domesticate aesthetic and religious sensibilities into a kind of global ritualistic *Muzak*. Too often even avant-garde art no longer seems to serve a genuinely communal function but rather can retreat into self-imposed 'reservations' of the spirit where one is momentarily freed from the wider technocratic culture.[11]In that context, how can we continue to hope that the modern genius at critique may not impede rather than enhance the disclosive and emancipatory powers of these retrieved symbolic forms? How can we continue to hope that the very power of authentic critique released by liberalism does not become captive to an *ethos* of technocracy?

This is, of course, a familiar charge laid at modernity's door: most often by such conservative critics of the modern experiment as such modern conservative theorists as Russell Kirk and Michael Oakeshott or on the question of religion by the latter stages of several new theological formulations of 'post-liberal' theologies.[12] What is of greater interest to those who fundamentally affirm the modern experiment of commitment to full-scale critique and emancipation, however, is not so much the familiar cannon-blasts from the right (although they too have hit many a target) but the more nuanced and ultimately more serious attacks from one's natural allies on the left.

For example, the Marxist social theorist, Jürgen Habermas, argues that our present societal situation is one where modernity's possibilities for critique are severely limited by a situation he describes as one of systematically distorted communication on every level of our complex culture—the political, economic, social, cultural, and intersubjective.[13] In such a situation it seems clear that conservative critics of the culture, whatever their other difficulties, are naive to hope that classical hermeneutical reflection upon the remaining and fragmented symbolic resources of the tradition will suffice. The more important question for us is how a liberal critique can best function in that kind of situation.[14] If the problem is really no longer one of mere social error but of far more radical societal illusion, our approach to religious questions can be neither merely a conservative return to symbol nor even such classical liberal strategies as the critical exposure of traditional errors with very little effort towards a constructive reappropriation of symbolic resources. Rather we need theories, practices, and symbols which, precisely by their fidelity to the critical spirit of modernity, can develop contemporary symbolic forms to help unmask the distortions and illusions of our societal lives in the same manner as the theories, practices, and symbolic systems of psychoanalysis provide an opportunity to unmask systematic distortions on an individual level. More specifically—and in more Anglo-American language—we need more, not less, commitment by the entire community of inquirers into religion on the need for publically available discourse, for argument—criteria, evidence, warrants, backing; for the increasingly sophisticated recognition of context-variant standards for so wide-ranging a subject-matter as religion and so field-encompassing a discipline as theology.[15]

For our present question on the revival of the symbolic imagination, I suggest, this situation implies that we need to concentrate more attention on unpacking the claims to existential significance and disclosive truth of the symbolic resources of our heritages. In that manner, the modern theological tradition would develop its fidelity to critical reason and argument in a direction where explicitly aesthetic and religious criteria could be more publically addressed. The critical resources of the modern traditions would direct their attention to the revival of interest in the symbolic imagination in such manner that the creative but not merely private resources of art and religion could be brought into the public light of critical reason and reappropriated for public disclosive and emancipatory use. As a single and limited example of that possibility, I will turn in the final section of this paper to an exposure of the kind of analysis and resources presently available for that task.

III. The Symbolic Imagination: Metaphor, Analogy, Ritual

In the context of affirmation of both tradition and critique, a plea for the relevance of the symbolic imagination may take a general or a more specific form. When contemporary philosophers and theologians approach the reality of *traditio* through the resource of the symbolic imagination, they are wont to appeal to the central category of possibility. More exactly, these thinkers no longer approach the reality of imagination in its classical philosophical form as merely another faculty of human knowing.[16] Indeed several contemporary philosophical and theological positions now approach the reality of the imagination as a central reality in all religious discourse and action. Moreover, the power of the creative imagination can now be understood not in merely general terms but in a context where a wealth of scholarly studies from several disciplines can actually provide the retrieved symbolic material needed: the actual non-linguistic images and rituals used in worship, the linguistic metaphors, stories, and myths of religious language, the models and analogies of theology.[17] Whenever a particular image, ritual, metaphor, myth, or analogy discloses some *permanent* possibility for the human spirit it may bear the distinctive title symbol. Symbol, therefore, has become the generic name for all those permanent imaginative possibilities for our common humanity disclosed in the reigning images, rituals, metaphors, myths, and analogies of our several traditions.[18] The appeal of symbols, to be sure, is an appeal fundamentally to the imagination and thereby to a redescription of possibility.[19] More specifically, symbols appeal to those kinds of imaginative redescriptions of human possibility which critical reason can illuminate by aesthetic analysis and can learn to discriminate through the development of explicitly aesthetic criteria analogous to those criteria already developed by classical liberalism in the metaphysical, ethical, and empirical realms.[20]

In Paul Ricoeur's well-known slogan to describe this situation, "The symbol gives rise to thought, but thought always returns to and is informed by symbol."[21] This slogan, as too many of its admirers fail to note, does not simply give a *carte blanche* to the symbolic imagination; it insists that our best critical reason *must* be employed on all our symbols (The symbol gives rise to thought), before suggesting that through such critical mediation, thought returns again to symbol. On the further side of demythologizing, we still find a disclosive and imaginative power to the Adamic myth over the Orphic and cosmogonic myths.[22] After the best historical-critical analysis of the central events and images of the tradition, we do seem to rediscover the still emancipatory force of the Exodus symbol.[23] After all the surely necessary critical restructuring of traditional forms of worship, we find that many traditional words and rituals bespeak transformative possibilities for our everyday lives.[24] After the most rigorous contemporary philosophical and theological critiques of the inherent difficulties in the conceptual analogies developed by a Maimonides, an Aquinas, a Calvin, we still find that these great symbolic-as-analogical visions of our theological traditions continue to disclose an imagined vision of human life as a whole which we ignore at the unwelcome price of self-impoverishment.

I will now risk showing how this new possibility may occur rather than simply stating that it does. I shall do so by appealing to an initially unlikely candidate for the symbolic imagination, the symbolic-as-analogical vision of Thomas Aquinas.[25] By concentrating the analysis on one acknowledged Western classic of theological languages, I also hope to encourage similar studies now occurring on the analogical language of a Maimondes or a Calvin. Although I have, in fact, made forays into the analogical language of the latter two theological giants, I will concentrate my own efforts here in trying to recover the imaginative possibilities present in the analogical language of Aquinas. That attempt, I trust, will prove resonant to those familiar with the better known studies of such symbolic forms as image, ritual, and myth. At any rate, the choice of Aquinas' analogical language should have the advantage of suggesting the kind of aesthetic and religious criteria relevant to any study of any rendering of the symbolic imagination, even one as highly conceptual as that of Aquinas.

The key to understanding the recent modern Catholic reappropriation of Aquinas by means of symbol and the imagination is to note that the study assumes earlier and more standard philosophical analysis and criteria (especially metaphysical and ethical criteria) and then turns to specifically aesthetic and religious criteria to analyze the symbolic dimension of the analogical language of Thomas as disclosive of certain possible modes-of-being-in-the-world.

It is important to note, however, that this present example of analogy in Thomas is confined to theological language. I understand that language to be a second-order, reflective language which claims fidelity to the originating religious languages of image, metaphor, symbol, myth and ritual. Although much reflection has recently been devoted to analyzing those originating religious languages—for Catholicism ordinarily under the general rubrics of the Catholic use of image, ritual, and sacrament in worship—very little work seems addressed to explicating the symbolic form of life disclosed in that properly theological language of analogy, so widely used by Catholic theologians and employed in Catholic creedal statements and worship services. Yet I have come to believe that even this highly conceptual language of Thomist analogy[26] may also profitably be studied to uncover a symbolic dimension which discloses certain possible modes-of-being-in-the-world, certain symbolic forms of life, certain distinctive projects for the imagination.

In order not to assume that everyone may prove as interested in Aquinas' use of analogical language as I am myself, however, I will discuss his usage by paralleling it to the more familiar work on that classical aesthetic figure of speech, the metaphor.[27] By that parallelism procedure, I hope to be able to suggest what kind of aesthetic and religious criteria can in fact be developed by theologians in any tradition to illuminate the symbolic resources of that tradition.

In fact, a partial consensus[28] seems to have emerged in recent studies of symbols. A major part of that consensus can be delineated by noting three characteristics of the religious use of that primary kind of symbolic language we name metaphor so dominant in both ritual and scripture. The first characteristic is a negative one: the traditional assumption (often shared by conservatives and liberals alike) that metaphors are merely rhetorical devices in the sense of decorative substitutions for the true-as-literal meaning has been effectively challenged by much recent linguistic and aesthetic study. On the question of the logic of the 'Kingdom of God' language in the New Testament parables, for example, the implications of this criterion have challenged both traditional (usually allegorical) and earlier liberal (often purely ethical) interpretations of the central Christian language forms of parables for a new generation of New Testament scholars.[29] The recognition of this peculiar aesthetic phenomenon of a more-than-literal meaning in metaphor suggests, therefore, the presence of a first aesthetic criterion: the non-reducibility of any truly symbolic reality, whether linguistic as in metaphor, or non-linguistic as in ritual, to merely literal meanings.

The second characteristic is a more positive one: whatever theory of the logic of metaphor is employed by its various proponents, the analyst will still note that a new meaning, not expressible without loss in literal terms, emerges from the very interaction of words not ordinarily—i.e. in terms of their 'literal' meanings— used conjunctively. Good metaphorical usage, as Aristotle long since observed, cannot be learned by formulating rules: the capacity to recognize similarity in dissimilarity is a mark of poetic genius. Good ritual, we might add, demands the same power of aesthetic and religious discrimination. As new emergent meanings explode in a culture's consciousness, the older and spent ones become merely dead metaphors and thereby enter our dictionaries. As we learn to hear in a more discriminating fashion the emergent meanings in any truly symbolic expression, whether metaphor, ritual, or analogy, we find a second aesthetic criterion for symbols: the presence of the peculiar logic of a non-reducible emergent meaning achieved through the interaction of literal words and actions whose conjunction is unlikely. This criterion may serve as the central positive clue to noting good aesthetic usage of metaphor or ritual.

The third characteristic is, from the viewpoint of the symbolic dimension of both theological language and religious action, the most important. Since I have tried to defend this conclusion at length elsewhere,[30] here I will simple state it. The conclusion can be variously formulated: in its more familiar form in contemporary linguistic philosophy of religion, one may recall Ian Ramsey's attempt to show that he nicely called the 'odd logic' of religious language.[31] In its less familiar but, for my part, more adequate formulation, one may cite the theory of Paul Ricoeur that the specificity of religious language lies in its character as a symbolic limit-language.[32] Alternatively, if I may presume to cite it, one may note my own attempted development of that limit-language tradition which suggests that careful attention to any explicitly religious use of symbolic forms shows the presence of two languages at work: a language expressive of a 'limit-to' our ordinary language and experience; and a second limit language which, precisely by stating that limit-to is also able to disclose or show a 'limit-of' language—i.e. a language which projects some aesthetically satisfying and religiously compelling vision of an imagined possibility for human life as a whole. More summarily, a genuinely religious use of any symbolic form seems to involve a limit-character wherein precisely by *stating* a limit-to the ordinary use of the language, also *shows* and *partly states* a symbolic language expressive of an imagined 'limit-of' possibility, some vision expressing a final meaningfulness to human life in relationship to the whole. An explicitly religious use, as limit-use, of symbolic forms, therefore, seems to serve as a third criterion needed to add to the two aesthetic criteria already advanced for appropriate theological discrimination.[33]

It is of some interest to note, moreover, that these same three criteria seem relevant to analyzing the symbolic dimension of the more conceptual and reflective language of theology itself. Allow me to return, therefore, to the question of Thomas Aquinas' actual use of analogical language with these same three criteria in mind.

In relationship to the first criterion, one may note that the same kind of initial move of negation is made by several contemporary linguistic interpreters of Thomas. Indeed, the most important criticism of the older Thomist tradition is not really that on most theological issues their position proved too often anti-modern (which it did), but that the classical modern Thomists failed to understand Aquinas' own highly pluralistic uses of analogical language in their own narrowly scholastic attempt to systematize a single Thomist doctrine of analogy.[34] That latter and almost canonical doctrine ended, ironically, in disclosing some form of a Scotist univocal language of 'common being' to 'bolster' what seems to be the too elusive, too pluralistic and even too symbolic use of analogical language by Thomas himself. Just as religious metaphors were once considered mere substitutions for literal meanings, so theological analogies—now implicitly rather than explicitly—were robbed of their symbolic function and considered substitutions for the real—the univocal—meaning. The first criterion which negates mere literal substitution language thereby seems to hold even for the highly conceptual language of Aquinas.

The second and more positive point of these theological studies of Thomas' analogical language parallels the second criterion, viz. the 'emergent meaning through interaction' theory of metaphor. For good analogies, like good metaphors and good rituals, depend on the capacity to recognize what Aristotle called similarity-in-dissimilarity. This capacity, so natural to the natively symbolic mind, allows us to break out of accustomed and deceptively univocal usage to describe either the unfamiliar or a forgotten dimension of the familiar. More specifically, analogical usage in both Aristotle and Aquinas is fundamentally a matter of good usage of 'focal meaning'—ordinary meanings expressive of human purpose and possibility—which provide a primary focus of meaning that is then proportionally employed in properly symbolic fashion for more extended usage.[35] In sum, the emergent meanings of analogous terms are not substitutions for a real, an univocal, meaning. Rather they are good language usage which, precisely as symbolic, relates all other uses to the focal meaning of the hopes, purposes, strivings and imagined possibilities of the human being.

The third criterion likewise is relevant. For the final clue to the proper use of analogical and symbolic language in Thomas may be found in noting how he too uses limit-language, now for strictly conceptual and reflective purposes. Recall, for example, that familiar analogical language of 'perfection terms' used by Aquinas to speak of God. The logic of perfection, as Aquinas knew, is an 'odd', even a 'limit' logic precisely as involved in the logical differences of all-some-or-none. Metaphysical criteria are thereby not merely relevant but necessary to adjudicating Aquinas' truth-claims. At the same time, the religious as limit-character of that very use of analogical language in theology should also turn an analyst's attention to the kind of focal meanings employed for these 'perfection-terms'. For the final symbolic focal meaning of those odd perfection-terms used for Thomist God-language may be found in the philosophical anthropology, the symbolic self-understandings of human possibility—its purposes, hopes, and desires—present in any particular religious and aesthetic tradition.[36]

Even in the highly conceptual language of Thomist analogy, therefore, a vision of properly theological speech for God-language is articulated which begins by a choice of aesthetic and religious criteria to describe human possibility as a focal meaning and ends in limit-language declarations, as Karl Rahner showed, of the disclosure of the radical mystery and intrinsic incomprehensibility of human existence itself and of the God religiously encountered in authentic faith.[37] Yet the basic route to this theological declaration is a familiar modern one with the addition of aesthetic criteria, now added to more familiar metaphysical and ethical criteria: a route which insists that reason can be trusted to bring one to just this point of disclosure of the symbols as revelatory of mystery and of aesthetic and religious criteria as appropriate to analyzing those symbols. This theological route also insists that even the reflective language of theology—if properly analogical language—can, by its fidelity to the logic of the symbols reflected upon, be trusted to lead the language-user to that aesthetic and religious self-discovery. Just this kind of development of aesthetic and religious criteria for the symbolic dimension of the analogical language of theology has led some contemporary Catholic theologicans, to an initially surprising enterprise: viz. the attempt to retrieve the embedded symbolic resources in Thomas' articulation of focal meanings disclosive of one imagined and possible way-of-being-in-the-world before God. For in its final moment, I think, any really masterful analogical vision in theology contains dimensions of the symbolic imagination well worth retrieving: dimensions which, once religiously engaged, seem to provide their proponents with a clearing, indeed what Hemingway called a clean, well-lighted place, which allows for a partial glimpse of the surrounding darkness and its possibly encompassing light.

If this example of three kinds of aesthetic and religious criteria relevant for the religious language—use of metaphor and the theological language—use of analogy is at all correct, it seems to shed some partial criteriological light on the wider question of all symbolic expressions. Any properly theological reflection on appropriate forms of worship and ritual, for example, will also seem to need these same kinds of aesthetic and religious criteria for its own process of discrimination: the first criterion to eliminate any temptations to literalization: the second criterion to retrieve those truly emergent meanings in the images, metaphors, myths, and rituals of the particular worship traditions; the third, religious-as-limit-language criterion, to discriminate a properly religious-as-limit-use of the particular symbolic forms employed in the ritual. With the aid of those three criteria, we may then attempt to imagine the possibilities for contemporary worship services that would be both aesthetically satisfying and religiously compelling. Yet that desired possibility seems unlikely to prove other than a project for the imagination unless theologians employ their critical powers, on other than an *ad hoc* basis, to understand the still enriching possibilities of the symbolic imagination embedded in every worship tradition by developing some such set of aesthetic and religious criteria as the three suggested here.

As the theological retrieval of the symbolic imagination continues on several fronts—on the realities of images, myths, metaphors, analogies, stories, and rituals—we may well find an increased interest among theologians for adding aesthetic criteria as a major component in the present post-modern determination of theological criteria. Indeed, such a possibility seems, to me at least, one of the most promising in the present révival of interest in the symbolic imagination and in linguistic, sociological, and anthropological studies. If that does in fact continue to occur then the ever delicate attempt of post-modernity to unite both critique and tradition, both emancipation and fidelity, both ritual and reflection, in a truly critical fashion can succeed.

In the meantime, some may justifiably wonder whether this kind of search for aesthetic and religious criteria can really—i.e. practically—suffice. The answer, of course, is no. Any theological determination of criteria never suffices. Yet the development of criteria, however partial, as these are, does serve by providing more appropriate modes of discrimination. The constructive theologian must usually rest content to work out a partial criteriological contribution to the larger whole and then turn to aid and be aided by those aesthetically and religiously creative spirits in any community who do not work out criteria but instinctively use them. At that point in the wider community's dialogue, the theologian finds that she/he has made, as best one can, the partial contribution of developing criteria relevant to the questions at issue. When asked for more specific advice, the same theologian may well feel rather like Saul Bellow's central character in his novel *Humboldt's Gift* who, in the final line of the novel, is asked just what is the name of certain flowers spotted in the early spring: "Search me", Bellow's protagonist says, "I'm a city boy myself. They must be crocuses."[38]

At least that is all this 'city boy' can say. It is a moment of no small amazement that another 'city boy', Andrew Greeley, has not only named but produced crocuses. How? Search me, I'm a New York city boy myself. It must have something to do with Chicago.

Notes

[1]The choice of the word "aesthetic" may prove confusing here. The argument may also be described as an argument on the "logic of the symbol." However, I have chosen to retain the adjective "aesthetic" to highlight the function of the imagination and thereby clarify the ontological locus of the discussion in relationship fundamentally to the "beautiful" rather than "the good" or the "the true." My hope is that precisely such a concentration may lead to the use of "ethical" and "metaphysical" criteria as well—but now in relationship to these earlier "aesthetic" criteria. In all three cases, of course, the form of argumentation is philosophical. In this specific case, to repeat, the basic argument is correctly described as an argument on the logical status of symbolic language (criteria 1 & 2) and the logically "odd" or "limit" status of the religious use of symbolic forms (criterion 3). The last criterion, of course, should indicate that the position represented by this argument is not, *in principle*, open to the charge of "reducing" religious to aesthetic experience. Whether *in fact* that occurs can only be decided on the basis of the analysis of the argument itself.

[2]The expression is Paul Ricoeur's. *Inter alia, The Symbolism of Evil* (New York: Harper & Row, 1967) 351-2. A less evocative but perhaps more accurate expression is a "critically mediated immediacy."

[3]For my own attempt to outline the basic contours of that "post-modern" situation, *Plurality and Ambiguity: Hermeneutics, Religion, Hope* (San Francisco: Harper & Row, 1987); for an alternative reading of "post-liberal" theology, see George Lindbeck, *The Nature of Doctrine: Religion and Theology in a Post-liberal Age* (Philadelphia: Westminster, 1984).

[4]Through this essay, I am employing symbol as a generic term expressive of *permanent* human possibilities. Symbolic expressions, therefore, may be formed in either non-linguistic images and rituals or linguistic metaphor, stories, myths, and rituals or even linguistic but second-order reflective concepts and analogies.

[5]Hans-Georg Gadamer, *Truth and Method* (New York: Seabury, 1975) 235-74.

[6]For a good contemporary theological formulation of this insistence from an ethical perspective, see Van A. Harvey, *The Historian and the Believer: The Morality of Historical Knowledge and Christian Belief* (New York: Macmillan, 1966).

[7]My dual assumption is, therefore, that the *symbolic* expressions of any particular tradition bear further analysis in the light of the possibilities for re-imagining human existence they may disclose.

[8]The distinction between *tradita* and *traditio* is a familiar one in Roman Catholic theology since the pioneering work on "development of doctrine" and "tradition" of John Henry Newman and Maurice Blondel. For a survey here, see James Mackey, *Modern Theology of Tradition* (New York: Herder and Herder, 1962).

[9]In my own Roman Catholic tradition, the early work of Don Gueranger is the most obvious example of this liturgical romanticism.

[10]Inter alia, see Max Horkheimer and Theodore W. Adorno, *Dialectic of Enlightenment* (New York: Herder and Herder, 1972); Herbert Marcuse, *One Dimensional Man* (Boston: Beacon, 1964). For a history of the Frankfurt School up to but not including

Jürgen Habermas, cf. Martin Jay, *The Dialectical Imagination: A History of the Frankfurt School and The Institute of Social Research. 1923-1950* (Boston: Little, Brown, 1973).

[11]The problem is not stated to be technological but the *ethos* of technology as technocracy. For analyses here, see Carl Mitcham and Robert Mackey, "Bibliography of the Philosophy of Technology", in *Technology and Culture* (14, 2, 1973), and the debate between Habermas and Luhmann in note 13.

[12]The clearest example in Christian theology remains the difference between the Karl Barth of *Romans* and the "later" Barth of the *Dogmatics*.

[13]Jürgen Habermas and Niklas Luhmann, *Theorie der Gesellschaft oder Sozialtechnologie?* (Frankfurt: Suhrkamp, 1970), esp. 119-20. In English, cf. "On Systematically Distorted Communication" and "Towards a Theory of Communicative Competence," in *Inquiry* 13 (1970), 205-18; 360-75.

[14]For Habermas' articulation of this possibility, cf. *Legitimation Crisis* (Boston: Beacon, 1973).

[15]Note Habermas' own appeal to the work of Stephen Toulmin, Ibid., 107. For Toulmin's notion of discipline, cf. *Human Understanding: Vol. I* (Princeton: Princeton UP, 1972), esp. 145-200 and 364-412.

[16]The clearest example of this shift is the contemporary reemergence of major interest in Kant's Third Critique: see Allan Megill, *Prophets of Extremity: Nietzsche, Heidegger, Foucault, Derrida* (Berkeley: Univ. of California Press, 1987).

[17]For example, Paul Ricoeur's attempts to develop a modern philosophy of the imagination appeal not merely to the Third Critique but also to the creative work on specific religious images in several traditions in the work of Mircea Eliade. For a clear example of Eliade's wide-ranging work here, see *Images and Symbols: Studies in Religious Symbolism* (New York: Sheed and Ward, 1969). On ritual, see also to the suggestive work of Victor Turner, esp. *The Ritual Process: Structure and Anti-Structure* (Chicago: Aldene, 1960).

[18]I am employing here the linguistic conventions developed in the work of Paul Ricoeur.

[19]On "fiction" as a redescription of possibility, see Wayne Booth, *The Rhetoric of Fiction* (Chicago: Univ. of Chicago Press, 1961), esp. 3-67.

[20]Cf. the attempt at clarification and caution in no. 1. For a fuller spelling-out of this position for hermeneutical theory, see my *The Analogical Imagination* (New York: Crossroad, 1981).

[21]Ricoeur, 347-57.

[22]Ricoeur, 330-47.

[23]Recall, for example, the appeal to the Exodus symbol as the primary symbol needed for a contemporary theology of liberation in Gustavo Gutierrez, *A Theology of Liberation* (Maryknoll, Orbis, 1973), 155-60. See also, Michael Walzer, *Exodus and Revolution* (New York: Basic Books, 1985).

[24]Inter alia., cf. Victor Turner's development of the notions of "liminality" and "communitas" in *The Ritual Process*, 94-131 or Mircea Eliade, *Rites and Symbols of Initiation* (New York: Harper, 1958), esp. IX-XV.

[25]See John Cobb and David Tracy, *Talking About God* (New York: Paulist, 1983).

[26]In the terms of the internal-Thomist discussion, my emphasis on "concepts" here is not meant to encourage the "conceptualism" that has plagued many forms of neo-Thomism. For a clear criticism of that danger and an argument for "intellectualism" (i.e., insights "over" concepts in Thomas) see Bernard Lonergan, *Verbum: Word and Idea in Aquinas* (Notre Dame: Notre Dame Press, 1969), esp. VII-XV. My own interpretation of the meaning of "concept" and "insight" in Aquinas continues to be influenced principally by Lonergan's masterful interpretation.

²⁷Cf. Paul Ricoeur, *LaMétaphore Vive* (Paris: Editions du Seuil, 1975) for the most constructive expression of this interpretation. My own interpretation unless otherwise cited here is heavily dependent upon this work.

²⁸For the most comprehensive survey-analysis of this emerging (if still partial) consensus, cf. *La Métaphore Vive*, 87-321; in the English-speaking context, cf. the representative work of Max Black, *Models and Metaphors* (Ithaca: Cornell UP 1967); Frederick Ferre, "Metaphors, Models, and Religion", in *Soundings* 51: 377-45; Mary Gerhart and Allan Russell, *Metaphoric Process* (Fort Worth: Texas Christian UP, 1984).

²⁹For a summary-analysis of this discussion in the work of Dominic Crossan, Robert Funk, Norman Perrin and Dan O. Via in New Testament parables, see my *Blessed Rage for Order* (New York: Seabury, 1975) 126-31.

³⁰*Blessed Rage*, 91-146.

³¹Cf. esp. Ian Ramsey, Religious Language: *An Empirical Placing of Theological Phrases* (New York: Macmillan, 1963).

³²Paul Ricoeur, "The Specificity of Religious Language," in *Semeia* (Scholars Press) (4, 1975) 107-45.

³³Hence, if this criterion of a "religious" use of aesthetic forms holds, the position presented is not reducible to a Santayana-like identification of "religion" and "art". I regret, of course, that present legitimate limitations of space force me to state my conclusion rather than argue it. Any reader interested in the argument proper may find it in the work referred to in n. 30.

³⁴Amidst the vast literature in the Thomist meaning of analogy, see especially the pioneering linguistic work of David Burrell, *Analogy and Philosophical Language* (New Haven: Yale UP, 1973). Although I reformulate his position in relationship to the present discussion, my interpretation of Thomas on analogy, unless otherwise cited, is heavily dependent upon Burrell's work here.

³⁵This "focal meaning" approach to analogical language is, in my judgment, the correct route to take; if taken, it challenges the Cajetan tradition of interpretation via "the analogy of proper proportionality." A modern logical defense of that latter tradition may be found in James F. Foss, "Analogy as a Rule of Meaning for Religious Language," in *Aquinas: A Collection of Critical Essays* (ed. Anthony Kenny), (New York: Anchor, 1969) 54-93.

³⁶A critical comparison of the Thomist and process traditions on each one's respective analogical God-language, therefore, should concentrate initially on the distinct anthropologies providing the "focal meanings" for the "perfection-language" employed and then upon the question of whether the "odd logic of perfection" is adhered to. It seems incorrect for Burrell to employ a similar logical series of steps to analyze Thomist analogical God-language, only to fail to do the same for the process analogical language of Charles Hartshorne and Schubert Ogden. Since I believe that the anthropology informing the "focal meanings" of the process tradition is more relatively adequate for contemporary self-understanding than the Thomist and since Hartshorne clearly meets the third criterion on the "odd logic" of perfection terms [cf. inter alia., *Man's Vision of God and the Logic of Theism* (Chicago: Willett, Clark, 1941)], this failure of Burrell's seems a central one for anyone desirous of a critical conversation between these two contemporary analogical languages. For further discussion, see my essays in the volume *Talking About God*.

³⁷Clear expressions of this familiar Rahnerian theme may be found in his "The Concept of Mystery in Catholic Theology," *Theological Investigations* IV, (London: Darton, Longman and Todd, 1964), 37-77 and *Foundations of Christian Faith* (New York: Crossroad, 1978).

³⁸Saul Bellow, *Humboldt's Gift* (New York: Viking, 1975) 487.

Sacred Space and Sacred Time: Reflections on Contemporary Catholicism

Lawrence S. Cunningham

Some few years ago I received a letter from Andrew Greeley telling me that he had run across one of my books and had read it with pleasure. Flattered, I wrote back and, almost immediately, he wrote back while sending, under separate cover, a manuscript of a novel for my comments. From that almost accidental beginning, we have become sporadic correspondents. As of this writing, we have never met but his presence is always close to me because I can espy in my study a pile of Greeley manuscripts (about nineteen inches worth) of drafts of works published and unpublished. I have also been the beneficiary of books, journals, and xeroxes on a wide range of subjects.

One does not have to be a close reader of Greeley's work to know that the texture of Catholicism in all of its iconic, communitarian, sacramental, and, yes, demonic threads is part and parcel of the imaginative world of his fiction and the very warp and woof of his intellectual worldview. Saint Paul, in one of his more protestant moments, says that faith comes from hearing. Greeley would argue, I suspect, that faith comes equally from looking and feeling and touching. When a Catholic, of a certain age, goes to midnight mass at Christmas that peculiar *gestalt* of odors (of incense, pine boughs, winter coats, candlewax) and sights of green and red and gold trigger, not just nostalgia, but a sense of community, togetherness, celebration, hope, and "rightness" which is (or: can be) a lens through which the values of the Gospel are assimilated, digested, and reified.

That experience (and many like them) is what constitutes tradition in the liturgical and historical sense of the term. Some argue that such traditions are part of a past which has eroded and is irretrievable and those who revel in its beauty are, quite simply, *laudatores temporis acti*. Now it is true that there is a tendency to want to recapture a past which is seen as superior to the present. Some Catholics pine for fiddleback vestments and the Tridentine Mass but their enthusiasms are rather like those Romantics who, in the last century, lauded the Gothic as paradigmatic for architecture or the painters before Raphael as the sole practitioners of authentically spiritual art. There is nothing intrinsically repugnant in a fascination with past periods but to make such interests normative is to end up, not with a Chartres but with a Saint Patrick's Cathedral; not with a Giotto but with an Edward Burne-Jones.

A more authentic sense of the Catholic tradition insists on the continuity of the past with the present while allowing for the paradoxical tension between the "unrecoveryness" (forgive the barbarism) of the past and the pertinence of that past for the present. Thus, for example, to recite the Lord's Prayer before communion is to pray as the first Christians prayed while the emphases and understandings of our ancient brethren may not be recuperable; may not resonate with our cultural life. But we pray as they pray and, in that continuity, we stand as part of the great church tradition in time and space. It should be a source of some consolation for those who emphasize change to remember that we use a eucharistic canon that was formulated in the early third century and still used today.

Such lines of continuity should not blind us to the profound changes that can take place within that stream of continuity. The last generation of Catholics has, in fact, undergone such a change of sensibility which I would characterize, borrowing the language of Mircea Eliade, as a shift from the experience of sacred space to a more intense encounter with sacred time. A recognition of this shift helps to understand some of the confusions of the present and offers hints about the crucial tasks of the church as we lurch towards the third millennium.

For the sake of clarity let me say, at the offset, that what I mean by a shift from sacred space to sacred time is something like this: an emphasis on the church not so much as a place where God dwells but as a locus for those times when the faithful gather to hear the Word of God and make sacramentally present Jesus who is the Christ. There is, obviously, not a chasm between those two concepts or even radical discontinuity. It is, I would suggest, an issue of nuance and emphasis. It is also a shift being aborn because of similar shifts both in ecclesiology and sacramental theology.

It is very difficult to convey to my Catholic students what the atmosphere of belonging to a parish was like before 1965. I do not mean atmosphere in the widest cultural sense but in that narrower sensibility which accompanied going to Sunday or daily mass or attending those paraliturgical services (e.g. Miraculous Medal Devotions on Monday evenings; Stations of the Cross during Lent; the annual parish mission; etc.) which were part of life or those daily visits to church which were signs of devout piety. Let us not overromanticize those exercises of devotion. The hymns were hackneyed and lugubrious; the sermons were, more often than not, ferverinos of uncertain quality; and the language (especially the language of devotions) reflected that inflated pseudo-Ciceronian orotundity favored by the Tridentine stylists. The point to be emphasized was the context in which that worship took place.

Over the arch of the main door of our parish church which led from the vestibule was the Latin phrase *Haec est porta coeli*—"This is the gate of heaven." To step through that portal was to leave the world of the profane (*profanum* means "outside the temple") for the world of the sacred. The boundary of vestibule/nave was further circumscribed by the communion rail beyond which priests and acolytes entered.

Women, we should remember, passed through the altar gate only for certain sacramental moments (like getting married) or, more typically, to clean.

If there was any doubt about the sacred nature of that space deduced from the architecture, the elaborate courtesy demanded of those who entered provided a forceful reminder of where they were. The holy water stoups, the covered heads of the women and the bare ones of the men (save for the various chapeaus of the clergy), the complex gestures of reverence (genuflections when the Blessed Sacrament was present; bows when it was not), the requirement of silence, and the orchestrations of sitting, standing, and kneeling all contributed to the sacred atmosphere of the church.

The elaborate protocols of modern Catholicism have a long history behind them but it is safe to say that their peculiar convergence derived from the increasingly large attention paid to the conviction of Christ's true and continuing presence in the Blessed Sacrament: The Prisoner of the Tabernacle. As I pointed out in *The Catholic Experience* (1985) one need only compare the floor plan of a sixth century basilica type church with any church built a millenium later to see the point: the altar moved to the wall in order to receive an elaborated frame to focus the eye on the tabernacle which assumed an absolute centrality on the altar and for the eye of the congregant.

The net result of this long historical evolution in which theology made demands on architecture and art was the sense that when one entered a Catholic church one, in fact, had stepped from the world into the anteroom of heaven where Christ, now sacramentally but in time "face to face," was worshipped. The church was, in fact, the *porta coeli*. At the level of symbolic theology both the congregation and the individual entered the church building in a kind of anticipation of the church triumphant in heaven. That is why, for instance, that in the Byzantine Liturgy the congregation can describe itself as representing the mystic Cherubim who stand before the throne of God in heaven.

Let us emphasize that there was a strong sense that the church building itself was a sacred place. That conviction is clearly behind the language of the rituals for the dedication, deconsecration, and purification of "profaned" church buildings. It was also behind the church practice of requiring a consecrated altar stone for the celebration of mass when no church was available; a practice familiar to every institutional and military chaplain. One of its most charming evocations was in the medieval custom of carving outflying gargoyles on cathedral roofs to serve the practical function of drains while symbolizing the flight of the demons from the holy precincts. The modern analogue to that notion was the very common practice of removing the Blessed Sacrament to a chapel when the church was painted or repaired lest the indecorous labors of the workmen in the church would somehow be injurious to the decorum of the Sacred precincts.

That strong sense of sacrality, closely linked to the doctrine of the Real Presence, was further enforced by simple gestures like the handling of sacred vessels. Altar boys or sacristans carrying chalices or ciboria to the altar prior to Mass never touched them. They were carried by wrapping a purificator around the node of the vessel. At Solemn Mass the subdeacon spent a fair amount of time with the paten wrapped in a humeral veil before it was used for the celebrant's communion. That same humeral veil was used by the priest when lifting the ostensorium for benediction and further refinements were added (like an elaborate canopy) should the Blessed Sacrament be taken in procession either within the church or, as in many Mediterranean countries, in processions through the streets on Corpus Christi.

That strong sense of the sacrality of space began to wane with the reforms of the liturgy mandated by the Second Vatican Council. While it has been a commonplace to note those changes it is my conviction that not enough attention has been paid either to the theological or social consequences of those changes. The loud cries of outrage and sorrow at those changes began in the 1960s and still can be found in conservative journals and newspapers. The one thing that is common to all these laments is the strong conviction that the Second Vatican Council's reforms "desacralized" the liturgy. My own conviction, and this is the thesis of this essay, is that the reforms of Vatican II resulted in a shift in Catholic worship from sacred space to sacred time and, as a consequence, from a strongly iconic to a more verbal matrix for the Catholic imagination. Because that shift (not complete but in process) is badly understood the church (read: the official church) squanders its not inconsiderable resources in its efforts to re-form the life of the church.

In the seventh chapter of the *Constitution on the Sacred Liturgy* the Fathers of the Second Vatican Council said that when churches are built "let great care be taken that they be suitable for the celebration of the liturgical services and for the active participation of the faithful." (*Sacrosanctum Concilium* VII.124). Using one of the fundamental buzzwords of the liturgical movement ("active participation"—*actuosa participatio*) the council, in effect, decreed churches whose spaces were to be designed, not for presence, but performance. The focal point of church architecture (and I use "architecture" as a synecdoche for the entire context of worship) was designed, not as the place for the Sacramental Christ, but for the liturgy as it was performed. To use my Eliadean language: there was a shift from the place where the liturgy was performed to the time when it was performed.

That shift occurred at the precise time when the same conciliar document made possible the use of the vernacular in the liturgy. The focus on the performance of the liturgy was accompanied by a change in the law which put a fundamental emphasis on *communication*. For the first time in centuries the people understood the hackneyed "Dominus vobiscum" as an English phrase which they could (or could not) directly assimilate in their consciousness. What was once "heard" as a sacral, other worldly incantation by many, now became an intelligible datum which required explanation, gloss, or interpretation: what do those words mean?

To spell out those changes and shifts in a different way would be simply to note that the priestly task focussed less on the priest as a custodian of the sacred mysteries of the Liturgy and more as a person who was expected to communicate those mysteries in a verbal form. The old custom (common in our very hot climate here in the Deep South) of dropping the homily in the Summer would be unthinkable today. Indeed, both the Second Vatican Council and the new Code of Canon Law (see: 767.2) made the Sunday homily obligatory and strongly recommend homilies for the weekday celebration of the liturgy. Those regulations reflect the contemporary concern of the church to emphasize the preaching function of the priest as complementary to his right to confect the eucharist.

The implications of that new focus on communication and performance are profound. An anecdote might help make the point. Many years ago, as a young student, I went to a morning mass in a parish church in Dublin. The priest, with a look of ineffable boredom on his face, appeared precisely at 8:00 and, twelve minutes later, he had finished mass and distributed communion to about forty people. His Latin was blurred, slipshod, and recited at breakneck speed while he glided from one side of the altar to the other. When, in the censorious tones and priggishness of pious youth, I recounted this horror to the landlady of our bed and breakfast hotel, she said, "Ah, yes. That would be Father X. He is a bit fast but what a blessing he is when one is trying to get a bus for work in the morning." Apart from her innate generosity, what she also said was that the priest got through the liturgy, consecrated the elements, and the people got to communion. Period. How Father X would have fit a homily into his performance defies my powers of imagination.

The world is not free of slovenly priests today by a long shot. What has changed, however, is the perception that the liturgy must communicate if for no other reasons than the fact it is in an intelligible language. While (Greeley's research has shown this) most Catholics are pleased with the new liturgy there is no doubt that the official church has meditated little on the profound implications for pastoral theology on this new focus on the timeliness of the liturgy as a form of communication especially as that communication becomes intensely *verbal.* Anyone who thinks that such a shift has not taken place might meditate on the observable fact that the most popular form of "low" liturgical art for the past two decades has been the liturgical banner: an art form that displays, not figures primarily, but messages. The other side of that example is the immense trove of now discarded liturgical paraphernalia now mouldering in church attics; a victim of a changing shape of liturgical space.

With a readily intelligible language and a priest facing the congregation there was the palpable expectation that the priest would reach across to the assembled people and *say* something. His very body language was oriented to the congregation instead of to the High One as in the older paradigm. A basic consequence of this change in paradigm was an increased emphasis not only on intelligible texts for the liturgy but the expectation that the homily would take on a central place in worship. That, in turn, created the tacit assumption that the priest and other ministers would know what to say and how to say it.

Has the church taken account of this shift in any serious and sustained manner? The answer, alas, is no, as any Catholic who goes to mass with regularity will attest. This is not to say, as the more rabid conservative critics would have it, that contemporary American Catholics are alienated from the church in any significant way. That, in fact, is not the case as studies dating back as far as 1978 have shown. Indeed, the compilation recently assembled by George Gallup, Jr. and Jim Castelli [published as *The American Catholic People: Their Beliefs, Practices, and Values*—

Doubleday, 1987] shows rather clearly that the majority of educated Catholics think themselves well served by the church. The increased attendance at Mass and the rise in converts would seem to give credence to that satisfaction. The point is that the "official" church has not encountered and does not seem ready to capitalize on the profound communications shifts that have occurred in the present day church.

This is not to argue that the church is unaware of the problem. It is to suggest that the thing which is most central to the church—the celebration of the presence of Christ in the public worship of the church—is so central and so much a part of the common experience of Catholics that the requirements of a heightened sense of language and a deeper appreciation of the context in which language must be used can be overlooked or ignored. The plain fact of the matter is that most Catholics contact the Good News in the encounter they have with the official liturgy. If that liturgy is not shaped by seriousness and conviction we are in danger handing out, not bread, but stones. The Sunday hour of worship is the timely occasion when the church gets to say what he has to say to the vast majority of Catholics— Catholics who exist in a surfeit of language and imagery from the mass media. A grasp of that simple fact should give urgency to any pastoral strategy of evangelization while setting before it some urgent tasks. It seem rather unlikely that there will be any real advance in the church's teaching capacity apart from the liturgy if the liturgy itself is poorly celebrated and the homily remains at the level of a perfunctory gloss on the readings of the day. We might also note, in passing, that until this basic level of communications is addressed more grandiose schemes of evangelization through the national media, etc. are doomed to mediocrity at best or complete failure at worst.

The first of these tasks concerns the education of the future clergy and the continuing education of those who already exercise a pastoral ministry. It is very clear that what is central to the priesthood today is the capacity of the priest to preside in a serious and intelligible way over the liturgy. That requires not only an ability to communicate in an intelligible manner the *mysterium* of the liturgy itself but, and this is crucial, to be able to extend the celebration of the liturgy qua liturgy through effective preaching in the homily. If this is not done, there is no reason to be confident that the other forms of catechesis or evangelization will be more effective.

In order to do that effectively we must relearn something about the ancient tradition of monastic theology which combined the traditional skills derived from the study of rhetoric (the *ars dictaminis*) with an intense meditation on sacred scripture. That tradition of a deeply contemplative study of scripture through a heightened awareness of the discipline of literary study provided the church with a synthesis which has been captured wonderfully in the title of Dom Jean Leclercq's magisterial study of this tradition: *The Love of Learning and the Desire for God.*

This is not to argue, in a retrograde fashion, for an abandonment of philosophical or systematic theology. It is very much a plea for a basic emphasis on the power of language in general and the manifestation of that power in the *Sacra Pagina* in particular studied in some kind of a contemplative setting. Obviously, that style of learning cannot be done by apeing the setting of either the medieval cloister or the *aula* of the Renaissance humanist. But it is obvious that those past traditions do have something to teach us. By a careful appreciation of that tradition we might overcome the gap that too often exists between academic theology and spirituality. David Tracy's program for the juxtaposition of classical text(s) and common human experience gives us some basis for rethinking how theology done in a precise pastoral mode might be accomplished.

Furthermore, that respect for the power of language does not only mean that the liturgical and sacramental leaders of our church need respect language (although that is surely a noble and necessary aim) but that they begin to re-appreciate the power and limitations of language as it used in public religious discourse. One could argue, after all, that the greatest problem concerning religious language today is that there is too much of it in a too familiar and trivialized setting. One need only think of the drumbeats of the electronic church to see the point. The old words of sin and grace and salvation are bandied about with such ease that one wonders whether they have lost their power to compel attention.

Those old words are part of "our" story—the story of salvation. The very emphases of some of Andrew Greeley's admitted mentors—John Shea's emphasis on story theology; David Tracy's focus on the classics—indicates how seriously he takes the task of juxtaposing our story with the old story of the Gospel. What all these folks have in common is the fundamental conviction that there must be the deepest respect for the polyvalence of language if it is to retain its power to convey the sense of the Transcendence to the contemporary world. Language cannot be the talisman it was in the past. It can no long inspire by its utterance. We require a language that evokes and provokes; a language that rises up from the babel around us to say something. It is not surprising that this need for a powerful religious language has been a concern of our more religiously literate novelists. I do not have in mind the "Catholic Nostalgia" school of writing but novels like Brian Moore's *Catholics* and both the novels and non-fiction of Walker Percy.

Let me not push the dichotomy of space and time too far. The older Catholic paradigm set a high standard for the sacrality of space precisely because the Real Presence of Jesus was emphasized. The newer paradigm in which the celebration of the liturgical mysteries re-call, and re-present the presence of Christ, proclaimed in the Word and actualized in the Eucharist, puts a premium on the moment(s) when the liturgy is celebrated. Those moments are preeminently moments of language. Language, in turn, provides a concomitant sense of the sacrality of place. The two, while separable, are not contraries. It is for that reason, as outrageous as it might seem at first mention, that the priest must also be a poet. The priest, like the poet, calls up those *Urworte* (as Karl Rahner has called them) which speak of transcendental mystery and ultimate purpose. Not to understand that fact is to miss a crucial part of the challenge of the Gospel in these heady days of the post-Vatican II church.

There are many reasons to hope that the contemporary challenge to energize both our religious language in general and our liturgical language can be met. Scriptural studies are done at a high level in Catholic circles while the newer emphasis on narrative theory, the meaning of symbol and metaphor, the attempts to construct a story theology, the emergence of new studies on the sources of the Christian tradition go on apace. That there is a serious dialogue between religious theorists and literary critics is a good sign. The great challenge ahead is to marry the field of theory with the ongoing praxis of the worshipping community. It has been the deepest conviction of scholars like Clifford Geertz and others that it is ritual that gives authenticity and coherence to religious belief. The great ritual act of the Christian liturgy is the *fons et origo* of Catholic identity and dynamism. To rise to the challenge of balancing the tradition and timeliness of that act is to act on the very central datum of Catholic life and vitality.

Discovering God Anew

Hans Küng

1. What Does it Mean to "Discover God Anew?"

The way this question is posed might lead to a twofold misinterpretation: To "discover" sounds like the finding of something previously invisible, the uncovering of some kind of object previously covered or concealed. To "discover anew" sounds like a religious fashion of the moment, like a new fad, like riding the very latest transcendental wave. Both forms of association arise out of misunderstandings which need to be cleared up at the very beginning.

The first concerns the word *"God."* If the word God is to have any meaning at all, then it cannot refer to one object among other objects, one being alongside other beings, one person like all other persons. If the word is to have any meaning today, then it must stand for the Invisible and Incomprehensible, the First and Last Reality determining and pervading all things. And this reality does not simply mean another level; it is a completely new dimension, not one to be easily discovered by the speculative equivalent of X-rays. No, God would not be God if he could be empirically perceived or calculated, mathematically or logically deduced.

This is why the *second* misunderstanding arises from the word *"discover."* "Discovering" God is, and will always be, a risk, a hazard for human beings, demanding everything of them, challenging both heart and head. Or, to put it positively and briefly: the fact that God really exists, though he can be neither perceived nor deduced, is not a matter of rational proof (as some Medieval Catholic theologians believed); nor is it a matter of irrational experience or feelings (as some Protestant theologians have assumed in view of difficulties arising in recent times)— but rather it is a matter of *reasonable trust*—something we Christians, along with Jews and Moslems, call "faith"—a reasoning trust, no more subject to rational proof than love, yet quite capable of being made comprehensible with the aid of many reasons. And why is this trust in a completely other "invisible" reality a reasoning and comprehensible trust? Because—this can be stated in principle at the outset and illustrated later—it is grounded and embedded in our everyday experience and can thus be confirmed, at least indirectly, can be proven and *verified* within the experiential horizons of our lives.

Finally, concerning the word *"anew"*: God—a new discovery by the human being? Such a thought would be arrogant or mindless. There is no absolutely new experience of God which has never been given in one form or the other! What, then, does it mean to discover God "anew" if the word "anew" is not to be understood as the extolling of the very latest religious trend? The only way to speak of discovering God anew is in terms of biography, of personal history. And this will be the topic of this paper.

Keeping in mind all these attempts at a precise definition, the basic theme of this essay can be expressed as a two-fold question. *What*, according to their structure, are experiences of God, discoveries of God, and *where* and *when* are experiences of God possible?

These questions must be considered within the context of a pluralistic audience representing diverse assumptions and expectations. Among readers, there will be atheists and agnostics with a thoroughly critical approach to religion. There will be many who, vacillating between faith and unbelief, ask themselves skeptically whether their faith and hope, their longing and their prayers might not end in a void after all, in an echoless room, emptiness swallowing everything. And finally, there will be those whose basic stance is one of faith. Some of them will find that the traditional formulas have nothing to say; others still utter the evening prayer of their childhood and have preserved a kind of childlike naiveté in their religious life which contrasts sharply with their professional life. Either way they cannot reconcile their religion with the everyday world, their personal experiences with pious expressions, the "external" language of life with the "internal" language of the church.

2. The Difficulty of Experiencing God in Prayer and Worship

In his novel *Halbzeit* (1960) the well-known German novelist Martin Walser tells of an experience shared by countless people: "With Lissa in church. Couldn't pray.... The solemn language in the church sounded foreign. Shop talk. Air of a hot, stifling *Föhn* wind.... My life can no longer accommodate itself to the language of prayer. I cannot contort myself like that any more. I have inherited God in these phrases, but now I am losing him on account of these phrases. He has been turned into a magical Privy Councillor whose eccentric use of language we adopt because, clearly, God belongs to yesterday."

Even today without doubt, countless people would answer the question of their concrete experience of God in terms of Bible study, receiving the sacraments, experiences with the community of believers, and worship services: faith-experiences, both individual and collective, in which they feel themselves to be confronted with the God who reveals Himself. When asked how God can be discovered, they would point to the Scriptures, the liturgy or the teachings of the Church.

Yet it is also true that although countless people have "inherited" God through the proclamation and teaching of the Church, through the Bible and worship, they have also "lost" him there: He is a "God of yesterday." How often indeed have churches been in fact "graves and gravestones of God" (F. Nietzsche) and not places where one could experience the *living* God! How often have the doctrines of the Church become empty phrases, the text of the Bible a collection of fairy tales of long ago? And who could dispute that for most people, life "can no longer be accommodated to the language of prayer?" Prayer in its traditional form is denied many people precisely because for them it represents childishness, regression, irrationalism, ideology, passivity and fatalism, flight from reality, flight from action, flight from responsibility and hence a "sell-out" to existing power structures. More often than not justifiably, prayer has indeed been criticized and denounced for having on occasions served as a *substitute* for action, enlightenment and social change. Instead of improving our disordered world and taking the initiative ourselves, we prefer to experience God and let him rule. It is a fact that more than anything else in the religious sphere, prayer can be the opium of the people, tranquilizer as well as intoxicant.

Many consider turning to the Bible an evasion of the real issue instead of a solution to the problem. Why? Because the *prayer contained in the Bible* also seems strangely naive to them. They ask: Is it really possible for today's men and women to pray like the devout (or not so devout) figures of the Bible? In such a natural, uncomplicated manner, in the middle of life and rooted in life, simply pouring out their hearts, asking to be heard, in simplicity and unbroken harmony with their practical reality; pleading for help, for mercy and grace, for their own salvation and that of others? Are we today still able to ask as spontaneously, to thank and to praise as honestly and well? Are we still capable of simply looking upwards and offering "praise to the Most Holy on High...?"

When they return to church services after a long absence some find the liturgical celebration before an omnipotent and omniscient God and especially the ritualistic formality of the event unbearable. How can one experience anything personal where everything appears prescribed, regulated, drilled, or at least devoid of spontaneity and imagination, often turned into a farce by artificial pathos or a mechanical attention to trivia? "Shop talk," hot, stifling "air of a *Föhn* wind"...

Some find comfort in simply *closing* their eyes right there in the church and *turning inwards*. And why not? For we know:

—God is *not* simply there *at the front*, where a minister, a bishop or a Pope "celebrates," "pontificates" or sometimes even stages the event.

—God is *not* simply *up there*, where the Hall of Heaven as the dwelling-place of God was dismantled with Copernicus and Galileo; where not even the heaven of a Baroque artist can magically restore it; where no smugly ruling church hierarchy, in its efforts to push its way in as a mediating canopy between God on high and the people below, can conceal it.

In view of this overshadowing of God in our churches—and often by our churches (the German psychoanalyst, T. Moser speaks of the "poisoning of God" from infancy)—do I have any choice but to close my eyes, turn inwards and find the all-embracing, all-pervading God *in the seclusion of my inner self*, to sense Him, to feel and experience Him in the center of my being?

3. Experiences of God In the Inner Self

To "*close*" one's mouth and eyes—*myein* in Greek, this is the root of the words "mystery" and "mystic;" this is the kind of religiosity which keeps its mouth closed to the world concerning its hidden secrets, which takes its eyes off the world in order to seek salvation in the inner self—in silence, retreat from the world and turning inwards, in the search for unity with the Absolute, with the one first and last Reality, which is known by a thousand names yet is unknown and unutterable.

Mystical experience of God: Is it any wonder that despite all the rhetoric which attacks the "new subjectivism" this kind of experience has become a magic word in our time? When asked where God is to be found, many will answer, along with Brecht's Galileo, "in us or nowhere." Having so often failed to experience God in the churches of a materialistic West, we search for such experiences wherever they can be found. Not only social drop-outs, rock stars and movie celebrities have carried this quest to Indian gurus and ashrams, but also state sovereigns and prominent Western intellectuals in their search for peace in a world haunted by external turbulence and inner desolation. The German physician and philosopher Carl Friedrich von Weizsäcker, for instance, speaks of an indescribable mystical experience at the grave of the Hindu saint Sri Ramana Maharshi.

Indeed many contemporary intellectuals overcome *the experiential crisis of Western religion and society with the help of mysticism*. It appears to provide a way of overcoming the doctrinal rigidity of traditional religion and the institutional inflexibility of conventional Christianity without actually giving up religion. It appears to provide a way of leaving behind conventional Western religion with its incessant confessional conflicts, without actually sinking into a spiritual vacuum. It appears to provide an opportunity to combine experience of God with experience of self, the physical with the rational, spiritual concentration with the highest degree of tolerance and "cosmic breadth."

The rapid rise in the number of self-actualization courses, of exercises in meditation and spirituality, of yoga and eutonics, is a typical and significant religious and cultural sign.

Whatever one thinks of its individual methods, its psycho-technics and systematics *Eastern meditation* holds a fascination for many who claim to have found in it what they have greatly missed elsewhere. For it is not a world of faith "above" or "beyond" into which such meditation, with all its various stages and stations, leads them, but rather the world of the "inner self," the realm of the deep. Methodically or systematically speaking, its aim is to lead a person to ultimate reality—seen as "fullness" (in Hinduism) or "emptiness" (in Buddhism). Hence it is a journey from the external world of the senses to the inner world of spirit, by means of an ordered advance through solitude, silence and seclusion, through the "dark night of the soul" to the light.

How can we relate what we know of experiences of God in the Western and Eastern traditions? At that point we touch upon a fundamental question concerning the very essence of contemporary understandings of God. It relates to the basic distinction drawn within religious studies between mystical and prophetic religions, which I can only outline briefly here.

The great *mystical* religions are of Indian origin. Their basic position is directed *toward the inner self*, toward liberation from desires, toward the extinguishing of a life lived according to the affections and the will, toward the renunciation and emptying of self—in short, toward annihilation. The *prophetic* religions, on the other hand—Judaism, Christianity and Islam—are of Semitic origin. They are characterized by the will to live, by the urge to assert themselves, by the motivating forces of values and tasks, as well as the passionate striving toward the fulfillment of particular ideals and goals. Hence prophetic experience of God is primarily directed outwards. It stands in open confrontation with the world, aims at asserting itself within the world and triumphing even in the severest defeat. In this sense, prophetically directed spirituality is aggressive, forcing its way from doubt to the assuredness of faith, from insecurity to trust, from the consciousness of sin to the attainment of salvation by grace. It is well known that according to St. Paul it is not the ecstatic ability to speak in tongues but faith, hope and love that are the highest gifts.

Discovering God anew? In view of such broad ecumenical horizons we must consider these two independently great streams of development of the early high religions which have gained global significance far beyond the lands of their origin. We are confronted with both the mystical tradition of Indian origin and the prophetic tradition with its roots among the Semitic peoples in the Middle East, a tradition which even today united Judaism, Christianity and Islam despite all their differences. We find ourselves facing the question of *which* God we are to discover, and under which circumstances he is to be *discovered anew*? Are we seeking the God of the mystics, "in" whom we live, and who lives in us—or the God of the prophets, "before" whom we live? Herein lies the crucial intellectual challenge!

How shall we meet this challenge? Are we faced with a clear choice between black and white, the one or the other? We need not go so far. In prayer and worship I have indicated already that Christians too have long since become familiar with mystical elements and practices. No: when we speak of experiences of God, we are *not* speaking of a *simple choice* between passive and active, the inner and the outer! Inwardness and involvement, sensitivity and solidarity, contemplation and action or, as Dorothee Solle has shown, "Hinreise" (the journey there—religious experience) and "Rückreise" (the journey back—translating the content of experience into everyday life) belong together, represent a single "round trip." And indeed the course of religious history has long witnessed the mingling, overlapping and interweaving of these major religious streams. Both divided into branches at an early stage and partially flowed into each other. Evidence of this tendency appears in Christianity as early as St. Paul and St. John, next in the Alexandrians Clement and Origen as well as the North African Augustine, and finally in many medieval and modern figures. Yet I do not wish to explore this in detail, either historically or theologically. In any case we should not dismiss the *mystical* experience of God as merely a preliminary form of (or derivation from) the prophetic experience; on the other hand, neither should we attempt to trace *prophetic* experience of God back to mystical experience as the "real" religion.

Assuming that we have no intention of creating either a shabby synthesis or a stark dissociation of one from the other, how is mutual permeation, enrichment and convergence possible? How can we, as children of the prophetic tradition, discover God anew? How can we talk of him and to him in a new way, precisely within this mystical perspective? In order to answer this question we must examine the basic structure of experience of God more closely.

4. The Basic Structure of Experience of God

I must admit one thing: for me personally, *music* is more often than not an important source of religious experience, and one does not need to travel to India to gain experiences of great spiritual intensity. What takes place in listening to music—for me and many others—is surely analogous *as far as its structure is concerned* to the experiences the religious person has with "his" or "her" God? What exactly does this mean?

Imagine that you are listening to music intently, completely free of outside disturbance, either at home alone or with others at a concert; perhaps your eyes are closed. Suddenly you notice that you are somehow no longer bound to sound as a physical, external "object;" that instead, you hear only music, nothing else. Now it is the music that embraces you fully, pervades you, and suddenly sings out from your own innermost core. What has happened? You sense that you are completely turned inward, with eyes and ears, with body and spirit; that you have overcome everything external, every posing of opposites, every division between subject and object. The music is no longer an *objective other*, but that which embraces, pervades and brings pleasure from within, that which fills and fulfills us completely. One might almost say, "In it we live and move and have our being." You will know that this is a passage from Scripture (Acts 17: 28), and it is not without risk that I introduce it here. It is taken from the speech (undoubtedly shaped by a Hellenistic Luke) the Apostle Paul made on the Areopagus in Athens. In it Paul speaks of searching for, groping for and finding God, who is far from none of us, in whom we live and move and have our being. But that particular word of Scripture is also an old Greek word of poetry, and that is where the border appears very fine between music, which is the most spiritual of all the arts, and religion, which has always had a special relationship to music. Why is that?

It is because in such moments I may succeed in opening myself, opening myself to the very depths of myself in that reasoning, more than reasoning trust of which we spoke at the beginning—in order to hear, in the eternally beautiful sound, the sound of the Eternal. It is when I open myself, open myself completely in trusting faith, that I can be grasped, in this wordless event of music, by the unutterable mystery; that in this overwhelmingly beautiful and pleasing experience I myself can sense and experience the presence of a depth within depth, for which the word of God stands.

This has nothing to do with rapturous effusiveness; neither is it a matter of ecstatic experience or being transported away. As an enlightened being of the twentieth century I do not suddenly let go of all reason: I take back nothing that I said critically at the beginning. Even in this utterly interior manner, recalling the inner light of the mystics in the depths of the soul, I cannot discover God as if by X-rays, cannot perceive him empirically as if I were a neutral observer, cannot manipulate him. There is nothing "self evident" here; nothing can take place without the relationship of a reasoning trust. For...

If I close myself against him, he will not disclose himself;

if I do not listen, he will not speak;
if I do not believe, he will not reveal himself.

This is the basic structure of *every* experience of God as experience of *God*.

Does this mean that it is my faith which leads to his revelation, my hearing to his speaking, my opening of myself in trust to his disclosing of himself? No: for even more than he is in me, I am in him. And he is before me—not only in a temporal sense, but in every respect. Not able to be grasped even in familiar presence, present even in experienced absence. No: for the first tenet is:

Unless he opens himself, I cannot open myself;
unless he speaks, I cannot hear;
unless he reveals himself, I cannot believe.

And more than this: even in the opening of myself, in this hearing and believing, *I do not "see" him.* Whoever sees him, says the Scripture, must die. We can turn this statement around and say, only he who dies can see him! A number of monistic mystics have exaggerated in their speculations to the same degree as other love mystics who emphasize feelings, and have spoken in rapturous ecstasy of the blessed unity with the One and only, or with the bridegroom of the soul. God alone is God. Even in our most completely inner and personal experience of God we should avoid mindless or disrespectful identification of our experience with the reality of God. After all, it is Paul himself—and he more than anyone could testify to mystical experience—who says that on this earth we will never see more than through a glass darkly: fragmented, puzzling—in any case never face to face.

Once and for all, let us remember that even in the most personal experience of God we do not experience the reality of God in its immediacy and totality. What we experience is *the presence, the nearness, the radiance of God*: the Bible expresses this in the Hebrew word *kabod* and the Greek *doxa*, which we translate with "glory". Considering that Moses himself, who at his calling saw only the burning (and yet not burning) bush, and who on the long journey through the desert wanted to see God at least once face to face—that even he could not look on God! When God passed by Moses as he stood in the narrow cleft of the rock, he had to hold his hand over him in protection, so that Moses would not be blinded by his glory. It was not until God had passed by, that Moses was permitted to look at him; he only saw God from the back, and not face to face.

Indeed, it is only the glory of God that we can, in retrospect, experience—the form of his appearing, his radiance, his reflection, his emanation—which can admittedly be experienced as well in the form of darkness, brokenness, absence. Just as we experience the radiance of the *sun* on us and *in us*, which, though it indeed permeates the whole of our being, warming us and bringing us light, always remains *transcendent*, even so it can also shine behind clouds. The transcendence of God is never removed, not even for an instant, despite his immanence. he is completely in the here and now, yet remains completely beyond us. And even when he has a hold on us completely, we do not gain a hold on him. Ultimately, he remains beyond our grasp, embrace, or comprehension. And even the most intensely moving religious experience is empty if it is not *his power and strength* which so deeply move us.

5. *The Second Form of Naiveté*

Since earliest times the Bible has known another word for this quality of "strength" or "power" emanating from God; interestingly enough, in Hebrew it is feminine (*ruach*), in New Testament Greek neutral (*pneuma*), and only in Latin, Latin derivatives, and in German is it masculine: *spiritus, der Geist,* the Spirit. Comprehensible, yet not to be comprehended, invisible yet powerful, as real as the energy-laden air, the wind, the storm, as vital to life as the air that we breathe: that is how people have imagined the "Spirit" of God and God's invisible working since antiquity. The strength or power emanating from God: in other words, God close to us in the Spirit, present in the Spirit, through the Spirit—as the Spirit. Whenever we experience God deep in the inner self, when we sense God as the wholly immanent transcendence, it is then that we experience the power and strength of God, his Spirit, God in the Spirit: God as that Spirit who is nearer to us than we are to ourselves, and yet as the Spirit of the Holy God, the Holy Spirit, not the same as our spirit, our spirit that is, as experience teaches, unholy throughout.

It is important for me to emphasize above all that in the light of mystical experience the Biblical manner of speaking of God, as naive and anthropomorphic as it seems, gains new breadth and depth. This is where a mutual enrichment, permeation and convergence is possible and urgently needed. To be precise: the person who experiences God in the act of mystical prayer will also speak of God in a completely different depth and breadth in the act of prophetic prayer. *A second form of naiveté, tested against contemporary reality,* now becomes possible. It is very different from the first, the childlike, natural naiveté. An example?

—After I have learned that God is *not a person* like you and I, but more than a human person, the eternal in the mortal; that he, the Eternal and Incomprehensible, is the sea that can never dry out (despite Nietzsche's "madman"), the horizon that never fades, the sun from which the earth and the mortal being can never be unfettered, the all-embracing, all-pervading Other, yet the One to whom we can, even as such, *speak* meaningfully in mortal words; after I have learned all of this I can address him again as *"You"*, I can pray again—in both praise and lament, in plea and rebellion.

—And since I have learned, inspired by the contributions of feminist theologians, that God is *neither male nor female* but transcends masculinity and femininity and humanity as a whole, and that as such he is the unutterable mystery of our reality, for which all our human terms, even the word "Father", are merely analogies, symbols, ciphers: I can, since we human beings have no names higher than human names, and since "Father" as a term of address says more to us than "the absolute" or "Being itself", I can also pray again, quite simply and at the same time post-patriarchally (without excluding God as Mother), as Jesus has taught us to pray for the past 2000 years, *"Our Father...."*

—And finally, having learned long ago that God is not *above us or "over there,"* but embraces and pervades the whole world and every human being here and now, I can, having had my eyes closed for so long, having looked inwards and found God in the depths of my being—I can open my eyes again and look upwards, to pray, in solitude or in community, *"Our Father, who is in heaven...."*

6. Experiences of God in the Everyday World

Now we look at the world differently because the world looks at us differently. And perhaps we are now able to discover not only in ourselves but in the world as well the dimensional depth which is submerged and foreign to the superficial human person alienated from himself. In any case, there are particular everyday experiences accessible to me which invite me to step past this everyday into another dimension and there to encounter deeper connections and an ultimate ground of meaning. But no: in so doing, we are not faced with any particular evidence, not forced by any transparency, and we can hardly communicate the experience adequately in language. Yet we have enough experiences—both positive and negative, interpersonal and of the world—which cause us to stop and allow us to look deeper.

Theologians and saints have written a great deal about this theme, especially since the *process of secularization* of the modern age appears to have left behind the Medieval-Romantic world, once so full of mystery, a world in which all temporal things were symbols of the Eternal. But it is precisely this contemporary, worldly, secularized, rational world which provides ample reason to see more in the everyday than the everyday itself. In any case, modern persons will not rid themselves of their "God complex" (H.E. Richter) as long as they fail to open themselves to the reality of God. Let me explain the problem:

There is a lack of mystery in modern life, as *Dietrich Bonhoeffer* pointed out. He made it clear that human beings, with their command over technical knowledge, their claims to power, their insistence on taking the world seriously only to the degree that it yields profit and can be exploited, destroy the mystery. This great Protestant theologian warned early that a life devoid of mystery meant failing to see, or even denying, the crucial processes of life. It is time we realized that the roots of a tree lie in the darkness of the earth; that everything which lives in the light comes from the darkness and hiddenness of the womb; that all our thoughts as well, our entire intellectual life comes from the hidden, mysterious Ground in this way, as does our love, as do all forms of life.

There are the great, pressing questions of humanity: Paul Tillich stressed that the modern person can find no answer to the question of the meaning of life until he regains the "lost dimension of the deep;" it is in the deep that people find answers to the questions of where they come from, what they are doing here and what they should make of their lives in the short time between birth and death.

There are the small signs and gestures of human life, interpreted by the sociologist of religion *Peter Berger* as ciphers of transcendence in our everyday life: gestures of protection and comfort, when a mother calms her frightened child, but also our strange desire for the restoration of order, our urge to play, our humor, our hope—all of these things are part of the human expression of being and indicate more than the human being: they indicate something that reaches above him, transcends him. They are parables of a possible salvation.

There are the basic experiences of human existence, as outlined by *Karl Rahner* on a number of occasions. How much in a human life cries out for interpretation: the concrete experience of need and loneliness which leads us to cry out for a solution; experience of calm, in which we hear a voice; experiences of total responsibility, so often the bearers of suffering, and of unconditional love which leaps over walls; experiences of unforgivable guilt, of ultimate fear and the longing for definitive meaning and peace.

And finally, *there are basic experiences in human history, in society and politics* so passionately defended by representatives of *political theology, liberation theology, and feminist theology.* They draw attention to the possibility of experiencing God in the history of the oppression and liberation of human beings—of the poor in particular, and especially of women—, and demand a new form of the discipleship of Jesus, one that is both mystical and political. These theologians have quite rightly opened our eyes to the fact that God can be experienced wherever alienation between races, classes and the sexes has been overcome, wherever injustice has been eliminated, peace has been established, and love has been put into practice. In short, they challenge us to find God in the spirit of Mt. 25: 35-46, in his humility, in the lowest of our brothers and sisters, in those who are scorned and despised— and to do so in the hope for the full justice that is to come, in which murderers will no longer triumph over their victims.

Thus in the course of every human life and in every form of human suffering there are strange facts, signs, events, situations and "coincidences" which can provide an impulse to thought and religious reflection. Our experiences are too valuable to be simply cast aside rather than preserved and reflected upon. And perhaps it will help you if I add—as a footnote, so to speak—some of my personal experiences which have given me cause to pause, reflect, and to think beyond. They are as follows:

Firstly, *the experience of being stopped*: it can happen in a small or a big way; at its most extreme it can be hard and bitter and cause many sleepless nights. In an undertaking that seems vitally important to both myself and others, there is suddenly no going on, and our opponents rejoice: "He's been stopped!" Somebody—whoever that may be—is preventing me, preventing us from carrying on, thus changing my situation completely. Only one thing is clear: nothing will ever be the same again, and I do not yet know what the outcome of the situation will be. I am supposed to adjust to it, but I cannot, must not: the work will not be abandoned. In short, my path is blocked, with no apparent way around the obstacle.

What should I do: resign myself to the situation once and for all, give up, revolt? Or view it as yet another sign of the absurdity of life? Whatever—this experience of being stopped is a clearly perceptible challenge not only to stop but also to pause and turn inwards. Whether it be an obstruction in one's profession, an unexpected illness or the failure of a personal relationship: all of these things can provide an impulse to reflect on the deeper dimensions of one's life, to open oneself anew in and to trusting faith. It is then a comfort to experience that even in this enforced stand-still there is a hold, an anchor, grounded in the basic reality of our lives, in the reality of God himself, who—and the Psalms testify repeatedly to this fact—is able to create new perspectives even in situations which otherwise lack all perspectives. As a result of this trust we are able to see our lives in a new light, to adopt a new standpoint, to correct our course and take hold of a task again. Indeed, "the Lord gives sight to the blind. The Lord lifts up those that were bowed down." (Ps. 146:8)

Secondly, *the experience of being held*: at the moment things come easily to me, not only in terms of work—things are accomplished almost of their own accord. Is it the weather, my horoscope or biorhythms? At any rate I am progressing, achieving something, and I am filled with self-confidence and good cheer. Of course my life will not always be like this; change is inevitable. But what does this matter to me today as I ride the high tide of the fulfilled moment! Why should I waste time with negative thoughts, negative feelings, negative moods...*Qui vivra verra.*

Yet something is not quite right! This consciousness of success, this untroubled good mood, is coupled more often than not with indifference, self-inflation and superficiality. We fail to perceive the deeper dimensions of life—to recognize that thinking has to do with thanking. For he (or she) who stops to think for just one moment will sense that happiness and success are not dependent on our work; that though we have achieved much, we have received even more; that our good fortune has come by chance, perhaps not without the wish for it, but, we must honestly admit, undeservedly: "Name something you have that you have not received?" writes Paul in the first letter to the Corinthians (4:7). Hence there is reason to be thankful, not only to other people, but to that other authority which confronts us and lends meaning to our lives despite all that is contrary to it. There is reason to trust anew, reason for renewing trust in the providence which bestows direction on our life's work, for recalling the debt we owe for our very existence. There is reason to rejoice that despite being continually driven we are in fact led and carried. In truth we can say:

My journeys and my rest you scrutinize,
    with all my ways you are familiar.
Even before a word is on my tongue,
    behold, O Lord, you know the whole of it.
Behind me and before, you hem me in
    and rest your hand upon me. (Ps. 139: 306)

Experiences of being stopped, of being held—so I, so we, could go on: experiences of suddenly feeling alienated within one's closest group of friends, in one's family, at work, at home, in this life as a whole. And yet, as well, there is always the opposite: to settle in somewhere, to become familiar with a new place, to feel at home. Not long ago the writer Heinrich Böll answered the question of why he personally believed in God by noting "that really all of us know—even if we fail to admit it—that we are not at home on the earth, *not completely at home*, that we belong somewhere else and come from somewhere else. I cannot imagine a person who has never realized—at least for a time, for an hour, for a day or even only for a minute—that he does not fully belong on this earth." It is, he says, the feeling of strangeness throughout, which keeps alive in a person the memory that this reality is not his home: "In no way does it have to do with a mere feeling, but perhaps with an ancient memory of something that exists outside of ourselves." Indeed it is no mere feeling, not simply a childhood memory, but "an ancient memory of something that exists outside ourselves."

7. God With a Human Face

Who would deny it, though we might have largely forgotten or suppressed it? All of us, no matter what our conscious opinion, live from this great memory, which has come to us in our particular Christian context through the Christian message, and which we continue to breathe even when we are no longer thinking of it. For myself, I admit gladly that I have spoken from this memory and have had it in mind continually, even when it has not been on my lips. It is a memory that binds us to the future!

Indeed how timelessly abstract and vague remains even the philosopher's understanding of God—quite apart from the fact that to a large extent contemporary philosophers have handed over their great classical heritage (the inquiry after God, the world, man and meaning) to history, sociology, psychology or theology itself, and that for this reason people of today certainly have no less to say than their great predecessors.

Unlike Pascal, I do not speak against the "God of the philosophers and the educated" when I speak for the "God of Abraham, Isaac and Jacob." And it is the "God of Abraham" in whom we as Christians, along with both our Jewish and our Moslem brothers and sisters, believe: that we must never forget. Admittedly even the Old Testament understanding of God remains in some respects very ambivalent, which is why Pascal adds the following vital words: "the God of Jesus Christ—only in those ways taught by the gospel is he to be found...is he to be preserved."

In fact it is not until the New Testament, in Jesus' proclamation of God as the father of the lost sons and daughters, that the Biblical understanding of God becomes completely unambiguous, because it is actually embodied, personalized, in this human person. Whereas the people of Israel heard only a voice, early Christians recognized a figure. Theirs it was to discover, for themselves and for others, that the one God not only had a name, but also a face. No, that is not blasphemy, as our Jewish and Moslem brothers and sisters believe, since we Christians have often understood this in such an un-Jewish, anti-Hellenistic, anti-Islamic way: even in Jesus one does not see God himself face to face; according to the whole of the New Testament, Jesus is not *the* God; *ho theos* is the Father alone. In Jesus one sees a *human* face, recognizable only by faith as the image of *God*, as his Christ and—an ancient royal title of Israel—as his Son.

Thus God appears to me in the life and teachings, in the suffering and death of Jesus, in yet another light, indicating that even the most meaningless human suffering and death can have a meaning, can take on meaning. This God is not a cruelly arbitrary and authoritarian God, is not a fearsome male, a theocratic God "from above," not a falsely omnipotent, omniscient, disassociated God-Father, as Elizabeth Moltmann-Wendel and other women rightly point out; instead he is a benevolent, empathetic God standing in solidarity with us. And there is no cross of this world that can refute the offer of meaning sent out by the crucified one, who was taken up into eternal life and installed in sonship by God. It is a God of love who reveals himself here, one who in the contradictions between our longings and reality not only challenges but gives, who is himself love in its fullness, and in whom the longing of countless people for justice in this unjust world, for genuine transcendence, for the "completely other," will be fulfilled. That is what we, as Christians, believe. But at this point we must leave off our believing reflection and come to a close.

8. Conclusion

What, then, does it mean to "discover" God, this all-determining, all-pervading Reality, to discover him anew in the ordinarily accessible experience of concrete life? We saw that *"discovering"* does not mean conclusively deducing him, the Incomprehensible-Uninvestigable, from a supposedly evident experience, nor *"uncovering"* him, in order that we might escape the necessity of deciding for ourselves. God is not "at the disposal" of the "neutral observer." Note: only to him who knocks in trust will the door be opened: "Return to me...then I will return to you." (Zec. 1:3)

"Discovering" God means shining a clarifying light on this our everyday experience, both external and internal, in its doubtlessly increasingly ambiguous and increasingly problematic nature; it means finding the key to a rational understanding of this experience and interpreting it verbally, in order to attain and appropriate, in a free and yet credible decision, a reasoning trust in this incomprehensible, uninvestigable, unutterable mystery of our reality, the mystery that embraces and pervades everything, that allowed its voice to be heard in Israel, and assumed form, took on a tangible face, in Jesus Christ. This God does not stand "at our disposal," yet stands surely "in expectation (readiness)." Note at the same time: the hidden One is open from the start to the one who opens himself. For here, in dialectical juxtaposition of trusting faith and benevolent grace, the other prophetic word applies: "Lead us back to you, O Lord, that we may be restored." (Lam. 5:21)

What about the conduct of the Christian; what about social and political practice? This has not been my theme, yet the answer should be obvious—the conduct of the Christian in social fields of conflict is accounted for, motivated and stimulated in quite another way by the experiences of God described here. In this way, God proves himself to be not only the completely Other but also the reality which completely changes things. Those who experience God anew as the mid-point of their lives in a new relationship of rationality and feeling, of inside and outside, above and below, of the beyond and the here-and-now, of mysticism and politics, will have their eyes opened, in new ways of seeing, to their own reality, in the form of new values, new priorities, new practices which free them, in a bond with the Absolute, from all false bonds. False gods are brought to a fall, whether in the Church or in politics.

Indeed in an epoch such as our own, in which many, and especially those in key positions, have been infected with that "universal, diffuse cynicism" of an "enlightened false consciousness," one which has already been reflexively and defensively shored up with a virtually out-of-tune, "dismal serenity" (if one is to believe the analysis of the German philosopher Peter Sloterdijk)—in a late culture such as our own, in which many values are worn out, many convictions for sale, the belief in progress run down, in which morality appears to have been replaced by selfish pursuit of private interests—in such a culture it will be necessary, for the sake of the survival of humanity, to adopt and live out an *alternative basic stance*, one whose focus is that reasoning trust in God, one whose guideline is his word and whose vitality his Spirit; yet whose center is freedom in love, and whose peak a new joy in life.

Indeed it is true: if "the Lord's are the earth and its fullness"—as Psalm 24 puts it—then the false rulers of this earth with their powers and authorities can be stripped of their magic and brought down from their thrones; then the benevolent God, who is everything but a patriarch and tyrant, can be honored and praised in a new way: in responsible service to the world and in a true service of worship. In a great synthesis of prophetical and mystical traditions, the message of Psalm. 24, so often misunderstood, that the earth is "the Lord's," can be understood in a new way:

The Lord's are the earth and its fullness;
    the world and those who dwell in it.
For he has founded it upon the seas
    and established it upon the rivers. (Ps. 24: 1-2)
Lift up, O gates, your lintels;
    reach up, you ancient portals,
that the King of glory may come in! (Ps. 24:7)

Married Love Stories:
Toward A Pastoral Theology
of Erotic-Romantic Love

Mary G. Durkin

As the Irish relatives would have said, "It was a *grand* wedding!"

The bride was radiant. The groom, despite a calm appearance, was a bit nervous. The mothers, grandmothers and sisters, true to their Celtic heritage, shed a few tears—sentimental tears, they said. The homilist spoke of God's delight with love stories. The groom's brother, a confirmed bachelor at age twenty-six, admitted in his best man's toast that even he was moved to believe in the possibility of marital happiness when observing the bride and groom. The groom's father read his poem about Celtic roots and thanked the bride and groom for the reminder "that life should be a thrill." The bride's brothers recounted tales about their sister's exuberance. The groom's sister delivered a message of *Cead Mille Failte* (a Hundred Thousand Welcomes) from the Irish relatives who could not attend. The groom recited an original love poem. The bride told how she had responded to all the previous week's queries about nervousness: "How could I be nervous when I'm marrying Dan?" she asked, her eyes sparkling. And the wedding guests ate, drank, danced and sang the night away, all a bit more hopeful about life after being part of a reenactment of what Pope John Paul II calls the "first feast of humanity:

Yahweh God fashioned the rib he had taken from the man into a woman, and brought her to the man. And the man said:

> This one at last is bone of my bones
> and flesh of my flesh!
> She is to be called Woman,
> because she was taken from Man.

This is why a man leaves his father and mother and becomes attached to his wife, and they become one flesh.

(Genesis 2:22-24)

For a short time, at least, the guests joined with the bride and groom and *imagined* the possibility of a life more exciting than the mundane existence of their day-to-day worlds. As the father's poem observed:

Oh yes, it's nice for us to think ahead and back.
But let's not forget this night we feel elation.
For we have come to witness God's great gift to us,
   that men and women are called to celebration.

This volume honors a man who firmly believes that love stories—real and fictional—tell about God. Furthermore, he argues convincingly that religious belief develops at two levels. Theological discourse with its emphasis on creedal beliefs and doctrines speaks to the intellect. However, the religious imagination, which has a profound effect on our views about God and on our religious practices, functions at an experiential level. Both are important avenues for discourse about religion and about a religious heritage.

Thus it is proper that a pastoral theology of sexual intimacy presented here be a theology of erotic-romantic love derived from the correlation of the love stories of marital intimacy and the faith stories of God's love for humankind. In other words, we begin with love stories that expose their participants to the extraordinary and encourage them to be hopeful. Then we turn to stories of faith that affirm that hopefulness, giving deeper insight into how to nurture the hopefulness even in the midst of ordinary events. Finally we will examine a strategy for action that evolves from this meeting of experience and faith. This strategy recommends a way pastoral leaders, pastoral workers, and individuals might make use of the creative imagination to develop a spirituality of sexuality. The methodology used in this theological exercise is that of correlation. The focus here will be on the Catholic faith tradition and its emphasis on sacramentality.

John Shea, who taught me the importance of the correlation method of theological reflection, considers pastoral theology an art as well as a science. According to Shea:

In a very real sense the pastoral theologian is analogous to the artist...called to be in Nietzsche's words "poet to our everyday lives." This reference to poetry brings out the pre-cognitive feel for the religious dimension of life that characterizes great pastoral theology....as a pastoral theologian the minister engages in, for himself and the community, the primordial act of interpreting the Really Real and trying to live in communion with it. This is a fundamental drive which, when exercised in the concrete, draws on the most creative aspects of the human personality.[1]

In other words, the pastoral theologian must be attuned to the role the creative imagination plays in the God/human relationship. At the same time the pastoral theologian seeks to enrich the pre-cognitive religious imagination by linking it to the creative stories of a faith tradition. By so doing, the pastoral theologian increases the possibility that peoples' religious imagination will help them recognize the God present in the various mystery experiences of human existence.

Obviously, this pastoral theology puts equal emphasis on *pastoral* and *theology*. The practitioners of this art believe that God lurks everywhere, waiting for humankind to discover the divine presence in a wide variety of experiences. When a faith tradition helps this discovery process, both the experience and the faith are enriched. A double prosecution takes place here. Experience demands that faith explain what is occurring; faith requires that the meaning of the experience be an authentic reflection of the tradition's faith. In the process of this prosecuting dialogue, the faith tradition constantly discovers meanings not considered in previous reflections; at the same time, the interpretation of experience is subject to evaluation.

The starting point for pastoral theology's reflection on the meaning of human sexuality is the experience of marital sexual intimacy. The opening wedding story does not speak explicitly about sexual intimacy. However, the erotic-romantic character of the attraction that leads to a wedding celebration is evident throughout the story. Indeed, the erotic-romantic nature of new love encourages lifelong commitment and supports partners when they find the commitment burdensome. The best man was right. Only the extraordinary power of erotic-romantic love could overcome all the rational reasons why two individuals should be wary of lifelong commitment. So a wedding love story encourages an examination of the religious dimensions of marital intimacy.

The mystery and revelation encountered in the powerful, playful, surprising, demanding, and, at times very frustrating, physical attraction between a husband and wife invites religious explanation. When the wisdom of the Catholic heritage with its emphasis on Creation, Incarnation, Redemption and Grace is linked with the experience of marital sexual intimacy, a pastoral theology of marital sexual intimacy emerges. This pastoral theology could serve as the basis for inspirational, challenging preaching and pastoral care.

Theological reflection begins with a consideration of the stories of sexual intimacy in marriage. These stories reveal the unique charisma of married people that Pope John Paul II said the church should listen to when it seeks to understand God's plan for marriage and family life. Stories of marital intimacy tell of the ongoing joys and struggles of a union that has the power to be a sign (sacrament) of God but that also has the power to destroy one or both partners.

An examination of marital sexual intimacy reveals that the sexual drive is a source of ambiguity for marriage partners. However, in a marriage where passion helps the partners as they strive to grow in intimacy, oftentimes the positive power of sex triumphs over the destructiveness that lurks in the feelings of ambiguity. Married love stories disclose the possibility of sex as a binding force in marriage. They also demonstrate how often this possibility is rejected.

When her husband of thirty years was feeling depressed, Anne surprised him with a trip to a "love motel" instead of to the local shopping center he thought was their destination. His comment" "If after thirty years of marriage my wife wants to take me to a "love motel" instead of to JC Penny's, I must be doing something right!" His winter doldrums quickly disappeared. Two years later he still smiles when someone mentions the surprise.

A couple, who both have busy work schedules and who are in many situations where they interact with attractive members of the other sex, arrange at least one weekend a month when they escape for a romantic interlude. They take turns planning the weekends, surprising each other with the destination and activities. The only rule is that they have privacy and plenty of time for lovemaking. Nothing will deter them from this time of renewal. Liz says: "A whole day of lovemaking and intense conversation recaptures those feelings and dreams we shared when we first fell in love. And the memories add spice to those times when our lovemaking might be just a quickie. I don't think our marriage would survive if we didn't nourish our passion for each other."

A man and woman quarreled violently and barely spoke for a week. Each was convinced that the other was impossible to live with; their marriage was definitely on the rocks. Their hostility was apparent to their children who worried that Mom and Dad were going to split. One night, in his sleep, the husband reached out for his wife and awoke to find her huddled next to him. They both wept as they apologized for the harm they had done to their love. They sealed their resolve to begin again with passionate and joyful lovemaking. He said: "I guess I must have been dreaming when I reached out. But I know that one of the hardest things I did during that week was resist my desire to take her in my arms and say 'I'm sorry,' I guess my subconscious won out in my dream. Thank God for that."

A mother and father, heartbroken at the news that their son's illness was serious—perhaps even fatal—, didn't know how they would face the long road ahead of them. They left the doctor's office overcome with fear, fear for their son, fear for each other, fear that they would be unable to cope. The fear created a wall between them because they weren't able to vocalize their feelings. Yet that night, in the midst of tender and passionate lovemaking, each experienced the other's promise of support. Later, after their son's death, the mother said: "That night was crucial. I knew then that Tom's agony was as deep as mine, something I hadn't realized when he was being the strong male in the doctor's office. I can see how a child's illness can destroy a relationship; it's so hard to express your anger and fear and sorrow. And you resent that your spouse doesn't feel the way you do or doesn't understand how you are feeling. Fortunately, when we weren't able to communicate our feelings verbally, our bodies did the talking."

In these four stories when the partners were willing gift for each other, sex became extraordinary. Their sexual intimacy acted as a mysterious force, fostering growth in their relationship. Religious language would describe this sexual intimacy as grace-filled, giving the partners an opportunity to savor their relationship as a gift from God. At times like this, partners are encouraged to continue to "cling together" and can appreciate why the *Genesis* writer believed that God looked upon sex and proclaimed that it was "good."

The goodness of God's creation is discovered and revealed in lovemaking that acknowledges the importance of the other person. Sex is seen as a bond that breaks down the obstacles that keep the partners from growth in intimacy. These stories of marital intimacy show that sex for pleasure, for fun,—sex that is recreational— actually strengthens the marital bond and increases the possibility that the marriage will be sacramental. Recreational sex in a marital relationship contributes to a re-creation of the sacramental, God-revealing love in the wedding story. From a Catholic perspective this sacramental power is the key that unlocks the door to the meaning of sexuality. Guidelines for sexual behavior that conforms to this meaning begin to surface.

Unfortunately, there are far too few of these grace-filled moments in most marriages. In addition, both individuals and religious thinkers ignore the sacramentality of the sex drive with it desire and passion. A female yuppie says she and her spouse are working so hard that they have gone for three months without sex. Three women married about thirty years discuss how they don't touch in their families—neither their spouses nor their children give or get many kisses or hugs. A man, married almost thirty years, hasn't hugged, kissed or made love to his wife in over five months. He claims they are "too old" for that.

A survey reveals that while men rank their marriage as good or better on a variety of issues—including sexual intimacy—their wives give it lower marks all around. This different interpretation of the same situation is evidenced in the story of the wife who wants love in the bed to be the inspiration for more cooperation in the rest of the marriage; her husband claims that if she were more responsive in bed, he might be more interested in exploring ways to grow in intimacy.

While there are also stories of sexual abuse—physical and psychological (treating the partner as nothing more than a sex object for another's satisfaction)—in marriage that demand condemnation, the far more prevalent misuse of sex in marriage occurs when partners neglect the positive reinforcement desire and passion give to their search for intimacy. As they find themselves caught up in the mundane world of day to day living, many partners begin to take each other for granted, sounding the death knell for growth in intimacy.

Periodically, they might wonder what happened to the dreams of their courtship days; but without a serious challenge to recapture the promise of those days, they easily dismiss their dreams as foolish romance. The strong genetically programmed human desires for independence and self-fulfillment encourage habits that often curtail the equally powerful desire for intimacy. The partners decide that real life is quite different. Sometimes they wind up like the woman who said she had been married forty-eight years to the wrong man, a man she had pursued aggressively and against the wishes of her parents.

Still, the periods when intimacy flourishes are the sacramental moments that reveal the meaning of sexuality and help harness it positive potential. At those moments, sex expresses both erotic and romantic love. The partners are lovers who in their passionate embrace are willing to overcome the barriers that keep them from deepening their marriage bond. They return in a very real sense to the time when they first fell in love. They remember the joy of their initial attraction and once again are willing to plunge ahead in their relationship. A marriage in which the romantic love of new lovers periodically flourishes and deepens reveals the bonding power of human sexuality.

The love of new lovers that must flourish if a marriage is to survive the inevitable barriers to growth in intimacy is best described as erotic-romantic love. Erotic-romantic love directs our strong sexual drive toward another who is loved as a person with his/her physical attractiveness, but also as a unique person to respect and cherish. Generally, sexual attraction is at the root of the initial allure between a man and a woman; it is the spark that moves them out of their self-centeredness and opens them to each other.

To a lover, love is indeed blind and rose-colored glasses filter out any defects in the beloved. At some point, the power of the physical attraction breaks down any previous hesitancy about commitment. The partners desire each other not just for the moment, but they want to share the rest of their lives with each other. They fantasize about the never-ending "high" that their life together will be. Anything and everything seems possible in their future. Their desire for each other overcomes all the obstacles anyone—themselves included—might try to put in the way of making a commitment.

A priest book reviewer once questioned how a married woman could support a romantic view of marriage since marriage was a serious business. He obviously had not listened to stories of marital intimacy. Otherwise he would know that the seriousness of lifelong commitment demands eroticism and romance if it is to be a sacrament of God's love. Perhaps he never heard that the pastoral theologian must be attuned to the pre-cognitive and the mysterious in human experience, including the experience of marital intimacy.

The best man in the opening story was aware of and frightened by the implications of marriage. So far in his life, he had not experienced the pull of the combination of eroticism and romance in a relationship. When he does, he, like the bride and groom, will live in the mysterious, pre-cognitive, romantic world of lovers. He, too, will believe that he and his beloved will be able to be true to each other in "good times and in bad, until death do us part." And, like all married people, he will discover that failure to keep erotic-romantic love alive will make it difficult to sustain the wedding promise.

The pastoral theologian, listening to stories of marital intimacy, soon discovers that it is erotic-romantic love that fosters growth in a marriage. Because this love encourages sex that is playful, caring, passionate, and committed, it helps the partners discover the wonder of the gift of human sexuality that alone of all animal sexuality allows sexual partners to choose to be united both physically and emotionally. The meaning of sexuality is linked to this impetus toward union. The challenge for the theologian is to discover how to illuminate this meaning through the double prism of erotic-romantic love and the religious heritage.

When the stories of marital intimacy with its erotic-romantic love are linked with stories of faith that flesh out some of the basic beliefs (doctrines of faith) of the Catholic heritage, they provide a tool for the pastoral theologian, the preacher, and the pastoral worker. The interplay between these stories speaks to the religious imagination of believers, inspiring them to discover the sacramentality of sex in their lives and at the same time challenging them to continue the revelation of God's gift of love that sexuality is meant to convey.

At this point the analogy between theologian and poet becomes obvious. The pastoral theologian who is aware of the religious dimension of marital intimacy now must do a poetic interpretation of the stories of faith that speak to that experience. Examining the stories of faith in light of the basic beliefs of the tradition so they will respond to the mystery encountered in marital intimacy is "the primordial act of interpreting the Really Real." The mystery encountered in marital intimacy points to a Mystery beyond the experience itself.

The pastoral theologian recognizes this as an experience of God. In the Catholic tradition this God is the God of Creation, Incarnation, Redemption, Grace and the Holy Spirit. These creedal categories, however, do not speak directly to the imaginative experience of Mystery. To address this experience, the theologian needs to tell, or perhaps retell, the biblical stories that capture the experiential basis of the creedal statements. These stories help illuminate the Mystery encountered in marital intimacy.

Pope John Paul II in his first fifty-six audience addresses on a theology of sexuality and the body does this retelling of biblical stories. He provides an example of a poetic response to the mystery of human sexuality. The Pope's interpretation of biblical stories helps clarify the ambiguity of erotic-romantic love. He shows how Christ directs those who want to know the meaning of human sexuality to the story of the "beginning" found in the first four chapters of the book of *Genesis*.[2] There they will find that God's plan for masculinity and femininity is for "two in one flesh" to be a revelation of Divine Love and a model for all human unity. The recognition of and respect for the personhood of the other required for a man and woman to "cling together" in a union that is the "image of God" are critical in all human relationships.

The "original nakedness" of which Adam and Eve were "not ashamed" was possible because they recognized that their sexuality was a gift (grace) from God. They celebrated this gift in "the first feast of humanity." This retelling of the Genesis story shows that an acceptance of the goodness of sexuality is intrinsic to the doctrine of Creation. So, too, is a recognition of the sacramental nature of the marital union with its erotic-romantic love.

Since the Pope is following Christ's directive to return to the "beginning," he is retelling the story in light of his belief in the Incarnation and Redemption. The "beginning" plan, though originally rejected, is still available. When Christ became human and brought the "redemption of the body," he was offering all those who still experience the desire for the unity of man and woman an opportunity once again to participate in God's plan. The Grace of the Holy Spirit, promised by Christ, includes the help to live according to God's plan for human sexuality.

For the purposes of a pastoral theology of marital intimacy, Adam and Eve are models of erotic-romantic lovers. In *Genesis* 2 they celebrate the giftedness of the human body and its sexual power that helps them acknowledge each other's personhood. Graced, and aware of their gracefulness, they experience the unity possible through erotic-romantic love. They are naked—both physically and psychologically—and "not ashamed."

But Adam and Eve, like all marital partners, are free to reject the grace of marital intimacy with its erotic-romantic love. They settle for less; they grow bored; they long for something exciting because they resist the continuing excitement available in growth in intimacy. Soon they find themselves ashamed of their bodily attractiveness and fearful of the grace available to them. They hide from God and from each other. However, in the Christian story, God and grace are not avoided easily. God, in the person of Jesus renews the offer of erotic-romantic love. In the person of the Holy Spirit, God continues to help married couples at every time and place in human history.

These biblical stories inspire the Catholic religious imagination. They give a message of hope about marital intimacy to those who believe the God of that imagination is the ultimate meaning of life. At the same time they challenge the believer to keep erotic-romantic love alive in marriage.

Another biblical story that speaks of the power of erotic-romantic love is *The Song of Songs*. This Old Testament poem celebrates erotic-romantic love for the joy and happiness it brings to the lovers. The lovers seek each other out. They long for each other when they are apart. They play when they are together. They fantasize about sexual union. They praise the beauty of each other's body. They never want their love to end. Though much of its imagery might be foreign to a contemporary audience, *The Song's* expression of the yearning of the lover and his beloved speaks to all lovers.

The presence of this erotic love poem in the Bible has been the subject of discussion almost from the beginning of its inclusion. Is it an allegory? Was it meant to describe the relationship of Yahweh and Israel? Were Christians correct in considering it a foretelling of the relationship of Christ and the Church? Was it composed by Solomon or was it a loose collection of love songs having no greater meaning than the celebration of love? These and other questions have occupied scholars through the ages. Whatever the final answer might be, if in fact there ever is a final answer, won't change the fact that the lover and his beloved speak the feelings of erotic-romantic lovers. The religious community that included this expression in its canon apparently found these feeling a proper expression of its belief.

The Song of Songs is a rich storehouse of imagery that speaks to the religious imaginations of marital partners concerned about keeping erotic-romantic love alive in their marriage. A widow, married during the Depression, tells the story of how she and her husband used to read *The Song of Songs* for entertainment during the early years of their marriage. From the smile on her face as she tells the story, you know the poetic imagery sparked their imaginations. The lovers in the poem spoke the thoughts and yearning they felt but lacked the skill to express.

Pope John Paul II sees *Genesis* 2:22-24 as a precursor of *The Song of Songs*. The latter certainly is an elaboration of the brief *Genesis* account. A careful reading of *The Song* reveals its paradigmatic character. Love poems, erotic art and love songs throughout human history seem to express many of the same ideas expressed by the lovers. Both *The Song* and these works of art tell us something about "the Really Real and how to live in communion with it."

The Song of Songs as a paradigm suggests a strategy for pastoral ministry that flows from the interaction of stories of marital intimacy and stories of faith. A religious imagination in tune with the imagery of *The Song* recognizes the importance of erotic-romantic love. *The Song* in conjunction with *Genesis* 2 nurtures a belief in the sacramentality of marital intimacy. When marriage partners become familiar with the paradigmatic message of *The Song*, they are inspired to grow in their intimacy. Pastoral ministry to the married should aim to excite the creative imagination of the partners. *The Song* is an excellent starting point for this strategy.

Consider, for example the imagery in the opening verses of *The Song*:

Bride

The Song of songs by Solomon.
Let him kiss me with kisses of his mouth!
  More delightful is your love than wine!
Your name spoken is a spreading perfume—
  that is why the maidens love you.
Draw me!—...

Bring me, o king, to your chambers...

I am as dark—but lovely,
  O daughters of Jerusalem—
As the tents of Kedar,
  as the curtains of Salma.
Do not stare at me because I am swarthy,
  because the sun has burned me.
My brothers have been angry with me;
  they charged me with the care of the vineyards:
  my own vineyard I have not cared for.

(1:1-6)

This opening selection from *The Song* introduces a recurring theme in love songs: the yearning of the beloved for the presence of an absent lover. Here, too, is a reference to the sensual nature of erotic-romantic love. Throughout the poem the senses describe a lover's feeling and at the same time enhance the love images. In this selection the maiden's love is more delightful than wine. Furthermore, when she hears her lover's name she feels herself engulfed by the perfume of his presence.

These verses capture how erotic-romantic love enhances the self-image of the individual lovers. The maiden's lover is a king in her eyes, though not in reality. At the same time, love makes her more self-confident about her own attractiveness. More than likely her lover has no problem with her swarthiness.

This same imagery appears in a tenth century poem from the Persian of Oumara:

Ah, would that I could hide within my songs
And every time you sang them, kiss your lips

and the words of an anonymous Elizabethan poet:

My Love bound me with a kiss.
    That I should no longer stay;
When I felt so sweet a bliss
    I had less power to part away:
Alas! that women do not know
Kisses make men loath to go.

Yes, she knows it but too well,
    For I heard when Venus' dove
In her ear did softly tell
    That kisses were the seals of love:
O muse not then though it be so,
Kisses make men loath to go.

Wherefore did she thus inflame
    My desires, heat my blood,
Instantly to quench the same
    And starve whom she had given food?
Ay, ay, the common sense can show,
Kisses make men loath to go.

Had she bid me go at first
    It would ne'er have grieved my heart.
Hope delayed had been the worst:
    But ah to kiss and then to part!
How deep it struck, speak, gods! you know
Kisses make men loath to go.

and the words of Robert Browning:

All the breath and the bloom of the year in the bag of one bee:
All the wonder and wealth of the mine in the heart of one gem:
In the core of one pearl all the shade and the shine of the sea:
Breath and bloom shade and shine,—wonder, wealth, and—
    how far above them—
    Truth, that's brighter than gem,
    Trust, that's purer than pearl,—
Brightest truth, purest trust in the universe—all were for me
    In the kiss of one girl.

and a host of other love poems. Love poems stir the imaginations of those who hear them, especially when they capture a yearning as deep as that expressed by the bride in *The Song*. A pastoral theology of erotic-romantic love finds value in the use of love poetry in pastoral ministry to the married.

Art works are another avenue of appeal to the imagination of married lovers. The opening verses of *The Song of Song* suggest that a plead for kisses is a symbol of a yearning for the continuing presence of a lover. Works of art that also convey the power of a kiss include the following:

1) Rodin's embracing lovers in his sculpture, *The Kiss;*

2) Klimt's elaborately ornamented lovers who seem to blend into one in his 1907/ 08 oil on canvas, *The Kiss*;

3) The adoring look of the lover in Ingres' painting of Francesca di Ramini and Paolo Malatesta;

4) The hunger of the lovers in *The Kiss* by Francesca Hayez.

An appeal to the imagination of married lovers through poetry and art makes them more attuned to the extraordinary possibilities of erotic-romantic love. The artist and the poet who capture the depth of our everyday life express the feelings that most lovers are unable to articulate. Yet when lovers see or hear these feelings expressed, they are able to say, "That's it. That's how I feel." When *The Song of Song* is linked with these feelings, a recognition of the Mystery (God) that lurks within the mystery encountered in marital intimacy is possible. Lovers are then in a better position to reveal this Mystery to others. The sacramentality of erotic-romantic love and its message that love of another as a unique person is possible becomes more apparent.

In summary, a linking of the stories of marital intimacy and the stories of faith indicates a need for a theology of erotic-romantic love to expresses the meaning of human sexuality. The God-revealing power of human sexuality revealed in the *Genesis* account of creation and in *The Song of Songs* is the basis for a Catholic understanding of sexuality. This love enriches a marriage and hints at the meaning of human sexuality. Erotic-romantic love was possible in the Garden of Eden because Adam and Eve were fully graced and always aware of their bodies as vehicles of Divine Love.

In a world where this consciousness of God's plan is not always present, religious thinkers need to remind people of God's grace, always available to married lovers. This grace will help them begin over and over again when they inevitably fail to appreciate the power of erotic-romantic love. A strategy for pastoral ministry that evolves from this theology should appeal to the creative imaginations of married lovers. *The Song of Songs* as a paradigm of the experience of erotic-romantic love and as an elaboration of *Genesis* 2:22-24 is a tool for helping lovers discover that they "witness to God's great gift to us."

The bride and groom in our opening story will find it easier "to be true to each other in good times and in bad for all the days of our lives" if they are challenged to keep alive the erotic-romantic love they felt on their wedding day. Their Catholic heritage gives them the hope their love will survive and at the same time challenges them to work at the growth in intimacy necessary to help it survive. When in the course of their marriage the bride experiences nervousness over her choice of a groom, as she will on innumerable occasions, *The Songs of Songs* and the memories of her wedding day can be the catalyst she needs to reawaken their marital love. At that point their love story, like all romantic love stories, will have survived another crisis. She and her spouse will believe that "life should be thrill."

Notes

[1]John Shea, "An Approach to Pastoral Theology," in Chicago Studies, XII (Spring, 1973): 20-21.

[2]For a more detailed analysis of these talks see: Mary G. Durkin, *Feast of Love: Pope John Paul II on Human Intimacy* (Chicago: Loyola UP 1983).

Stories of the Love of God

John Shea

In 1979 Andrew Greeley celebrated his twenty-fifth anniversary of his priesthood. Friends gathered for a liturgy at St. Barnabas parish on the South side of Chicago and afterwards continued the celebration at Beverly Country Club. One of the after-dinner speakers was Todd Brennan, representing Dan Herr and the Thomas More Association. Todd's speech was simply to read the titles of Andy's books. It was not a short talk. And today it would be considerably longer. As one wag commented, "Thank God he left out the articles."

Andy's writings, which are only part of what this present volume celebrates, are not only voluminous but wide ranging. The titles which Todd read would not be located in only one part of the library. Andy has infiltrated every section of the Dewey Decimal System. On Todd's list were books of poetry and fiction, studies in religion, theology, and history, sociological investigations into ethnicity, education, politics, and aspects of American culture ranging from sexuality to mystical experiences.

Many of us listening to this impressive list have been exposed to metaphysics. Some have caught the disease and others have gloried in their immunity. But even those who steadfastly refuse to consider the question of the one and many either before or after dinner puzzled about whether there was a invisible unity to this highly visible multiplicity. Did these printed planets revolve around a single sun or were they off on their own? Were these horses galloping wild or did an overall purpose harness them?

My suggestion is that the love of God is the hidden unity of Andy's prodigious writings. If I were more of a detail person, I would attempt to back up this intuition by carefully collecting citations. I would note how divine love is a recurring theme in his works on theology and sociology of religion. I would suggest that the fullest interpretation of his novels must acknowledge them as stories of sin and grace, adventures of divine love and human freedom. Furthermore, I would contend that Andy's passionate interest in every aspect of the human condition, his deep desire to find out what is actually going on in the minds and hearts of people,—in other words the imagination and discipline of sociology—comes from a sense of the abiding value and dignity of all things sustained and transformed by the love of God. Finally, I would make a case that the many struggles of Andy's career within Church, academia, and society could be traced to concerns which he thought were either "in or out of sync" with belief in a loving divine reality. But the rigorous research necessary to bolster this intuition will have to await another day.

Instead I would like to focus on one way the experience of the love of God is expressed and communicated—storytelling. To reflect on stories is a laudable hermeneutic activity. To tell stories is a slightly different enterprise. Permit me to tell four brief stories of the love of God. They have all been inspired by the Christian tradition and so they all attempt to articulate and communicate the felt-perceptions of that tradition. "The Father of Ice Cream" takes a clue about divine love from the perhaps rhetorical remark of Jesus, "What father among you will give his son a snake if he asks for a fish, or hand him a scorpion if he asks for an egg?" (Lk. 11:12) "The Penny Planter" borrows a incident that Annie Dillard tells about her childhood in *Pilgrim at Tinker's Creek* and combines it with the dynamism of the sower and the seed parable in Mark 4. "Martha the Good" reflects the intriguing story in Luke about Jesus, hospitality and two sisters. "Let Them Be Who They Will Be" is not so much a story as three monologues from the main characters of Jesus' most famous parable—The Prodigal Son. Hopefully they all say something about the central conviction of Christian faith—God is love.

The Father of Ice Cream

Tom, eleven, was the first in the door at 31 flavors. He shouted over his back to the people behind him. Everyone in the store heard his ultimatum. "I said I get the window on the way back."

Alice, the oldest at thirteen, followed. She was somewhere between collecting stuffed animals and riding in cars with boys who would tell her, "I'm the type of guy your mother hoped you wouldn't meet." She looked bored.

Next Janet, who was nine, was shoved through the door by Jeff, who was aggressively eight. Finally, the smallest of the group, a boy by the name of Paul, came through the door, holding the hand of the tallest of the group, a man by the name of Daddy.

They all lined up in front of the plate glass wonderland. "Whatever you want," said the father. His arms spread out, indicating all 31 flavors.

"I want a scoop of rocky road and licorice in a cup," grinned Jeff the eight year old.

"Daddy, Dadddy, Daddddy!" Janet the nine year old was sputtering. "That's what I was going to get. I told Jeff in the car that I was going to get that. That's why he got it."

"Janet, I'm sure they have enough rocky road and licorice for two," the great mediator assured her. She glared at her father.

Meanwhile Tom, the eleven year old, had conned the teenage girl behind the counter into giving him a taste of of pralines 'n cream and double chocolate. He was now pushing along into bannana fudge and pineapple swirl.

"Tom!" shouted his father. Tom backed off and returned the little pink tasting spoon to the girl. His father said only one word; but the communication was unmistakable. They had had the conversation before.

"Daddy," said Alice in a refined voice, "I'll have two scoops of lime sherbet in a cup." She got her ice cream and drifted away from her embarrassing family toward a group of teenagers in the corner.

Paul, the five year old, had said, "Daddy," three times and tugged vigorously on his father's pants before Daddy looked down. "I want bubblegum peppermint."

"Don't get the bubblegum peppermint," coaxed his father. "You like chocolate chip."

"I want bubblegum peppermint," Paul's voice moved toward tears.

"O.K. But you are going to finish it," said the father, doing his imitation of a stern parent.

The father turned back to Janet who was pouting in the corner. "What'll you have, honey?"

"Vanilla." Her voice was as cold as the ice cream.

Jeff said, "Boy, this rocky road and licorice is good."

"Jeff!" said the father. It was the same one word conversation he had had with Tom. Jeff walked away.

The father bent down for a private conversation with Janet. "Janet honey, don't cut off your nose to spite your face. Get the rocky road and licorice."

She looked at her father as if he were the dumbest man on the face of the earth. He knew nothing about life. "Vanilla in a plain cone," she said adamantly. She would not be denied the wrong done to her.

Tom was pacing up and down in front of the glassed-in choices.

"You'll have to make up your mind," said his father.

"O.K. I'll have a hot fudge banana split with four scoops of ice cream—chocolate, double chocolate, chocolate chip, and chocolate ripple."

"No extra nuts?" suggested the father.

"Extra nuts!" echoed the son.

"And two maraschino cherries for my son," added the father.

"I don't like this bubblegum peppermint," came a voice from the floor.

"Give it to me, Paul," said the father. "And give him a scoop of chocolate chip in a plain cone." The teenage girl behind the counter hurried it up.

The father licked the bubblegum peppermint. He didn't like it either.

Then, out of the wealth of his pockets, the father paid for it all.

The father was herding his children out the door when Alice, his oldest said, "Daddy, I'm going to stay with these kids I met."

He looked over at the teenagers in the corner with that steely parental appraisal that withers all wrongdoing.

"Be home by five," he said and he was startled by the tenderness in his voice.

From outside came Tom's voice, "I said I had the window on the way home."

The father turned immediately and pushed out the door. His children needed him.

The Penny Planter

Patricia planted pennies.

She lived on Farmer Ave. It was called Farmer Ave. because years ago it was the road the farmers took into town to sell their produce. It was a popular road. The adults would pull their wagons over to the side and talk, catching up on the news, hugging friends not seen for some time, and making dates and deals. The children would run and play in the fields and sneak up behind the wagons and snitch apples and pears, carrots and tomatoes. Going to town was an excuse for a picnic.

Time and the new highway changed all that. Now Farmer Ave. was a quiet, tree-lined, residential section. Its only traffic was a morning and evening rush hour flow of men and women trying to catch or trying to escape from the buses which stopped at the corner. These hassled, unsuspecting people were the special subjects of Patricia's ministrations.

Patricia was ten; and the initial burst of summer excitement at being out of school had faded. Although she filled her days with baseball and swimming, her nights with rock tapes, and as much time as she could with Tim Freemont who was a grade ahead of her in school, she was bored—like totally. But her mother had put a lid on it. "Young lady, I don't want to hear you say one more time that you're bored." So Patricia would lock the bathroom door and drone into the sympathetically listening mirror, "Boring! Boring!"

It was in this sorry state of soul that she began drawing arrows on the sidewalk. She started one house down from her own. With a large yellow chalk she scratched out an arrow and attached the message: TREASURE AHEAD. Then three sidewalk squares later, a second arrow with the same message. Then, directly in front of her house, the arrow pointed sideways and the message changed to: TREASURE NEAR. Any eyes interested enough to follow the chalk arrow would see a large, very old oak tree that grew in the middle of Patricia's front yard. The trunk of the tree had split for the first time only four feet from the ground. In the flat space of this split, shiny as a new-born baby, lay a penny.

From the window of her room on the second floor Patricia could see it all.

No two people reacted the exact same way. Some people just stomped on by, like they never even noticed the signs they were stepping on.

Others briefly glanced down but were in too much of a hurry to follow the leads.

Some hesitated; their eyes followed the arrow to the tree; then their no-nonsense feet took them to the bus.

Some stood on the sidewalk for awhile, then tiptoed across the grass toward the tree. When they found the penny in the nook, they flipped it in the air with a laugh and pocketed it.

One man picked it up, examined it like a rare coin collector, and put it back.

Each morning and evening Patricia would watch them and pray that the hurriers would stop, and the stoppers would seek, and the seekers would find, and the finders would rejoice; and she would get to sneak out of her house and plant another penny in the tree. The sheer stealth of it all delighted her so much that she completely abandoned her mirror conversations.

Patricia's favorite was a thin, young man. He wore a three-piece suit and carried a brown attache case; but that did not fool her. She knew that as soon as he reached home, he put on cut-offs and a T-shirt and shot baskets before dinner. The first day he strolled on by, not to be bothered. The second day he read the signs of the sidewalk. The third day he glanced at the tree. The fourth day he walked very slowly, genuflected to tie his shoelace, looked around to see who was watching, and then kept on going. The fifth day he ran by.

He needs help, thought Patricia.

And so she put her not inconsiderable mind to it. In fact it was what she was pondering right before bed when she looked out her window and saw a figure on the sidewalk. The blend of the street light and the leafy branches of the tree covered the figure in shadows. But she could see it was a thin, young man in cut-offs and a T-shirt. She threw open her window and thundered, "Go for it!"

The young man stiffened as if he had been suddenly drenched by a storm he did not see coming. He turned and bolted down the sidewalk.

"I'll have to try something else," said Patricia outloud to whoever might be listening. "But make no mistake. I'm going to get him."

Martha the Good

Martha is as good as a butter cookie. The Good Samaritan could take lessons from her. If someone is sick, she is first down the block with a meal and chatter. "If you need anything just let me know." She means it.

But her mothering is never neglected. After dinner with the dishes cleared, she sits with her two daughters at the kitchen table and helps them with their homework. She guides Janet, who is fourteen, through the maze of algebra. Next she listens to Alice, her fifth grader, spell the ever elusive "b-o-u-q-u-e-t-."

When the girls are finished and off in their own room, she joins her husband before the television set. "They're doing well," she says with a nod.

"They have a good helper," Tom says.

Martha's husband, Tom, is proud of her. He basks in her goodness. She likes it when she can feel him feeling good about her. It gives her the support she needs to go on.

Martha is also socially concerned. She deplores media hype, government lies, big business ploys. She cannot understand the cruelty and apathy everyone seems to take for granted. At the center of it all, she tells whomever will listen, is rampant self-interest.

"No one cares for anyone but themselves," she says, mounting her soapbox.

"Martha to the rescue," chides Tom.

"Well, they don't," she insists, calmed down a bit. She is determined she will not be that way.

Her parish staffs a soup kitchen in the downtown district. The name of the kitchen is Nazareth. One night a week Martha and her oldest daughter go down there and prepare sandwiches and soup for whoever comes in off the street. While the street people are eating, Martha and Janet clean the kitchen. When the street people are done and gone, mother and daughter straighten up and head for home.

On their "social action" night Tom cooks and has dinner waiting for them. The conversation usually goes the same way.

"How many tonight?" Tom asks.
"About ten," Martha answers.
"It's a good work."
"It's little enough."
"It's a lot."
"I feel sorry for them."
"You should."
"I guess so."

One Tuesday night at 11:30 the doorbell rang. "Who could that be at this hour." Tom said as he got out of bed to answer it.

"Oh my God!" Martha heard Tom say. She put on her robe and went to the door.

It was Tom's father. The last time they had seen him was at the wedding seventeen years ago. He was drunk then too.

"Martha, honey," he smiled and gave her a hug. Liquor had wasted him. When he grinned, all the bones of his face showed.

The first night he slept on the couch. But by the end of the week the den had been turned into a temporary bedroom. He would sleep away the days and prowl at night. Whatever liquor was in the house always disappeared.

It was Alice, the youngest, who said it. "Gee, Mom. We have our own personal street person."

Martha was not amused. "Tom, how long is he going to stay?" Her voice had an edge to it.

"He's my father. I can't just throw him out." Tom snapped. Then he playfully grabbed and rubbed the back of Martha's neck. "Give me time," he pleaded.

A month passed and Tom had not found the time.

One night at supper, after the girls had left the table, the family street person slurred, "That Janet of yours is really growing into a ripe young woman."

That night in bed Martha said, "He has to go."

"As soon as I can." Tom turned toward the wall.

Two days later they found him on the floor of the den. The ambulance got him to the hospital in time. The heart attack was not fatal.

He had no insurance. Tom and Martha dug into their savings for a two week hospital stay. When he was released, they rented a hospital bed. The den was rearranged into a permanent sick room. And Martha the good became a full time nurse to a cranky, unappreciative, foul-mouthed old man.

One afternoon he yelled from his bed, "God-damnit Martha, bring me a beer."

In the kitchen Martha stood perfectly still. Her voice was a whispered monotone; but her ears heard what her mouth said. "God, I hope the son of a bitch dies." Her whole heart was in every word.

And it was as if she caught God in a rare moment when He had nothing to do but listen; and as a reward for her years of goodness, He tickled her father-in-law's heart into thrombosis, and left her staring into the coffin with her answered prayer, wondering how she would ever get back into the garden now that she lived so far east of Eden.

The day of the funeral was also Martha's "social action" night.

"Stay home, tonight," Tom said.

"I'm going," Martha said. Her teeth were clenched.

She and Janet opened Nazareth and prepared the soup and sandwiches. But she did not clean the kitchen while the street people ate. For some reason she does not till this day understand, she sat at a table with a bowl of soup.

Tears came with the first taste and did not stop. But she finished the soup like a medicine she had long avoided.

On the way home in the car her daughter asked, "You o.k., mom?"

The words came out slow, with audible sighs between them, the result of some interior, labored birth.

"Next week we'll bring flowers for the tables. Maybe your father and sister will come with us. We'll all eat at Nazareth."

LET THEM BE WHO THEY WILL BE

The Younger Son

On beef,
the meat around the bone is best
On woman,
though, I prefer the plump parts,

What a feast my father throws!
O belly, we're back!
No more watch and rumble
while the swine swill and snort
and I bite through my lip and drool
for a munch on one of their carob pods.
But a love slap on their unclean rumps!
They made me remember my own trough-
DADDY.

I rehearsed a speech,
a mumble masterpiece.
With a mouth turned down,
an eyeful of mist,
repentant as a whore with clap:
I whimper:
"Father, I have sinned against heaven
and against thee." (voice falters)
    (Daddy, your little boy has done wrong
    and he's so worry that he'll never do it again.
    Really, he won't.)
"Do not take me back as a Son:
take me back as a hired hand."
    (But TAKE ME BACK,

my belly and I do beg.
you large-lardered,
stuffed-saddlebagged,
wine-drenched
old Daddy.)

Grovel a little to guzzle a lot:
crawl on your belly to feed it.
That is my philosophy.
But the old man upstaged me.
He fell upon me in mid-sentence
ruining my clever act.
But the script was magic.
A robe, ring, and sandals
suddenly appeared;
and this feast fell from heaven.
It was like I was,
what can I say,
a long lost son,
a dead man come back to life.
But I suspect Father is up to something.
No one can be that happy
to see the return of an appetite
that swallowed half an inheritance.
But, then again, I always was his favorite
and I could make him dance to any tune I piped.
Gushy old men are my specialty.
Anyway, the calf is succulent.
I have what I want,
and that is what I have always wanted.

The Older Brother

All these years!
Even the servant boy sensed it.
He would not look at me
as he told me the news:
"Your brother is home;
and your father has killed the fatted calf
because he has him back safe and sound."

He has had ME home-
all these years-
and no music ever greeted ME
as I dragged in
from our fields.
All those mornings!
With him coughing up his night phlegm
and complaining of the cold,
and me throwing a blanket around his bones,
and sitting him on a bench in the sun.
All those days!

With him staring off in the opposite direction
of wherever I was,
growing weary from watching
for the one who does not come,
and me looking up from the earth
to find his back blocking the sky.
All those harvests!
With me, giddy as a child who had found a coin,
yelling for him to come
see the hundredfold crop and sagging vine,
and him coming and sighing
like the wheat was dust and grapes were rocks.
All those nights!
With him droning a prayer
and nodding over his food,
and forgetting to bless me before bed.
And me waiting for the embrace
he was saving,
hoping for the words
he was hoarding,
eager for an unfeigned arm
around my shoulder,
for a kiss strong enough
to bring blood to my cheek.

Now he tells me that
all these years
we have been
together
and have become
one.
"You have been with me always;
and all I have is yours."
I need more, Father
I need you to run to ME
out of breath and heart-bursting,
not as you are now
with your sensible "Now see here" logic
about the fittingness of feasting
for someone else.
All these years!

The Father

I have two sons,
neither of whom want Me for a father.
So they make me into the father they want.

One makes me into a pimp for his belly.
He thinks he tricks me into concessions,
cons a calf from a sentimental old fool.
He credits my dancing to his piping:
but the music I hear has another source.

He is always empty
so my fullness is hidden from him.
His cunning gives him no rest
so my peace eludes him.

He secretly seizes in the night
what I freely offer in the day.
He want a father he can steal from.
Instead he has me,
a vine with more wine
than he can drink.
It is hard for him to forgive me
for providing more than he can plunder.
I am abundance.
He must learn to live with it.

The other one counts my kisses.
He wants me to count his.
"For two days ploughing,
take this hug.
For a plentiful harvest,
receive this blessing."
He is so unsure of himself,
He cannot share my assurance.
He lives by measuring what he does not have.
An eye anywhere else
Is an eye lost to him.
He thinks I take him for granted;
but I lean him like a staff.
He is the privileged companion
Of my morning pain and evening praise.
I would allow no one else to see
the stumble of my memory,
the embarrassment of my body.

But he credits my love to his loyalty.
He want a father, indentured to him,
Paying him back in affection
for his back-breaking labor.
Instead he has me,
an ancient tree with its own soil.
He does not understand
that he cannot calm his panic with a bargain.
There will be no chain between us.
I freely tie my wrist to his.

I have two sons.
Wherever they are,
I go to meet them.
I am their father.
But I am who I am.
Let them be
who they will be.

The Wedding Gown

Alice S. Rossi

Preface

When Ingrid Shafer first approached me to do an essay for a volume in honor of Andrew Greeley on the occasion of his 60th birthday, I leaped at the opportunity, since it was a lovely idea in the hands of one who would be sympathetic to the many-sided nature of this Renaissance man of many talents.

But time passed, the academic year ended, and a sabbatical year's agenda bulged with 'serious' sociological research and writing. By early summer, I wrote to express my regrets that no inspiration had hit me concerning a theme relevant to creativity that I might undertake, and hence I had to sadly withdraw as a potential contributor to the volume Ingrid Shafer was planning.

Undaunted, Ingrid came back with a last ditch appeal, and one I found impossible not to consider. She wrote that the theme of creativity need not be pursued by writing as a social scientist *about* it, but to "manifest it." Further, she wrote "there's a poet hiding within the scholar in you; why not let her out?"

Ingrid's challenge gave me no peace for days, as I toyed with the suggestion, tempted to try but fearful of the consequences. The theme of the Wedding Gown, also suggested by Ingrid from the personal news I included in my letter to her, began to obsess me, and I slowly realized that to write such an essay would be most fitting in a volume honoring my friend, Andy Greeley, who had himself shifted his life's priorities to "let the poet out" in his fiction.

I spent two of the happiest days of my life writing the essay that follows. Though creative writing has as many constraints as social science writing, they are of a different order, and I found it not confining but liberating to work within their parsimonious parameters.

Much social science writing takes many words to say little. Creative writing, by contrast, takes few words to say much. I hope my essay speaks to the heart and mind, and that it is not vain to suggest that it "thinks in the marrow bone," where Yeats reminds us, one finds all "lasting songs."

Aroused from the first deep sleep of a late winter night, Alice reached for the phone while running through a litany of worries: Was it her mother, living alone in New York at eighty-seven? Her husband Pete, ill in a Washington hotel? An accident involving her windsurfing daughter Kris in the southwest? A break-in and harm done to her son Peter or his family in Chicago?

"Mom?"

"Neen! Is that you? What's wrong?"

"Of course it's me, and nothing's wrong." Catching her mother's anxiety, Nina lowered her voice and smiled to herself, "old worry-wort mom!"

"What's up? Why are you calling after midnight?" Alice asked, anxiety giving way to annoyance.

"My God! I had no idea it was so late.... I have great news! Mark and I are going to get married. We just decided an hour ago, and wanted to tell you right away."

"You ARE? Is it for real?" Alice asked, uncertain whether to take her daughter seriously at first.

"Very much 'for real' " Nina responded, her voice trembling.

"Fantastic!" Alice's heart took a leap, catching her daughter's joy. "When's the wedding?"

"Not so fast! We're not in a hurry about that. It depends...on a lot of things. But I suggested September to Mark."

"September? When in September?" her mother asked.

"Well, I thought it would be neat to be married the same day you and Dad were, but I couldn't remember the date of your anniversary. Was it the 26th? All I could remember was that it's near your birthday."

"No, the 29th. Why the same date?"

Nina hesitated a moment, then in a quiet, small voice, she said: "Oh, I thought it would be a good omen. I'd like to think Mark and I can be as good a team as you two have been. But say, there's something else I'd like to ask you."

"What's that?" her mother asked, responding in the same quiet voice as she cradled the phone to her ear and wished she could cradle her daughter in gratitude for the sweet accord hinted at by a "shared anniversary."

"Could we get married in your garden? I have this old feeling from the years in Kenwood. Remember how you used to talk about Kris and me getting married in that house? Coming down the stairs to the huge foyer, all full of flowers from the garden?"

The tears welled as Alice said, "Of course I remember. It was that kind of house, just made for weddings and parties. The first time I saw it, I imagined you and Kris coming down those winding stairs in your wedding gowns. And the two of you all of 6 and 2 years old!"

Nina laughed and said, "Well, that was just a pipedream wasn't it? Your new house doesn't have a staircase, but it does have an old-fashioned garden. Think of the great wedding pictures with those flowers and trees in the background!"

Alice thought a moment and warned "But September is hardly the best time of year in the garden, you know."

"Oh Mom! I know you'll figure out ways to make it beautiful. After all, September is months away! But just one last question and then I have to sign off. Mark wants to call his folks tonight."

"What's the last question?" Alice asked, wondering what was still to come.

After a moment's pause, Nina said, "Well, would you be willing to make my wedding gown?"

"ME? You really want me to make your dress?"

"Yes, And I want it to be satin and lace and snug as can be, and...old fashioned."

"Old fashioned?" Alice asked. "You mean to say you want a traditional wedding? Bridal bouquet, white satin and all that?" She could not keep surprise from her voice, thinking of her daughter's usual jeans and boots.

"Well, yes. Yes I do. But now I must go. We can talk tomorrow. Mark's ready to grab the phone if I don't hang up. Take care...be in touch."

Alice put the phone down softly, a smile on her lips. She propped up the pillows, lit a cigarette, and began to muse about the wedding to come, how to assure colorful blooms in a September garden, what could be done to make the gown specially memorable for this last of her children's weddings. And she thought of the miracle of this last child, the only unplanned and unexpected one of the three, and the one that had brought such joy and such pain to their experience of parenthood. Wishing Pete was beside her, she fell asleep reliving the birth of their ten-pound "butterball" of a baby daughter.

*****

Alice thought of Nina's birth many times in the following few months, as she did of all the peaks and valleys of the child's life since 1960. This was especially so on the long nights devoted to work on the wedding gown: with Pete already asleep and her lectures prepared for the next day, she spent many nights from nine to midnight working on the dress. She came to feel there were memories sewn into the very stitches of the garment. Indeed, she realized that happy thoughts translated into tiny smooth stitches, while unhappy ones produced ragged tight stitches she had to remove and redo. Too bad we can't as easily replace the unhappy experiences themselves as we can these untidy stitches, she often thought.

But there was a cathartic effect to finger work: the peaks from the past loomed larger, and the valleys dimmed. The trauma of dealing with a third baby while coping with complex little creatures of three and four was remembered with wry amusement now, as Alice recalled her argument that an additional parent ought to be added to a family with each birth so there would be enough hands and hearts to go around! Her heart still went out to three year old Kris who took to incessant rhythmic rocking while Alice nursed Nina, and who created her own imaginary "super-mom," a female not with two but twelve breasts. Like many last-borns, Nina was a cheerful happy toddler, grateful for the least little gesture toward her, tolerant of the clumsy rough affection from her brother, a willing victim of her ambivalent sister's alternation of acceptance and rejection. Who would have imagined that these two little girls would grow into the loving sisters they are today?

In her quiet way, Nina found her own special place in the hearts of all: her ready confidences, hugs and squeezes of the hand, her gestures of thoughtfulness for others, and her unusual creative talents with thread or paintbrush, endeared her to many. By four, it was clear that she would share her mother's love of design and sewing. At seven, she began a project of building a dollhouse herself, making all the dolls, their clothes, and much of the furniture. Alice remembered with a chuckle her discovery that the mother and father dolls were Nina herself and Father Greeley, who removed his priest's collar when he entered the dollhouse. There was even a half-inch tiny book on the dollhouse bookshelf, entitled "I Married a Priest," authored by Nina herself! Clearly, Andy had impressed the child during the Kenwood years when he was collaborating with Pete on research projects, while secretly creating a conspiratorial alliance with the children against the "grown ups," Alice and Pete.

While the actual sewing of the wedding gown was largely a solitary nighttime venture, the selection of design and fabric that preceded the sewing was a daytime delight shared by mother and daughter. Pouring over gown patterns, rejecting most of them, the two women were in instant agreement on those they liked. Gradually the choice narrowed, and one was selected, with a boat-shaped neckline, snug through the bodice to the dropped waistline, a triangular dip in midcenter of both front and back, a very full skirt with taffeta slip beneath to hold it out, puffed sleeves narrowing to a slim forearm, some 36 tiny buttons down the back and on the cuffs, appliqued lace motifs on bodice, neckline, cuffs, and in an artful array on the skirt. Very traditional indeed, but something the like of which Alice had never attempted before.

The fabric selection was quite another matter. Nothing suitable was in the local shops in Alice's small town or surrounding cities. Eventually she consulted with her favorite fabric house in the midwest. Swatches went back and forth through the mails, with Alice and Nina debating the virtues of duchess satin, 4-ply French silk, silk Barathea, chartreuse satin, peau de soie, the choice made more difficult by the fact that Nina did not want a white bridal gown, but as she put it, a "very pale pink, like the blush on your French pussy willows when they first emerge from their little brown shells in February." Eventually, the decision was made for a Col. Cloud Marshall chartreuse crepe satin for the dress, in a pale peach-pink, and an ivory peau de soie taffeta for the slip. But the final touch was to be the French Alencon champagne-toned lace, so beautiful and so expensive Alice worried in anticipation of the delicate task of cutting out each small lace motif from its net backing, to say nothing of appliqueing some 65 of them to the gown itself.

To reduce error and avert catastrophe, a batiste bodice was first made, fitted, and altered several times, until the exacting snug fit was achieved, and the satin itself could be cut. Best of all were the frequent visits from Nina as the dress progressed, each fitting giving a clearer image of how close the wedding gown would come to the dream mother and daughter shared.

Many things blossomed in thought as did the gown in revealing its promise. Past and present met and merged in Alice's thoughts as she sewed. The sewing machine itself evoked milestones in her life with Pete. Still holding out against the encroachment of technology, she had stuck to the machine they bought in their first year of marriage thirty-six years before. That was a peak in her own life and marriage. Poor as only indebted academics could be in the 1950s, Pete noticed an ad in a Boston paper for a second-hand sewing machine for only twenty-five dollars. Knowing Alice's passion for sewing, and the pleasure she took in it as a relief from professional work, he suggested they "take a look" at the machine that Saturday morning. It was clearly impossible, a mere "come-on" to gain access to potential customers for new machines. Alice couldn't remember if they finally paid fifty or a hundred dollars for the new portable Modern Age Japanese machine, but the memory was sharp and wonderful of leaving the store, Pete carrying the machine while she literally skipped down the street to the car, happy in the totally physical way that children show so much more often than adults.

That same machine has been her companion over the years, as children's clothes, Pete's jackets, her own suits and coats, drapes, slipcovers, and bedspreads were made on it. Even today, all three children report fond memories of being snug in their beds, falling asleep to the purr of the sewing machine and the sound of music coming up the stairs, secure in the sure knowledge of their mother's presence below, knowing the familiar look on her face when she sewed—a frown of concentration combined with the smile that comes from doing something she loved.

Alice remembered that same combination of frown and smile from her own childhood memories of her mother's head bent over a sewing machine purchased by her father at the beginning of the depression, and still in use to this day. Suddenly, with a rush of insight, Alice realized that the three women—her daughter Nina, her mother, and herself—shared this passion. Indeed, to wear a traditional wedding gown sewn by her mother was itself only another example of Nina's deep love of the past, of ritual, and of old things. In fact, her own sewing machine is older than her mother's and grandmother's: a treadle machine made when the century was young that her father renovated with new black lacquer and gold paint for a Christmas present.

These memories crowded in as Alice faced the last step of appliqueing the lace motifs onto the gown, and an inspiration hit her—to invite her mother for a week-end visit to share the hand-sewing, knowing without a doubt that her mother would experience the same deep pleasure from contributing stitches and loving thoughts to the project that she did.

And so it came to be. And the middle of that week-end lovefeast of sewing found three smiling, frowning women under a tree on a sunny Sunday afternoon, silk-threaded needles in hand stitching their memories, hopes, and dreams into the happiest, most beautiful gown the family has yet produced.

*****

The wedding itself was a fitting climax to the months of anticipation. Pink, rose, and white mums filled the bare spots in the garden, while the blue and pink ageratum, white alyssum, pastel asters and phlox, and the stately white cimicifuga graced the background for the ceremony and reception, Nina and her gown the glowing centerpiece of the dramatic scene. Alice and her mother exchanged glances over the head of the bride, privately feeling that the Sunday afternoon of three generations of fingers appliqueing the lace was second only to the wedding ceremony itself in its love and magic. The gown had worked its charm in merging past and present. Now it worked yet another one, for it spoke to the future and its fruit in a fourth generation to come.

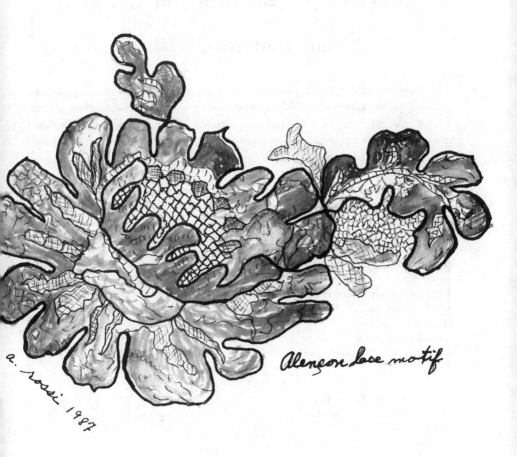

a. rossi 1987

Alençon lace motif

Limericks on the Study of Religion

Wendy Doniger O'Flaherty

These bits of doggerel were scribbled during the longueurs of many meetings and conferences; they were in many cases the *only* product of those academic sessions. I hope that they will be found an appropriate offering in honor of a man who has combined the academic and the creative modalities in far more consistent ways, who never loses his sense of humor, and who knows that Limerick is a town in Ireland.

A. On the Religions of the World

When the sky and the earth were still close,
And the planets were wedged tail to nose,
All still might have been well,
Without heaven or hell,
Had the gods not become otiose.

The bases of every cosmology
Are symmetry, law, and homology.
Micro- and macro-
Are front-row and back-row
Within the one church of Ontology.

B. On Christianity

"Theology," said David Tracy,
"Need not be all saintly and gracey.
If order's a rage
On a blessed rampage,
Then the scriptures may be rather racy."

An atheist and a Fascist
Who hated the priestly classes
Became quite allergical
To parsons clergical,
Shouting, "Let's kick some masses."

C. Hinduism

"The Indian sage," said the Pope,
"Theologically is just a dope.
For the world, so it seems,
Is just one of His dreams,
And He can't tell a snake from a rope."

The yogis and naths and hakkims
Tell their pupils, "It's not as it seems.
Though you think that your mind
Made up God, you may find
You're a figment of one of *His* dreams."

There once was a young Bengali
Who covered his dog, a Kali,
With snakes and an eel
Till it looked so surreal
That his friends shouted, "Hello, Dali!"

A Jew with cirrhosis of liver
Jumped into the pure Ganges river.
His sons all drew lots
On the funeral ghats
And the loser was forced to sit Shiva.

"A goddess's fury when scorned,"
Said a Babu, "is not to be borned."
So this pious Bengali
Made statues to Kali
And argued, "Four-armed is fore-warned."

A worshipper of Minakshi
Objected to strict orthodoxy.
He said, "If I wish to
I'll also praise Vishnu
In person, or else by proxy."

"In India," said the Mahatma,
"We honor the thin or the fat ma.
That a wife should be modest
And act like a goddess
We hold, not as dogma, but catma."

D. On Buddhism

A worldly young Buddhist complained,
"I hate what Gautama explained.
I won't seek *nirvana*
Because I don't wanna.
And so, on the Wheel he remained.

When Gautama preached to the masses,
He mixed with all castes and all classes.
He talked about *dukkha*
With pimp and with hooker
And made nuns of all kinds of lasses.

E. On Indian Islam

A certain young Turk, great and noble,
Regarded the world as his bauble.
He conquered afar,
Shouting, "Allah Akbar!"
For Babur was upwardly Mogul.

F. On Greek Religion

A student of Greek theodicy
Asked, "What kind of a god is he?
He uses his magic
To render too tragic
The *Iliad* and the *Odyssey*."

According to old Parmenides,
The world is a cluster of entities.
People who say,
"Very well, but *pan rei*,"
Have forgotten about the Eumenides.

G. On Feminism

Though women are getting much faster
At winning a license to Pastor,
It still seems profane
To the church to ordain
A mistress instead of a master.

A feminist makes synonyms
By laws quite different from Grimm's.
Instead of "A-men"
It's "A-women," and then
She sings hers instead of hymns.

H. On Methodology

The eclectic method can yield
Insights from many a field,
Serendipitous finds
For people whose minds
Are not hermeneutically sealed.

The pluralist tends to boast
That he covers his field coast to coast.
He thinks of religion
As his private pigeon,
Part Brahma-goose, part holy ghost.

Kitchen Window Sacrament

Ingrid H. Shafer

It is a little after midnight as I begin to make final revisions on my intended contribution (written months ago) to the Greeley *Festschrift*. Scanning the twenty odd single spaced pages on the monitor, I am struck by my philosophic pedantry and the absence of precisely what I had envisioned at the very core of this volume: the live spark of the creative imagination. Relentlessly, paragraphs like the following keep scrolling up and off the screen:

> In the emphasis on the experience of active reception in literature as well as the interaction of reader and text, Jauss criticizes Adorno's "negative dialectics" of the radically monadic individuality of isolated subjects (who know via a general principle of non-identity) by placing individuals within interpretive communities of shared experiences, thus restoring the hermeneutic dimension of the early Dilthey and recapturing Kant's notion of intersubjectivity for our postmodern deliberations.
>
> Like Lonergan, Doran and others, Lyotard is conscious of the characteristic convergence of art and philosophy. "A postmodern artist or writer is in the position of a philosopher: the text he writes, the work he produces are not in principle governed by preestablished rules, and they cannot be judged according to a determining judgment, by applying familiar categories..."(81). Postmodern works of art are themselves the process of establishing the very principles and rules "of *what will have been done*" (81). They are *events* to be understood "according to the paradox of the future (*post*) anterior (*modo*)"(81). Relationship, process and context have taken the place of transcendence, entity, and totality.

The paper literally bristles with references to Rahner, Lonergan, Tracy, Hegel, Jauss, Ricoeur, Whitehead, Eliade, Jung, Lyotard, Scheler, and, of course, the honoree himself (among others), before it reaches its oddly muted finale:

> The analogical or religious imagination thus appears particularly well suited to developing modes of knowing and being responsive to the needs of a pluralistic world and "strange loop" hemisphere-bridging epistemological models. It is an invitation to engage in a dialogue, a conversation with countless traditions and texts. In its rootedness within the preconscious, creative, symbol-bearing matrix of individuals and cultures, it presents us with a method of dynamic intra—and inter-human communication not possible with discursive logical analysis, and superbly adapted to the exploration and unpacking of those kinds of concerns traditionally called religious or theological.

Related to Schelling's Romantic *Einbilden* (literally, to form into one picture) which unites Spirit and Nature, it is the epistemological corollary of Incarnationalism and provides an ongoing opportunity for engaging in Lyotard's "future anterior" process of constituting the very syntax of the new language of post-modernity being birthed; an interactive, dynamic, poetically-philosophic language capable—like love—of plying between opposites and articulating similarity-in-difference (without dissolving authentic conflict in lazy relativism or freezing it in rigid, authoritarian univocity); a language of reflexively reflective allusion which can witness *simultaneously* to the unpresentable we intuit as *deus absconditus, anatta,* "the silence between the words" *and* the proleptic event of the Incarnation, "the futural eschatological ideal of a self committed to the reign of love and justice" (Tracy 1986:434).

Would I use this terminology to communicate with anyone not associated with the Harvard/Berkeley/Chicago Religious Studies summer institute at the University of Chicago Divinity School I attended in 1986? Would I dare give this kind of talk in one of my guest lectures on creativity to under-graduates? Is it even what the creative imagination, this "lover who is also a mate" (Greeley, "Theology" 15), this "dimension of the self which knows the end of a journey before it even begins" (17), means to me? Of course not! This is an exercise in "third level discourse"— abstract, theoretical, and definitely "left brain." Maybe even just a bit of what I might jokingly refer to as "academic gobbledegook" in my Logic and Critical Thinking classes. Valid in its place, but somehow inappropriate for an interdisciplinary volume honoring Andrew Greeley who has spent most of his life in a concerted effort to present complex ideas in popularly accessible language. I push ALT F7 2 to reveal a lengthy explanatory note near the end of the article:

Both Jauss' "reception aesthetics" and Lyotard's "future anterior" event reflect (consciously or unconsciously) what may be the most striking characteristic of contemporary epistemological horizons: the computer-inspired (or at least computer-manifested) emphasis on dynamic *interactivity* as epistemological category. It is precisely this issue which Paul Ricoeur appears to confront in *Time and Narrative* as he points to the meaning-constituting event of the intersection of the "world projected by the text" and the "life world of the reader" and insists that this new focus will demand the "radical reformulation of the problem of truth" to include "the capacity of the work of art to indicate and to transform human action" (160). Ricoeur sees this new focus as a possible center of approachment and interweaving of the truth claims of fictional and historical narrative. It seems that this focus also opens a further horizon (inextricably linked to the stated one): the sublation of the traditional opposition of poetry and religion in a new Lonerganian transcendental aesthetic woven into the foundations of theology.

In the summer of 1986 I read hundreds of letters sent to Andrew Greeley by readers of his theological novels. A large percentage of those readers described at length how their lives had been radically affected, how they had literally been forced to take a new look at themselves, their relationships to others and their unexamined religious presuppositions in the process of imaginatively joining Greeley's fictional world with their personal experiences. Obviously, in the minds of the readers, the stories (texts) took on a life of their own, becoming occasions for imagination leaping to imagination, generating totally new creative syntheses. This concept of "interactivity" opens up as yet unforeseeable opportunities for entirely new models of communicating and expressing.

The paradigms will both depend on and develop the human imagination, and may demand that we redefine the notion of "conceptual act" (completed) as "conceptual event" (open-ended) and broaden it to include the process of "imaging" as epistemological category.

Not bad. Still, few if any phrases in this paper are likely to inspire imaginative leaps or precipitate creative syntheses, at least among any but the initiated. I had woven a tight and philosophically coherent net of more than ten thousand words in an effort to capture a mysterious SOMETHING called creative imagination which I considered inexplicably and inexorably linked to the experience of the sacred. Immediately after writing the piece I was rather pleased with my effort, but now I suspect that my wily prey has eluded me after all, leaving behind not even its Cheshire smile. How pompous and anemic my article somehow seems, compared to the fascinating chapters on the religious imagination in Greeley's current manuscript "A Catholic Theology of Popular Culture" which I read earlier in the evening. "What do I mean by creative imagination?" Greeley asks, answering his own question, "Either you have it, like rhythm, and no definition is necessary or you don't have it and no definition is possible." Is this what Lao Tzu meant 2500 years ago when he said, "The Tao that can be told of is not the eternal Tao;/ The name that can be named is not the eternal name" (Chan: 139).

Suddenly my mind drifts and I see my daughter (now herself a mother) as a toddler. She is less than two years old, a tow-headed charmer sitting on the kitchen floor, trying to catch a stray ray of sunshine in her tiny palms. Again and again she opens her hands and then quickly cups them to trap the light. She stomps in frustration, her large blue eyes brimming with angry tears, when time after time she peeks into the darkness of her fist. I remember writing a poem to her that night. The last stanza read "Too soon you will learn there are things/which die if you hold them tight/like snowflakes and butterfly wings/and love, and rays of light."

With clumsy eagerness and intellectual arrogance my academic fist had managed to chase off, choke or crush the three central aspects (according to Greeley) of religious imagination: experience, image, and story. What a shame, there is no legitimate way for me to invite the honoree to do a paper for his own *Festschrift*! He should be part of this project in a manner even more essential than as the one to whom the volume is dedicated. I am grasped by the alarming feeling that if I am to do this right I will have to start all over again. And there is so little time. Hans Küng's ambivalent grace "experience of being stopped" comes to mind.

What now? I go to the kitchen to fix a cup of coffee. I am definitely not ready to go to sleep. As I stand at the sink, waiting for the tap water to get hot (a trick which cuts down on microwave time), I disconsolately and absentmindedly stare at whatever is in front of me. An appallingly dirty window (on the outside which is accessible only to the likes of orangutans and blue jays), but also a kitchen window unlike any I have ever seen elsewhere, and now that I really SEE it for the first time ever, a window which I can't even imagine anywhere but in my house. A window, I realize in a sudden flash of insight, which is almost entirely the product of what Andrew Greeley calls the Catholic Imagination, in, of course, its unique Ingrid Shafer incarnation.

"Just as I have a beginning, a middle, and a conclusion, so the cosmos of which I am a part has a beginning, a middle, and a conclusion. It has a story and I have a story, and my experience of grace links these stories." (Greeley, *Religion* 47). A passage from Robert Doran's *Subject and Psyche* comes to mind. Something about the unfolding of a post-critical symbolic consciousness, evolving a transcendental aesthetic of immediacy which passes beyond the self-appropriation of the cognitional subject to the self-appropriation of the existential subject by exploring imaginal and trans-temporal or synchronistic "inner space", the *unus mundus imaginalis et physica* (14). An eschatological psychic self-appropriation which yields to the *Anima/Sophia* with her primordial archetypes and leads to "the poetic enjoyment of the truth about man and God" (25).

Steam pours up from the sink, the coffee momentarily forgotten. An idea begins to take form and crystallize, tantalizing in its anti-academic appeal to subjective experience: why not apply Greeley's categories to my window—and myself? Why not do something Father Feeney might call an "autobiography of the religious imagination?" Why not link my story to the cosmic story?

I don't recall exactly how and why the window area happens to be "decorated" the way it is. Over the years I simply put certain items on the thin ledge which separates the upper pane from the lower pane (the window cannot be opened) and attached an assortment of additional objects to the hanging cabinet ends on either side. Before my children left home and my husband died I spent much time around the sink, doing routine chores while my mind was busy simultaneously composing culinary delights, lectures, and poems (I once even thought of writing a "Philosopher's Cookbook"). Even now whenever I feel stuck while working on one of my writing projects, when the right ideas or words won't come, I tend to get up, away from the computer, and head for the kitchen, to fix a cup of tea or coffee, but just as often to stand for a few moments at the sink and absentmindedly contemplate the view. Sometimes I simply turn on the water and listen to its tranquil, calming sound.

More than any other part of my house this space is the result of preconscious, seemingly random additions and deletions over a period of eight years. None of the items (apart, possibly, from an egg timer, never used as such, however) have any overt association with the room's function. There is absolutely no practical justification for their presence. They add clutter and catch dust. To the casual observer they would be little more than cheap old junk. A discriminating critic would dismiss the majority as nostalgic kitsch, symptomatic of my lack of aesthetic refinement.

Almost everything on and surrounding the window seems associated with my Austrian childhood. There are other such spaces in my home—but most of them, more deliberately arranged, contain artifacts from many cultures and eras. This window is different and special, a private and peculiarly sacred space which represents peace, hope, life, love; a constant, subtle reminder that resolution is possible. In times of major and minor frustration, when everything seems to be going wrong,

I find myself in front of the sink, just standing there, letting my unseeing gaze travel from object to object, my mind unwinding, relaxing, letting go, opening up. *Opening up!* Erika Fromm's "gate" to primary process thoughts and images comes to mind. Is this "sacred space" a sort of "gate" for me? I have done this for as long as I can remember, in other houses in front of other sink areas decorated in ways appropriate to those particular stages of my life. Still, it is not until tonight that I am struck by the true significance of my window, and its relevance to the topic at hand.

The window is a multi-level metaphor, containing layers and layers of superimposed meaning which can be "unpacked" like those in a painting or poem; read and decoded in a way analogous to turning the pages of anatomical transparencies from epidermis to organs, nerves, and skeletal structures. As I ponder the window I see a symbolic web connecting this individual twentieth century American woman scholar not only to her European childhood but also to the Catholic imaginative universe and beyond that to the realm of primordial, cosmic archetypes, those "channels" through which the Ineffable communicates Itself to us. Furthermore, by being a *window*, it is part of a "nested" metaphor, a metaphor *within* a metaphor, transparent to the natural world outside which is in turn transparent to the mystery beyond. "A symbol," according to Coleridge, "is characterized by a translucence of the special in the particular, or of the general in the special, or of the universal in the general: above all by the translucence of the eternal through and in the temporal." "This paradox," notes John Shea, "an imageless God available through images, is at the heart of the sacramental imagination" (100).

Suddenly I understand just exactly what it was about Andrew Greeley's stories which drew me into their magic circle from that copy of *The Cardinal Sins* I had picked up in a University of California book store four years ago, captured by the verse on the flyleaf: "Stern as death is love,/Relentless as the nether world is passion./Its flames are a blazing fire;/Deep waters cannot quench love,/Nor floods sweep it away." I read the book that afternoon, and for the first time in more than twenty years, I knew—with Ellen Foley—that I could go home again or, more accurately, that I had never really left. Andrew Greeley and I (as well as millions of his readers) inhabit congruent imaginative cosmoi. As Greeley put it in *The Religious Imagination*, "Religion as story leaps from imagination to imagination, and only then, if at all, from intellect to intellect" (17). His stories make contact with my (their) preconscious, activating and validating a number of essential components of "my" (their) master narrative which the scholar in me subsequently turns into interpretative categories to be applied to Greeley's work (after they have allowed the human being simultaneously to deepen her sense of Self and of Divine Presence). Our biographic differences are insignificant compared to our common rootedness in a pre- or post- "Garrison Church" Catholic analogical (as contrasted to the Protestant dialectical) imaginative universe with its faith in the graciousness of the Really Real and its fundamental acceptance of the sacramentality of the world.

Let me take you on an imaginary guided tour of my kitchen window:

Centered on the ledge, flush against the window pane, you see a piece of glass, painted in translucent, slightly faded yellows, reds and greens with fairly abstract bells and holly outlined in black, and the calligraphy inscription "Christmas 1975". Outside the window, beyond the red Oklahoma dirt film and the spider webs, a makeshift wire trellis supports a large wild climbing rose bush. For a few weeks each spring its meandering branches explode in what seems like a million blossoms, pale pink, almost white, a fitting wedding gown to celebrate the beginning of yet another seasonal cycle.

In front of the "stained glass" stands a six inch fir or spruce cone I picked up years ago on a mountain forest path near my native Innsbruck. To the left of the cone is an amber bee's wax candle in a nine-point three dimensional lead crystal star shaped holder covered with amber wax "tears". On the other side of the cone a two inch dark brown glazed pottery vase containing three white straw flowers with dark golden centers perches on a tiny wreath of cloves, miniature pink and white starched cloth blossoms, and opalescent white pearls. The vase and candle are flanked by a porcelain hare (European cousin to the New World rabbit) and owl, neither more than an inch tall.

On either side of the "wild life" stands a Tyrolean liqueur glass shaped like a miniature wine goblet and decorated with folk art slightly stylized flower motifs. The chalices hold blown out eggs, a post-War Easter gift for my parents, on which I had painted a little girl, a brunette picking up an Easter basket (complete with pin head eggs and rabbit) and a blonde (like me at the time) reaching up toward a pink blossom in a tree. Next to the goblets two yellow china baby chicks are frozen in chirping silence, their backs bearing egg cups, each containing a relatively large bluish pink blossom with leaves of undetermined identity cut earlier today from a tall mystery shrub in the back yard.

Next to each of the egg cup chicks lies a deep purple garnet crystal, a bit over an inch in diameter. A third garnet, still embedded in a miniature pillar of silver grey shale, is propped up against the interior window frame, concealing a small cigarette lighter I keep in back of it for cases of nocturnal power failures. At the opposite end of the ledge stands a delicate silver bell with a wooden handle. When I was small I used to wait impatiently for its ethereal sound on Christmas Eve, pressing my ear to the smooth coolness of the door which separated me from the room which had been kept locked all day to give the *Christkind* and angels a chance to bring the tree and gifts without being disturbed.

On the side of the cabinet to the left, about seven inches below the central ledge, three little plush-and-wire devils (called *Krampus* in Austria and associated with St. Nicholas' Day), the smallest one black, the medium one green, and the tallest one red, are rather uncomfortably seated in a two inch wooden match box holder which used to hang in my mother's kitchen (containing matches, not devils). A portable light fixture is attached to the same surface, several inches above the ledge. Its bulb illuminates the scene on the ledge and the other cabinet side, but the radiance does little to brighten up the *Krampus* family's gloom.

Another Easter egg (obviously of duck or goose origin), painted with flowers, dangles from an unused cafe curtain rod holder where the right cabinet butts up against the window frame. From a nail in that cabinet, next to a heart stitched of cloves and "gold" braid, hangs a round woven corn husk plaque with dry mountain leaves, berries, seed pods, and blossoms. A tiny plastic white and red heart with the message "to my Valentine" is pinned to the edge of the basket plaque. On the wall above the window several stalks of ripe golden wheat are woven into a traditional American Indian "god's eye." Below, on the bottom window ledge are two stubby candles, bracketing from left to right an egg-timer "hourglass", a centrally placed carved horn sail boat, and a small glass mug with hand painted dark blue gentians and white edelweiss.

Let me peel back the layers. The two major cycles of the Catholic liturgical calendar are represented: Christmas and Easter, plus St. Nicholas (by association) and St. Valentine. The physical arrangement of various objects parallels the medieval model of a three level universe, symbolized by the pageant wagon with its vertical Heaven-Earth-Hell construction. The central ledge, separating Heaven from Hell represents the main stage of natural life on earth. It is on this ledge that the images "interact" in my miniature world. There is something Theilhardian about the presence of various levels of matter from shale and garnet crystal through several forms and stages of plant life to animal images and traces of human activity. Despite the obvious significance of the Catholic connection, however, my window world, like Christianity itself, is inextricably rooted in its un-baptized past. The tree (in the form of an erect pine cone) is centrally placed, reaching up toward the "sky/ heaven" from "earth," surrounded by its woodland friends, owl and hare, ancient symbols of wisdom and fertility.

Below dwell the dark spirits. In my version of the Catholic universe they are definitely not absolutely evil. They are pathetic and even somewhat comic figures, deprived of light because they prefer darkness, temporarily installed in their counter nativity scene (Dad, Mom, and Infant—even devils shouldn't be lonely!), tricksters or maybe even God's reluctant helpers, in a fundamentally gracious cosmos. No matter how loudly church officials (and more recently child psychologists) grumble, to Austrian children the Eve of St. Nicholas means above all "Krampus," the deliciously scary night when the Expected Dreaded One arrives with his horns and limp and long, lolling tongue, carrying a switch, and rattling a chain. Sometimes he carries a basket on his back, large enough to stash a hollering kid who has been particularly ill behaved and haul her off to hell. Still, generally, after much chain rattling and switch swishing, Krampus relents, and passes out apples, oranges, candy and small toys, along with the inevitable pieces of coal. At times (if two "actors" to play the parts are available), he is accompanied by white and gold robed Saint Nicholas with miter and staff. Then it is td staff. Then it is the worthy "bishop" who distributes the goodies.

Look again. The window is located above the sink, the indoor contemporary equivalent of the pre-Christian fountain, spring, and spring-fed pond. Could it be haunted by displaced nymphs and water sprites, gently impish spirits of transformation, fertility, and wisdom? To the ancients, water, particularly in the form of spring-fed ponds (running water filling the sink) represented perfect potentiality, prophetic power, and the inexhaustible cyclical principle of life, death, and regeneration. When in times of crisis I stand at the sink, letting the water wash across my wrists and fingers, listening to it flow down the drain, am I unconsciously appealing to those sister spirits, cleansing myself symbolically from whatever troubles I have encountered, making contact with those primal forces of life?

Actually, the entire sink-window area can be considered a hybrid shrine, dedicated at once to powers of forests, fields, springs, and the hearth; to the anonymous forces of animism, the gods and goddesses of the ancient world, the Judeo-Christian God. The central motif is obviously fertility, a celebration of masculinity and femininity. Symbols of the Feminine include water, a variety of containers or vessels, eggs, plants (both live and in representation), blossoms, seeds and fruit. Symbols of the Masculine are the candle/fire, the cone/tree, and the garnet "pillar". It is easy to forget that even in the modern home, with its air-conditioned rooms, synthetic floors and counter tops, the ancient deities of fire, water, and vegetation still live, most especially in the kitchen.

I look at the tiny vase next to the cone-tree and suddenly its hourglass shape brings the Minoan Great Mother to mind, complete with tiara, long ringlets, bare breasts, tiny waist, full skirt, and a snake coiled around each arm. The ancient Cretans worshiped her in association with sacred trees, divine mediators whose roots were thought to reach into the lower world while their branches pierced the heavens, and sacred phallic pillars. She turns into brown-skinned androgynous Isis beneath the "Eye of Horus," next to the pine cone, itself a symbol of Osiris' resurrection. But this Great Mother is a vessel, open to the "God's Eye" above, three white straw-flower stars in her crown, standing in a wreath of fragrant spices, pearls and blossoms. She is at once dark feminine depth, the Black Madonna of Einsiedeln, Our Lady, the Mother of God, the Womanly Face of God; she is symbol *per excellence* of Catholic Christianity.

My mind travels back across the years to the mighty oak and spruce and chestnut trees which surrounded a castle where my parents and I shared a room during two final years of World War Two. There, sitting in a rainbow striped wood and cloth lawn chair, the *Alte Dame* (Old Lady, with none of the patronizing American vernacular connotations), as we called her, the owner's baroness mother, with her dark dresses and white lace edged collars and wrists, would hold me on her soft lap and tell me stories of hedge hogs and hares, of goblins and fairies, of Prinz Liebling's adventures, of Mary and Jesus, of the angels and the Saints. Her soothing voice made the night terrors go away, the screaming sirens, the solitary dangling light bulb in the cellar, the haggard faces of adults, their hollow eyes pools of darkness, the distant explosions, the tales of death and destruction.

Somehow I had acquired a little picture of a blue-robed young woman with a bright golden halo round her gently smiling face. I loved the picture, and decided to build a special secret place for it, in a moist, dark, miniature cave between and beneath gnarled roots next to one of the several ponds. I would carry "offerings" of acorns and fresh violets to my "shrine," stretch out on my tummy, and use a small mirror to reflect light into its darkness. I don't ever recall being taken to church in those days (my parents rarely if ever attended), but there must have been some early experience which inspired those shrines.

Thus Mary to me is inextricably bound to the tree, and the tree to Mary, and somehow, here in my 1987 kitchen, going from cone to tree to vase to Mary to Christmas to Christ all happens in one smooth imaginary linking process in which each element is related to, and implicitly contained within, all the others. Mary is present in my window garden not as an actual image but through memory fragments, associations and analogy. Mary is both like and not like that star crowned brown vase. "If Jesus became man, if Jesus took on human flesh, if Jesus was part of the material things of this world, then everything is sanctified, everything is Christian, everything will tell us something about God" (Greeley:47). Greeley is right. Karl Rahner was right. But only if we are as open and unpretentious and empty as that humble little pottery vessel; only if we *allow* grace to make the everyday both a pointer towards and transparent to the mystery.

Three items in my miniature window world are archetypally phallic: the cone/tree, the garnet "pillar," and the candle/fire.

The tree is a complex, multivalent symbol, of life as well as death, of womanliness (as bearer of fruit) as well as masculinity. The ancient Egyptians identified the evergreen sycamore with both Osiris, the dead and risen Lord, and the womb of gentle Nut, his mother. The Aryans, living in a world largely covered with primeval forest, worshiped in sacred groves, offered sacrifices to sacred trees. In the Roman Forum, figuratively the very center of the Empire, stood the sacred fig tree of Romulus, its welfare linked by people and priests to the fate of the city and realm. The May Pole, with its colorful ribbons and blossom garlands, is a tree. So are the gallows. So is the cross.

I have loved trees for almost as long as I can remember. Bare trees in winter, with their dark limbs etched against the evening sky; blossom covered trees in spring; cherry and apple trees bowed low with fruit in summer and autumn; and the most wondrous tree of all, brought down from heaven by Jesus and His angels: the Christmas Tree with shiny glass ornaments, flickering candles, and the scent of fresh spruce and bee's wax and *Lebkuchen* all intermingled. Yet one of my earliest memories of a forest is of a different kind. I was about three, and my parents had taken me into the foothills of the Tatra mountains. I will never forget the immensity of the forest, the height of the trees, the darkness, the silence. Our steps were muffled by a thick carpet of brown needles. Not a speck of sunlight pierced the gloom. Tree trunks reared up and up and up toward a sky infinitely distant, and visible only in a few tiny patches of blinding brightness. These were not Christmas trees of light and celebration, these were somber terror trees. Never had I been filled with such absolute dread. I screamed and screamed, and buried my head against my father's neck, until we were safely out of this awe-full place.

When I re-call, re-live, this episode I understand in a small way what those ancient Germanic peoples must have felt like when the days grew shorter and darkness seemed about to swallow their summer world. Greeley writes about pre-Christian winter solstice festivals: "They drank and they loved and they celebrated and in the center of the celebration was a sacred evergreen tree which perhaps they had moved into the camp and put next to the sacred stone. The tree and the stone were the same thing. They were earth reaching to heaven.... They put lights around the tree because they said the lights represented the light that's coming back into the world."

It was a cold, gloomy winter day in 1944, when Mama brought home a large spruce wreath, attached four candles to it, and Papa hung it from the chandelier with wide red ribbons. That Sunday night they lit a candle and turned out the light. I stood in the dark, holding my parents' hands and listened to my mother talk of the most special baby ever born, in a stable many, many years ago, a child so good, so filled with love, that when it grew up its love brought peace to the world and turned enemies into friends. I had heard the story before, many times, but I never grew tired of it. I didn't think of the Christ Child as a boy or a girl, but simply as a child like myself, my very best friend, different from me only in never even thinking of being naughty or mean or selfish or dishonest. Soon this special friend would come down from heaven and visit all the children and parents in the world to help them celebrate his birthday, and maybe, just maybe stop the sirens from screaming and the black boots from marching and people from hating each other for no reason at all.

I looked at that bright flame and suddenly all her fears went away. There in the dark room with that one steady flame I knew for the first time that everything would be alright, that light was more powerful than darkness.

Thus, like the Madonna, Christ is present in my microcosm, in all the complex associations which surround the vase, the candle, and the tree, and specifically evoked in the Christmas stained glass pane behind the window ledge display. He is the Incarnate Christ, a "humanized" God, both fully within this world and fully transcendent. The word human comes from the Latin *homo* which in turn derives from *humus*, earth or soil. Christ is the union of spirit and nature, God-in-the-word, God-in-the-earth, the sanctification of the soil and her bounty and terror, the sanctification of the carnal sphere. Mary as *theotokos*, who is she but the Great Earth Mother as God-Bearer, the one who engenders this union of opposites through the fluids and cells of her body? It seems significant that the Temple of Athena (whose bird was the owl) in Athens is now dedicated to the *Theotokos*. The Incarnation, stumbling block to Greek Reason, the ultimate paradox, can be readily grasped, "grokked" (to use a term from Heinlein's *Stranger in a Strange Land*) through the analogical imagination. In this perspective Art and Religion are no longer at war, the former seeking idolatrously to make the finite infinite and the latter to express the infinite in finite terms. Both movements are complementary correlatives in a non-dualistic cosmology.

Art, as the German Romantic philosopher Friedrich Schelling recognized, is the product of the creative imagination and reflects the union of spirit and nature, *Geist und Natur*, which is, in the spirit of Karl Rahner's Incarnationalism, ultimately...Christ. Thus it appears that the most appropriate way to communicate "knowledge" concerning God Incarnate is through the affective "language" of art and poetry, the language Andrew Greeley has chosen for his own, but a "language" which has been intuitively used by the Catholic imagination since it scratched the ichthys on catacomb walls, illuminated the Gospel in the *Book of Kells*, composed romances such as *Parzival*, designed the windows and gargoyles of St. Denis (to St. Bernard's distress), and painted such works as Rubens' allegorical hymn to conjugal passion, the *Garden of Love*.

Thus the position of the two chalices on my window ledge, particularly in association with the Easter eggs and next to the egg cup chicks takes on major significance. They are the Catholic liturgical symbols of the pre-Christian natural conception/incarnation motif at the center of the display. The chalices represent at once the holy grail and the eucharistic cup, reminding us of the symbolic substructure for the central Catholic mystery of transubstantiation, the moment of the consecration of bread and wine, which evokes the instant of the Incarnation, the merging of the infinite and the finite, the "enfleshment" of God, fertilization by the Holy Spirit within a woman's ovarian duct and descent of the *conceptus* into her womb, signified by the eucharistic cup. This most sacred of all human rituals (in the Catholic perspective) is ultimately a symbolic re-enactment of the pro-creative event, just as communion is a baptized form of the pagan ritual of the eating of the god.

Each of my chalices holds an Easter egg (painted with images of myself as I was—a blonde, and as I wanted to be—a brunette, a Romantic "double heroine"). Among the pagan Teutonic tribes (such as the Angels and Saxons), eggs were offered the Eostre, goddess of Dawn, Spring and Fertility who would be officially deposed by the likes of Charlemagne's zealous battle axe wielding "missionaries" but did not yield without bequeathing to the Germanic peoples her name for Passover, Easter (English) and *Ostern* (German), along with her messengers of vernal fruitfulness, the egg and the hare (also symbol of fertility among the ancient Egyptians). Three hundred years ago, the German poet/mystic Angelus Silesius wrote: "My body is a shell containing a chick waiting to be hatched by the spirit of eternity." This analogy captures both the pagan egg and Jesus' reference to himself as brood hen. Once again, the boundaries between the Christian world and the unbaptized past merge, the layers interpenetrate.

Like the characters in Greeley's stories, the allegorical objects on my window stage, attached to the marionette strings of my imagination, dance round the eternal flame of Eros/Agape, forever re-enacting the primordial *hieros gamos* of Mother Earth and Father Sky, the kabbalistic union of Malchuth and Tifereth in the garden of pomegranates, symbolically represented by the garnets (from Latin *granatum*, pomegranate). My kitchen is sacred space, this house is sacred space, through their archetypal association with the consummation of the first and greatest of all sacraments, pre-Christian in its origin, the cosmos constituting sacred marriage of the Primal Pair, the joining of fire and water. Greeley often reminds us that the erotic dimensions of divine love are revealed rather than concealed in the traditional Tridentine Easter Vigil ritual of blessing the Baptismal waters by having the celebrant plunge the lighted Easter Candle three times into the font. Catholicism is indeed "a religion of fertility ritual and of self-transcendence" (34).

My parents come to mind. Married for almost fifty years, and prone to disagree violently on many issues, they fought and loved with equal passion. According to my mother, it was their continued sexual hunger for each other, their joyous oneness of the flesh which had sustained them through all those decades. "In his eyes," Mama (fifty pounds overweight, but never matronly) smiled shortly before Papa died, "I'll always be the girl he married, only more beautiful than I ever was." They did not go to church. When I tried to change their ways, mother commented wryly, that they weren't about to have some shriveled up old celibate tell them that they were committing mortal sins (by practicing birth control) when they were simply doing what God intended them to do. Ours was not a formalist Catholic home. Half a century ago my parents were "do it yourself" Catholics (apparently for the same reason that has been changing the American laity since *Humanae Vitae*, as Greeley's research shows); they lit candles on the Advent wreath; they put up the old creche and hugged each other and me under the Christmas tree; they mourned on Good Friday and celebrated on Easter Sunday. One year we kept the Christmas tree until Candlemas; Mama couldn't bear to part with it.

At 4:12 in the morning a little over two years ago I was putting the final touches on my *Eros and the Womanliness of God* manuscript. The phone rang and a stranger's voice told me in German that my mother had died (three years after my father's death). The room, my monitor screen, everything slipped out of focus, and I saw my Dad, a short and somewhat square version of my son, hair falling into his eyes where his imposing forehead should have been (he was thirty-four and balding when I was born), in the middle of a sunny meadow, holding a bouquet of snapdragons, and looking sheepish, excited, expectant, nervous. Then my mother stepped out from among the dark trees to the right of the clearing, younger and more lovely than I had ever known her. They started running, almost flying, toward each other, and embraced in the longest, most passionate kiss I had ever seen. She took his flowers, and then, hand in hand, they headed for the bushes to pick raspberries and, I was sure, renew their love affair. Love stronger than Death. As Father Greeley had written in a poem, "We shall be young once more, we shall laugh again."

Death, My gaze travels to the lower window ledge. Suddenly, each of the objects seems associated with death and transition. I turn the miniature hourglass. The fine pink sand flows in a thin, steady stream through the tiny opening. I remember Schlob Ambras, the imperial Habsburg hunting lodge turned 20th century museum. One of the display cases holds a late Gothic wooden box with intricately inlaid doors. You open the doors and the interior is revealed: the figure of death, carved from ivory, holding a scythe and hour glass, the skeletal body twisted as though frozen in midst of a *danse macabre*.

I look at the painted gentians. "Bavarian Gentians" comes to mind, D. H. Lawrence's haunting poem, written a few days before he died. "...Torch-flowers of the blue-smoking darkness, Pluto's dark blue blaze/Black lamps from the halls of Dis, smoking dark blue/Giving off darkness, blue darkness, upon Demeter's yellowpale day.... Give me a flower on a tall stem, and three dark flames,/For

I will go to the wedding, and be a wedding-guest/At the marriage of the living dark."

Between the hourglass and Pluto's blue chalices sails the boat, archetypal mediatrix between this world and the next. The ancient Egyptians pictured their gods raised in boats to the skies and turned into sun, moon, and stars by heavenly Nut, and celebrated the great festival of the death and resurrection of Osiris by floating the god's image in the Neshmet-boat on a lake. Charon used to row the shades of the dead across the river Lethe or Styx, while a Buddhist ferry man still guides the faithful across the stream of *samsara*. Celtic bards sang of boat journeys to the Island of the Ever Living Women. For Christians the boat signifies both the church building (with its "nave" from the Latin *navis*, ship) and the Church, as the ark or ship of the Lord containing the Christian community. Ships are of immense importance as paradigms for the human situation, particularly in conjunction with the quest motif, in popular tales and allegories such as Sebastian Brant's *Ship of Fools* and the stories of Joseph Conrad and Hermann Melville. The haunting melody of a 15th century advent hymn resounds in my head: "Es kommt ein Schiff geladen...," the German words conjuring up the image of a boat (Mary) carrying Christ, headed toward the earthly shore, the Holy Spirit as its mast, and Love for its sail. Finally, the boat signifies forgiveness and grace. Skimming across the waves in a white-sailed blur, it allows us to suspend the forces of gravity and merge with the primal rhythms of the universe—and God.

I look up. The Indian God's Eye looks back at me, surrounded by golden wheat rays. I look at it, through it, beyond it, and suddenly I find myself in a vast Gothic cathedral, much like St. Stephen's in Vienna (where I as a poor student used to munch my cheese roll lunch almost every day, discreetly concealed in a dark pew behind a convenient pillar). Above the main altar hovers the mightiest Christian God's Eye I have ever seen, its triangle shape surrounded by a brilliant halo of luminous rays. Is that what Greeley means by calling God the "Divine Voyeur"? The brightness dazzles, confounds, blinds. I lower my eyes and focus on the familiar scene before me. The pine cone, flanked by vase and candle emerge out of the mists. To find God in the everyday....

Water is pouring from the faucet. Steam is rising from the sink. I better fix that cup of coffee and get started on those revisions. With luck I'll have a paper by sunrise.

References

Doran, Robert M. *Subject and Psyche: Ricoeur, Jung, and the Search for Foundations.* Washington: UP of America, 1979.

Jauss, Hans Robert. *Aesthetic Experience and Literary Hermeneutics.* Trans. Michael Shaw. Intro. Wlad Godzich. *Theory and History of Literature.* Vol. 3. Minneapolis: Univ. of Minnesota Press, 1982.

Greeley, Andrew M. *The Religious Imagination.* Los Angeles: Sadlier, 1981.

_____*Religion: A Secular Theory.* New York: The Free Press, 1982.

_____"A Catholic Theology of Popular Culture." (Unpublished manuscript).

Lyotard, Jean-Francois. *The Postmodern Condition: A Report on Knowledge.* Trans. Geoff Bennington and Brian Massumi. Foreword by Fredric Jameson. *Theory and History of Literature.* Vol. 10. Minneapolis: Univ. of Minnesota Press, 1984.

Ricoeur, Paul. *Time and Narrative.* Trans. Kathleen McLaughlin and David Pellauer. Chicago: Univ. of Chicago Press, 1985.

Shea, John. *Stories of Faith.* Chicago: Thomas More, 1980.

Tracy, David. *The Analogical Imagination: Christian Theology and the Culture of Pluralism.* New York: Crossroad, 1986.

Chan, Wing-Tsit. *A Source Book in Chinese Philosophy.* Princeton: Princeton UP, 1963.

Contributors

Albert Bergesen is Professor of Sociology at the University of Arizona. His research centers on the sociology of art and culture, and the political economy of the international system. His books include *Cultural Analysis: The Work of Peter Berger, Mary Douglas, Michel Foucault, and Jürgen Habermas* (co-author 1984), *The Sacred and the Subversive: Political Witch-Hunts as National Rituals* (1984), *Studies of the Modern World-System* (1980), *Crisis in the World-System* (1983), and *America's Changing Role in the World-System* (1987). He is presently completing a new book, *The Ritual Order*, to be published by the University of California Press.

Joseph Blotner is Professor of English at the University of Michigan. At the University of Virginia he was a member, and eventually chairman, of the Balch Committee, under whose auspices William Faulkner became Writer-in-Residence there. His writings on Faulkner include *Faulkner in the University* (1959), with Frederick L. Gwynn, *William Faulkner's Library: A Catalogue*, and *Faulkner: A Biography* (1974). He served as editor of *Selected Letters of William Faulkner* (1978) and *Uncollected Stories of William Faulkner* (1981), and is one of the editors of the Garland Faulkner Facsimile edition as well as co-editor of the first Faulkner volume in the Library of America series. His other books are *The Political Novel* (1955), *The Fiction of J.D. Salinger*, and *The Modern American Political Novel: 1900-1960*.

Ray B. Browne is Editor of the *Journal of Popular Culture* and *Journal of American Culture*, and author and editor of 35 books, the latest of which are *Heroes and Humanities: Detective Fiction and Culture* and *The Spirit of Australia: The Crime Fiction of Arthur W. Upfield*.

Lawrence S. Cunningham is Professor of Religion at the Florida State University, Tallahassee. The author or co-author of twelve books, he serves as editor of the American Academy of Religion's monograph series and is an associate editor of the journal *Horizons*. Among his works are *The Meaning of Saints* (1980), *The Catholic Heritage: Martyrs, Ascetics, Pilgrims, Warriors, Mystics, Theologians, Artists, Humanists, Activists, Outsiders and Saints* (1983) and *The Catholic Faith: An Introduction* (1987). He is currently at work on a book about prayer and the Catholic tradition.

Mary G. Durkin is a pastoral theologian who earned her doctorate from the University of Chicago. She taught at De Paul University, Loyola University and the University of Dayton. She was involved in the early formation of the School for New Learning, the adult college of De Paul University, starting its first external learning center and teaching its initial course. She has written and lectured on various pastoral

316   The Incarnate Imagination

issues including marriage, family life, sexuality, women, parish and young adults. Her most recent published work is *Guidelines for Contemporary Catholics: Sexuality* (Thomas More Press). Thomas More Press will soon be publishing her latest book tentatively titled *Making Your Family Work*, a self-help book on family relationships. She is presently completing a book, *Making Peace With Your Family*, that addresses the need for adults to understand their psychological roots. She and her husband, the parents of seven young adults, reside in a Chicago suburb.

Charles Fanning is Professor of English at Bridgewater State College in Massachusetts. He has written widely on the history and literature of the Irish in America. His books include *Finley Peter Dunne and Mr. Dooley: The Chicago Years* (1978), which won the Frederick Jackson Turner Award of the Organization of American Historians, and *The Exiles of Erin: Nineteenth Century Irish-American Fiction*, published in December 1987. He has held fellowships from the National Endowment for the Humanities, the Rockefeller Foundation, and the American Council of Learned Societies, and served as a Fulbright senior lecturer in American Studies in New Zealand.

Joseph J. Feeney, S.J., is Professor of English at Saint Joseph's University in Philadelphia. He received his doctorate from the University of Pennsylvania and has published mainly on Gerard Manley Hopkins, contemporary British drama, the contemporary American religious imagination, and American novelists. His research has appeared in such journals as *The Hopkins Quarterly*, the *Victorians Institute Journal, Studies in American Fiction, Minority Voices*, and *American Studies*. More popular essays have appeared in *America, The Critic*, and *The Philadelphia Inquirer*. He has lectured in Europe and the United States, did an NEH Summer Seminar at the University of Kansas, and in 1986-87 held the Jesuit Chair at Georgetown University.

Erika Fromm has been Professor of Psychology at the University of Chicago since 1960, and guest lectures widely on psychoanalytic topics, hypnotherapy, and hypnoanalysis at other universities. She has taught many workshops on hypnosis all across the U.S. and Europe. Dr. Fromm has co-authored three books, *Dream Interpretation: A New Approach* (1964, second edition 1986, with Thomas M. French), *Hypnotherapy and Hypnoanalysis* (1986, with Daniel P. Brown), and *Hypnosis and Behavioral Medicine* (1987, also with Daniel P. Brown). She edited the by now classic book on experimental hypnosis, *Hypnosis: Developments in Research and New Perspectives* (1972, second edition 1979). She has published more than eighty scientific articles. Since 1969 Dr. Fromm has been the Clinical Editor of the *International Journal of Clinical and Experimental Hypnosis*. She also serves on editorial boards of various other psychological journals. Among her many scientific honors, Dr. Fromm received the American Psychological Association (Division of Psychoanalysis) 1985 Award for outstanding contributions to psychoanalysis, the 1986 Award of the Society for Clinical and Experimental Hypnosis for best clinical paper, and its 1987 Award (together with Daniel P. Brown) for the best book written in the field of hypnosis.

Fran Gillespie, S.J. holds a doctorate in sociology from the University of Texas at Austin. He is the President of CARA (Center for Applied Research in the Apostolate) in Washington, D.C. His ten years of teaching experience in Catholic Higher Education include St. Joseph's University in Philadelphia and the Catholic University of America.

Henry C. Kenski is Associate Professor holding joint appointments in the Departments of Communication and Political Science at the University of Arizona. He has published numerous journal articles and book chapters on American politics.

Margaret Corgan Kenski holds a doctorate in political science from Georgetown University, has published a number of journal articles and book chapters on American and comparative politics, and is president of Arizona Opinion and Political Research.

Hans Küng is Professor of Dogmatic and Ecumenical Studies and Director of the Institute of Ecumenical Research at Tübingen University. He studied at the Gregorianum in Rome, the Sorbonne, and the Institute Catholique in Paris. He first gained the attention of the international theological community with the publication of his doctoral dissertation which demonstrated the convergence in thought between Karl Barth and the Council of Trent concerning the central Reformation issue of justification by faith. Two years after the publication of *The Council, Reform and Reunion* (1960) he was appointed official theological adviser to Vatican Two by Pope John XXIII. Among his many subsequent books are *The Church* (1967), *Infallible? An Inquiry* (1971), *On Being a Christian* (1976), *Does God Exist? An Answer for Today* (1980), *Structures of the Church* (1982), *Eternal Life: Life After Death as a Medical, Philosophical & Theological Problem* (1984). He has edited or co-edited numerous *Concilium* volumes and other journals. He has been Visiting Professor at Union Theological Seminary, the University of Chicago, The University of Michigan at Ann Arbor, and Rice University.

William Lockwood is a computer analyst in the Department of Political Science and a doctoral candidate in the Department of Sociology at the University of Arizona.

Michael T. Marsden is Professor of Popular Culture and Associate Dean of the College of Arts and Sciences at Bowling Green State University. In addition to authoring numerous articles and co-editing several volumes dealing with various aspects of Popular Culture Studies, he also co-edits the quarterly *Journal of Popular Film and Television*. His teaching and research interests include popular literature, popular entertainment forms, films and television studies, and culture theory.

Martin E. Marty is Fairfax M. Cone Distinguished Service Professor of the History of Modern Christianity at the University of Chicago, senior editor of *The Christian Century*, editor of *Context*, co-editor of *Church History*. He has been president of the American Society of Church History and the American Catholic Historical Association and is president of the American Academy of Religion. He is an elected member of the American Antiquarian Association, which seeks to keep documents for the "creatively irrelevant" and of the Society of American Historians, which honors writing style and imagination within the profession. He has written many books, but not as many or as profitable ones (he observes) as has his birthday-mate Father Greeley. His most recent books are *Modern American Religion Volume*

One, 1893-1919: The Irony of it All and *Religion and Republic: The American Circumstance.*

John David Mooney executes and exhibits large-scale public sculptures in Europe, North America, North Africa, Eurasia, and Australia. Major permanent sculptures in the U.S. include "Chrystars," a suspended atrium sculpture made of Waterford Crystal and aluminum, at the University of Chicago, and "Starsteps," a 135 foot long rooftop sculpture which adds three stories in height to a building at the corner of the Hollywood Freeway and Sunset Boulevard in Los Angeles. His works are in the collections of such museums as the Museum of Modern Art in New York, the Art Institute in Chicago, and most recently, the Crawford Municipal Gallery of Cork, Ireland. From his Chicago studio, John David Mooney is currently working on the *Great River Project*, the design of floating performing arts centers and barge designs, to travel down the Illinois and Mississippi rivers in the U.S. and down the Seine in France.

Roland E. Murphy O. Carm., is George Washington Ivey Emeritus Professor of Biblical Studies at Duke, where he joined the Divinity School faculty in 1971 after twenty-two years at Catholic University. In addition to degrees in Semitic languages and in philosophy, and a doctorate in theology from Catholic University, Father Murphy holds the Licentiate in Scripture from the Pontifical Biblical Institute in Rome. He has been Visiting Professor at Pittsburgh Theological Seminary, Yale University Divinity School, Princeton Theological Seminary, and Notre Dame. He has served as editor-in-chief of the *Catholic Biblical Quarterly* and as member of editorial boards of a number of journals such as *Concilium, Vetus Testamentum, Interpretation, Theological Studies, Old Testament Abstracts*, and the *Hermeneia* Biblical Commentary series. The author of many scholarly articles, he was one of the co-editors and contributors to *The Jerome Biblical Commentary*, cooperated in the translation known as the *New American Bible*, and is currently a member of the board for the revision of the Revised Standard Version. Among his recent publications are *Psalms, Job* (1977), *Wisdom Literature* (1981), and *Wisdom Literature and Psalms* (1983). He has been president of the Catholic Biblical Association and the Society of Biblical Literature. He has been actively engaged in ecumenical dialogue.

Jacob Neusner is University Professor and Ungerleider Distinguished Scholar of Judaic Studies at Brown University. He was educated at HarvardCollege (A.B. Magna Cum Laude), Oxford, the Jewish Theological Seminary of America (M.H.L.), Hebrew University and Columbia (Ph.D.) and taught at Columbia, University of Wisconsin-Milwaukee, Brandeis, and Dartmouth before he was called to Brown in 1968. His writings range from specialized scholarly works to books for undergraduate instruction and the public at large (including children). The editor of numerous scholarly journals, and several monograph and textbook series, Professor Neusner is the author of over two-hundred and fifty volumes of translation, analysis, exegesis, history, interpretation and exposition. Among the more than a dozen books he published in 1987 alone are *What Is Midrash?; Vanquished Nation, Broken Spirit. The Virtues of the Heart in Formative Judaism; Self-Fulfilling Prophecy: Exile and Return in the History of Judaism; The Making of the Mind* *of Judaism; Christian Faith and the Bible of Judaism.* Professor Neusner holds honorary degrees from Brown (A.M. *Ad Eundem*), University of Cologne (Ph.D.,h.c.) and the University of Chicago (L.H.D.). and has addressed audiences at major centers of learning on several continents. He is scheduled to deliver the opening address at the 1989 International Conference on Judaism, University of Bologna.

Wendy Doniger O'Flaherty is Mircea Eliade Professor of History of Religions at the University of Chicago. She holds doctorates in Sanskrit (Harvard) and Oriental Studies (Oxford), and has taught at Harvard, Oxford, the University of London, and the University of California at Berkeley. Among her many books are two Penguin Classics, *Hindu Myths: A Sourcebook translated from the Sanskrit* (1975), and *The Rig Veda: An Anthology, 108 Hymns translated from the Sanskrit* (1981), and several books with the University of Chicago Press: *Women, Androgynes, and Other Mythical Beasts* (1980); *Tales of Sex and Violence: Folklore, Sacrifice, and Danger in the Jaiminiya Brahmana* (1985). In press are *Other Peoples' Myths* (Macmillan, 1988), and the English-language edition of Yves Bonnefoy's *Dictionnaire des Mythologies* (Chicago, 1990). In progress are books on the *Mythology of Horses in India, Sexual Doubles and Sexual Masquerades*, and a translation (with Brian K. Smith) of *The Laws of Manu.*

David Riesman is Henry Ford II Emeritus Professor of Social Sciences at Harvard. Before being called to Harvard in 1958, he was a practicing lawyer, Professor of Law, Deputy Assistant District Attorney, student of psychoanalysis, member of the Social Science staff at the University of Chicago, and Lecturer at Yale and Johns Hopkins. While at Harvard he spent a year each at Sussex, Stanford, and Princeton. In addition to essays on Freud, aging, and higher education, Mr. Riesman has written many books including *The Lonely Crowd* (1950, with Nathan Glazer and Reuel Denney), *Faces in the Crowd* (1952, with Nathan Glazer), *Conversations in Japan: Modernization, Politics & Culture* (1967, with Evelyn T. Riesman), *The Academic Revolution* (1968, with Christopher Jencks), *The Perpetual Dream: Reform and Experiment in the American College* (1978, with Gerald Grant). He has been a member of the Carnegie Commission on Higher Education since 1967. *On Higher Education: The Academic Enterprise in an Era of Rising Student Consumerism* (1980) is the final volume of the Carnegie Council on Policy Studies in Higher Education series. His many honors include the Prix Tocqueville (1980), the Distinguished Contributions to Teaching Award of the American Sociological Association (1983), and the award of the Association for the Study of Higher Education for distinguished lifetime contribution (1986).

Alice S. Rossi is Harriet Martineau Professor of Sociology at the University of Massachusetts (Amherst). She holds the Ph. D. in sociology from Columbia University, and five honorary degrees; and she has held research or faculty appointments at Cornell University, Harvard University, the University of Chicago, the Johns Hopkins University, and Goucher College prior to her appointment at the University of Massachusetts in 1974. She has served as President of the Eastern Sociological Society and the American Sociological Association. She has published widely on family and kinship, adult development, biosocial science, sex discrimination, and political movements. Among the books she has authored or

320   The Incarnate Imagination

edited are *The Feminist Papers* (1973), *Feminists in Politics* (1982), *Gender and the Life Course* (1985), and *Parenting and Offspring Development; Biosocial Perspectives* (1987). Her current research is on the parent-adult child relationship in a life course framework, with a book in progress during a sabbatical year's leave.

Charles Scribner III holds a Ph.D. from Princeton University where he taught Baroque Art before joining his family's publishing firm, Charles Scribner's Sons. He is now a Vice President of Macmillan Publishing Company and continues to write and lecture on literature, publishing and art history, with special focus on the art of the Counter-Reformation and the Baroque masters Rubens, Caravaggio, and Bernini. He made a PBS television documentary on Rubens' Eucharist Tapestries (1977) and is the author of *The Triumph of the Eucharist, Tapestries Designed by Rubens* (UMI Research Press, 1982). In press is his book on Rubens' life and art (Harry N. Abrams, 1989).

Ingrid H. Shafer is Associate Professor of Philosophy and Religion at the University of Science and Arts of Oklahoma. A native of Austria, she studied literature (American and German), human relations, and philosophy at the Universities of Vienna, Innsbruck, and Oklahoma. As N.E.H. Fellow, she did post-doctoral work at the University of Chicago Divinity School (Summer 1986). For twenty years she has been responsible for developing, coordinating, and teaching a sequence of required interdisciplinary world thought and culture and contemporary world society courses. Her articles have appeared in *Chicago Studies, The Journal of Ideology, The Owl of Minerva: Biannual Journal of the Hegel Society of America*, and *The Journal of Evolutionary Psychology*. She is the author of *Eros and the Womanliness of God: Andrew Greeley's Romances of Renewal* (Loyola, 1986) and the editor of a special Greeley issue of *The Journal of Popular Literature* (Spring 1988). In progress is a book tentatively titled *Religious Experience as Focus for an Interdisciplinary World Thought & Culture Program: Theory and Practice*, and a translation of Max Stirner's *Kleinere Schriften* (with Lawrence Stepelevich).

John Shea is director of the Doctor of Ministry Program at St. Mary of the Lake Seminary where he himself received the Licentiate and Doctorate in Theology. He has also taught at the University of Notre Dame and Niles College of Loyola University. As much story teller and poet as theologian, Father Shea has written many articles and a number of books including *The Hour of the Unexpected* (1977), *Stories of God: An Unauthorized Biography* (1978), *The God Who Fell from Heaven* (1979), *Stories of Faith* (1980), *An Experience Named Spirit* (1983), *The Challenge of Jesus* (1984), and *The Spirit Master* (1987).

Teresa A. Sullivan is Professor of Sociology at the University of Texas at Austin where she has taught since 1981. She completed her Ph.D. at the University of Chicago in 1975. Among the books she has authored or co-authored are *Marginal Workers, Marginal Jobs: The Underutilization of American Workers* (1978), *Young Catholics in the United States and Canada* (with J. Fee et al; 1981), and *The Dilemma of American Immigration: Beyond the Golden Door* (with P. Cafferty et al; 1983). She has contributed chapters to more than a dozen books. Her articles have appeared in periodicals such as *Social Forces, International Migration Review, Work and Occupations, America, Concilium, University of Chicago Law Review*, and

University of Wisconsin Law Review. Professor Sullivan's most recent academic honors include that of Research Fellow, East-West Population Institute, Honolulu (Summer 1986) and the Liberals Arts Council Teaching Excellence Award (1985).

David Tracy is Andrew Thomas Greeley and Grace McNichols Greeley Distinguished Service Professor of Modern Catholic Studies at the University of Chicago Divinity School. He holds both the Licentiate and Doctorate in Theology from the Gregorian University in Rome and has been at Chicago since 1969. His books include *The Achievement of Bernard Lonergan* (1970), *Blessed Rage for Order: The New Pluralism in Theology* (1975), *The Analogical Imagination: Christian Theology and the Culture of Pluralism* (1981), *Plurality and Ambiguity: Hermeneutics, Religion and Hope* (1987), and *Religion and the Public Realm* (1988). He has served as co-editor of special volumes of *Concilium, Religious Studies Review*, and *The Journal of Religion*. His articles have appeared in *The Journal of Religion, Theological Studies, Theology Today, New Literary History, Critical Inquiry, Daedalus, The Thomist, Thought, Dialogue, Journal of the American Academy of Religion*, and *Concilium*. He has addressed international audiences at Beijing Institute for the Scientific Study of Religion, the World Council of Churches (Geneva), Gregorian University (Rome), Trinity College (Dublin), and Tübingen University, and has lectured in North America at Toronto, Harvard, Yale, Catholic University of America, Vanderbilt, Boston University, Union Theological Seminary, Southern Methodist, and University of the South.

Harrison White is Head of the Department and Professor, Department of Sociology, and Eller Professor of Management & Policy, College of Business and Public Administration at the University of Arizona, where he was called in 1986 after twenty three years at Harvard. He holds doctorates in Theoretical Physics (Massachusetts Institute of Technology) and Sociology (Princeton), and has also taught at Carnegie-Mellon, The University of Chicago (where he directed a certain young priest's thesis on the sociology of country clubs) and the University of Edinburgh. In his books, book chapters, and articles, Harrison White has dealt with vacancy chains and classificatory kinship, developing mathematical models of complex systems. His papers have appeared in such journals as the *American Journal of Sociology, Behavioral Science, Urban Affairs Quarterly, Journal of Mathematical Psychology, Transaction, Sociological Forum*, and the *Journal of Institutional and Theoretical Economics*. His books include *Chains of Opportunity: System Models of Mobility in Organizations* (1975), *Research and Development as a Pattern in Industrial Management: A Case Study of Institutionalization and Uncertainty* (1981), and *Canvas and Careers: Institutional Change in the French Painting World* (1986, with Cynthia A. White).